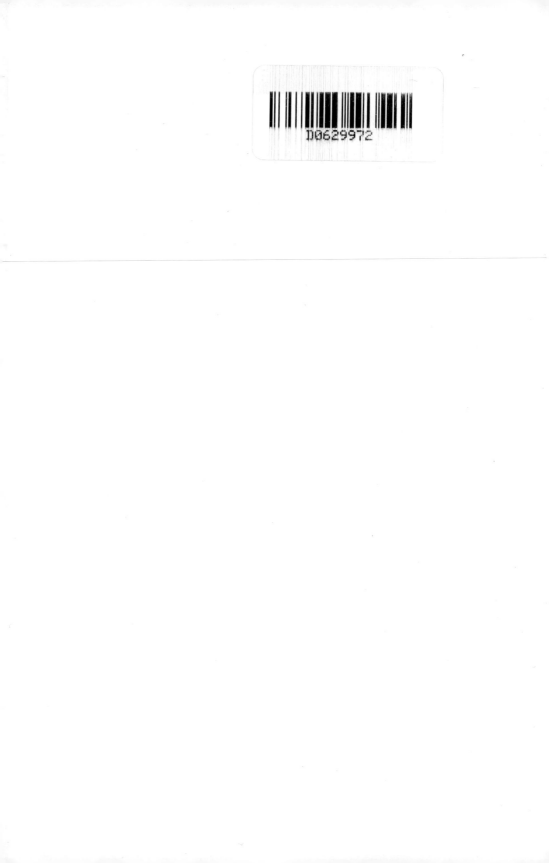

# Cecil B. DeMille's
# Hollywood

11515-01-2/18

# Cecil B. DeMille's
# Hollywood

## ROBERT S. BIRCHARD

With a foreword
by Kevin Thomas

THE UNIVERSITY PRESS OF KENTUCKY

Publication of this volume was made possible in part by a grant
from the National Endowment for the Humanities.

The University Press of Kentucky
Scholarly publisher for the Commonwealth,
serving Bellarmine University, Berea College, Centre College of Kentucky,
Eastern Kentucky University, The Filson Historical Society, Georgetown College,
Kentucky Historical Society, Kentucky State University, Morehead State University,
Murray State University, Northern Kentucky University, Transylvania University,
University of Kentucky, University of Louisville, and Western Kentucky University.
All rights reserved.

*Editorial and Sales Offices:* The University Press of Kentucky
663 South Limestone Street, Lexington, Kentucky 40508-4008
www.kentuckypress.com

08 07 06 05 04   5 4 3 2 1

*Frontispiece:* Handing down the Law. Cecil B. DeMille and Charlton Heston during
production of *The Ten Commandments* (Paramount, 1956). (Author's collection)

**Library of Congress Cataloging-in-Publication Data**

Birchard, Robert S.
    Cecil B. DeMille's Hollywood / Robert S. Birchard.
        p.   cm.
    Includes bibliographical references and index.
    ISBN 0-8131-2324-0 (alk. paper)
    1. DeMille, Cecil B. (Cecil Blount), 1881-1959. 2. Motion pictures—United
States—History. I. Title.
PN1998.3.D39B57 2004
791.4302'33'092—dc22                                        2003024585

Member of the Association of
American University Presses

*For Grace Houghton
who kept the faith*

# Contents

**Appendices**

*Illustrations follow
pages 112, 208, and 304*

# Foreword

In 1989 I had the honor of introducing the Silent Society's seventy-fifth anniversary screening of Cecil B. DeMille's *The Squaw Man* in the Lasky-DeMille Barn, home of the Hollywood Heritage Museum today and the very building from which DeMille's first film was produced. It was a special thrill for me because my relatives' citrus orchards once began across the street from the Barn's original location at Vine Street and Selma Avenue, extending many blocks to where the Egyptian Theater stands today. But I quickly brought Robert Birchard to the stage, knowing of his passion and knowledge of DeMille. His remarks then and there made it clear that he was the man to write this definitive survey of the films and career of Cecil B. DeMille.

As a veteran film editor and an experienced film historian, Birchard is uniquely qualified to judge DeMille and his accomplishments—artistically, technically, and historically. We learn how much DeMille's movies cost, how much they made (or on occasion, lost), and how long they took to make, where they were made, and under what conditions. *Cecil B. DeMille's Hollywood* is a detailed study of DeMille's films and their impact, not a biography of the director. Yet Birchard illuminates the director's relations with his colleagues so thoroughly that we get an idea of what DeMille was like through this documented history perhaps more strongly than we would through the inherently conjectural nature of conventional biography. DeMille emerges as a man of tremendous drive and dedication, concerned with making a contribution through his work, and on the whole much more likable than one would have imagined.

Today DeMille is best remembered for his colossal 1956 remake of his 1923 silent *The Ten Commandments,* for which Charlton Heston has good-naturedly endured a zillion Parting-of-the-Red-Sea jokes. It is the epitome of the biblical spectacles for which DeMille was so famous, those with a seeming cast of thousands and filled with pagan revels featuring scantily clad beauties, as the director was a firm believer in showing sin in action in order to effectively condemn it. DeMille is also remembered for his 1952 circus extravaganza, *The Greatest Show on Earth,* which won the Oscar for Best Picture, and for his 1927 silent story of Jesus, *The King of Kings,* which has a simple beauty and deep spirituality that surprise many who only think of DeMille as the most unabashed of showmen.

That DeMille showed an instinct for the cinema and its endless possibilities is startlingly evident right from the beginning with *The Squaw Man,* which may be an adaptation of a play, but in its unfolding makes excellent use of its expansive natural locales. Also from the start, DeMille loved to mix highly theatrical hokum with often pious sentiments and technical finesse, which made him more cherished by audiences than critics. Yet it was his natural flair for screen storytelling and his patent sincerity that make his films so enduringly entertaining and their messages, in some instances, valid even still. It is important to see his work and those of his contemporaries, most notably D.W. Griffith, as expressions of a Victorian sensibility committed to uplift as much as entertainment.

Nobody would ever place DeMille on the same level of artistic genius as Griffith, but time and again Birchard shows how far more complex and wide-ranging a filmmaker DeMille really was, capable of sympathies and concerns for the individual and for society that are at odds with his conservative political image. What is also surprising to learn is that Paramount head Adolph Zukor kept as tight a rein as possible on his star director and especially resented maintaining a separate production unit for him. Long simmering tension between the two men would finally erupt in the wake of cost overruns on the original *Ten Commandments,* leading DeMille to be forced out of Paramount for a difficult seven-year period, during which he nevertheless showed just as strong a flair for talkies as he had for silents. DeMille returned to Paramount in the depths of the Great Depression and soon hit the long successful stride that would sustain his career until the end of his life in 1959.

DeMille had a reputation for being the most imperial of directors on the set, but Birchard argues effectively that this was his way of keeping outsized egos on either side of the camera in line, and that DeMille was remarkably loyal, going to great lengths to ensure work for veteran players whose moment of fame and fortune had long since passed. *Cecil B. DeMille's Hollywood* is a major achievement, a model of clarity, judgment, and informative and revealing detail, and constitutes a long-overdue comprehensive and serious evaluation of the wide-ranging accomplishments and contributions of a legendary, enduringly successful Hollywood pioneer.

Kevin Thomas
*Los Angeles Times* film critic

# Preface

In those days there were three great directors . . . D.W. Griffith, Cecil B. DeMille, and Max von Mayerling." Erich von Stroheim speaks this line in Billy Wilder's *film à clef, Sunset Boulevard* (Paramount, 1950). In the film Stroheim portrays the fictional von Mayerling, a once-famous filmmaker reduced to serving as butler to one of his former stars. The dialogue is poignant because in some sense Stroheim the actor is speaking of himself and his own vanished career as a director. Similarly, D.W. Griffith was ultimately unable to find work in the industry he helped create. But what of Cecil B. DeMille? In *Sunset Boulevard* we see DeMille busy on the set directing his sixty-eighth picture, *Samson and Delilah* (1949), still a power in the motion picture industry and seemingly untouched by Hollywood's adversities. Yet, DeMille's *Joan the Woman* (1916) was as big a failure as Griffith's *Intolerance* (1916), and DeMille was even more profligate with studio money on *The Ten Commandments* (1923) than Stroheim was on *Greed* (1925).

What set DeMille apart? Why did he remain successful when other filmmakers fell from professional and public favor? Early in his career Cecil B. DeMille's films were highly regarded, while his later work sometimes met with critical derision; but the fact remains that no other director was a major force in the film world over such an extended period of time. Allan Dwan's career (1910–61) was longer than DeMille's (1913–59), but Dwan started out making one-reelers and ended up making low-budget features. John Ford spent his first ten years as a director making inconsequential Westerns and program pictures. George Marshall had the staying power, but many of his projects were trivial at best. DeMille, on the other hand, could lay claim to creating prestigious major attractions in each of his five decades as a filmmaker.

DeMille's box-office success was staggering. In Hollywood, where the dollar is almighty, it is easy to see why he was considered the greatest filmmaker of them all. Charlie Chaplin? Chaplin had big box-office grosses, but he made relatively few pictures. Ernst Lubitsch? Despite his prestige, virtually all the Lubitsch films lost money. Josef von Sternberg? *Blonde Venus* (1932) was a modest hit; *The Scarlet Empress* (1934) kept people out of theaters in droves. Many found DeMille's success revolting. He was criticized for pandering to the lowest common denominator, and damned with faint praise in phrases like "Master of Spectacle" or "Great Showman" or "the director who brought the bathtub to the screen."

When Andrew Sarris wrote *The American Cinema*, his testament to the auteur theory, he rated Cecil B. DeMille highly—not quite in the "Pantheon," but firmly on "The Far Side of Paradise." He observed, however, that "Griffith, Chaplin, Lubitsch, Murnau, Eisenstein, Ford, Hawks, Capra, Welles, Renoir, Ophuls, and all the others came and went without influencing his style in the slightest." One could argue that the very hallmark of being an auteur is a consistency of theme and visual style, and that Sarris could just as easily have substituted the name of any one of these filmmakers for DeMille's and made an equally valid critical observation. What Sarris was really trying to say, of course, is that for all his virtues as a filmmaker, DeMille was somehow hopelessly out of step with the dialectical march of the cinema as an art form.

It is clear, from films like *Kindling* (1915) or *The Golden Chance* (1916), that Cecil B. DeMille was perfectly capable of creating naturalistic films, but as his career progressed he chose to work in what *New York Times* critic Mordaunt Hall called the "queer flamboyant style" that became his trademark.

As early as the 1920s the story was told that DeMille put his heart and soul into making *The Whispering Chorus* (1917), and when audiences proved indifferent to his artistic efforts he decided to give up on art and offer the public what it wanted: SEX, SIN, and SATAN with a half reel of REDEMPTION thrown in for good measure.

Was Cecil B. DeMille a mere cynic who sold out to popular taste, or was he an artist who was misunderstood by his critics? As is often the case with such questions, the answer is not simple.

Although DeMille projected a carefully crafted image as an all-powerful producer-director who worked in a rarefied atmosphere above the dog-eat-dog politics of Hollywood, the truth is that commercial realities sometimes conspired to force DeMille to turn out pictures he had little interest in making. He was also deprived of the opportunity to make several cherished projects. And, DeMille's standing in Hollywood was far from secure. There were several critical junctures in his career when he could easily have ended up as a dimly remembered has-been not unlike James Cruze, Herbert Brenon, Fred Niblo, Edwin Carewe, Sidney Olcott, Irvin Willat, and other leading directors from the silent era.

Anyone with an interest in Hollywood lore has heard tales of DeMille's colorful exploits as a filmmaker. The punch lines alone conjure up humorous anecdotes of an autocratic figure who demanded far more than the mere mortals who worked for him could offer. "Ready when you are, C.B.," shouts the cameraman who just missed a once-in-a-lifetime action shot. "When is the old bald-headed bastard going to call lunch?" whines an embarrassed extra to the assembled cast and crew when forced by DeMille to share what she was whispering during the great director's instructions for a scene. And, without missing a beat, DeMille calls, "Lunch!" Then there is the new associate who is escorted to his office in the DeMille bungalow at Paramount studio, and C.B. tells the young man, "This is an old building, you'll notice the floor slants down and to the left, and I put you here on the left side at the end of the hall on purpose so you can see the heads as they roll by." All great stories . . . and maybe some of them are true. I'd like to think so. But such anecdotes obscure DeMille's real accomplishments, even as they seek to illuminate his personality.

There has been no shortage of biographical interest in Cecil B. DeMille over the years; but it is extraordinary for a director of DeMille's stature that his critical reputation has been based on a mere handful of his seventy pictures—all the more remarkable because the majority of his fifty-two silent films and all of his sound films survive. *Cecil B. DeMille's Hollywood* is an effort to go beyond anecdote and reminiscence to create a portrait of DeMille the filmmaker. It is based in large part on original documents that erase the blur of nostalgia and preserve the immediacy of a time when Cecil B. DeMille helped create the art of motion pictures.

My own interest in Cecil B. DeMille and his work goes back to my earliest days as a film fan in the early 1960s, but my appreciation for his skill as a filmmaker was a long time coming. I first saw *The King of Kings* (1927) and *Union Pacific* (1939) when I was twelve or so and was impressed with the historical sweep of these epics. When I was in college I saw *The Road to Yesterday* (1925) and thought it was one of the worst films I'd ever seen. Later, working in a theater where a reissue of DeMille's *The Ten Commandments* (1956) was playing, I couldn't help feeling that the film was a work of incredible banality—and yet I'd see looks of religious rapture on the faces of patrons leaving the screenings. These people were either crazy, or there was something to this 1956 relic that I was missing . . . since I was about twenty at the time, I was pretty certain that they were crazy.

In the 1980s I came to do some unpaid work making a detailed inventory of the films in a vault on the grounds of DeMille's estate. The two houses on the property, connected by a glass-paneled hallway, had served as living quarters and offices through most of DeMille's years in Hollywood, and they remained largely untouched by time in the nearly thirty years since his passing. His suits still hung in the closet, fresh flowers were still placed on his desk each morning, and it was impossible to ignore the notion that everything was in place for an anticipated second coming.

The reward of my endeavor as volunteer film archivist was being able to borrow and screen 16mm prints of most of DeMille's surviving silents. It was an impressive body of work. But it was only when I saw *The Golden Chance* (1916) that I began to reevaluate my impressions of DeMille's artistry. Here was a true masterpiece unmentioned in any history of the cinema. This film had been completely overshadowed by *The Cheat* (1915) which had come to stand in as a sort of shorthand filmography for critics and historians seeking to define DeMille's early career. Ironically, *The Cheat* was not a film that was particularly close to DeMille's heart, although he was happy to accept the critical accolades for it when French film critics embraced the film shortly after the First World War. *The Golden Chance*, on the other hand, went largely unseen after its initial release.

For me, *The Golden Chance* revealed DeMille's themes and techniques in a way I had not experienced before, and I began to look again at many DeMille films that I had earlier dismissed.

In 1988 Richard Koszarski, then working for the American Museum of the Moving Image in Astoria, Long Island, asked me to write program notes for what would be the first comprehensive retrospective of DeMille's films. Richard was an old friend, but I don't think it was friendship that caused him to hand me this assignment; rather it was a short lead time and the fact that, by virtue of my work with the DeMille estate, I was one of the few people in the world at the time who had seen virtually all of DeMille's surviving films.

In some ways *Cecil B. DeMille's Hollywood* betrays its origins in those early program notes. It is organized as a series of chapters headed by film titles, release dates and credits, but the text and historical content have been greatly expanded—to the point that little survives from that earlier endeavor in this present volume. I gave some thought to arranging this book in a more traditional fashion, especially since there is a narrative thread that carries through the text, and the sequence sometimes strays beyond the strict limits of the film title headings. Ultimately I felt the structure did not detract from the narrative flow for "cover-to-cover" readers and also allowed more casual readers the opportunity to jump around or revisit areas of particular interest.

I am most grateful to those who have helped along the way. Richard Koszarski, for reasons cited above. Grace Houghton, who first expressed interest in my transforming the DeMille program notes into this book. Cecilia DeMille Presley, granddaughter of Cecil B. DeMille, for her friendship and interest in my work. Helen Cohen, who first welcomed me to the DeMille estate when she ran the office there. Betty Lasky, daughter of film pioneer Jesse Lasky, who provided photocopies of some early correspondence between her father and DeMille that first took me behind the scenes to a Hollywood that was just beginning to feel its oats. Marc Wanamaker/Bison Archives—the name and company are inseparable in credits, but Marc has been a friend for many years and has generously shared his own research and many behind-the-scenes stills from his collection. Russell Merritt, for offering some of his own research about road-show playoffs in the 1910s. Kevin Brownlow, for providing a number of references from his own extraordinary researches into the history of early Hollywood and for reading and commenting on the manuscript. Karl Thiede, for sharing his research into motion picture costs and grosses. Miles Kreuger and Danny Schwartz, who contributed several photos. Stan Taffel for information about DeMille's location jaunts to Idyllwild, California.

Special mention should go to James D'Arc and the staff of the L. Tom Perry Special Collections Library in the Harold B. Lee Library at Brigham Young University in Provo, Utah, where Cecil B. DeMille's correspondence and business records are housed, for their help and courtesy. As always, Linda Mehr, and the staff of the Margaret Herrick Library of the Academy of Motion Picture Arts and Sciences in Beverly Hills, California, offered unfailing help. Robert Cushman, photo archivist at the Academy Library also showed great generosity in reading, correcting, and commenting on the manuscript.

Janet Bergstrom, Rudy Behlmer, James Curtis, Steve Hulett, J.B. Kaufman, Gordon Kent, David Kiehn, Kelly Kiernan, Leonard Maltin, Kevin Thomas, Lisa Mitchell, and Anthony Slide also read and remarked on the manuscript.

At the University Press of Kentucky I want to tip my hat to former director Ken Cherry, who took on this book just as he was about to retire. Also, Leila W. Salisbury, who wears two hats at the press as acquisitions editor for film-related projects and as marketing manager; she is quite literally responsible for this book coming and going. Jim Russo copyedited the manuscript with great skill and patient good humor. Richard Farkas designed the book and David L. Cobb guided it through proof corrections.

Others deserving thanks are Richard deMille, adopted son of Cecil B. DeMille, for observations about his father; Mark Haggard for reminiscences of his visit to the set of *The Buccaneer* (1959); Marvin Paige for his help in arranging an interview with Laraine Day; the late George Turner, former editor of *American Cinematographer* magazine, who first published earlier versions of chapters on *The Squaw Man* (1913) and *The Ten Commandments* (1923); the late Agnes deMille, who read and critiqued early chapters; the late George Mitchell, for sharing memories of his visit to the set of *The Story of Dr. Wassell* (1944); and the late Irvin Willat, who shared stories of his days in Hollywood. The Hollywood Heritage Museum, operated by Hollywood Heritage, Inc., deserves mention for preserving and maintaining "The Barn" where Cecil B. DeMille first made movies in 1913–14.

# The Squaw Man

Produced by the Jesse L. Lasky Feature Play Company. Distributed via states rights. Directors: Oscar C. Apfel and Cecil B. DeMille. Scenario by Apfel and DeMille, from the play by Edwin Milton Royle. Photography: Alfred Gandolfi. Assistant cameramen: Johnny Cramer and Bert Longenecker. Film editor: Mamie Wagner

Picture started: December 29, 1913. Eighteen shooting days (the company is known to have been shooting on January 20, 1914, on location at a mansion on West Adams Boulevard in Los Angeles). Length: six reels. Cost: $15,450.25. Released: February 23, 1914. Net producer's profit: $244,700.00

Cast: Dustin Farnum (James Wynnegate), Winifred Kingston (Lady Diana), Red Wing (Nat-U-Rich), Monroe Salisbury (Sir Henry), Joseph E. Singleton (Tabywana), Billy Elmer (Cash Hawkins), Dick Le Strange (Grouchy Bill), Baby DeRue (Hal), Dick La Reno (Big Bill), Foster Knox (Sir John), and Fred Montague (Mr. Petrie)

In the fall of 1913 Cecil B. DeMille faced a bleak future. He was thirty-two years old with a wife and daughter to support, and only a mountain of debt to show for his years in the theater. DeMille's wife, actress Constance Adams, showed great patience. His creditors, on the other hand, were becoming aggressively insistent that Mr. DeMille meet his outstanding obligations.

In a November 10, 1913, letter to theatrical entrepreneur George Pelton, DeMille complained, "The present conditions, theatrically, are the most unfavorable in the twelve years that I have been associated with them. The pieces that are absolute knock-outs are doing business. Nothing else is. Business on the road is ghastly."[1]

Cecil was born on August 12, 1881, in Ashfield, Massachusetts, the second son of Henry Churchill deMille (1853–93) and Matilda Beatrice Samuel deMille (1853–1923).[2] Cecil's father was a lay minister in the Episcopal Church and a leading playwright noted for his collaborations with David Belasco, the "Wizard of Broadway." Cecil's older brother, William (1878–1955), found equal success as a writer, with plays like

*The Woman* and *The Warrens of Virginia*. But Cecil's early professional life was spotty. After attending Pennsylvania Military College and the American Academy of Dramatic Arts he pursued careers as an actor, play broker, producer, and writer with great enthusiasm but with only modest success. The possibility for even modest success in the theater was rapidly disappearing in 1913, and the reason was the movies. In the early 1900s, when Cecil DeMille first set foot on stage, there were well over three hundred theatrical touring companies. By 1912, only two hundred remained, and the number continued to decline. In New York City the devastation was even worse. Where once forty theaters flourished with popular melodrama, only one still catered to that market in 1912.

The Broadway theater was alive and well, and vaudeville was in its heyday; but the audience for the "ten, twent', thirt'" shows[3] had switched its allegiance to the "theater of science," where silent shadows danced on a silver screen. The most elaborate stage setting for a theatrical warhorse like *The Squaw Man* could not compete with the genuine cactus and sagebrush seen in the one- and two-reel oaters cranked out by the likes of Broncho Billy Anderson in Niles, California; Romaine Fielding in Texas, New Mexico, and Colorado; or Thomas Ince in the Pacific Palisades near Los Angeles. A man of the theater could easily dismiss the movies as simplistic, childish, and lacking in real dramatic values—but, principles aside, motion pictures had become the entertainment of choice for the largest segment of the audience.

At least one man believed in Cecil B. DeMille's talents, and that was producer Jesse L. Lasky. Along the way, Lasky and DeMille collaborated on several one-act operettas for the vaudeville stage, and the association led to a lasting friendship. But the royalties DeMille earned from his vaudeville playlets were not enough to live on, and even though he had an "unquestioned success"[4] producing *The Reckless Age* on his own in the spring of 1913, by the fall Cecil was looking for a way out of his financial woes.

Jesse Lasky's brother-in-law, glove salesman Sam Goldfish, was fascinated by the movies, and this fascination led him to study the picture business. He even mounted a one-man campaign to persuade Lasky to get into film production, but the vaudeville producer would have none of it. "When Sam kept urging me to start a picture company," Lasky wrote, "I told him hotly that I would have nothing to do with a business that chased people out of theatres. . . ."[5]

Over lunch one afternoon, DeMille confided to Lasky that he wanted an adventure. Perhaps he would check out the revolution raging in Mexico and write about his experiences. If DeMille was serious, and Jesse Lasky certainly thought he was, this sudden desire to become a foreign correspondent demonstrated just how desperately DeMille saw his situation. Lasky made a sudden decision. If his friend wanted adventure, why not the movies? DeMille was excited. Goldfish was thrilled. And even though Lasky had grave doubts about the enterprise, the Jesse L. Lasky Feature Play Company was formed with Lasky as president, Goldfish as general manager, DeMille as director general, and attorney Arthur Friend as secretary.

For once DeMille was in the right place at the right time. Up to 1913, American filmmakers had concentrated on the production of short one- and two-reel pictures, and movie theaters offered two or three such films with a daily change of program. The economics were simple and rewarding. A one-reel film could be produced for as little as three hundred to five hundred dollars. The release prints were sold to exchanges at the rate of ten cents per foot—or one hundred dollars for a thousand-foot reel. A sale of thirty prints would bring three thousand dollars. Making movies in the nickelodeon age gave every appearance of being a license to mint money.

But just as live theater was in upheaval, so were the movies. A number of European features had been exported to America, notably the Italian *Quo Vadis?* (1913) and the four-reel French production of *Queen Elizabeth* (1912), starring Sarah Bernhardt. These films played in Broadway theaters at advanced prices, and theater producers like William A. Brady, Daniel Frohman, Marcus Loew, and the Shuberts began to see feature films as a replacement for the popular theater. They were also quick to see the possibility of additional revenues both by licensing their play catalogues for "picturization" and by renting their theaters to the movies between legit engagements.

In Hollywood legend, DeMille, Lasky, and Goldfish were shoestring operators ill-equipped to take on the moving picture world, but the founders of the Jesse L. Lasky Feature Play Company did not just happen into the picture business. According to Lasky, Goldfish first became interested in movies in 1911 and "had been nosing around the General Film Company ever since."[6] General Film was the distribution arm of the Motion Picture Patents Company—the so-called "film trust"—whose members were the leading producers of the day. Apparently Goldfish had a solid understanding of the picture business and its pitfalls long before the Lasky Company was born. Lasky himself had acts playing in vaudeville houses throughout the country; and even if DeMille's career was less successful, he did have a solid background in theatrical production. The Jesse L. Lasky Feature Play Company was not a spur-of-the-moment enterprise, as evidenced by the announcement of the company's officers in July of 1913, many months before its formal incorporation in November.

*The Squaw Man* seemed a natural for the new company's first production. It was a well-known play; author Edwin Milton Royle was willing to sell the motion picture rights at an affordable price; and being a Western, most of *The Squaw Man*'s action could be staged outdoors—eliminating the necessity for costly lighting equipment. In his autobiography, Lasky claims to have paid fifteen thousand dollars for the play, but he almost certainly exaggerates. At the time, play brokers typically sought advances ranging from fifteen hundred to six thousand dollars against a percentage of the profits.

In preparation for making *The Squaw Man*, Cecil B. DeMille spent a day at the Edison studio in the Bronx, observing how pictures were made, yet another indication that the Lasky forces had done their homework. The Edison Company was the foremost member of the Motion Picture Patents combine, and it seems unlikely that DeMille, as an independent filmmaker from an unlicensed company, could have visited the Edison studio unless some sort of detente had been reached before the start of the first Lasky production. Despite (or perhaps because of) DeMille's day of training, it was felt that a production of the scope of *The Squaw Man* required a director with more film experience. Oscar C. Apfel was selected to direct the production under DeMille's supervision. A veteran of the stage, Apfel made films for Edison, Reliance, and Pathé before signing with Lasky. Along with Apfel came cinematographer Alfred Gandolfi, a fellow alumnus from Pathé who started his career at the Cines and Itala studios in his native Italy. Gandolfi claimed to have invented the lens shade and to be the first to shoot double-exposures in motion pictures; he later asserted that he was the first cameraman to use a foreground reflector in California.

Matinee idol Dustin Farnum was chosen to play the lead in the picture. A star of some standing in the theater, Farnum had appeared in *The Squaw Man* on stage (although William Faversham originated the role), but equally important, he had recently completed his first feature-film role in *Soldiers of Fortune* for the All-Star Feature Corporation. The nature of Farnum's participation in the Lasky Company's first production has long been a matter of dispute. DeMille claimed Farnum was offered a 25 percent interest in the company in lieu of salary, but turned it down for a flat $250 a week. In Jesse Lasky's version Farnum agreed to the stock offer, but insisted on $5,000 in cash before leaving New York for the West. In fact Farnum's contract called for the actor to receive $250 a week for each week that he actually played before the camera, and "twenty-five (25%) per cent of the net profits derived from the sale of the picture throughout the entire world." In later years Lasky and DeMille preferred to gloat over Farnum's lack of foresight in taking the stock, rather than admit that they had agreed to give away 25 percent of the profits.[7]

The selection of the leading lady for *The Squaw Man* was a relatively simple matter. Winifred Kingston had been Dustin Farnum's co-star in *Soldiers of Fortune*, and, more to the point, she was his leading lady offscreen as well. They later married. The rest of the cast and crew were to be picked up on location.

Leaving Lasky and Goldfish in New York, DeMille and his small troupe set out for Flagstaff, Arizona, where they planned to shoot the picture. While on the train, he and Apfel set about adapting *The Squaw Man* into a suitable moving picture scenario. Arriving in Arizona, the filmmakers were disappointed by the high desert country around Flagstaff. It did not suit the Wyoming locales specified in Royle's play, and even though many film companies had sent units to Arizona for winter filming, the location must have seemed incredibly remote. As DeMille remembered it: "When I got to Flagstaff there were high mountains, and I didn't want high mountains. I wanted plains with mountains in the distance . . . Dustin Farnum said to me, 'Well . . . I think we ought to go on to Los Angeles where the other picture companies are and have a look around.'"[8]

Arriving in the City of the Angels on December 20, DeMille and company took up residence in the Alexandria Hotel. Today, despite a not-so-long-ago restoration, the Alexandria is a faded lady, but in 1913 it was the hotel of choice for travelers to L.A. Soon it also became the hub of motion picture deal-making, and the rug in the lobby was dubbed the "million dollar carpet" in honor of the many film deals consummated there. By late 1913 Los Angeles was already a major production center. The New York–based Biograph Company had sent units to the city each winter since 1906. The Selig Polyscope Company of Chicago followed with the first permanent Los Angeles studio in 1909. In 1911 David Horsley and Al Christie brought their Nestor Company to Hollywood, and the New York Motion Picture Corporation opened studios in Edendale and Santa Monica. By 1912, Vitagraph, Kalem, Universal, Edison, and Lubin all had branch studios in the Los Angeles area; so it was no surprise that as DeMille and Apfel prepared to shoot *The Squaw Man*, word spread quickly through the picture community.

During his years in the theater, Cecil B. DeMille had come to know E.A. Martin, who was now making pictures in Los Angeles. Martin had just completed a film titled *Opportunity* for the Efsco Film Company, using the Burns and Revier Studio in Hollywood to shoot his interior scenes. According to Martin's daughter, DeMille looked up his old friend, and Martin suggested that the Lasky Company rent the facility for its base of operations. L.L. Burns was the founder of Western Costume Company. His partner, Harry Revier, owned a number of movie theaters and had worked in pictures for both American Gaumont and Universal before joining forces with Burns in June 1912. Together they set up a studio and film laboratory in East Hollywood where Sunset and Hollywood Boulevards cross. They leased the studio to the Kinemacolor Company in March 1913 and moved their own operations to a lot located at the corner of Selma Avenue and Vine Street on property owned by Hollywood pioneer Jacob Stern. The main building on the property was a barn that Burns and Revier adapted to serve as offices, dressing rooms, and film laboratory. They also built an outdoor stage. By the time the Lasky Company arrived, the Burns and Revier Studio was known to be one of the best-equipped rental lots in Los Angeles.

On December 22, 1913, DeMille and Burns signed a letter of understanding for the sublease of the Burns and Revier Studio. Contrary to Jesse Lasky's recollection, the term of the lease was not month-to-month at $50.00 per month, but for four months at $250.00 per month, with a three-year renewal option. Burns and Revier agreed to enlarge the existing open-air stage to forty-by-seventy feet and to "erect new and modern diffusers." They also agreed to build a second stage for their own use, which the Lasky Company could utilize when it was not otherwise occupied. In addition the Burns and Revier laboratory offered to develop film negative and make one print at the rate of 1.5 cents per foot.

Two days later the agreement was formalized, with Burns and Revier further promising to "extend all partitions to the ceiling in all dressing rooms now on said premises," and to reduce the price for developing and work-printing to 3/4 cents per foot, including "tinting, toning and dyeing of the positive film."[9] With the studio facilities arranged, DeMille and

Apfel settled down to a preproduction schedule that lasted all of seven days.

To round out the cast, the producers turned to the large pool of film and theatrical talent in Los Angeles. Dick Le Strange, who played Grouchy the ranch hand, was the first actor to be signed. A native of Germany, Le Strange began his stage career in 1900. DeMille's first choice for the role of Nat-U-Rich was Princess Mona Darkfeather. Darkfeather was billed as a full-blooded Seminole during her earliest days in pictures, but her real name was Josephine Workman, and by 1913, as the market for Indian-themed pictures began to wane, she claimed she was of Spanish descent and capable of playing a wide range of roles. Darkfeather and her husband, Frank Montgomery, were producing their own films independently for release through the Kalem Company, and she was not available to take the role in *The Squaw Man*.

DeMille's second choice for the role was Red Wing. Born February 13, 1884, in Winnebago, Nebraska, Red Wing was a full-blooded Winnebago whose real name, phonetically at least, was Ah-Hoo-Sooch-Wing-Gah. She also used the Anglicized name of Lillian St. Cyr through much of her professional life. Princess Red Wing started her picture career in the East with the Kalem Company as early as 1908 in a picture called *The White Squaw*, but she first came to prominence with the Bison unit of the New York Motion Picture Company,[10] working with actor-director Charles K. French in *The Cowboy's Narrow Escape* (released June 1909). She spent a year with Bison and then went to work for the Western unit of Pathé Freres, where she again worked with French and James Young Deer. "I remember going to the Van Nuys Hotel to meet Mr. DeMille," Red Wing told a reporter in 1935. "He said I was too short. But just then Dustin Farnum, who played the lead, came in and looked at me and said, 'Don't go any farther; she'll do.' That's how I got the part."[11]

Authenticity in Native American casting ended with Red Wing. Joseph Singleton, who played Tabywana, was Australian. He started his stage career Down Under and came to the States in 1894. After years in stock, his first film work was for Universal in 1912. He appeared in several features for Bosworth, Inc., before his assignment in *The Squaw Man*.

Monroe Salisbury was a New York stage actor who had appeared with Richard Mansfield, Minnie Maddern Fiske, and Nance O'Neil, among others. Billy Elmer, who portrayed the villainous Cash Hawkins, was a onetime boxer turned actor who gained screen experience with Biograph and Selig before joining the Lasky forces. Although he would never gain any lasting screen fame, Elmer became a familiar member of DeMille's stock company, appearing in bit parts in the director's films well into the 1940s. Young Hal, the Squaw Man's son, would be billed simply as Baby DeRue so as not to give away the fact that the little boy was actually a little girl named Carmen. For Big Bill, the Squaw Man's friend, DeMille and Apfel selected Dick La Reno. Born in England and a veteran of over twenty years in the theater, La Reno had played film roles for a half dozen companies before signing on for *The Squaw Man*. Among the extras were two who went on to greater fame. Rodeo champion Art Acord became a Western star at Universal in the 1920s, and Hal E. Roach became a producer and brought the talents of Harold Lloyd, Laurel and Hardy, and Our Gang to the screen.

*The Squaw Man* went before the camera on December 29, 1913, at the Burns and Revier Studio. The extent of DeMille's involvement with the direction of the picture is unclear. A photograph taken on the first day of shooting clearly shows Oscar Apfel directing, while DeMille stands with other members of the company offstage. Surviving prints give the credit "Produced by Oscar C. Apfel and Cecil B. DeMille" (the word "producer" meant director in 1914), but the main titles are from an early reissue, reflecting the graphic style of the Lasky films of the 1915–16 period.[12] It would be another three months after the completion of *The Squaw Man* before DeMille had a solo outing as a director. However, if he was not actively involved in directing *The Squaw Man*, he was certainly heavily involved in editing the picture.[13]

The first scenes shot for *The Squaw Man* were also the first scenes in the story—the dinner in the officers' barracks, the charity bazaar, and the theft of charity funds by the earl of Kerhill. With the exception of a few other interiors—a New York hotel room, a ship's stateroom, the Squaw Man's cabin, and Tabywana's teepee—the rest of the picture was shot on location. Stories in the trade paper *Moving Picture World* told of the Lasky Company's travels to Utah, Arizona, and Wyoming in search of authentic scenery, but DeMille and crew never left Southern California. Although the story opens in Britain, the scenes of the English Derby were bought from a stock-footage service and intercut with scenes of Farnum, Kingston, and Salisbury in a decidedly un-grand grandstand. Harbor scenes were shot in San Pedro, California, and the Western saloon set was built beside railroad tracks in the vast desert that was once the San Fernando Valley. The company did go as far afield as Keen Camp in Idyllwild and Hemet, California, to shoot footage of cattle on the open range and Mount Palomar for snow scenes. The English manor house was a mansion in the fashionable West Adams District of Los Angeles, and the exterior sets of the Squaw Man's cabin were built at the Universal ranch (now Universal City). The imaginary stories of the far-flung locations did help generate exhibitor interest, however, and Sam Goldfish took advantage of the publicity in selling the picture.

Principal photography took eighteen days, and the production went smoothly enough on the set, but serious and potentially deadly problems arose offstage. Aware that the nitrate film stock they were using was highly flammable, DeMille ordered two usable takes shot on every scene— one negative to be stored at the studio, the other at the director general's rented home. One night, DeMille went to the laboratory and found a length of the precious *Squaw Man* negative unspooled on the floor and irreparably damaged. Another evening, while DeMille rode home on horseback through the Cahuenga Pass, a bushwhacker took a shot at him. Both incidents were assumed to have been perpetrated by goons hired by the Motion Picture Patents Company, though in interviews conducted for his own autobiography DeMille refused to blame the Patents Company, hinting instead that the acts might have been perpetrated by a lab technician he had fired.

By the end of January 1914, *The Squaw Man* was cut and titled. Jesse Lasky later claimed he came west for the first screening, relating that "Everyone connected with the picture . . . was invited to the first showing in the barn. It was such a proud occasion that the men put on collars and coats and brought their wives. There were about fifty of us."[14] According to Lasky, he crossed his fingers as the operator began to crank the projector. The six reels of film represented an investment of $15,450.25—his own money, and the money of family and friends. *The Squaw Man* had to be a success.[15]

Then, as if in a nightmare, the picture jumped and staggered on the screen, stubbornly refusing to stay in frame. They checked the projector and found it to be in perfect working order. The problem was with the film itself, and it looked as if Lasky's motion picture career would be over before it had begun. Reluctantly, Lasky and DeMille wired Sam Goldfish to break the bad news. At least this is the story, filtered through forty-odd years of memory and retelling, that both Lasky and DeMille related in their autobiographies. The truth, as far as it can be pieced together from copies of original telegrams between DeMille and Goldfish, was considered much less of a disaster at the time.

At least part of *The Squaw Man* negative had been misperforated with sixty-five sprocket holes to the foot instead of the customary sixty-four, causing the frame line to roll on-screen when the picture was projected. DeMille, though certainly aware of the problem, did not seem overly concerned. He wired Sam Goldfish on January 24, 1914: "CAN'T AR-RANGE PERFORATION UNLESS YOU CAN FORCE EASTMAN TO GIVE YOU POSITIVE [print film] TO MATCH FIRST NEGATIVE. [or] RUSH PERFORATING MACHINE... WITH FIFTY THOUSAND FEET UNPERFORATED POSITIVE .... SQUAW MAN A GREAT PICTURE. CAN SEND FIRST PRINT FIVE DAYS AFTER RECEIVING PERFORATOR OR SIXTY-FIVE [perforations to the foot] POSITIVE." The telegram reveals DeMille's belief that simply matching the number of sprocket hole perforations on the positive prints to the sixty-five perforation negative would solve the problem. This was incorrect, of course. The projector sprocket wheels would still turn at the rate of sixty-four to the foot, and the picture would still appear to roll.

Several days later DeMille wired, "RAN 'SQUAW MAN' COMPLETE FOR FIRST TIME. ALL WHO SAW IT VERY ENTHUSIASTIC. FARNUM WILL DELIVER TO YOU SUNDAY NIGHT. PROPER CUTTING TAKES GREAT DEAL OF TIME. [The picture] RUNS JUST SIX THOUSAND FEET.... YOU MAY BE SATISFIED YOU HAVE A GOOD PICTURE."

No evidence exists that Lasky was present at the screening, nor does any evidence indicate a serious problem with the film in California. The fact that Dustin Farnum would carry the print on his return to New York strongly suggests DeMille felt no apprehension about the picture.[16] In later years, while being interviewed by Art Arthur in preparation for writing his autobiography, DeMille stated, "I think [Jesse Lasky] recollected wrong. It did run off the screen here [in Hollywood], but not as badly as it did there [in New York]. I think probably because our operator or whoever was running the projection machine was alert to where it [the problem] came and was ready with the framing. You could frame it quite easily, you know. Then it would run alright for awhile, and then it would go off [frame] again."[17]

There is no question, however, that when Sam Goldfish saw *The Squaw Man* in New York the rolling image made the picture unmarketable. One simply couldn't rely on projectionists in hundreds of theaters to constantly ride herd on the framing lever through the film's ninety-minute running time. Faced with potential disaster, Goldfish decided on a desperate course of action. He arranged for DeMille to take *The Squaw Man* to the Lubin Manufacturing Company in Philadelphia, Pennsylvania, generally acknowledged to have the finest motion picture laboratory facilities in the United States at the time.

As a member of the Patents Company, Lubin was theoretically unable to take work from independent producers. However, Sigmund Lubin, affectionately known as "Pop," was a bit of a rebel. In his earlier years in the business he had run afoul of Edison's patents himself and was forced to leave the country for a time to avoid the long arm of the Edison attorneys. Now he was in the "establishment" but not of it, and he agreed to help the novice filmmakers. The Lubin laboratory glued a celluloid strip over the existing sprocket holes in the problem areas and reperforated the film. In extant prints of *The Squaw Man* several scenes are splattered with white sprocket-hole-shaped "snowflakes." During re-perforation, bits of celluloid adhered to the negative and "printed through," causing them to appear on-screen when the picture is projected.

In solving the problem, Lubin earned a contract for Lasky's release printing, and *The Squaw Man* was finally screened for an invited trade show audience at the Longacre Theater in New York on February 17, 1914.

As a movie, *The Squaw Man* is more of a moving illustration than a work of real dramatic power and does not measure up to the best Biograph and Vitagraph shorts of the period. Somewhat cryptic in its presentation—especially in the early scenes that establish the motivation for Jim Wynnegate's self-exile to the American West—the film requires a certain familiarity with the source play. But 1913 audiences were acquainted with the play that had toured the country in various forms since 1906 and were eager for longer narrative films with established stage stars.

With no national distribution network, the Lasky Feature Play Company sold *The Squaw Man* on a states rights basis—territory by territory. Although no extant records indicate what price Sam Goldfish was able to demand from various territorial distributors, terms were probably similar to those outlined by Frank Paret, New York representative of the California Motion Picture Corporation, in a letter to his general manager, Alex E. Beyfuss, dated July 3, 1914:

> Herewith I am giving you the prices which a Standard-Play
> may be expected to bring at the present time, if sold on a

State-Right Basis, also the number of prints necessary for each territory.

| | | |
|---|---|---|
| New England States | (2 prints) | $3000. |
| City and State of New York | (3 prints) | $6000. |
| New Jersey | (1 print) | $1200. |
| Eastern Pennsylvania, Delaware, Maryland, D.C. | (2 prints) | $3000. |
| Western Pennsylvania, Ohio, Kentucky, West Virginia | (2 prints) | $2750. |
| Illinois and Indiana | (2 prints) | $3500. |
| Kansas, No. and Sou. Dakota, Oklahoma | (2 prints) | $2200. |
| Texas | (2 prints) | $3000. |
| Oregon, Washington, Nevada | (1 print) | $2000. |
| California, Arizona, New Mexico | (1 print) | $3000. |
| Colorado, Wyoming, Utah | (1 print) | $1750. |
| Minnesota and Wisconsin | (2 prints) | $2500. |
| Michigan | (1 print) | $2000. |
| Dominion of Canada | (2 prints) | $2000. |
| Southern States not included above | (3 prints) | $3500. |
| TOTAL | (27 prints) | $41,400. |

These figures are compiled from the books of the biggest producing companies and strike a very fair average. The prices secured naturally vary, according to the merit of the picture, the demand for a special picture in a certain territory and other influences.

In addition to the total given above, the producer can figure on a fair profit from selling lithographs [posters], advertising, etc. I understand that the expenses of the New York office of the All-Star Feature Corp. are paid from this income.

The figures given above refer to the present time and are lower than the prices obtained even a year ago.[18]

The territorial sales prices described by Frank Paret were advances against rentals. The regional distributors recouped their investments before splitting overages (the income over and above their advances) with the producer on a percentage basis. Eventually, after the term of the distribution agreement (usually five or seven years), all rights reverted to the producer. For all practical purposes, however, such cash advances often were the only receipts realized by the producers.

Within two weeks of the February 17 trade screening, the Lasky Feature Play Company sold territorial rights for thirty-one of the forty-eight states. A week later, only Iowa, Kansas, Missouri, and Nebraska were up for grabs, and they soon fell into line. A list of costs and grosses on all of his pictures prepared for Cecil DeMille in 1936 lists *The Squaw Man* as having shown a net producer's profit of $244,700—an extraordinary figure for 1914, and far in advance of anything his other pictures would do over the next several years. The figure is somewhat suspect, but there is no question that for Lasky, Goldfish, and DeMille the picture was a spectacular success.[19]

The triumph of *The Squaw Man* was noted by W.W. Hodkinson, whose Progressive Motion Picture Company held the West Coast rights to the Lasky production. With exhibitors clamoring for feature pictures, Hodkinson dreamed of setting up a national distribution organization that could guarantee theater owners fifty-two feature pictures a year, much as the older, established distributors were able to provide a full program of short films. Hodkinson joined forces with a number of regional distributors to form Paramount Pictures in May 1914 and contracted with Bosworth, Inc., Adolph Zukor's Famous Players Film Company, and the Jesse L. Lasky Feature Play Company to produce pictures for the Paramount program.

# 2

# The Virginian

Produced by the Jesse L. Lasky Feature Play Company. Released through Paramount Pictures. Director: Cecil B. DeMille. Scenario by Cecil B. DeMille, from the novel by Owen Wister and the play by Owen Wister and Kirk La Shelle. Photography: Alvin Wyckoff

Picture started: April 25, 1914. Length: 3,743 feet (four reels). Cost: $17,022.06. Released: September 7, 1914. Gross: $111,518.85

Cast: Dustin Farnum (The Virginian), Winifred Kingston (Molly Wood), Billy Elmer (Trampas), Monroe Salisbury (Mr. Ogden), Anita King (Mrs. Ogden), Tex Driscoll (Shorty), J.W. Johnston (Steve), Horace B. Carpenter (Spanish Ed), Sydney Deane (Uncle Hughey), Hosea Steelman (Lin McLean), James Griswold (stage driver), Dick La Reno (Balaam), and Mrs. Lewis McCord (Mrs. Balaam)

E ven before *The Squaw Man* was completed, the Lasky Feature Play Company was moving ahead on its second production, a film version of the popular novel and play *Brewster's Millions,* with Edward Abeles recreating his stage role as heir to that delightful and frustrating legacy. Although Jesse Lasky and Sam Goldfish were committed to the project, the strain on the young company's capital assets was tremendous. On January 23, 1914, Sam Goldfish wired DeMille: "GIVE US BY RETURN WIRE SOME IDEA HOW MUCH MONEY YOU WILL REQUIRE TO START 'BREWSTER'S MILLIONS' AS UNTIL 'SQUAW MAN' IS RELEASED WE HAVE VERY LOW FUNDS AND CANNOT PROCEED EXCEPT VERY CAREFULLY." DeMille's request seems Lilliputian in today's world of $100-million-plus budgets, but Lasky and his brother-in-law probably went pale when they read: "WILL NEED NOT LESS THAN SIX THOUSAND DOLLARS TO BEGIN 'BREWSTER' AND FINISH 'SQUAW.'"

Just how much DeMille had to do with the direction of *Brewster's Millions* (released April 1914) and the following three Lasky productions—*The Master Mind* (May 1914), *The Only Son* (June 1914), and *The Man on the Box* (July 1914)—is difficult to judge. Although DeMille did not include these titles among his personal credits in later years, he was listed as co-producer with Oscar Apfel on all of them when they were first released; most likely, he played a collaborative role, as he had on *The Squaw Man*. Perhaps the lesser historical significance of these pictures kept DeMille from taking credit, or perhaps at the time he was so busily engaged with the day-to-day business of running the studio, writing scenarios, and editing Apfel's footage that he was necessarily less involved in their production.[1] However, because of the pending affiliation with Paramount Pictures Corporation, the Lasky Feature Play Company needed to greatly increase its production schedule and consequently it was no longer practical to have two directors working on one picture together when they might be shooting two separately.

The alliance that became the basis for Paramount Pictures was a natural extension of the intricate business alliances of W.W. Hodkinson, Jesse L. Lasky, Los Angeles businessman Frank A. Garbutt, and Adolph Zukor. Zukor's Famous Players Film Company also operated the Famous Players Exchange, with offices in New York and Philadelphia, and Famous Players Film Service, with offices in Pittsburgh and Detroit. Through these exchanges Famous Players acquired territorial rights to the productions of Garbutt's Bosworth, Inc., which had as its home base the same facility that Famous Players rented for its West Coast studio— the old Bradbury Mansion on Court Street in Los Angeles.[2] W.W. Hodkinson's Progressive Motion Picture Company had rights to the Bosworth, Lasky, and Famous Players pictures for California, Oregon, Washington, Nevada, Arizona, and New Mexico.[3]

Under the arrangement announced in May 1914, Famous Players Exchange and Film Service combined with Progressive Motion Picture Company, the William L. Sherry Feature Film Company of New York, and Master Productions Film Company (headed by Hiram Abrams in Boston) to form Paramount Pictures Corporation. Paramount in turn signed exclusive contracts with Famous Players Film Company, Bosworth, Inc., and the Jesse L. Lasky Feature Play Company guaranteeing to advance production costs of $17,500.00 per film, provide national advertising, and split profits in return for each company's total feature output for a period of twenty-five years. The goal was to supply exhibitors with 104 feature films a year—enough to provide for twice-weekly changes of program. Famous Players was to produce fifty-two, Bosworth twenty-two, and Lasky thirty pictures a year. By providing up-front financing Paramount pulled the fat out of the fire for the three film companies, allowing them to continue making pictures without having to rely on uncertain regional sales to bankroll their ongoing production expenses.

After the impressive success of *The Squaw Man*, reaction to *Brewster's Millions* and *The Master Mind* was mixed, in part because the trickle of feature films that began in 1912 had become a torrent by early 1914. *The Virginian* was an attempt to duplicate the formula that had made *The Squaw Man* so successful. Dustin Farnum was signed on April 2, 1914, to repeat his Broadway stage role and appear in three additional pictures under the same terms as his *Squaw Man* engagement. A hand-written amendment to the contract stipulated: "It is further agreed the 'billing' of 'The Virginian' shall read 'Dustin Farnum in The Virginian.'"[4] (Contractual credit demands by actors are not a recent phenomenon.)

*The Virginian* demonstrates that Cecil B. DeMille had developed a grasp of the medium that is not evident in the Apfel-DeMille *Squaw Man* collaboration. The shot compositions are more assured, and DeMille moves his camera closer to the players, showing a greater reliance on personality and subtlety of performance. Story exposition is also more clear-cut and lucid. While *The Squaw Man* required six reels, *The Virginian* tells its story of friendship, honor, and betrayal in something less than four reels, although it must be said that Owen Wister's original relies on a far less complicated narrative than Royle's novel and play.

The main plot developments of Wister's novel—the friendship of the Virginian and Steve, their rivalry over Molly, and Steve's falling in with Trampas and his band of rustlers—are treated in a matter-of-fact manner. DeMille's approach emphasizes character over plot, and a great deal of footage is devoted to a prank played on the town's proud parents by Steve and the Virginian, who switch babies in their cradles while mom and dad are having a night out at the Saturday dance. This sort of non-narrative interlude was unusual at the time and made DeMille's film seem different from other directors' films.

In early 1914 no standard length existed for feature pictures. Bosworth's *The Sea Wolf* (1913) was seven reels long, *The Squaw Man* six, Selig's *The Spoilers* nine, and the Vitagraph production of *The Christian* eight. It was felt that longer was better if features were to play in legitimate theaters at advanced prices. However, as the novelty of feature films wore off and they began to play movie houses for ten and twenty-five cent admissions, exhibitors forced producers to standardize their features at five reels—or roughly seventy-five to eighty minutes of screen time. Any shorter and the public would feel cheated, any longer and the exhibitor could not get in enough shows per day to justify the higher film rentals demanded by distributors.

Because cameraman Alfred Gandolfi continued to work with Oscar Apfel, DeMille hired Alvin Wyckoff from the West Coast studio of the Selig Polyscope Company to be his cinematographer. Wyckoff remained with DeMille from *The Virginian* through *Adam's Rib* in 1923, and his work was excellent. DeMille sought to bring more dramatic and realistic lighting to the screen, and Wyckoff helped the director achieve the effects he desired, though their collaboration was often a stormy one. Their association ended when DeMille became more interested in decor and setting than in lighting effects, but in the 1910s DeMille and Wyckoff set a much-imitated standard for visual excellence.

"[Wyckoff] made a funny mistake," DeMille recalled in the 1950s. "When I was trying to get composition and light and shadows into my pictures, I would say to him: 'You mustn't make this part [of the scene] so light. Under the table . . . it should be dark, and the back corner of the room should be dark.' So [Wyckoff] would say: 'He [DeMille] likes everything contrasty.' There were some terrible battles because of that, because [building contrast] means making the blacks blacker and the whites whiter, [while I was interested in] putting them [the shadows] in the right place. I don't know that he still knows the difference [between contrast and shadows]. He will tell you that I liked everything very 'contrasty.'"[5]

DeMille's interest in lighting is evident in *The Virginian* even when there are few opportunities for lighting effects. In one scene, the afternoon sun streams through a window to give backlight and texture to a romantic moment. When the Virginian catches up with the cattle rustlers in their camp at night, flares hidden in the campfire provide the scene's only illumination. The effect is somewhat overpowering—the flares giving off much more smoke than any mesquite fire—but such use of dramatic lighting was very rare in 1914.

In *The Virginian* DeMille was clearly influenced by the Westerns of D.W. Griffith and producer Thomas Ince. He employs parallel action—cutting from one location to another at the same moment in narrative time—as in Griffith's work, and he uses dynamic screen compositions with characters close in the foreground watching riders approach in extreme background long shot, as in the Ince pictures.

Even at this early stage in his filmmaking career, DeMille was not content to accept nature as he found it if visual interest could be heightened. Nine years before he parted the Red Sea in his first version of *The Ten Commandments* he managed to divert a river from its course for *The Virginian*. "One great personal feature in pictures that I find conducive to artistic results and the best that is in a man," he wrote Sam Goldfish on July 23, 1914,

> is the out-door life that their production entails. The fascinating problems that confront one: for instance, in *The Virginian*, we needed a great water hold in a certain river in order that the stage-coach might plunge into it and become fast in the mire. We found the exact spot that we wanted, but to get the best lighting effect, the camera could only take in a portion of the river. We were eighty miles from a railroad and with only the tools and equipment necessary for our outfit. It would have done your heart good to see forty cowboys strip, make dray horses of their cow-ponies, harness of their lariats, make dredges of the sheets of iron we used for stoves and start to turn the course of the river. I felt quite like Colonel Goethals digging the Panama Canal.[6]

In 1918 Paramount reevaluated its produced properties and began to reissue or remake several early successes. *The Virginian, The Cheat, Carmen*, and several other DeMille films were rereleased at that time. Although picture content was substantially the same as in the original releases, the titles and subtitles were modified to make these films seem more up-to-date. It is the 1918 reissue version of *The Virginian* that survives. Titles in the print credit art direction to Wilfred Buckland, but Buckland was not signed by the Lasky Feature Play Company until several weeks after *The Virginian* started production, and considering the week's train-travel time from New York to Los Angeles, it is unlikely that he had anything to do with the picture.

# 3

# The Call of the North

Produced by the Jesse L. Lasky Feature Play Company for Paramount release. Director: Cecil B. DeMille. Scenario by Cecil B. DeMille from the play by George Broadhurst, and based on the novel *The Conjuror's House,* by Stewart Edward White. Art director: Wilfred Buckland. Photography: Alvin Wyckoff

Picture started: June 6, 1914. Length: 4,789 feet (five reels). Cost: $16,540.52. Released: August 11, 1914. Gross: $52,284.48

Cast: Robert Edeson (Graehme Stewart, the father, and Ned Stewart, the son), Theodore Roberts (Galen Albret, the factor [broker or agent]), Winifred Kingston (Virginia, the factor's daughter), Vera McGarry (Julie), Jode Mullally (Picard, Julie's lover), Florence Dagmar (Elodie), Milton Brown (Me-En-Gan), Horace B. Carpenter (Rand), Cecilia deMille (a small child), Sydney Deane (McTavish), and Fred Montague (Jack Wilson)

Although contracts were in place by May 1914, the Paramount distribution agreement was not scheduled to go into effect until August of that year. To finance production in the interim the Lasky Company printed its own money by means of an elaborate stock maneuver. "We realize that we must have Fifty Thousand Dollars more in cash in order to be more comfortable during the summer months," Jesse Lasky wrote DeMille on May 26, 1914.

> . . . There is now Thirty-five Hundred Dollars in the Treasury stock, which we are going to divide among the present stockholders by way of stock dividends. . . . [An additional five hundred thousand shares will be created.] Then there will be Fifty Thousand Dollars of stock actually issued [i.e., sold] and each stockholder will get a stock dividend of seven hundred percent. . . .
>
> That will make Four Hundred Thousand Dollars issued and outstanding and as we are increasing to Five Hundred Thousand Dollars [in stock], it leaves One Hundred Thousand Dollars [in stock] in the Treasury.[1]

With this sort of wizardry going on, it is no wonder there was a stock market panic in 1914. By selling 10 percent of their new stock issue and using an immediate stock dividend as a sales incentive, while at the same time protecting and increasing the majority interest of the original principals and diluting the equity position of the new investors, the Lasky Feature Play Company managed to raise the fifty thousand dollars. Today the Securities and Exchange Commission would require a disclaimer stating that "motion pictures are a highly speculative investment." Still, the foolhardy souls who bought into Lasky's half-million-dollar house of cards soon reaped benefits beyond their wildest dreams. As the financial wheels were turning in New York, Cecil B. DeMille was preparing his second solo production in Hollywood.

The Call of the North was based on a 1908 play by George Broadhurst, which in turn was adapted from Stewart Edward White's 1903 novel The Conjuror's House. Today a novelist might sell paperback rights and motion-picture rights to reap the greatest benefit from his literary labors. In the early 1900s writers sold serialization rights, low-price hardcover reprint rights, and theatrical adaptation rights. That a story set in the great outdoors like The Conjuror's House could inspire a stage adaptation seems odd, but the situation was not unusual. Jack London sold theatrical rights to his novel The Sea Wolf, which over the years was adapted into an unsuccessful full-length play and a highly popular vaudeville playlet. D.W. Griffith's epic film The Birth of a Nation (1915) was based not so much on the Reverend Thomas Dixon's 1906 novel The Clansman as it was on Dixon's theatrical adaptation of his own book.

Before movies, American theater was dominated by melodramatic plays that relied on elaborate mechanical devices to create their effects. In 1890 Joseph Arthur's Blue Jeans featured a hero lashed to a log inching ever closer to the blade of a buzz saw. By 1899 Gen. Lew Wallace's Ben-Hur was playing on Broadway, complete with chariot race! Train crashes, horse races, and pitched battles all found their way to the stage, and audiences accepted the conventions of theatrical "realism" used in their presentation.

Early films sought to exploit this theatrical tradition, but the results were often surreal. In The Miller's Daughter (Edison, 1905), the despondent heroine walks along a real New York street in one shot and jumps from an obviously painted stage setting of a bridge in another. Movie audiences quickly rejected the substitution of painted backdrops for natural settings, but interior scenes continued to be staged against trompe l'oeil painted flats when DeMille started making pictures.

After *The Squaw Man*'s success, the Lasky Company met with grumbling over the shoddiness of the interior sets in its next several pictures. Audiences and exhibitors were becoming more sophisticated and feature films were proliferating at an exponential rate. The seller's market of only a few months before was now a buyer's market, and audience demands for more realistic settings forced producers to address their appeals. To stem the tide of criticism, Jesse Lasky hired Wilfred Buckland as artistic director for the Hollywood studio. Buckland signed a contract on May 19, 1914, that ran through September 1, 1915, at a starting salary of $75 a week and escalating in four steps over the length of the agreement to $150 a week. He came to films after a long career in the theater, most significantly a twelve-year tenure as designer, lighting director, and stage manager for David Belasco. He was also a successful stage producer in his own right, but the movies presented a new challenge. As Buckland later told William deMille, with a gesture to the great outdoors, "[T]his is the first time in my life I ever had a big enough stage to work on."[2] Cecil B. DeMille knew Buckland from their days as students at the American Academy of Dramatic Arts, and he welcomed the art director's arrival.

One can only speculate on Buckland's contribution to *The Call of the North*. He arrived in Hollywood barely a week before the picture went into production and received no screen credit on the finished film. However, one scene in particular suggests Buckland's involvement—a rather elaborate night exterior of a cabin in the woods. The setting consists of three elements—a painted silhouette of trees in the far background; a miniature cabin, which by forced perspective appears to be several hundred yards away; and a foreground of real pine trees and shrubbery. Lost in the woods, Galen Albret stumbles through the dark in a weakened state. He sees a light in a distant cabin window and calls out. A woman (in fact an articulated puppet silhouette) comes to the cabin door. Albret calls and waves and exits scene stage left as he sets off for the cabin. Today, of course, the effect is somewhat ludicrous, but this is exactly the kind of "realistic" stagecraft for which the Belasco plays were noted.

Buckland soon rejected this sort of stage trickery, but his real contribution to screen art direction emerged in the way he dressed his interior sets, abandoning painted decor in favor of three-dimensional detailing with extensive practical set dressing. Other producers quickly took notice of Buckland's contributions and adopted them for their own pictures.

As with *The Squaw Man*, Sam Goldfish proclaimed that *The Call of the North* was shot on locations appropriate to the story—in this case, Moose Factory, Canada. And again, DeMille and his company never left Southern California. Big Bear Lake proved a more-than-adequate substitute for the Canadian woods.

Over the years, DeMille delighted in playing himself on camera. The original main titles on *The Call of the North* survive, and it is possible to see the first evidence of DeMille's penchant for self-promotion. A common practice in feature films of the 1910s was to introduce the players by means of an introductory vignette, much as stage actors might take an opening bow. DeMille dressed up his credits by appearing on-screen against a black backdrop with author Stewart Edward White. As DeMille points out the actors' names and the characters they play in the script, the performers dissolve into scene while White nods his approval.

Cecil B. DeMille often pointed with pride to the accurate historical detail in his films, as if accuracy alone were sufficient to justify the value of his work. This aspect of DeMille's personality was also evident from the beginning. "I will challenge anyone to find an incorrect detail in 'The Call of the North,' he wrote Sam Goldfish on July 23, 1914, ". . . in matters of detail, there is no stone left unturned. . . . The only point in this picture which I believe might be opened to criticism is, that the piece of plug tobacco used in the second reel is wrapped in a piece of paper, and paper was a rare article on Dog River; but Stewart Edward White, the author, sportsman, explorer, informs me that it is not at all impossible . . . or even improbable that some special treasure might have reached Dog River wrapped in a piece of paper."[3]

Although *The Virginian* and *The Call of the North* were produced several months before Paramount took over distribution of Lasky films, they were held for release through the new company. The sequence of release was also changed, and *The Call of the North* became Cecil B. DeMille's first Paramount Picture.

# 4

# What's-His-Name

Produced by the Jesse L. Lasky Feature Play Company for Paramount release. Director: Cecil B. DeMille. Scenario by Cecil B. DeMille, from the novel by George Barr McCutcheon. Art director: Wilfred Buckland. Photography: Alvin Wyckoff

Picture started: July 13, 1914. Length: 4,966 feet (five reels). Cost: $12,233.97. Released: October 22, 1914. Gross: $61,560.19

Cast: Max Figman (Harvey), Lolita Robertson (Nellie), Sydney Deane (Uncle Peter), Fred Montague (Fairfax), Cecilia deMille (Phoebe, the child), Dick Le Strange (best man), Merta Carpenter (Nellie's friend), Theodore Roberts (a doctor [Roberts also portrays a theatrical bill-poster in the introductory credit sequence]), Billy Elmer (stage manager), Horace B. Carpenter, and Dick La Reno

In the 1910s, as women migrated into the workforce and gained some successes in their long-fought struggle for universal suffrage, there was a knee-jerk reaction against the women's movement. Movies were quick to exploit these issues in dozens of short comedies like *The Cowboys and the Bachelor Girls* (G. Melies, 1910), *A Suffragette in Spite of Himself* (Edison, 1912), and *Future Man* (Rolma-Metro, 1916), which were filled with brow-beaten house-husbands, ball-busting wives with the physical dimensions of defensive tackles, and supposedly innocent sweet young things who could more than hold their own in a man's world.

Continuing this tradition in the feature film, Cecil B. DeMille's adaptation of George Barr McCutcheon's *What's-His-Name* tells the story of a young wife and mother who succumbs to the lure of the footlights and leaves home, husband, and child to pursue a career on stage. The film offers a reversal of the classic "he-done-her-wrong" situation of so many melodramas. To DeMille's credit, *What's-His-Name* is sympathetic to both husband and wife and never descends to the level of caricature evident in so many "today's woman" films of the period.

The stars, Max Figman and Lolita Robertson, were husband and wife offscreen. Both had distinguished stage careers, but their success in films was limited. The bulk of their movie work was in a series of single-reel domestic comedies produced for Metro Pictures between 1915 and 1917.

*What's-His-Name* offers ample evidence that DeMille still had much to learn about narrative technique in motion pictures. Without the strong physical action of *The Squaw Man* or *The Virginian*, he has difficulty conveying the details of his story. His reliance on stage technique contributes to a lack of audience involvement with the characters on-screen, due not so much to theatricality in the performances—Figman and Robertson are quite restrained in their playing—but to the mistaken notion that the story was being "put across" by the actors when in fact the absence of dialogue and the limited use of explanatory titles make it difficult to follow the action on-screen.

As Nellie Duluth rises to fame as an actress she is pursued by a wealthy stage-door-Johnnie named Fairfax. At a dinner party one evening, Fairfax learns that Nellie Duluth is married. In McCutcheon's novel the scene is played largely in dialogue:

> And it was at the table, moreover, that Nellie received Harvey's note. She saw the special delivery stamp; naturally her mother's heart leaped to the thought of Phoebe.
>
> "This may be urgent," she said, turning to Fairfax, who sat at her side. They had reached the stage of coffee and liqueurs. "You'll excuse me while I read it?"
>
> He nodded; she tore open the envelope and read. And then she laughed, helplessly, until the tears rolled down her cheeks.
>
> "Oh, dear me!" she said. "That is so funny!"
>
> "May I share the jest?" asked Fairfax.
>
> "Why—Harvey's been discharging the cook! And he thinks he has to write me about it!"
>
> "Harvey?" he said curiously, a strange look coming into his steel blue eyes.
>
> "My little hubby!" she explained—and was startled at the change that came over him.
>
> "Do you mean that?" he said, in a moment.
>
> "What? About my husband? Of course!"
>
> "I've known you three months," he said. "And this is the first I've heard of him. What's the game?"

"You might call it a guessing game, I suppose," she said, rather coldly. She held out her left hand. "Why do you suppose I wear that plain gold ring on my third finger?"

"I never noticed it," he said huskily. "I never thought of you as being married."

"Did you think I was divorced?" she asked.

"I didn't think of it at all, I tell you," he replied. "But—well, you girls seem to get divorces very easily."

"Not me," she said, with a flashing smile. "He's the nicest little hubby you ever saw, and we get along beautifully, even if we don't see one another all the time. And I've the dearest little girl—she's four—no—five!"

He glowered.

"Don't joke about it," he said. "You must guess what it means to me—how I—"

"Don't say any more," she warned him. "You might be sorry—and I might be angry."[1]

Today's readers may find McCutcheon's purple prose a little hard to take, but the scene has many subtle shadings of character that are lost in DeMille's adaptation. In the film, DeMille dispenses with the delivery of the note and has Fairfax lean close to Nellie. She backs off slightly and points to her third finger, left hand. Fairfax is shocked. Lip-readers can see that he says: "You're married?" Then, via subtitle, Nellie says, "Be careful, my husband is a regular fire eater." The dinner party breaks up and Fairfax leaves, giving Nellie a sly and knowing parting glance. The scene is economical—too economical. The nuances of Nellie's ambivalence toward her husband and child and Fairfax's relatively honorable hope that she will get a divorce and marry him are all lost in translation, and because the action is played in a single shot that takes in the entire dining room, the action of Nellie showing off her wedding ring is easily missed.

Contemporary reviewers commented on the "convincing detail" of the backstage action in *What's-His-Name*, much of which, of course, came from DeMille's own experience in the theater. Unfortunately, this most theatrical of all directors never really utilized the theater as a setting for a story. The few times he did venture backstage, as in *What's-His-Name*, *Temptation* (1917), and *Triumph* (1924), the theatrical environments seemed almost superfluous to his narratives. Even the motion picture studio setting of *We Can't Have Everything* (1919) was only a minor element of that film. DeMille's one extended exploration of life behind the scenes was *The Greatest Show on Earth* (1952), which proved to be one of his most critically acclaimed films.

About the time DeMille completed *What's-His-Name* he wrote to Sam Goldfish at some length about his attitude toward the movies. "Why did I desert my natural vocation and avocation of play writing to dabble in this most alluring art of picture making?" he asked.

> . . . . because where one member of the paying public will see a play, there are two thousand who will see a picture; whereas one or perhaps two countries would see my play, practically all the countries of the world will see my pictures. Again, and as has been probably said before, the scope of the photoplay is so much wider than that of the legitimate drama. In the first place we DO things instead of acting them. When a big effect is necessary, such as the burning of a ship, the blowing up of a mine, the wrecking of a train, we do not have to trick the effect with lights and scenery, we DO it. If it is necessary to burn a certain house, we do not employ the time honored lycopodium torches; we buy the house and burn it. We do not have to stage firemen, we employ the fire department. . . . It is the same with personal combat. If we had a great struggle to stage in the legitimate drama, I would have to so arrange the "business" that the actor participating would not be in any way injured as the struggle would have to be portrayed each night; but, in the case of the picture where the struggle is portrayed but once, the fight is real. True, the actor may be incapacitated for two or three days afterwards, but the wonderful effect on the screen acts as a balm for his wounds.[2]

Whether his actors shared this enthusiasm is not a matter of record, but it is fascinating that from his very first days behind the camera DeMille saw the movies as a vehicle for financial success and worldwide celebrity, and he seemed to have a clear vision of the public persona he would soon project to audiences around the world.

# 5

# The Man from Home

Produced by the Jesse L. Lasky Feature Play Company for Paramount release. Director: Cecil B. DeMille. Scenario by Cecil B. DeMille, from the play by Booth Tarkington and Harry Leon Wilson. Art director: Wilfred Buckland. Photography: Alvin Wyckoff

Picture started: August 19, 1914. Length: 4,900 feet (five reels). Cost: $14,221.99. Released: November 9, 1914. Gross: $62,090.77

Cast: Charles Richman (Daniel Vorhees Pike), Theodore Roberts (Grand Duke Vasili), Mabel Van Buren (Ethel Granger-Simpson), Anita King (Countess de Champigny), Fred Montague (Earl of Hawcastle), Monroe Salisbury (Hon. Almeric St. Aubyn), Horace B. Carpenter (Ivanoff), Jode Mullaly (Horace Granger-Simpson), Dick La Reno (Old Man Simpson), James Neill (officer of the carabiniere), Robert Fleming (Ribiere), J.W. Johnston (prefect of the Italian police), and Florence Dagmar (Ivanoff's maid)

One of the enduring themes of American literature is the tale of the innocent abroad. For a young nation with a decided inferiority complex there was great comfort to be gained from stories that revealed haughty, superior, and highly cultured European society to be corrupt and morally bankrupt. *The Man from Home* clearly followed in this tradition, and was all the more timely as Europe settled into the "Great War," which most Americans of 1914 viewed as the height of European folly.

*The Man from Home* was based on a play by two of the greatest purveyors of Americana, Booth Tarkington and Harry Leon Wilson. Tarkington, who would go on to win the Pulitzer Prize for literature with *The Magnificent Ambersons*, was beloved for his tales of American youth, *Penrod, Penrod and Sam,* and *Seventeen*. Wilson's novels included *Merton of the Movies, Ruggles of Red Gap*, and *His Majesty Bunker Bean.*

As a play, *The Man from Home* was a phenomenal success. It opened at the Studebaker Theatre in Chicago under the management of Liebler & Co. on September 29, 1907, and played there through the theatrical season before moving to Broadway's Astor Theatre on August 17, 1908.

The plot involves Ethel and Horace Granger-Simpson, two young Americans who have spent their school years in Europe, soaking up culture and living down their past as the children of plain John Simpson of Kokomo, Indiana. Ethel, who wants to marry a European title, sets her cap for the Honorable Almeric St. Aubyn, son of the earl of Hawcastle. Hawcastle consents to the liaison, even encourages it, but he persuades Ethel that she must be prepared to bestow a settlement on the house of St. Aubyn—a mere £150,000—something like $750,000 at then-current exchange rates. Ethel is quite comfortable committing her inheritance to the glory of the name of St. Aubyn, for the settlement will bring her a name that goes back centuries and erase her vulgar background as a mere American. But there is a fly in the ointment: her guardian, Daniel Vorhees Pike—the "man from home" of the title—is not prepared to concede that the American aristocracy of hard work and democratic decency is not equal to an ancient family with merely inherited social standing.

*The Man from Home* works on several levels, both as a sly comedy of manners and a parody of the conventions of melodramatic storytelling. In bringing the play to the screen, DeMille lost much of the comic subtlety of the original. Reviewers of the time gave the director the benefit of the doubt and noted that the emphasis was on the dramatic rather than the comedic elements of the play, but, as in *What's-His-Name,* some subtleties in the source material simply did not translate to the new medium. Still, *The Man from Home* was universally regarded as the finest Lasky feature to date.

The scenes of the play include the outdoor terrace of the Hotel Regina Margherita on a cliff at Sorrento overlooking the Bay of Naples, Italy, and the garden at the same hotel. In 1914 the sunny and open California countryside with its Mediterranean Revival style homes could easily pass for Italy—especially for the majority of the audience who had never been to either California or Italy. Today, one marvels at the idyllic setting, and can sense the appeal of Southern California for the transplanted troupers of Thespis who were used to cold winters in drafty theaters and long hot summers of unemployment.

For DeMille, California was invigorating, and he quickly adopted the "uniform" for which he would become famous—jodhpurs and puttees, open-necked shirt, and slouch hat, often set off with holster and revolver. He justified the costume because of the weeds, snakes, and relentless sun found in the vast tracts of vacant land that surrounded Hollywood—but it cannot be denied that these costume pieces lent an air of authority to DeMille's presence around the studio. Although he was imperial and domineering on the set, DeMille was said to be rather shy when away from the limelight, and it may well be that CECIL B. DEMILLE was Cecil B. deMille's greatest creation.

# 6

# The Rose of the Rancho

Produced by the Jesse L. Lasky Feature Play Company for Paramount release. Director: Cecil B. DeMille. Scenario by Cecil B. DeMille, from the play by David Belasco and Richard Walton Tully. Art director: Wilfred Buckland. Photography: Alvin Wyckoff

Picture started: September 30, 1914. Picture finished: October 22, 1914. Length: 4,991 (five reels). Cost: $16,988.01. Released: November 30, 1914. Gross: $87,028.35

Cast: Bessie Barriscale (Juanita), Jane Darwell (Senora Kenton), Monroe Salisbury (Don Luis), Dick La Reno (Ezra Kincaid), J.W. Johnston (Kearney), James Neill (Padre Antonio), Sydney Deane (Espinoza), Jeanie Macpherson (Isabelita, Espinoza's daughter), and Billy Elmer (half-breed)

As the Lasky Feature Play Company expanded its production schedule to meet the Paramount commitment, Jesse Lasky concluded an agreement with David Belasco to buy the film rights to ten Belasco plays. For DeMille the Belasco deal was a personal and professional triumph. His career in the theater developed in Belasco's shadow. His father and brother had their greatest successes working with the silver-haired Wizard of Broadway, and Cecil acted in several Belasco productions. But beyond this long-standing family dependence, Belasco had caused Cecil a humiliating professional embarrassment.

In 1910 he hired DeMille to write a play—*The Return of Peter Grimm*. By the time it reached the stage of the Belasco Theater in October 1911, the play had been completely rewritten and bore the name of Belasco as author, merely giving credit for the idea to DeMille. "It was evident from the first night," wrote DeMille in his autobiography, "that *The Return of Peter Grimm* would be a greater success than any play I had been associated with up to then. It would have meant much to have joint author's credit."[1] To the end of his days DeMille said that he understood why Belasco had appropriated and changed his work, but the explanations rang hollow. In 1911 DeMille simply could not afford to cross Belasco; but in 1914 he had the opportunity to bring Belasco's plays to the screen and the power to change his mentor's work at will. DeMille must have been amused by the irony, but to his credit he never gloated publicly over his triumph.

Gloating would have been premature in October 1914, for the rapid expansion of production, combined with slow box-office returns, devoured the cash resources of the Lasky Company at an alarming rate. In the midst of production on *The Rose of the Rancho*, Samuel Goldfish sent a letter to DeMille stressing the need to economize. "If you will go over my salary sheets," the beleaguered director replied on October 10, 1914,

you will appreciate the impossibility of any reduction there, with the exception of the one you name [Oscar] Apfel. With this exception, a cut anywhere in the salaries is an impossibility, for the reason that the cut was made at the time of employment. For instance: Do you realize that two of the principle parts in "The Man From Home" received a weekly salary of $15.00. In "The Ringmaster" [directed by Apfel, and finally released as *The Circus Man* in November 1914] the star [Theodore Roberts] receives $100.00 and the leading woman [Mabel Van Buren] $15.00 and the leading juvenile [Jode Mullally] $25.00. Comparatively, the rest of the salaries are the same. We pay from 30% to 60% less, per capita, in salaries than any company operating on the Coast. In other words, I am giving you features that have taken first place in the country at a less price than Universal can make it's one reel abhortions or Ford Sterling his one reel grotesques.[2]

"Let me correct you on your average," DeMille continued.

You state that the pictures on this end average over $14,000.00. According to your statement enclosed, they average about $12,250.00, a difference of $1,750.00 per picture. From this, take an average price of $4,000.00 for a star. This reduces the total cost [of production] on my end, including present overhead expense, to an average of $8,000.00 and I defy Man, God, or Devil to accomplish even one half as good results for that amount of money.

. . . I feel that you are entirely inappreciative of the fact that I have given the company work that can compete with [D.W.] Griffith, at a cost that theatrically can compete with the 5 and 10 cent store.[3]

. . . As to cutting down scenically, that I can do easily . . . [I can] do away with [art director Wilfred] Buckland and his entire department and go back scenically to the type of stuff used in "Brewster's Millions" and "The Master Mind" . . . but with the disastrous results that you know.

If you find that the $35,000.00 basis does not warrant our making productions at a cost around $12,000.00 or $13,000.00 including the star, then the only possible thing to do on this end is to cut down on the cost of productions. We can cut [Theodore] Roberts, though in my opinion he is one of the strongest cards we have and is the only actor we have getting a semi-decent salary. . . .[4]

I would suggest your writing Apfel direct yourself, telling him just how much you want him to know, and with this exception, will you look over the salary list and suggest where you think cuts might be made. I am free to confess that the problem has got me stumped.[5]

In the end DeMille prevailed. Wilfred Buckland and Theodore Roberts remained on the payroll, while Oscar Apfel and Dustin Farnum left the Lasky ranks and joined Frank Garbutt's Bosworth, Inc., Previous Bosworth pictures met with heavy exhibitor complaints, dragging the Paramount program down with them. Apfel and Farnum added box-office appeal to the Bosworth slate, and eliminating their salaries brought cost savings to the Lasky organization.

In his letter to Goldfish, DeMille said that he would complete *The Rose of the Rancho* on October 17, "a week earlier than I had anticipated," but his meticulously kept records indicate that the picture was actually finished on October 22. It was an impressive production, due largely to the contributions of Wilfred Buckland. Buckland's centerpiece was an elaborate set for the Castro hacienda; but for all its scale and authentic detail, the house was a near duplicate of his original stage setting. The scenery outside the upstage archway is real, but it might as well be a painted backdrop.

DeMille staged his action much as he would for the theater. Horsemen ride into scene from stage left or right and are seen through the archway as they dismount. The camera never ventures beyond the archway to show the hacienda exterior. But DeMille was learning.

In the legitimate theater, the final siege of the rancho was suggested by offstage gunshots and shouts while onstage defenders fired into the wings. In a clever bit of staging for the film, DeMille placed his camera on the side of a hill immediately above a portion of the hacienda roof. From this angle he was able to show the defenders on the roof in the foreground and the invaders circling the house in the distance. Suddenly all the conventions of "realistic" stagecraft became laughable, and Cecil B. DeMille sounded the death knell for David Belasco as a force in the theater. Belasco, blissfully unaware that his crown was about to be passed to DeMille, enthusiastically wrote that "It was like a dream to sit in my theater . . . and see my production of *The Rose of the Rancho* unfold in all its beautiful color and with all its dramatic action. You have caught the very shadows of the land of my childhood."[6]

Whether those "very shadows" were seen to the same advantage by general audiences is open to question. After Sigmund Lubin solved the *The Squaw Man*'s technical problems, the Lasky Company used Lubin's laboratory in Philadelphia for its release printing. With its Liberty Bell logo, the Lubin Mfg. Co. proclaimed its lab work was "clear as a bell," but Cecil's mother, Beatrice deMille, saw Lubin's print of *The Rose of the Rancho* and wrote to her son that "Lubin made such a bad print of The Rose, I wondered if I had seen the original film at the Belasco [Theater] through rose-colored spectacles, and called about it to find out that the one I had just seen at the Strand [Theater in New York] was Lubin's print—not yours. In the moonlight [scenes] the faces came out almost black. . . . Jesse [Lasky] says Belasco . . . saw it at the Strand and noticed no difference——!!!! and there you are."[7]

# 7

# The Girl of the Golden West

Produced by the Jesse L. Lasky Feature Play Company for Paramount release. Director: Cecil B. DeMille. Scenario by Cecil B. DeMille, from the play by David Belasco. Art director: Wilfred Buckland. Photography: Alvin Wyckoff

Picture started: October 30, 1914. Picture finished: November 7, 1914. Length: 4,420 feet (five reels). Cost: $15,109.69. Released: January 4, 1915. Gross: $102,224.46

Cast: Mabel Van Buren (The Girl), Theodore Roberts (Jack Rance), House Peters (Ramerrez), Anita King (Wowkle), Sydney Deane (Sidney Buck), Billy Elmer (Ashby), Jeanie Macpherson (Nina), Raymond Hatton (Castro), Dick Le Strange (Senor Slim), Tex Driscoll (Nick, the bartender), Art Ortego (Antonio), James Griswold (guard), and Ed Harley (old minstrel)

*T*he Girl of the Golden West was a "sure-fire" theatrical property that found success as a dramatic play and was later adapted into a popular opera before Cecil B. DeMille brought it to the screen in 1915. Three film remakes followed in 1923, 1930, and 1938 before Belasco's 1905 original ran its course. DeMille's version of *The Girl of the Golden West* was a frugal production, cranked out in a mere eight days, and the film must be considered one of the director's weaker early efforts. The settings by Wilfred Buckland were solid and realistic for the time, and DeMille attempted to recreate the Belasco lighting effects; but the hurried schedule made for some very sloppy photography. Although deep blacks and bright highlights became a feature of the lighting in DeMille's pictures in the 1910s, the lighting treatment in *The Girl of the Golden West* is haphazard, or, to paraphrase DeMille, the contrast is there but the shadows are in the wrong places. The shadowy outline of overhead muslin diffusers cut across the floor of the set at times, and in several scenes the actors are half in harsh sunlight and half in the dark. Whether this uneven lighting resulted from experimentation gone awry or sloppiness on the part of Alvin Wyckoff, we'll never know, but no other surviving DeMille film from the period has such an inconsistent photographic style.

For the first time DeMille employed a moving camera in staging a scene. When Theodore Roberts enters Mabel Van Buren's cabin in search of the wounded House Peters, the scene begins in a full shot and dollies into a tight two-shot of Van Buren and Roberts. DeMille was never noted for his use of moving camera, but he did employ the technique from time to time with great skill. For DeMille, the play was the thing, and he never called undue attention to his camera. Perhaps for this reason he has never been given his due as a creative filmmaker. In fact, DeMille's visual approach became the predominant style of the Hollywood film, and his early technique has much more in common with films of the 1930s than with the work of D.W. Griffith or his other contemporaries.

*The Girl of the Golden West* also suffers from poor casting. Mabel Van Buren came to Lasky from the Selig Polyscope Company, where cinematographer Alvin Wyckoff photographed several of her pictures. Van Buren's screen personality was pleasant but nondescript. Her days as a leading lady were brief, although she had a long career as a bit player and character actress. House Peters came to *The Girl of the Golden West* fresh from an engagement with the California Motion Picture Corporation of San Rafael, where he played the mysterious "Man" in the screen adaptation of Bret Harte's *Salomy Jane*. His screen personality was long on dignity and short on verve. Jesse Lasky, however, saw the players as an asset to the company. In a letter to Sam Goldfish he wrote, "Cecil is making good progress on 'The Girl of the Golden West' and I like what I have seen of it very much. Miss Van Buren is particularly good and House Peters, in the lead, promises to be one of the handsomest figures ever seen on the screen. I am trying very hard to get him to remain in stock. It is only a question of getting him at the right figure. He seems to be just what we need, a handsome, clever leading man."[1]

Today, *The Girl of the Golden West* is more interesting for its minor players. Anita King has a small role as Wowkle, the Girl's Indian maid, but DeMille indelibly etches her character in the minds of the audience in a matter of seconds. In the scene, Mabel Van Buren brings home groceries for a dinner she is preparing. As Anita King opens the packages, she secretly and ravenously licks the wrappers and stashes away a few morsels for herself. The externalizing of character through bits of "business" turns a walk-on part into a character role and enriches the whole work. Two other actors in *The Girl of the Golden West* had great impact in DeMille's later career. Jeanie Macpherson played her first significant role in a DeMille picture (after a minor part in *The Rose of the*

*Rancho*), and Raymond Hatton also made his first appearance for the director.

Jesse Lasky visited the West Coast about the time DeMille completed principal photography on *The Girl of the Golden West*, and he offered this assessment of studio operations:

> The plant here is run simply and systematically. The moment instructions are received, every department is notified and Cecil never forgives, or excuses, any failure of any of his subordinates to carry out his instructions. . . .
>
> We are experiencing the same old trouble again with having discovered spots in the negative [film] stock. Our technical force here feel sure these spots are in the negative which Lubin furnishes us. I don't know this is the case, but some "CAMEO KIRBY" scenes just finished will now have to be retaken; this causes the loss of a little time and some money. However it is all part of the game.
>
> [Frank] Garbutt wired his man, Pierce, yesterday in answer to a telegram he received, offering him Douglas Fairbanks. He wanted to know if I wanted him and I said "Yes". . . the "GENTLEMAN OF LEISURE". . . will make a good vehicle for Fairbanks, but if we do not secure him, we will have no trouble in filling the lead in that play.[2]
>
> I am still holding out on Blanche Sweet, as I hate to pay her over $300.00, but I will not lose her and, if by the time I leave I cannot bring her around, will give her more money. . . .[3]

# 8

# The Warrens of Virginia

Produced by the Jesse L. Lasky Feature Play Company for Paramount release. Director: Cecil B. DeMille. Scenario: William C. deMille, from his own play. Photography: Alvin Wyckoff. Art director: Wilfred Buckland

Picture started: December 5, 1914. Picture completed: January 9, 1915. Length: 4,178 feet (five reels). Cost: $28,359.59. Released: February 15, 1915. Gross: $85,769.96

Cast: James Neill (General Warren), Mabel Van Buren (his wife), Blanche Sweet (Agatha Warren), Page Peters (her brother), House Peters (Ned Burton), Marjorie Daw (Betty Warren), Gerald Ward (Bob Warren), and Mildred Harris

Cecil B. DeMille had a long association with *The Warrens of Virginia* before he brought it to the screen. He played a leading role in David Belasco's 1907 Broadway production of his brother William's original play, which was loosely based on their grandfather's exploits in the Civil War. Even though Belasco had produced the play, *The Warrens of Virginia* was not part of the ten-play Lasky-Belasco agreement. The Lasky Feature Play Company carried the play on its books as an asset at the time *The Squaw Man* was in production, but whether Lasky paid for the rights or William deMille offered them to the company as an in-kind investment is not known.

In his 1939 autobiography, *Hollywood Saga*, William belittled his movie adventure, claiming that when offered a 25 percent interest in the Lasky Company he flatly turned down the proposition because he didn't feel he could invest good money in one of his brother's harebrained schemes. Later, when he realized the error of his ways, William condescended to come to Hollywood for three months to lend his talents to the "flickers." But in 1939 William deMille was out of the picture business, and his Broadway triumphs were long forgotten. His autobiography was an attempt to justify his life's work. It cannot be determined whether or not he was actually offered an interest in the Lasky Company, but when he finally came to the movies he certainly hoped his career would last longer than three months. On September 17, 1914, he wrote to his brother:

> Dear C.:
>     . . . by the time this reaches you, I will be on the train bound for Hollywood.
>     I suppose Sam [Goldfish] and Jesse [Lasky] have written you that they have arranged for me to join your forces. I am coming, prepared to jump right in and if I fit stay a year or two. . . .
>     I expect to leave New York on Tuesday the 22d, on the Santa Fe limited, which should bring me to Hollywood, I think, on Saturday evening.
>
> Best wishes and love from us all,
>
> Billy[1]

On his first day in Hollywood, William deMille was pressed into service as a bit-actor in *The Rose of the Rancho*, but he quickly settled down to writing and was put to work adapting Booth Tarkington and Harry Leon Wilson's *Cameo Kirby* for Oscar Apfel to direct. After he'd proven his ability in the screen trade, William set about converting *The Warrens of Virginia* into scenario form.

In 1910, with the fiftieth anniversary of the Civil War approaching, the movies became fascinated with tales of what was still known in the North as the War of the Rebellion and in the South as the War between the States. Hundreds of Civil War films poured out of the studios, from the somber *The House with Closed Shutters* (Biograph, 1910) to the raucous *Cohen Saves the Flag* (Keystone, 1913), but the cycle reached its peak with such films as *The Birth of a Nation* (Epoch Producing Corp., 1915) and *The Coward* (Triangle-KayBee, 1915).

*The Warrens of Virginia* was the Lasky Feature Play Company's contribution to the cycle, and no expense was spared in bringing it to the screen. The cost was nearly double that of any previous Lasky production—in part because the film required a large number of extras and period costumes. But for all the extra money that went into the picture, little attempt was made to enlarge the action of the stage play.

In *The Birth of a Nation* D.W. Griffith took a bold cinematic approach to Thomas Dixon's stage script for *The Clansman*. The battle of

Petersburg and the ride of the Klan were played for spectacle, and the action jumped from location to location in a frenzy of cross-cutting that became Griffith's trademark. DeMille, on the other hand, remained relatively true to the theatrical context of *The Warrens of Virginia*. Although he expanded the action to include a supply train raid that occurred off-stage in the play, the picture lacked big battle scenes. His treatment was in keeping with the Lasky policy of producing Broadway plays on film.

The real difference between Griffith and DeMille was rooted in their theatrical careers. Griffith, a product of popular melodrama, was also influenced by the naturalistic dramas of Henrik Ibsen; DeMille's background was in the mainstream Broadway theater. He almost never succumbed to the manipulation of Griffith's last-minute rescues, nor did he paint his villains only in shades of black. Griffith, in contrast, was not bound by DeMille's devotion to narrative logic.

Whatever their differences in approach, DeMille's Civil War picture simply could not compete with Griffith's. *The Birth of a Nation* was a cultural sensation, and in a very real sense it became the Civil War picture to end all Civil War pictures. Released at virtually the same time as Griffith's picture, *The Warrens of Virginia* was everyone's second choice. Little wonder that it was only a modest success.

It was a great coup for Lasky to lure leading lady Blanche Sweet away from Griffith's Reliance-Majestic stock company. Sweet's talent blossomed under the guidance of D.W. Griffith, but he was notorious for paying low wages. The $500.00 per week Lasky offered Sweet was a substantial increase over her previous weekly salary, and she could not refuse the offer—especially because Griffith showed no inclination to meet it. Regarded as one of the screen's finest actresses, Blanche Sweet was naturally assumed to be a great asset to the Lasky Feature Play Company. But Sweet never really clicked with the public during the time she spent with Lasky. Certainly her performance in *The Warrens of Virginia* is rather lackluster: she comes across as a competent leading lady and nothing more. The differences in her performances for Griffith and DeMille force one to consider how each director affected her way of working. Those who acted under Griffith's direction often commented on his almost hypnotic power in coaxing performances from his players. Griffith had his actors compete for plum roles, and he was known to change actors in the middle of rehearsal. While shooting a picture, he lavished special attention on individual close-ups for Lillian Gish or Mae Marsh or Blanche Sweet. Griffith was an actor's director.

In contrast, Cecil B. DeMille believed that telling an actor how to act was not the director's job. He hired people he felt were competent to play the roles as he envisioned them, and he left the details of the performance to the actors. Perhaps Blanche Sweet needed the attention that DeMille was unwilling or unable to give. It is a matter of record that they never got along. She was appalled by his public bravado and what she perceived to be his lack of sensitivity. DeMille soon left the guidance of her performances to other directors. She barely rates a mention in his posthumously published autobiography, and her name does not appear in the index.

Although *The Warrens of Virginia* did not match the commercial success of *The Birth of a Nation*, it was nonetheless an influential film. DeMille, art director Wilfred Buckland, and cinematographer Alvin Wyckoff continued to refine the visual style they derived from "Belasco" lighting in the theater. The photography in *The Warrens of Virginia* emphasizes source lighting from windows, lamps, and fires and successfully creates a dark, moody look. Lasky sales manager Sam Goldfish feared exhibitors would complain that the picture was too dark and grumbled that the picture was not properly exposed. But DeMille argued that the film's lighting followed Rembrandt's treatment of light in his painted masterpieces. Armed with this artistic imprimatur, Goldfish was confident he could tell exhibitors he was giving them more for their money—not less. "Rembrandt lighting" became known as "Lasky lighting" in the trade and set the standard for motion picture photography between 1915 and 1918.

# 9

# The Unafraid

Produced by the Jesse L. Lasky Feature Play Company for Paramount release. Director: Cecil B. DeMille. Scenario by Cecil B. DeMille, from the novel by Eleanor M. Ingram. Art director: Wilfred Buckland. Photography: Alvin Wyckoff

Picture started: January 19, 1915. Picture finished: February 12, 1915. Length: 4,008 feet (four reels). Cost: $14,226.50. Released: April 1, 1915. Gross: $63,944.02

Cast: Rita Jolivet (Delight Warren), House Peters (Stefan Balsic), Page Peters (Michael Balsic), Billy Elmer (Jack McCarty), Larry Peyton (Danilo Lesendra), Theodore Roberts (secret agent of the "Dual Empire"), Marjorie Daw (Irenya), Raymond Hatton (valet), Gertrude Kellar (Countess Novna), James Neill (Delight Warren's uncle), Jane Darwell (her aunt), and Allan Garcia (Joseph)

Committed to making thirty feature films a year for Paramount, the Lasky Company gave Director-General DeMille the responsibility for supervising the entire output of the studio. To say that DeMille took his responsibilities seriously would be an understatement. In 1915 he wrote scripts for eighteen of the thirty Lasky pictures and directed no fewer than thirteen of them himself, as well as parts of several others.

With the Great War raging in Europe, American audiences took an interest in Serbia and other exotic, little-known principalities of eastern Europe. Part of the attraction of Eleanor Ingram's 1913 novel *The Unafraid* was its setting—the rugged, mountainous Montenegro, which would soon be absorbed into the state of Yugoslavia. The story revolves around an Austro-Hungarian plot to subvert and annex the principality of Montenegro. Because the United States was still neutral in 1915, Austria-Hungary is referred to euphemistically throughout the film as "The Dual Empire."

Playboy prince Michael Balsic (Page Peters) is bribed by an agent of the Dual Empire (Theodore Roberts) to start a revolution in Montenegro. Michael's brother Stefan (House Peters) suspects his brother's treachery, but there is little he can do to stop it. In Paris, Michael squanders the money he was paid. His life threatened by the Dual Empire, Michael

**41**

determines to marry Delight Warren (Rita Jolivet), a rich American heiress, with the intention of using her money to cover his losses. To thwart his brother, Stefan kidnaps Delight and forces her to marry him. In the time-honored tradition of the romantic novel, her initial revulsion turns to love when she is made to realize Michael's evil intentions.

The central conflict in *The Unafraid*—two brothers (or, in other stories, best friends), one not entirely good, the other not completely evil, and both vying for the same woman—was a theme that appealed to DeMille, and he used it often in films such as *The Ten Commandments* (1923), *Union Pacific* (1939), *North West Mounted Police* (1940), and *Reap the Wild Wind* (1942).

Wilfred Buckland's art direction in *The Unafraid* shows a growing sophistication, although many indications remain of the great economy with which the Lasky features of the period were made. After the kidnapping, for example, Delight Warren and her captor ride to a church where the forced marriage will take place. The coach pulls up and stops on a dirt road in medium shot. Delight and Stefan step out. Next, DeMille cuts to inside the sanctuary where the priest will perform the ceremony. The exterior of the church is never shown, saving the building of an expensive but relatively unimportant set. This sort of economy is lost on modern audiences who have come to expect obligatory establishing shots.

Although the Lasky Company continued to walk a precarious financial tightwire, the studio showed signs of growing prosperity as the Hollywood facilities underwent almost continuous capital improvement. Sometime before the production of *The Rose of the Rancho,* a long row of wood-frame dressing rooms was erected, followed by rapid expansion and improvement of stage facilities. By the time *The Unafraid* went before the camera in January 1915, the Lasky studio had a large new glass-covered stage that allowed for both better lighting control and filming during bad weather.

As early as February 1914, Cecil B. DeMille bought Harry Revier's interest in the Burns and Revier studio and his interest in the ground lease for $2,250. Shortly thereafter, L.L. Burns also exited the picture and DeMille entered into a three-year lease agreement with Jacob Stern, owner of the property, that apparently superseded the sublease with Burns and Revier.[1]

Across town, Frank Garbutt sought to shore up his faltering Bosworth, Inc., by creating the Oliver Morosco Photoplay Company. Like David Belasco, Oliver Morosco was an important theatrical impresario in Los

Angeles and New York. Although Morosco had little to do with the film company that bore his name, his lieutenant, Charles Eyton, took up residence at the Bosworth-Morosco Studio on Occidental Boulevard near downtown Los Angeles to supervise the Morosco productions.

Three of the actors in *The Unafraid*—leading lady Rita Jolivet and supporting players Allan Garcia and Larry Peyton—were members of the Bosworth-Morosco stock company—an indication of the growing cooperation between Garbutt and the Lasky Company. Rita Jolivet became a footnote in history when she survived the sinking of the *Lusitania*. One of her fellow passengers was prominent theatrical manager Charles Frohman, who gave Cecil DeMille his first opportunity on the stage. Frohman was not so lucky. He was among the 1,198 passengers and crew to go down with the ship on that fateful May 7, 1915.

# The Captive

Produced by the Jesse L. Lasky Feature Play Company for Paramount release. Director: Cecil B. DeMille. Original story and scenario by Cecil B. DeMille and Jeanie Macpherson. Art director: Wilfred Buckland. Photography: Alvin Wyckoff

Picture started: February 15, 1915. Picture finished: March 4, 1915. Length: 4,596 feet (five reels). Cost: $12,153.54. Released: April 22, 1915. Gross: $56,074.88

Cast: Blanche Sweet (Sonya Martinovitch), House Peters (Mahmud Hassan), Page Peters (Marko), Jeanie Macpherson (Milka), Theodore Roberts (Burgomaster), Billy Elmer (Turkish officer), and Marjorie Daw

Although Jeanie Macpherson appeared in several DeMille films beginning with *The Rose of the Rancho*, *The Captive* marked her first screenplay collaboration with the director. She quickly became his favorite screenwriter. Macpherson began her film career in 1909 acting in D.W. Griffith's Biograph stock company. By 1913 she was a triple hyphenate at Universal: actress-writer-director. According to an official studio biography, Macpherson encountered Cecil DeMille several times before actually meeting him.

> She played for a few months in the musical production, *Havana*. Then she secured a part in the William deMille production *Strongheart*, with Edgar Selwyn in the lead. Cecil B. DeMille was in the crowd at the dress rehearsal, but she did not meet him for many years. She crossed the path of DeMille on another occasion, when she went to the DeMille Play Agency in New York and asked for Mrs. [Beatrice] DeMille [Cecil's mother and head of the agency]. Mrs. DeMille was not in but she was told that Cecil DeMille was. She said, "No, I won't see Mr. DeMille."
> Several years later, when Miss Macpherson was with Universal she saw Mr. DeMille at lunch, and asked [fellow actress-writer-director] Lois Weber, "Who is that brooding

man with the black eyes?" Again she crossed DeMille's path without meeting him.[1]

Another time she was directing a one-reel picture for Universal. She happened at that time to choose the same desert location as Mr. DeMille. When she was all set for her long shot she found Mr. DeMille's company in the foreground. . . . Still they did not meet, the companies exchanging greetings from a distance and choosing new locations.[2]

Macpherson came to the Lasky studio after being fired from Universal for going over schedule on one of her short productions. She is said to have laid siege to DeMille's office until she was given an opportunity, but she was initially hired as an actress only and not as a writer-director. Macpherson managed to impress DeMille with her story sense, however, and proved to be an ideal collaborator. She shared DeMille's enthusiasm for melodrama and brought a distinct, if somewhat eccentric, sensibility to her writing.

*The Captive* seems to have been designed to take advantage of the costumes already used for *The Unafraid*. Again the setting is an eastern European country, and again the heroine falls in love with her enemy, though in this story the dramatic tension is greatly increased. Mahmud Hassan (House Peters) is a Turkish nobleman who is captured and given to Sonya (Blanche Sweet) to work the family farm in the absence of her brother, Marko (Page Peters), who has been killed in the Great War. Sonya first dominates the captive Turk, then falls in love with him. He later rescues her in defiance of his own countrymen. The lovers' lives are shattered before they can start anew. In finding each other Sonya Martinovitch and Mahmud Hassan lose everything they have lived and worked for: friends, property, and position. This ambiguous and disturbing approach to typical romantic novel claptrap was a quality that distinguished Macpherson's work. As everyone in the audience expected, love conquered all in *The Captive*—but at what price? An element of this theme appears in Belasco's *The Girl of the Golden West*, but Ramerrez and the girl make a lesser sacrifice when vigilantes only force them to leave the state.

A freak accident killed an extra during production of *The Captive*. Actors portraying soldiers stormed a door, smashing it with their rifle butts. One of the guns was loaded with live ammunition and went off, dropping thirty-year-old Charles Chandler dead in his tracks. In his autobiography, DeMille asserts that he told the extras to reload their rifles with blanks before the scene was taken. Blanche Sweet contended that DeMille's demand for realism led the director to encourage the use of live ammunition.[3]

Not among the films that DeMille kept in his personal collection, *The Captive* was long thought to be lost. In 1970 Paramount donated studio prints of its pre-1948 sound film library to the UCLA Film and Television Archive. While removing these films from the Paramount vaults, Bob Epstein and Richard Simonton Jr. discovered a treasure-trove of silent films, including *The Captive*, and it was arranged for the American Film Institute to take possession of the films and preserve them.

# The Wild Goose Chase

Produced by the Jesse L. Lasky Feature Play Company for Paramount release. Director: Cecil B. DeMille. Scenario: William C. deMille, from his play. Art director: Wilfred Buckland. Photography: Alvin Wyckoff

Picture started: March 15, 1915. Pictured finished: March 25, 1915. Length: 4,286 feet (five reels). Cost: $10,611.85. Released: May 27, 1915. Gross: $60,630.68

Cast: Ina Claire (Betty Wright), Tom Forman (Bob Randall), Lucien Littlefield (Grind), Helen Marlborough (Betty's mother), Raymond Hatton (Betty's father), Theodore Roberts (Horatio Brutus Bangs), Ernest Joy (Bob's father), and Florence Smith (Bob's mother)

*T*he Wild Goose Chase brought stage favorite Ina Claire to the screen in a quickly and cheaply made production that the star later chose to ignore—to the point of forgetting she ever made it, according to DeMille.[1] Today, no print of *The Wild Goose Chase* is known to exist in any archive or private collection, and it is a pity. Ina Claire was a delightful theatrical personality, and from contemporary reviews it seems that DeMille was able to capture much of her stage presence on film. Claire made only two other silent films, *The Puppet Crown* (Lasky Feature Play Company, 1915) and *Polly with a Past* (Metro, 1920), and a mere handful of talkies—most notably *The Royal Family of Broadway* (Paramount, 1930), *The Greeks Had a Word for Them* (Goldwyn-United Artists, 1932), and the long-unseen first sound version of *The Awful Truth* (Pathé, 1929).

During his early career, Cecil B. DeMille made no effort to keep prints of his films. When he left Famous Players-Lasky to form his own company in 1925, he made an agreement with Jesse Lasky to strike prints of his earlier productions for his personal use.[2] DeMille received prints of all but seven of his first forty-eight films, and in the early 1960s his family made arrangements to give the 35mm nitrate prints to the George Eastman House in Rochester, New York, for preservation. The majority of his work survives because of DeMille's foresight. While *The Squaw*

*Man* (1914), *The Cheat* (1915), *The Little American* (1917), *The Affairs of Anatol* (1921), *Manslaughter* (1922), *The Ten Commandments* (1923), and a handful of his other Paramount silents have surfaced elsewhere, the bulk of DeMille's pre-1925 output would have been lost to the ravages of nitrate decomposition and studio neglect if he had not kept his own prints in a concrete vault at his Hollywood home. By contrast, William deMille, who was an equally prolific silent-screen director, left his celluloid posterity in the hands of Paramount, and his surviving films can be counted on the pitching hand of "Three-Finger" Brown.

When Cecil B. DeMille received the Screen Producers Guild Milestone Award on January 22, 1956, he said in his acceptance address:

> I cannot stand here surrounded by so many friends . . . without thinking also of the others who did so much to make our industry great and are now gone out of this world of shadows and images into the Light.
>
> I cannot think of them and their work without wishing again, as I have wished many times, that we and the public were more aware of the dramatic riches we have stored in our vaults—the classics of the screen.
>
> Of course, we have occasional reissues, if one must use that detestable word. We do not say that someone reissues Hamlet or Lohengrin—or that, the next time you go to the Louvre, you can see a reissue of the Mona Lisa. You might as well say that God reissues the sunset every evening.
>
> When we think in terms of "reissues," we automatically condemn the picture to second-rate treatment by the publicity and advertising departments, by the exhibitors—and by the public. The great classics of the screen deserve better treatment than that—for they remain not second-rate, but first-rate specimens of the dramatic art.
>
> And I include among them a number of the old silent pictures—which, for pure motion picture art, have not been surpassed by sound—and which should be presented to the public on special projecting machines running at 60 feet a minute, instead of the present 90 feet a minute, that makes great artists jump about like Woody Woodpecker.[3]
>
> The [motion picture] industry will not come of age until it makes a determined effort to keep its own great classics

alive—and to present them regularly to the public in a manner worthy of their merit and worthy of the great names who made them.[4]

Today, "preservation" is a buzzword in Hollywood, but in the 1950s Cecil B. DeMille was a voice in the wilderness.

# 12

# The Arab

Produced by the Jesse L. Lasky Feature Play Company for Paramount release. Director: Cecil B. DeMille. Scenario: Cecil B. DeMille, from the play by Edgar Selwyn. Art director: Wilfred Buckland. Photography: Alvin Wyckoff

Picture started: April 5, 1915. Picture finished: April 21, 1915. Length: 4,844 feet (5 reels). Cost: $18,327.88 Released: June 14, 1915. Gross: $68,526.84

Cast: Edgar Selwyn (Jamil, the son), Horace B. Carpenter (the Sheik, his father), Milton Brown (Abdullah), Billy Elmer (Meshur, his enemy), Gertrude Robinson (Mary), Sydney Deane (Dr. Hilbert, her father), Theodore Roberts (Kyamil Pasha), Raymond Hatton (messenger), J. Parke Jones (Ibrahim), and Irvin S. Cobb (an American tourist)

I n the 1920s, after Rudolph Valentino created a sensation in *The Sheik* (Famous Players-Lasky/Paramount, 1921), Paramount sold remake rights for *The Arab* to Metro Pictures as a vehicle for director Rex Ingram and his new discovery, Ramon Novarro (nee Samaniegos). There was a certain irony in this, because it was Ingram who plucked Valentino from the ranks of bit players to star in *The Four Horsemen of the Apocalypse* and *The Conquering Power* for Metro in 1921. However, Metro failed to recognize Valentino's appeal, and the screen's first Latin lover was signed by Paramount. Meanwhile, DeMille used Novarro as a bit player in *Joan the Woman* and *The Little American*, but Paramount paid no attention, and Novarro was allowed to slip away and gain his greatest fame at Metro.

By the time DeMille ordered prints of his early pictures, the 1915 version of *The Arab* was no longer available. When a studio sold remake rights, it commonly conveyed the master film elements to the purchasing studio to keep the original from competing with the remake. Although Metro-Goldwyn-Mayer launched an ambitious preservation program in the 1970s, neither DeMille's version of *The Arab* nor their own 1924 remake were found in the studio vaults. Since then a print of the Ingram/ Novarro picture was discovered at the Czech Film Archive, but DeMille's 1915 original remains a lost film.

In addition to marking the film debut of famed American humorist Irvin S. Cobb, DeMille's production of *The Arab* featured Edgar Selwyn, who wrote and produced the original play. Edgar Selwyn and his brother, Archibald, were respected theatrical producer-managers who had been involved in the formation of the All-Star Feature Film Corporation in 1913. All-Star was a short-lived proposition, although some elements of the company were incorporated into Metro Pictures in 1915.

When Famous Players and the Lasky Feature Play Company merged in 1916, Sam Goldfish and Adolph Zukor discovered that the company wasn't big enough for the two of them. Goldfish was asked to leave, and he set up shop in partnership with the Selwyn brothers to form Goldwyn Pictures—the name was an amalgam of Goldfish and Selwyn. Sam liked the name Goldwyn so much he took it for his own, though some Hollywood wags were said to have quipped that "Sel-fish" was a more appropriate combination.

# 13

# Chimmie Fadden

Produced by the Jesse L. Lasky Feature Play Company for Paramount release. Director: Cecil B. DeMille. Scenario by Cecil B. DeMille, from the book by E.W. Townsend and the play by Augustus Thomas. Art director: Wilfred Buckland. Photography: Alvin Wyckoff

Picture started: May 3, 1915. Picture finished: May 18, 1915. Length: 4,809 feet (five reels). Cost: $10,504.39. Released: June 28, 1915. Gross: $78,944.49

Cast: Victor Moore (Chimmie Fadden), Raymond Hatton (Larry Fadden, his brother), Mrs. Lewis McCord (their mother), Ernest Joy (Van Cortlandt), Anita King (Fanny, his daughter), Camille Astor (Hortense—"the Duchess," her maid), Tom Forman (Antoine, Van Cortlandt's valet), and Harry deRoy (Perkins, the butler)

*Chimmie Fadden* was created by E.W. Townsend, a writer for the *New York Sun*, who based his fictional character on the toughs and pugs who were a fixture on the Bowery in the 1890s. First appearing in a series of newspaper sketches, the Chimmie Fadden stories were collected and published as a book in 1895 and transformed into a stage play by Augustus Thomas the following year.

Thomas fleshed out Townsend's character pieces with a plot that has Chimmie befriended by a society woman and hired as a rather bumbling butler. Complications arise when Fadden's brother robs the home of Chimmie's patron. DeMille and Jeanie Macpherson would later rework some of these elements in a more serious vein in creating the scenario for *The Golden Chance*.

Having seen Victor Moore in *Chimmie Fadden* on Broadway, Beatrice deMille persuaded her son that Moore was the only actor for the screen role. A good part of Moore's appeal was the distinctive nasal whine of his voice. The silent screen deprived the star of this vocal trademark, but Moore nevertheless created a strong impression in *Chimmie Fadden*. According to DeMille, and based on the evidence of their second film, *Chimmie Fadden Out West*, the director and star deliberately avoided wild slapstick in favor of a quiet but amusing style of character comedy. Unfortunately, we can only imagine how funny *Chimmie Fadden* was, because today no prints of the film are known to exist in any archive or private collection.

# 14

# Kindling

Produced by the Jesse L. Lasky Feature Play Company for Paramount release. By arrangement with E.J. Bowes. Director: Cecil B. DeMille. Scenario by Cecil B. DeMille, from the play by Charles Kenyon. Art director: Wilfred Buckland. Photography: Alvin Wyckoff

Picture started: May 24, 1915. Picture finished: June 10, 1915. Length: five reels. Cost: $10,039.52. Released: July 12, 1915. Gross: $66,036.42

Cast: Charlotte Walker (Maggie Schultz), Thomas Meighan ("Honest" Heine Schultz), Raymond Hatton (Steve, a crook), Mrs. Lewis McCord (Mrs. Bates), Billy Elmer (Rafferty, of the central office), Lillian Langdon (Mrs. Burke-Smith), Florence Dagmar (Alice, her niece), and Tom Forman (young Dr. Taylor)

In 1915 Cecil B. DeMille created some of his finest films. Seeing them today, it is easy to understand why critics and audiences so highly regarded the director's work. From the first shots of a skid-row street corner at night, one is aware that *Kindling* is a very special picture and that DeMille is at last in full command of his medium.

*Kindling* is DeMille's most claustrophobic film. All of the action is played in tightly composed shots emphasizing the oppressive nature of tenement life. In many ways the film is a polemic rather than a drama. At one point the narrative stops dead as Heine Schultz takes his wife, Maggie, on a tour of their poverty-stricken neighborhood. Children are seen eating out of garbage cans, and a drunk initiates a six-year-old in the dubious pleasures of John Barleycorn by pouring beer down her throat. Deadbeats and petty criminals infest the area. The depiction of life in the slums is ugly and uncompromising. "In this environment children burn up like kindling," Heine Schultz tells his wife. "I'd rather kill a child of ours the day it is born than send it up against a life like that." Unknown to Heine, Maggie is pregnant and afraid to tell him he is to become a father. After seeing "The toll of the tenement," we meet "The receiver of the toll," Mrs. Burke-Smith, who accepts payments from her rental agent as she pampers her pet dog with lavender baths and custom-made sweaters.

A neighbor tells Maggie Schultz of a government program that provides farmland out west. Maggie sees her salvation in leaving the slums for wide-open spaces. She will be able to tell Heine about the baby and overcome his objections to children. The problem: they will need one hundred dollars to make the trip.

In one of those beau gestes that salve the conscience of the rich, Mrs. Burke-Smith is persuaded by her niece to visit her tenants in the slums. "I am glad to see you have no children," Burke-Smith reinforces the sentiments of Maggie's husband. "They are an economic error in the tenements." She offers Maggie a job as a seamstress for five dollars a week. With her husband now on strike, Maggie accepts, but the job brings only bitterness as she finds that she is to sew a wardrobe for Mrs. Burke-Smith's pet. "Clothes for a dog. She'd do this for a mutt and let my baby starve."

The squalor and misery depicted in *Kindling* offer stark contrast to the nostalgic Norman Rockwell *Saturday Evening Post* world often called to mind when we think of America before the Great War, yet literature, theater, and film regularly explored social ills in the 1910s. Of course, melodramatic exaggeration often shrouded social themes in the arts, and *Kindling* is no exception. Steve, a petty criminal in the neighborhood, offers Maggie a chance for a quick hundred dollars if she will help him rob the Burke-Smith mansion. She agrees, and suffers predictable consequences. Despite several unconvincing plot complications, DeMille manages to keep the plight of the characters believable.

The one false note in *Kindling* is the rather simpering performance of Charlotte Walker. Walker had a long career in the theater beginning in 1895 and extending into the mid-1930s. She appeared in the original stage productions of *The Warrens of Virginia* and *The Trail of the Lonesome Pine*. Her film career was spotty, although she worked intermittently on-screen as a character actress into the early 1940s. Thomas Meighan, however, plays the role of Heine Schultz with the skill and restraint that were his hallmark. Meighan gained his greatest popularity in DeMille's *Male and Female* and George Loane Tucker's *The Miracle Man* (both 1919) and remained a top star throughout the silent era.

Charles Kenyon made his reputation as a playwright with gritty, realistic dramas like *Kindling, Husband and Wife*, and *The Claim*. In the 1920s, however, the San Francisco writer spent much of his time writing slick Western screenplays for Tom Mix.

DeMille himself was not immune to the swing of the artistic pendulum. One of his great talents was reading the public mood, and in the late 1910s and early 1920s he gave up the exploration of social ills in favor of illuminating the vagaries of human folly in a series of sophisticated comedies. Yet, for all the glamour and spectacle of DeMille's later work, *Kindling* was not simply an early aberration. Charles Kenyon's play exerted a strong influence on the director. He borrowed elements from it for several of his later pictures including *The Golden Chance* and its remake, *Forbidden Fruit*, as well as *The Whispering Chorus* and *Saturday Night*.

**15**

# María Rosa

Produced by the Jesse L. Lasky Feature Play Company for Paramount release. Director: Cecil B. DeMille. Scenario by William C. deMille, from the play by Angel Guimera, as translated and adapted by Guido Marburg and Wallace Gilpatrick. Art director: Wilfred Buckland. Photography: Alvin Wyckoff

Picture started: June 14, 1915. Picture finished: June 25, 1915. Length: 4,253 feet (five reels). Cost: $18,574.97. Released: May 8, 1916. Gross: $102,767.81

Cast: Geraldine Farrar (Maria Rosa), Wallace Reid (Andreas), Pedro de Cordoba (Ramon), Ernest Joy (Carlos), Anita King (Ana), Horace B. Carpenter (Pedro), James Neill (a priest), and Billy Elmer (a policeman)

When Geraldine Farrar appeared for her last performance in the current season at the Metropolitan Opera House in New York City," wrote an anonymous reporter for *Paramount Progress* in 1915, "the audience, at the conclusion of the opera, flatly refused to leave the auditorium. The deafening applause continued without ceasing while Miss Farrar came repeatedly before the curtain, bowing her thanks. . . ."[1] Geraldine Farrar, one of the great stars of the Metropolitan Opera, was beloved by the American public; they were proud that this homegrown daughter of a professional baseball player was an internationally recognized celebrity in a European art form.

Farrar came to pictures at a crucial time in her career. "The European war, ruining opera on the continent," wrote Morris Gest, "had deprived her of her customary summer of international activity."[2] A longtime friend of Farrar and the son-in-law of Mrs. David Belasco, Gest was a vaudeville producer long connected with Hammerstein's Victoria Theater, where he handled "everything from a Caucasus bear to a Russian giant or a fake Sultan with a large family. . . ." After dinner at Farrar's home one evening, Gest recalled,

> She led us to her library, where she has . . . a painting of the Emperor of Germany in the full flower of early maturity. It

57

was a favorite portrait, presented to her by the Emperor himself.

"How different he is now," she said. "Really—to perpetuate one's youth one should have a photograph taken every day—until age begins."

"The only way to really live forever," I answered, "is on a picture screen. . . ."

That evening, according to Gest, the Lasky production of *The Girl of the Golden West* opened at the Strand Theater in New York. "Miss Farrar was very glad to attend," continued Gest, "but in the limousine en route confessed to me that she had seen but one 'picture show' in her life—*Quo Vadis?*, only a year ago at the Cinema Theater, in Paris."

In his article Gest insisted that his efforts to bring Geraldine Farrar to the movies were completely unselfish. "I at length made her see that my interest was a friendly one," he wrote,"and that I had not entered her home as a friend to make personal profit." But whatever his motive, he went about his task with great zeal. First he had to persuade the opera star that the public might be interested in seeing her on-screen:

At length I endeavored to show her what a wonderful thing it would be if her performance of *Carmen* could be perpetuated in motion photography. There are nine million [phonograph] records of your voice to-day . . . and everyone who owns Farrar records has a *Carmen* record.[3] Every one of those people, as well as many others, would be more than glad of the opportunity to see you as an actress even as they now hear you as a singer. Your voice is heard in every American town and city of consequence, and yet you've been in comparatively few of these places. Do you think that your actual moving personality would have less appeal?

Next, Morris Gest invited Jesse Lasky to see Farrar at the Met in *Madame Butterfly,* and let it be known that Miss Farrar would consider film offers. It was Lasky's intention that *Carmen* would provide the vehicle for her screen debut.[4]

Farrar left the East Coast on June 8, 1915, traveling with an entourage that included Morris Gest and his wife, her parents, and several others in a private Pullman car named "Superb." Her arrival in Los Angeles was greeted as a major event with Los Angeles mayor Henry Rose and a delegation from City Hall in attendance along with Lasky, DeMille, and others from the studio.

Because grand opera often emphasized the "grand" in performance and gesture, DeMille had doubts that Farrar could make an easy transition to the screen. He proposed making *Maria Rosa* as her first picture to help the star become accustomed to screen technique. He needn't have worried. Farrar was a natural. Charming, believable, and capable of great range, she lit up the screen just as she created excitement on the operatic stage, and with the release of *Carmen* (produced after *Maria Rosa*, but released first) she became a top film star—at least for a time.

*Maria Rosa* is an outstanding film, notable not only for Farrar's performance, but also for the excellence of its photography. Alvin Wyckoff used lighting to create dramatic moods in a manner fairly unique for 1915. The contrasts of light and dark, dim interiors with bright exteriors seen through windows or doors, were extremely difficult photographic feats with the low-speed, high-contrast film stocks of the time.

Although *Maria Rosa* was written in 1890, Angel Guimera's play had its first American performance in New York in 1914. William deMille's screenplay is a free adaptation of the Guimera original: In the play the character played by Wallace Reid is already dead and only referred to in dialogue. In the movie, the Reid character is framed for murder and sent to prison. His rival for the hand of Maria Rosa causes her to believe that her lover has died while incarcerated. She consents to marry the rival, only to have Reid appear on her wedding day.

Wallace Reid had his first starring role in a DeMille picture with *Maria Rosa*. DeMille claimed that Reid's bit part as a blacksmith in *The Birth of a Nation* first drew his attention to the young actor, but by 1915 Reid was already a veteran of four or five years in the business with the American Film Company, Vitagraph, and Reliance-Majestic. He even directed a number of the films in which he starred before he joined the Lasky forces.

By coincidence, the star of the New York production of *Maria Rosa*, Lou-Tellegen, was also under contract to the Lasky Company. Though he was not scheduled to appear in the picture (Pedro de Cordoba played the role of Ramon), Lou-Tellegen sat in on some of the story sessions with Cecil and William deMille. During one of these sessions he met Farrar for the first time; they were married in 1916.[5]

# 16

# Carmen

Produced by the Jesse L. Lasky Feature Play Company for Paramount release. Director: Cecil B. DeMille. Scenario by William C. deMille, from the story by Prosper Merimée. Art director: Wilfred Buckland. Photography: Alvin Wyckoff

Picture started: June 28, 1915. Picture finished: July 13, 1915. Length: 4,512 feet (five reels). Cost: $23,429.97. Released: Oct. 1, 1915 (Boston premiere), general release November 1, 1915. Gross: $147,599.81

Cast: Geraldine Farrar (Carmen), Wallace Reid (Don José), Pedro de Cordoba (Escamillo), Billy Elmer (Morales), Horace B. Carpenter (Pastia), Jeanie Macpherson (Frasquita), and Anita King (Mercedes)

In 1915 a critic for the *New York Dramatic Mirror* wrote, "Geraldine Farrar has put her heart and soul and body into this picture, and without the aid of the magic of her voice, has proved herself one of the greatest actresses of all times. Her picture, *Carmen*, will live long after her operatic characterization has died in the limbo of forgotten singers. Her acting in this production is one of the marvels of the stage and screen, so natural, so realistic that it is hard to believe that it is acting." Twenty years later, in 1935, William deMille sat in a Paramount screening room to watch *Carmen*. Two decades had passed since he had written the screenplay and seen its images flash across any screen but the one in his mind's eye. "It was hard to believe that what I saw on the screen was actually the same work upon which so much honest effort had been expended. . . . Looking at it with 1935 eyes, our picture was badly photographed, the lighting was childish, the acting was awful, the writing atrocious and—may Allah be merciful—the direction terrible." In the end, William deMille found comfort only in "the fact that we had taken the same pride in it as Henry Ford took in his Model T, or the Wright Brothers in their first plane. As I watched the bizarre affair flicker by I reflected that perhaps it is just as well we have no film recordings of David Garrick, Edwin Booth or Salvini: they might only shatter cherished ideals."[1]

The bewildered William deMille was at a loss to explain what he had seen, and today we can only have an imperfect sense of the shock he must have felt. Television, radio, videocassettes, and sound recordings have made the past a part of the present. Fifty-year-old episodes of *I Love Lucy* and forty-year-old recordings by the Beatles are so much a part of our lives that we forget they are the products of another time. Imagine a favorite film—*Casablanca* (Warner Bros., 1943), for example—locked in a vault unseen for nearly sixty years. Would we respond with emotion or smug snickers to the story of Rick and Ilsa and her husband, Victor Laszlo? The performances are believable in their familiarity, but the technique of Humphrey Bogart and Ingrid Bergman is so different from the technique of Gwyneth Paltrow or Kevin Spacey that their artistry might not be immediately apparent to those acquainted only with the conventions of American film acting in the first decade of the twenty-first century.

Film preserves not only action and performance but the aesthetic sensibilities of a moment in time. If we reread a novel or see a revival of a play, we unconsciously adapt our perceptions to our current sensibilities. When seeing an old film we are forced to watch with two sets of eyes—our own in the present, and those of the filmmakers in the past—a sort of technological necromancy. In that screening room in 1935 William deMille came face-to-face with a phenomenon we have yet to fully comprehend.

His perception of the film was wrong, though he could not see it at the time. Geraldine Farrar was born to play Carmen, and she brings a vibrancy to the portrayal that is still exciting to watch nearly ninety years after it was first screened. *Carmen* lacks some of the visual style of *Maria Rosa*, but the characters and motivations are more strongly developed, and on balance it is a better film. The writing and direction need no apology, and if the picture lacks "glorious Technicolor, breathtaking CinemaScope, and stereophonic sound," there are more than enough virtues for those who can see them.

What is evident in both *Maria Rosa* and *Carmen* is that Wilfred Buckland's settings, though elaborate, still owe much to the theater—suggesting great scale, but showing very little. When forced to economize in later years, Cecil B. DeMille returned to this sort of suggested grandeur for *The Volga Boatman* (1926), *The Sign of the Cross* (1932), and *Cleopatra* (1934).

The scenario presented a special problem for William deMille because the Lasky Company announced that *Carmen* would be the first

Geraldine Farrar picture, then discovered that Bizet's opera was still under copyright and that the owners wanted a small fortune for the screen rights. William was forced to tear up his first draft and turn to the Prosper Merimée story, which was the basis for the opera, and which was in the public domain. He recalled that Cecil chided him: "You've got smugglers, and a tavern, and soldiers, and a fight between two dames (and give that the works, too), and a camp in the mountains, and, best of all, the bullfight. All that's in Merimée, and you're supposed to be a dramatist, so if you can't make the audience think they're seeing the opera without butting into their damn copyright, you'd better go right home and take a big dose of Lydia Pinkham's Compound. . . ."[2]

DeMille's *Carmen* directly affected future presentations of the opera. The fight in the cigarette factory was an element of the Merimée story not included in Bizet's musical adaptation. At a later staging of the opera Farrar included the fight—perhaps as a prank—and it was so well received that it has become a part of most subsequent operatic productions.[3]

By all accounts Geraldine Farrar was a star without temperament. She had "warmth and laughter and down-to-earthiness, and a total lack of airs or affectations," wrote Cecil B. DeMille in his autobiography, but she did make one request that other Hollywood stars soon demanded. "I asked Mr. DeMille if we might have music during our scenes, as I was so accustomed to orchestral accompaniment for certain tempi and phrasings," wrote Farrar. Consequently, the director hired Melville Ellis to play mood music on the set during production, a practice that became standard for most filmmakers through the end of the silent era.[4]

Farrar also asked that *Carmen* be premiered in her hometown at the Boston Symphony Hall. The opening was entrusted to Samuel L. Rothapfel, the father of deluxe motion picture presentation, known to the world by his nickname—"Roxy." "You will be pleased to know that Rothapfel has planned the Smuggler's Motive from Carmen all the way through the picture," Sam Goldfish wrote DeMille two days before the October 1 Boston screening. "From what I understand the music is positively wonderful and I think it would have been worth $5,000 to this company to have had you see the opening of this picture in Boston as I am certain that if you could see the way the picture is to be presented you would be inspired to do [greater] things than [you] have ever done in the past, and it would make you feel that the good work that you are doing is being appreciated."[5]

The picture made Geraldine Farrar an overnight film star. Jesse Lasky, visiting Los Angeles at the time, sent this observation to Goldfish in New York: "Carmen at Tally's is in its second week. It is doing the biggest business in the history of the Theatre. In fact no exhibitor in his wildest dreams ever conceived of a picture doing such an enormous business. The Theatre opens at 10:00 a.m and there is a crowd all day with two lines, running in either direction."[6]

With all of the advance publicity surrounding the Farrar *Carmen*, and with Merimée's story in the public domain, rival producer William Fox took advantage of the situation by turning out a *Carmen* of his own. The Fox Film Corporation version, directed by Raoul Walsh and starring screen "vamp" Theda Bara, opened day and date with the Lasky picture, but the competition had little impact on the success of the Lasky film.[7] With block-booking practices in place at the time, the Fox picture would never play a Paramount contract theater. Comparing the two films would be interesting, but unfortunately no copies of Fox's *Carmen* are known to exist.

# 17

# Temptation

Produced by the Jesse L. Lasky Feature Play Company for Paramount release. Director: Cecil B. DeMille. Original story and scenario by Hector Turnbull (additional, uncredited writing by Cecil B. DeMille and Jeanie Macpherson). Art director: Wilfred Buckland. Photography: Alvin Wyckoff

Picture started: July 27, 1915. Picture finished: August 10, 1915. Length: 5,550 feet (six reels). Cost: $22,472.25. Released: January 2, 1916. Gross: $102,437.47

Cast: Geraldine Farrar (Renee Dupree), Pedro de Cordoba (Julien), Theodore Roberts (Otto Muller), Elsie Jane Wilson (Madame Maroff), Raymond Hatton (the baron), and Sessue Hayakawa

The third of DeMille's films with Geraldine Farrar, *Temptation* was the second to be distributed—presumably to separate the release of *Maria Rosa* and *Carmen,* the two Spanish-themed films. The film is not known to exist in any archive or private collection.

*Temptation* was the first screenwriting effort of Hector Turnbull, former drama critic of the *New York Tribune.* Turnbull, recruited to the silent drama by William deMille, went on to marry Jesse Lasky's sister after her divorce from Sam Goldfish. Cecil DeMille's low regard for Turnbull's abilities as a screenwriter became a source of friction when William deMille took charge of the West Coast office and Turnbull was picked to head up the Lasky scenario department in New York.

*Temptation* tells the story of an aspiring opera singer, Renee Dupree, who is engaged to a struggling composer, Julien. Impresario Otto Muller has eyes for Renee and offers her a role in the upcoming production being written by Julien. When she refuses his advances, Muller fires both Renee and Julien. Months of poverty lead Renee to temptation and she accepts Muller's proposition, but when she arrives at his apartments for their tryst she finds Muller has been killed by an irate mistress.

In a letter to Sam Goldfish, DeMille wrote, "I want to thank you for your letter . . . regarding 'The Temptation.' I have extended your congratulations [for a job well done] to those whom you mentioned—even to Hector Turnbull, which I must admit, I did most reluctantly, as he had about as much to do with the writing of 'Temptation' as you did."[1]

Turnbull went on to write *The Cheat*, which DeMille claimed was "so far superior to his first, *Temptation*, that to this day film historians, especially in Europe, regard *The Cheat* as a landmark in the development of the cinema." Yet, *The Cheat* is praised primarily for DeMille's visual treatment of its lurid melodrama, not for its unenlightened story values. The director never warmed up to Turnbull personally or to his taste in story material. "While there is no question in anybody's mind that the New York office is the seat of government [for this company]," DeMille wrote Lasky, "there is considerable doubt in our minds [here in Hollywood] that it is the seat of great literary and dramatic discernment."[2]

# 18

# Chimmie Fadden Out West

Produced by the Jesse L. Lasky Feature Play Company for Paramount release. Director: Cecil B. DeMille. Original story and scenario by Cecil B. DeMille and Jeanie Macpherson, founded on the stories by E.W. Townsend. Art director: Wilfred Buckland. Photography: Alvin Wyckoff

Picture started: September 27, 1915. Picture completed: October 18, 1915. Length: 5,211 feet (six reels). Cost: $16,069.67. Released: November 22, 1915. Gross: $72,036.24

Cast: Victor Moore (Chimmie Fadden), Camille Astor ("The Duchess"), Ernest Joy (Van Courtlandt), Mrs. Lewis McCord (Mother Fadden), Raymond Hatton (Larry Fadden, Chimmie's brother), Tom Forman (Antoine), Florence Dagmar (Betty Van Courtlandt), Harry Hadfield (Preston), and Henry Bergman (hotel clerk)

*C**himmie Fadden* had a better box-office reception than any of DeMille's films in the first half of 1915, so the decision was made to produce a second film featuring Victor Moore as the lovable, street-wise oaf. *Chimmie Fadden Out West,* an amusing, unpretentious picture, shows a flair for farce comedy that, except for Eddie Quillan's sequences in *The Godless Girl* (1928), DeMille would never exercise again. Critical reception of the picture was excellent, and a third Moore/Fadden picture was scheduled to go into production.

However, Jesse Lasky got cold feet when he saw *Chimmie Fadden Out West* at Tally's Theater in Los Angeles. He wrote DeMille that "In spite of our decision to do another picture with "Chimmie" as the central character, after watching the picture at Tally's [Broadway Theater] last night, and talking with [Thomas] Tally and others, I have come to the conclusion that the 'Chimmie Fadden' type of picture will never do business, and therefore, I think it might be well to try an entirely different type of subject for Moore."[1] Lasky's judgment in the matter was less than perceptive. *Chimmie Fadden Out West* performed nearly as well as *Chimmie Fadden*; Moore's next two Lasky productions, *The Race* (directed by George Melford) and *The Clown* (directed by William C.

deMille), marked the end of the comedian's Hollywood career—at least until the1930s. Moore made a series of one-reel shorts for Klever Comedies in Florida in 1916 and 1917 that were released on the Paramount program, and he appeared in a minor role in *The Man Who Found Himself* (Famous Players-Lasky/Paramount, 1925), but, until sound came to the movies, he found his greatest success on the stage.

The scenario that Cecil B. DeMille and Jeanie Macpherson wrote for *Chimmie Fadden Out West* could just as easily have played as a drama. Chimmie is hired by a railroad to stage a publicity stunt. He will go west, pretend to find gold, and then hire the fastest train east—which will bring attention to the rail line. Chimmie agrees to the proposition in order to gather "enough coin to get spliced" to his girlfriend, "The Duchess"—maid to the rail tycoon's family. The scheme works like a charm, but the rail king gets greedy and sells phony stock in Chimmie's imaginary mine. The humor in *Chimmie Fadden Out West* rises from Victor Moore's characterization. At a time when Charlie Chaplin was still working in rough knockabout shorts for the Essanay Film Manufacturing Company, and the only feature-length comedy of any consequence was Mack Sennett's six-reel slapstick extravaganza *Tillie's Punctured Romance* (Keystone-Alco, 1914), Cecil B. DeMille was creating the type of emotionally believable, character-centered comedy that would be hailed as a stunning screen achievement when Chaplin made *The Kid* (Chaplin-United Artists, 1921) and Harold Lloyd released *Grandma's Boy* (Hal Roach-Pathé, 1922).

For Cecil B. DeMille, however, the huge returns generated by *Carmen, The Cheat,* and *Temptation* later in 1915 made the better-than-average success of *Chimmie Fadden Out West* look like small potatoes by comparison. The Lasky Company recognized that DeMille's efforts were better expended on melodrama than comedy—at least for the foreseeable future.

# 19

# The Cheat

Produced by the Jesse L. Lasky Feature Play Company for Paramount release. Director: Cecil B. DeMille. Original story by Hector Turnbull. Scenario by Hector Turnbull and Jeanie Macpherson. Art director: Wilfred Buckland. Photography: Alvin Wyckoff

Picture started: October 20, 1915. Picture finished: November 10, 1915. Length: 4,243 feet (five reels). Cost: $17,311.29. Released: December 13, 1915. Gross: $137,364.87

Cast: Fannie Ward (Edith Hardy), Jack Dean (Dick Hardy), Sessue Hayakawa (Tori), James Neill (Jones), Utake Abe (Tori's valet), Dana Ong (district attorney), Hazel Childers (Mrs. Reynolds), and Judge Arthur H. Williams (judge)

W hen this film first appeared in France in the middle of the war [WWI], audiences were entranced and producers thunderstruck," wrote Maurice Bardeche and Robert Brasillach. "It seemed to make everything that had preceded it quite meaningless."[1] Cecil B. DeMille's early critical reputation is based almost entirely on *The Cheat* and its French acceptance as a masterpiece. Not coincidentally, until recently it has been the only one of DeMille's early films generally available for reappraisal.

For all its sensationalism and box-office success, *The Cheat* was not a project close to DeMille's heart, though he was more than willing to accept the critical praise the film received. For the second time he was working with an original story by Hector Turnbull, and for the second time Jeanie Macpherson was given the job of reworking the script.[2]

*The Cheat* is a lurid tale. Edith Hardy (Fannie Ward) is a bored spendthrift who finds excitement in the companionship of Tori (Sessue Hayakawa), a wealthy Japanese, while her husband (Jack Dean) tries to put over a big business deal. Edith "borrows" ten thousand dollars from a Red Cross fund to invest in a stock deal touted by a business rival of her husband. Of course, the "loan" is lost in the market, and Edith is forced to borrow from Tori to avoid a scandal. She promises to make herself available in exchange for the favor. Her husband's business deal succeeds and she tries to repay Tori in cash—but he insists she honor her bargain. When she refuses he brands her with his mark of ownership. Edith shoots Tori and escapes, but her husband discovers the wounded Japanese and is arrested for the crime. At trial he is convicted and is about to be sentenced when Edith reveals the wound Tori seared into her flesh. The crowd in the courtroom riots and nearly kills Tori. Hardy is released and leaves the courtroom with Edith in his arms.

Although DeMille did emulate some elements of *The Cheat* in later films, the film has few links to his usual thematic concerns. Tori is painted strictly as a villain with no redeeming features, and Edith's selfishness and perfidy go unpunished. The blatant racism that allows Edith to go free after committing robbery and assault while the riled courtroom mob tries to kill Tori for merely enforcing his dark bargain is also uncharacteristic of DeMille.[3]

Whatever his feelings about the material, however, DeMille pulled out all the stops in his direction of *The Cheat*. Tori's attempted rape of Edith is terrifying in its realism, and the courtroom riot, with seemingly hundreds of seething extras, is staged on a grand scale.

Fannie Ward, known as the "eternal flapper," was nearing forty when *The Cheat* was made. Her youthful appearance was said to be the result of paraffin injected into her cheeks. The wax kept Ward's skin tight and smooth, but it tended to melt under hot lights. Frequent ice pack applications were needed to keep her jowls from sagging. Her on-screen husband, Jack Dean, was her husband offscreen as well.

DeMille was not particularly fond of Fannie Ward, and he kept two precious shots of accidents involving the actress on his private outtake reel. In one scene, from *The Cheat*, Ward falls into a pond while leaving Tori's house. In another scene, from *Witchcraft* (Lasky/Paramount, 1916), directed by Frank Reicher, actor Frank Clark inadvertently hits Ward on the head with his cane.[4] One must assume that DeMille took some special pleasure in seeing Fannie Ward get knocked around.

For Sessue Hayakawa *The Cheat* was a turning point. His wife, Tsuru Aoki, was by far the more successful of the two, having starred in several films for Thomas Ince, but after *The Cheat* Hayakawa became a major star in American films until he went to Europe in 1923. Today he is best known for his work as the Japanese commander in *The Bridge on the River Kwai* (Columbia, 1957).

Although a restoration of the original intertitles is currently contemplated by the George Eastman House, the surviving version of *The Cheat* is the 1918 reissue, which contains a number of minor changes. In the original film, Hayakawa's character is clearly identified as Japanese. When *The Cheat* was first released in 1915, the Japanese American community howled in outrage, although the protests fell on deaf ears. In 1918, with Japan as an ally in the World War, the character's name and nationality were changed, and the terse subtitles of the original were inflated for literary effect. As an example, in 1915 Tori's introductory title read "One of Long Island's Smart Set." But 1918 audiences were introduced to "Haka Arakau, a Burmese ivory king to whom the Long Island smart-set is paying social tribute." Presumably it was felt there were not enough Burmese in the country to raise a credible protest.

*The Cheat* was remade twice in America—in 1923 with Pola Negri and in 1931 with Tallulah Bankhead. It also served as the basis for the opera *Forfaiture*, and Hayakawa reprised his role in a 1937 French film remake, also called *Forfaiture*.

# 20

# The Golden Chance

Produced by the Jesse L. Lasky Feature Play Company for Paramount release. Director: Cecil B. DeMille. Original story and scenario by Jeanie Macpherson. Art director: Wilfred Buckland. Photography: Alvin Wyckoff

Picture started: October 26, 1915. Picture resumed: November 5, 1915. Picture completed: November 26, 1915. Cost: $18,710.81. Length: 5,274 feet (six reels). Released: January 31, 1916. Gross: $83,504.03

Cast: Cleo Ridgely (Mary Denby), Wallace Reid (Roger Manning), Horace B. Carpenter (Steven Denby), Ernest Joy (Mr. Hillary), Edythe Chapman (Mrs. Hillary), and Raymond Hatton (an underworld rat)

Although he often explored similar themes in film after film, Cecil B. DeMille officially remade only three of his pictures. It is easy to see why he remade *The Squaw Man* twice, in 1918 and again in 1931—he had a strong personal connection to the property. His 1956 version of *The Ten Commandments,* containing none of the modern elements of the 1923 original, was barely a remake at all. Besides, DeMille's first *Ten Commandments* was one of the biggest box-office hits of the silent era, and the remake complemented the cycle of Biblical spectacles that Hollywood found profitable in the 1950s. But why would DeMille remake *The Golden Chance*, which was called *Forbidden Fruit* in its 1920 incarnation? The original movie was a solid but hardly spectacular success that was soon forgotten after its initial release. What was the attraction?

According to Jesse Lasky both *The Cheat* and *The Golden Chance* were written in response to his request for original screen stories to supplement the theatrical adaptations that were the mainstay of the studio's output.[1] *The Cheat* was written in New York by Hector Turnbull, a personal favorite of Lasky's who would soon replace Sam Goldfish as Lasky's brother-in-law. *The Golden Chance* was written by Jeanie Macpherson, DeMille's screenwriter of choice.

Today, when a prolific filmmaker may make one picture a year, we have difficulty believing that DeMille made no fewer than thirteen feature films in 1915. What is more remarkable is that *The Golden Chance* and *The Cheat* were produced simultaneously—*The Cheat* during the day, *The Golden Chance* at night. Lasky suggests that contractual obligations made it necessary for both pictures to be shot at the same time in order to meet the studio release schedule. William deMille remembered that a problem with the director assigned to *The Golden Chance* compelled Cecil to step in. In his autobiography DeMille characteristically says that he felt it was necessary to prove by example to other directors on the Lasky lot that they were not overworked, despite their protests to the contrary. Surviving documents suggest that William deMille's memory was faulty—Cecil clearly was the original director of *The Golden Chance*. Production problems forced the picture to shut down, and what seems more likely is that Lasky assigned Hector Turnbull's story to DeMille, and, with both pictures scheduled for early release, the director was unwilling to trust the making of Jeanie Macpherson's script to another filmmaker.

DeMille began shooting *The Golden Chance* with Edna Goodrich in the leading role. Surviving stills indicate that a good portion of the film was completed with Goodrich, but the actress exhibited a fondness for the bottle, and when she arrived on the set in a drunken stupor DeMille fired her from the picture and shut down production. In a letter to Sam Goldfish dated November 2, 1915, Jesse Lasky wrote, "Edna Goodrich will not be with us after her ten weeks have expired. She is hopelessly bad and, as far as Cecil is concerned, I don't believe he could ever be persuaded to direct her again. On Sunday Cecil sent for me and wanted to leave Goodrich out, pay her off and put someone in her picture which is already half finished. Cecil has a fine story but he claims she is killing it. She cannot act and also screens very poorly."[2] The Goodrich footage was scrapped and the balance of her Lasky contract was parceled off to the Bosworth-Morosco studio. The role of Mary Denby was given to Cleo Ridgely, and DeMille resumed shooting *The Golden Chance* while *The Cheat* was still in production.

After a stint in the chorus at New York's famed Hippodrome Theatre, Cleo Ridgely began her screen career with the Kalem Company at its Jacksonville, Florida, studio in 1910. She later worked for Lubin in Philadelphia and the Rex Company back in New York. On August 26, 1912, she set out on one of the earliest movie publicity stunts, riding on horseback from New York to Los Angeles with her then husband, Richard Ridgely, as a representative of *Motion Picture Story*, stopping at theaters along the way to promote the fan magazine. On arriving in L.A. she rejoined Kalem at its Glendale studio.

In early 1915 Cleo Ridgely signed with the Lasky Company, and after several supporting roles she was given the lead in *The Chorus Lady* opposite Wallace Reid. *The Golden Chance* was her second pairing with Reid, and they were promoted as a screen team in several later pictures. Although she made occasional appearances in films into the early 1920s, Ridgely essentially retired from the screen in 1916 to settle down to domestic life with her second husband, director James Horne. It is a pity, because *The Golden Chance* shows that Cleo Ridgely was an exceptionally gifted actress.

The scenario for *The Golden Chance* borrows narrative threads from several sources, including the fairy tale *Cinderella* and Charles Kenyon's play *Kindling*, but Jeanie Macpherson wove these elements into a complex and disturbing psychological drama that is better than the sum of its parts.

The daughter of a respectable judge, Mary Denby lives in tenement squalor with a drunken lout of a husband. She married Steve Denby over her parents' objection and now, with rent due and her husband demanding food on the table, she searches the want ads and finds employment as a seamstress for the wealthy Mrs. Hillary.

Mr. Hillary has a dilemma. He wants to interest young Roger Manning in a business proposition, but Manning is about to return to his home in the West and doesn't have time to entertain Hillary's offer. Mrs. Hillary intervenes by inviting Manning to dinner where she promises he will meet the most beautiful young woman in the city. However, the woman Mrs. Hillary plans to invite is ill, and she can find no adequate substitute. Aware that her seamstress has a sophisticated bearing that belies her skid-row address, she offers Mary extra money to attend the dinner party and work her charms on Manning in an effort to persuade him to stay in town. Mrs. Hillary's scheme works too well—Mary and Roger fall in love.

Steve Denby attempts to rob the Hillary home, not realizing his wife is their weekend houseguest. Manning catches Denby and learns that Mary is married to the thief and that his hosts have deceived him to promote their own interests. Sick at heart, Manning allows Steve Denby to escape.

Realizing Mary's love for Manning, Denby sends a note to the young millionaire threatening to harm Mary unless he is paid a healthy ransom. In the fight that ultimately follows, Denby is killed by the police. Roger and Mary are free to wed, but the film ends with an extraordinary image.

After Manning tells Mary that Steve is dead, the young lovers turn their backs to each other, lost in their own thoughts, as the picture fades to black.

Surviving prints of *The Golden Chance* are missing the end title card, and some have speculated that the final scenes of the picture must be missing as well; but the musical selections suggested in the January 27, 1916, issue of *Paramount Progress* prove that the prints are complete. To the accompaniment of "Hurry No. 2" by Otto Langey, the action is described:

> Interior—Fight continues. Police break in. Steve out of window, Police shoot him. He falls. Street—crowd around body. Interior—Steve's body brought in. Carried into bedroom. Manning enters bedroom.

With the changing mood, the music becomes "Moonbeams Shining" by Victor Herbert, and the action continues:

> Door—Manning comes out and stands at door with Mary.
> THE END.

Despite the derivative nature of its screenplay, *The Golden Chance* proves to be one of DeMille's early masterpieces, every bit the equal of *The Cheat* in its use of the medium, and closer to the director's heart in its exploration of theme. Mary Denby is a classic DeMille heroine who pays a great price for love—but the film paints an especially dark vision of the consequences of romance. As the story begins, Mary has already lost her social position by marrying Denby. At the fade-out, the sense of guilt over Denby's violent death threatens to cast a pall over her future relationship with Manning. Audiences are conditioned to seeing a clinch and a kiss before a love story fades from the screen. The ambiguity of the final scene in *The Golden Chance* is especially disturbing because it contradicts all conventional expectations.

As in the director's other films from this period, DeMille and Wilfred Buckland use a sort of visual shorthand in the settings. Hillary's office is little more than a desktop and a single wall. The barroom where Steve Denby finds his pleasure is merely sketched in the backlit silhouette of a beer sign painted on a window. The Denby apartment is a slight redressing of the set used in *Kindling* earlier in the year, and even the Hillary mansion is suggested more than it is shown. Alvin Wyckoff's moody photography contributes to the overall effect.

*The Golden Chance* marked Edythe Chapman's first appearance in a DeMille picture. Chapman, whose real name was Edith Van Renssaleer, was a Rochester, New York, schoolmarm who went to New York at the age of twenty to pursue a career in the theater. Among her early stage credits was *The Charity Ball* by Henry C. deMille. In 1897 she married fellow actor James Neill. Both Chapman and Neill became regulars in Cecil B. DeMille's stock company.

# The Trail of the Lonesome Pine

Produced by the Jesse L. Lasky Feature Play Company for Paramount release. Director: Cecil B. DeMille. Scenario by Jeanie Macpherson, from the novel by John Fox Jr. and the play by Eugene Walter (additional, uncredited writing by Cecil B. DeMille). Art director: Wilfred Buckland. Photography: Alvin Wyckoff

Picture started: December 28, 1915. Picture finished: January 20, 1916. Length: 4,613 feet (five reels). Cost: $22,249.12. Released: February 14, 1916. Gross: $77,944.00

Cast: Charlotte Walker (June Tolliver), Thomas Meighan (Jack Hale), Theodore Roberts ("Devil" Judd Tolliver), Earle Foxe (Dave Tolliver), Milton Brown, and Hosea Steelman (Tolliver men)

Cecil B. DeMille's production of *The Trail of the Lonesome Pine* was the first version of John Fox's famous story to reach the screen, but it was not the first film version made of the novel. In early 1914 the Broadway Picture Producing Company started production on *The Trail of the Lonesome Pine* with Dixie Compton in the lead. The film was to have been the second Broadway Picture release.

That same year the California Motion Picture Corporation asked Frank Paret to negotiate for film rights to the play with theatrical managers Klaw and Erlanger, who controlled Eugene Walter's play based on the novel. Paret found that a film version of the story was already in production. On May 15, 1914, he wrote to the general manager of the California Motion Picture Corporation: "Mr. David Young, President of Broadway Picture Producing Co., said three-fourths of the picture 'Trail of the Lonesome Pine' has been completed in the woods of New Jersey and he had already been in receipt of offers for Eastern State rights. He would not dispose of his interest for any amount of money that could reasonably be offered him. [However] The Western States territorial rights are still open."[1] Little more than a month later, Paret reported, "I understand the Broadway Picture Producing Co. has been or will be enjoined by Klaw & Erlanger from marketing 'Trail of the Lonesome Pine' film. . . . Even if Klaw & Erlanger do not win out, a lot of money will be tied up meanwhile, and I am glad negotiations for this play have been abandoned."[2]

Although the Broadway Picture Producing Company's version of *The Trail of the Lonesome Pine* seems to have been produced in good faith with permission of the publisher of the novel, theatrical entrepreneurs Klaw and Erlanger felt that this film version infringed on their dramatic rights, leaving the screen rights available for acquisition by the Lasky Company.

As in *The Golden Chance*, Macpherson and DeMille's adaptation of *The Trail of the Lonesome Pine* treats the romantic element in a grim and pessimistic manner. "I love him more than home, more than my people, more than God," declares June Tolliver in one of the film's more florid subtitles. Whether penned by John Fox Jr., playwright Eugene Walter, or Macpherson herself, this line is the clearest statement of a theme that runs through much of her work with DeMille. The willingness to destroy one's world for the sake of love is a melodramatic plot convention that predates DeMille by several centuries, but it is usually handled in a romantic manner as in Shakespeare's *Romeo and Juliet*, where the heroine kills herself to be with her lover in death. DeMille and Macpherson, however, emphasize the devastation caused by a great love, not its transcendent joys.

In *The Trail of the Lonesome Pine*, June Tolliver sees her cousin killed, her family's livelihood (albeit an illegal one) wiped out, and her once-powerful father reduced to ineffectual madness all for the sake of love. In the end only a vague hope of some future happiness remains. The film does not end with a lovers' kiss; instead, Jack Hale leaves the Blue Ridge Mountains with only a promise that he will return to make June Tolliver his wife. DeMille and Macpherson are said to have had a long-standing affair, and this decidedly negative approach to romantic subjects may have been a reflection of their own emotional states.[3]

Perhaps because she now had more experience acting for the camera, Charlotte Walker gives a stronger performance in *The Trail of the Lonesome Pine* than in *Kindling*. Walker originated the role of June Tolliver on stage, which may also account for the strength she brought to the part. Certainly after *The Cheat* and *The Golden Chance*, DeMille was more confident of his abilities as a filmmaker, and the acting in *The Trail of the Lonesome Pine* is more consistent than in many of his earlier films.

The manner in which Lasky pictures used subtitles distinguished the company's pictures from other films of the period. In the 1910s, titles commonly described the action that followed. In D.W. Griffith's *Intolerance* (1916), for example, one reads:

> Dividends of the Jenkins Mills failing to
> meet the increasing demand of Miss Jenkins'
> charities, she complains to her brother,
> which helps decide him to action.

The subtitle is followed by a shot of Miss Jenkins entering her brother's office and pleading her case in pantomime.

DeMille, however, utilized dialogue titles to carry the narrative in his films. In *The Trail of the Lonesome Pine*, Jack Hale is wounded, and June tries to get help for him. Another filmmaker might have used a title such as

> Playing on his love, June Tolliver
> sends her cousin for the doctor.

DeMille, however, shows June urging Dave Tolliver into the wounded man's room. Then she asks, via title,

> "Do Yo' love me—Dave Tolliver?"

Dave grabs June and tries to kiss her. She pulls away. Another title:

> "If yo' do love me—I'm askin' yo'
> to ride for a doctor!"

Griffith's approach was considered more cinematic at the time because the dramatic action was not interrupted with reading matter, but such an approach makes the picture irrelevant because it merely illustrates what is essentially a literary narrative. DeMille's technique of using dialogue to carry the story owes more to the theater than to literature and makes it possible for an audience to more closely identify with the emotions of the characters. By the 1920s his method became standard practice in Hollywood films, and Griffith's technique was considered old-fashioned.

# The Heart of Nora Flynn

Produced by the Jesse L. Feature Play Company for Paramount release. Director: Cecil B. DeMille. Scenario by Jeanie Macpherson. Original story by Hector Turnbull. Art director: Wilfred Buckland. Photography: Alvin Wyckoff

Picture started: March 7, 1916. Picture completed: March 27, 1916. Length: 4,819 feet (five reels). Cost: $21,998.57. Released: April 24, 1916. Gross: $87,738.27

Cast: Marie Doro (Nora Flynn), Elliott Dexter (Nolan), Ernest Joy (Brantley Stone), Lola May (his wife), "Little" Billy Jacobs (Tommy Stone, their son), Peggy George [Margaret deMille] (Anne Stone, their daughter), Charles West (Jack Murray), and Mrs. Lewis McCord (Maggie, the cook)

*The Heart of Nora Flynn* is little more than a pleasant program picture, notable for the appearance of stage star Marie Doro and her future husband, Elliott Dexter. Doro acted with William Gillette in his stage adaptation of *Sherlock Holmes* and was famous for her portrayal of Oliver Twist in a play based on the Dickens novel. She was a gifted actress with large, sad, dark eyes. Elliott Dexter became one of DeMille's favorite leading men. Solid, pleasant, capable—he never set the screen on fire, but he embodied the middle-class man in crisis that became the central character of so many DeMille productions of the late 1910s and 1920s. The rest of the cast included DeMille standby Ernest Joy, Griffith-Biograph alumnus Charles West, and the particularly untalented Lola May. Six-year-old "Little" Billy Jacobs (already a four-year veteran of the picture business) played one of the Stone children, and Peggy George (in reality DeMille's niece Margaret deMille) played his sister.

Even though DeMille was director-general of the Jesse L. Lasky Feature Play Company, his projects were for the most part assigned by Lasky, and he didn't work up much enthusiasm for yet another Hector Turnbull story. The feud between DeMille and Lasky over Turnbull's abilities as a writer continued, and the film's main title reads:

Marie Doro in
The Heart of Nora Flynn
By Jeanie Macpherson
from the story by
Hector Turnbull

DeMille was simply unwilling to concede that Turnbull could produce a usable scenario without assistance, although Turnbull went on to a long and reasonably distinguished career as a screenwriter.

The story for *The Heart of Nora Flynn* bears some resemblance to Turnbull's earlier scenario for *The Cheat*. Mrs. Brantley Stone is bored with her workaholic husband and encourages the attentions of playboy Jack Murray. *The Cheat* concentrates on the love triangle, but *The Heart of Nora Flynn* plays its tale of marital infidelity against the love story of Nora, the Brantley's Irish nanny, and Nolan, the family chauffeur. As in *The Cheat*, the wife's lover is shot (this time by the chauffeur, not the wife) and a great deal of legal confusion arises over who really pulled the trigger, but the central conceit of the film is the old saw about the maid with a heart of gold taking the rap to save her mistress from social ruin.

DeMille manages to build some on-screen excitement, however, as Nolan and his employer, Brantley Stone, return to Stone's home. Stone is certain that Jack Murray is keeping company with his wife, while Nolan is equally sure that Murray's attentions are directed toward Nora. The sequence takes on the appearance of an "old dark house" thriller as Brantley hovers over his wife and Nolan searches for Nora, while she tries to sneak Murray out of the house to protect Mrs. Stone's honor. Unfortunately, the rest of the film never develops the energy of this extended sequence, and the overall plot lacks focus.

*The Heart of Nora Flynn* demonstrates DeMille's growing sense of staging scenes for the camera. Composition and movement within the frame combine in a deceptively simple visual approach. From his first film DeMille preferred to stage his scenes in a modified "American foreground" style—working close to the actors, but favoring two-shots over single close-ups or long shots.[1] He saved the visual pyrotechnics for emphasis and effect.

In part this was simply practical technique. The closer one worked, the more one could save on building sets. But such considerations were only part of the reason for DeMille's fondness for the mid-shot. If D.W. Griffith favored isolated close-ups to delve into his characters' thoughts (the equivalent of the "aside" on the melodramatic stage), DeMille pre-ferred to explore character by showing actors' interactions and also by relying on illustrative props.

In 1916 the attention of audience and critic was riveted on D.W. Griffith's super-production, *The Birth of a Nation*, and his forthcoming four-story epic, *Intolerance*. Paramount had no room for films that went beyond the strict budget and length limitations of the "program" picture, and DeMille was marking time to find an opportunity to display his talents on a larger canvas.

# 23

# The Dream Girl

Produced by the Jesse L. Lasky Feature Play Company for Paramount release. Director: Cecil B. DeMille. Original story and scenario by Jeanie Macpherson. Art director: Wilfred Buckland. Photography: Alvin Wyckoff

Picture started: April 17, 1916. Picture finished: May 4, 1916. Length: 4,825 feet (five reels). Cost: $13,523.19. Released: July 17, 1916. Gross: $66,724.59

Cast: Mae Murray (Meg Dugan), Theodore Roberts (her father), James Neill (Benjamin Merton), Earle Foxe (his grandson Tom), Charles West ("English" Hal), Mary Mersch (Alice Merton), and Mrs. Lewis McCord (matron of orphanage)

Cecil B. DeMille drastically cut back his production schedule in 1916. In part because of the prestige he gained with the Geraldine Farrar pictures and as a reward for his contributions to the success of the Lasky Feature Play Company, DeMille was given the opportunity to make larger-scale, special productions outside the quota of Paramount program pictures. During the year he concentrated his efforts on his first "big picture," *Joan the Woman*, and directed only three other films. The third of his programmers for the year, *The Dream Girl* was made very cheaply and cannot have been of much interest to the director, yet there are indications that it was a pivotal film in his career.

The plot bears some similarity to *The Golden Chance*. Meg Dugan escapes from a reformatory and is taken in by the wealthy Merton family. A con man named "English" Hal poses as a British aristocrat and tries to infiltrate the Merton home. Meg falls in love with young Tom Merton and exposes "English" Hal as a fraud. In turn, "English" Hal produces Meg's reprobate father, who tries to sell her to the Mertons for a fee that will ensure his departure from their lives. Benjamin Merton is outraged and drives the Dugans from his house but finally relents and allows Tom and Meg to wed.

What set *The Dream Girl* apart is that it contained the first example in DeMille's work of the dream of ancient times, or "flashback," which became a virtually obligatory device for him in the years following the

First World War. Meg is enthralled by the legends of King Arthur and his Knights of the Round Table, and she imagines Tom Merton to be Sir Galahad. In light of DeMille's later work, seeing how he handled these dream sequences would be fascinating. Unfortunately, *The Dream Girl* is not known to exist in any archive or private collection.

Early feature films played short runs, changing twice a week—and sometimes every day; often no more than forty prints were made to cover the entire country. For these reasons, the theatrical play-off of a picture took considerable time—often two to three years. The consequently slow return on a producer's investment made it absolutely essential for studios to keep production costs to a minimum. At the same time, great strides were being made in film technique; so there was every reason to fear that a film might become obsolete before it played out its run.

The function of a distribution company like Paramount, or its rivals Metro Pictures and the Mutual Film Corporation, was to provide production financing as an advance against projected rentals, enabling the producer to meet overhead expenses and providing the promise of eventual profits. The Lasky features were popular with audiences and exhibitors; but, except for the films of certain breakthrough stars like Geraldine Farrar, box-office returns hovered in a narrow range.

Although Paramount was the idea of W.W. Hodkinson, it was Frank A. Garbutt who helped cement relations between Hodkinson, Lasky, and Zukor and made the company's formation possible. Garbutt came to Los Angeles as a boy in the 1880s. Spurning his parents' socialist politics, he set up shop as a job printer and also worked as a photographer and millwright before he made his fortune sinking one of the first oil wells in Los Angeles. He became a director of the Union Oil Company and was involved with at least a half dozen other oil concerns. By 1900 he was one of the wealthiest and most respected businessmen in Los Angeles.

Garbutt bankrolled Bosworth, Inc., in 1913 and quickly formed informal alliances with Adolph Zukor and Jesse Lasky. It was Garbutt who helped to pave over differences and petty jealousies the various producers and regional distributors felt when Hodkinson first made the Paramount proposal.

Almost from the beginning, Hodkinson was a problem for the producers. "For your information, and not as a criticism of Mr. Hodkinson," Garbutt wrote in November 1914, "I will say that his accounts were in extremely bad shape, no proper books of record having been kept on our

[Bosworth, Inc.'s] business. There is no question in my mind but what he is honest and but what he is honestly accounting for our money but these accounts were in such shape that no one but an expert auditor could make anything out of them. As to the Paramount Picture Corporation, I have insisted that its books be audited weekly by Price, Waterhouse and Company. . . ."[1]

Added to his sloppiness in conducting business, Hodkinson was also deeply committed to keeping production and distribution separate. With some justification he felt product quality would be higher if producers were beholden to the distributor for their survival rather than the distributor merely being a conduit for whatever the producers happened to turn out.

Zukor, Lasky, and Garbutt tolerated Hodkinson's shortcomings because he knew motion picture distribution and because they needed him. In early 1914 when the Paramount negotiations began, Famous Players Film Company was in desperate straits. The profits from its Mary Pickford pictures barely kept pace with the mediocre performance of the other films on the company's slate. Bosworth, Inc., had several pictures completed and in the can, but no adequate distribution, and the Jesse L. Lasky Feature Play Company had just completed *The Squaw Man*.

Paramount brought stability and profits to the three producers, but problems continued. In 1916, by all accounts, the Lasky pictures carried the Paramount program, while Mary Pickford was still the major asset of Famous Players, and Bosworth, Inc. (now releasing as Pallas-Morosco), was a constant drain on the financial resources of Frank Garbutt.

Zukor saw the future of the film industry much differently than Hodkinson. He felt that by combining production and distribution the 35 percent distribution fee paid to Paramount could be put to better use. At the annual Paramount directors meeting on June 13, 1916, Zukor pulled a palace coup and installed Hiram Abrams as president of Paramount. With Hodkinson out of the picture, Zukor moved quickly to consolidate his position and to allay the fears of his associates. On June 24, 1916, Lasky wired DeMille:

HAVE BEEN NEGOTIATING FOR MERGER FAMOUS
WITH US AND HAVE ZUKOR'S CONSENT TO FIFTY
FIFTY BASIS WHICH WE FEEL MAKES ATTRACTIVE
PROPOSITION. ALL OF US INCLUDING YOURSELF
WILL BE OFFICERS AND DIRECTORS AND WILL

HAVE FIVE YEAR CONTRACTS WITH NEW CORPO-
RATION TO BE CALLED FAMOUS PLAYERS LASKY
CORPORATION. CONTROL OF PRODUCING END WILL
VEST IN US SO THERE WILL BE NO CHANGE IN
YOUR POSITION OR PLANS FOR SPECIAL RELEASES
BUT FEEL CERTAIN MERGER WILL MAKE
EVERYBODY'S STOCK MORE VALUABLE. . . . THIS
DEAL JUST BETWEEN FAMOUS AND US, NO
BANKER, NO BROKERS OR OTHER LEECHES. IMPOR-
TANT TO CLOSE IMMEDIATELY ANXIOUS YOUR
APPROVAL.[2]

DeMille responded immediately:

APPROVE MERGER. RELY ON YOU TO REPRESENT
MY PERSONAL INTERESTS. PRINCIPLE POINTS ARE: I
TO REMAIN IN COMPLETE AUTHORITY OF WHAT-
EVER STUDIO AM CONNECTED WITH AND THAT I
MAY NOT BE MOVED FROM CALIFORNIA WITHOUT
CONSENT. YOU KNOW ME WELL ENOUGH TO AR-
GUE ALL MY POINTS BETTER THAN I COULD.[3]

The merger talks went smoothly enough, and by June 29 Lasky could
report to DeMille:

THE STORY OF THE MERGER OF LASKY AND FA-
MOUS WAS WIDELY PUBLISHED IN TODAYS NEW
YORK DAILYS THE TRADE GENERALLY HAVE BEEN
CONGRATULATING US ON THE NEW COMBINATION
WE ALL ARE VERY MUCH PLEASED AND CON-
GRATULATE THE NEW DIRECTOR GENERAL OF THE
FAMOUS PLAYERS LASKY CORPORATION.[4]

The merger was formalized on July 19, 1916, and both sides gained
from the deal. Zukor was a businessman who freely admitted that the
Lasky "product was better than mine . . . ,"[5] and Lasky, who always felt
more comfortable dealing with creative people, was content to let Zukor
shoulder the larger part of the business concerns.

DeMille was heavily into production on *Joan the Woman* when the merger concluded, and after Jesse Lasky's initial glowing accounts of the deal he probably felt secure in the arrangement. However, there were subtle shadings in the agreement that would have great impact on DeMille's future. Lasky wired DeMille:

REMEMBERING MY PROMISE TO ALWAYS IN YOUR ABSENCE LOOK AFTER YOUR PERSONAL INTERESTS AS I DO MY OWN I WANT TO EXPLAIN TO YOU IN MY OWN LANGUAGE THE SITUATION REGARDING YOUR FIVE YEAR CONTRACT[.] PERSONALLY I WOULD HAVE PREFERRED A FIVE YEAR CONTRACT THE SAME AS YOU ARE GETTING BUT ZUKOR FELT THAT IT WOULD NOT BE QUITE FAIR AND HONORABLE FOR WE EXECUTIVES WHO ARE NONPRODUCERS TO BIND OURSELVES TO RECEIVE OUR VERY LARGE SALARIES FOR A PERIOD OF FIVE YEARS REGARDLESS OF THE FACT THAT THE CORPORATION MIGHT NOT BE ABLE TO PAY THEM AT SOME TIME DURING THIS PERIOD[.] WE FEEL THAT WE HAVE NO MARKET VALUE AND THAT OUR SALARIES DEPENDED UPON THE FINANCIAL SUCCESS OF THE CORPORATION YOU HOWEVER BEING AN ACTIVE PRODUCER HAVE A MARKET VALUE AND JUST BECAUSE YOU ARE ON OUR BOARD YOUR SALARY SHOULD NOT BE SUBJECTED TO ANY POSSIBLE REDUCTION ON ACCOUNT OF THE FUTURE FINANCIAL CONDITION OF THE CORPORATION[.] WE ARE READY TO SIGN CONTRACTS THEREFORE WHICH BIND US FOR FIVE YEARS TO THE CORPORATION BUT GIVE THE CORPORATION THE RIGHT TO TERMINATE OUR CONTRACTS OR REDUCE OUR SALARIES BUT YOU ARE TO HAVE A CONTRACT THAT NOT ALONE BINDS YOU BUT BINDS THE CORPORATION TO PAY YOUR SALARY.[6]

No doubt Lasky felt he was looking after DeMille's interests, and the contract did provide a financial safety net, but this amounted only to job security. DeMille was no longer a principal in the Famous Players-Lasky Corporation.

Paramount still had a twenty-five-year agreement with Bosworth, Inc., and it was deemed essential that Frank Garbutt's company be brought into the new combine. In the early 1920s Garbutt prepared a history of his motion picture activities to give his attorney background for pending tax litigation. While the document is somewhat self-serving, it does offer insight into the manner in which the Bosworth, Inc., merger with Famous Players-Lasky was negotiated.

"In the late summer of 1916," wrote Garbutt,

Samuel Goldfish visited me in Los Angeles with a suggestion that [Bosworth, Inc.] form a consolidation with the Famous Players-Lasky Corporation.

. . . The propositions made by Mr. Goldfish were not satisfactory to us and nothing came of the negotiations except that Mr. [Arthur] Friend [attorney for Famous Players-Lasky] came out from New York to see if the matter could not be fixed up. As a result of these talks . . . it was decided that I should go to New York with them and discuss the matter with Mr. Lasky and Mr. Zukor and the other directors there. . . .

On arriving in New York Mr. Goldfish, for internal reasons, severed his connection with the Famous Players-Lasky Corporation, and our negotiations were not progressing satisfactorily . . . due to my disinclination to put the assets [of Bosworth, Inc., Pallas Pictures, and the Oliver Morosco Photoplay Co.] wholly in the control of other people no matter how friendly or competent they might be. . . .[7]

I would negotiate . . . during the day and return to the hotel at night and tell my family the results. [My daughter] Melodile Garbutt [who was officially the president of Bosworth, Inc. at the time] was spending her time going through the books and affairs of the Famous Players-Lasky Corporation with a view of acquiring all of the information she could in regard to their business as a guide to me in pursuing the negotiations.[8] One of these evenings when I was particularly tired and rather disappointed at the result of the day's work, Mrs. Garbutt urged me to not be so particular about the deal but to close it up and get out of the [picture] business. . . .

Mr. [Oliver] Morosco was in New York and I consulted

him in person and on one or two occasions he went with me to the Famous Players-Lasky Corporation's offices to negotiate with them.

. . . I was advised by them, and especially by Mr. Zukor, that they did not wish to complicate matters by negotiating with more than one person . . . and to simplify matters I did the negotiating and the contracting. Whenever we reached a point where I was exceeding my authority . . . I would ask for further time or adjourn the conference and . . . consult with my family and Mr. Morosco. . . .

Shortly after I renewed negotiations the thought came into my mind that we could solve our differences . . . by only trading them part of our assets and have them pay us cash for the balance. They objected to doing this, and finally the plan was evolved whereby we consolidated with them on one-half of our interests and liquidated the balance in the orderly course of business. This was the scheme that was ultimately worked out and closed on October 7, 1916 by a letter which was drafted by Mr. Arthur Friend, then Treasurer and attorney for the Company. This letter was drafted in Mr. Friend's office late on the evening of the 6th, as I remember it, after I had come in and turned down coldly a proposition which they had previously made me that day.

This letter of October 7, 1916 was signed by Mr. Lasky, as Vice President, the next day, Mr. Zukor being absent for a day or two. . . . [9]

Garbutt's account of the merger talks is as interesting for what it implies as for what it actually says. In his book *Goldwyn*, Scott Berg suggests that Goldfish's insensitive handling of Mary Pickford was the source of the rift with Zukor that resulted in Goldfish's forced resignation from Famous Players-Lasky.[10] But Garbutt's statement implies that at least part of the antagonism between Zukor and Goldfish was due to Goldfish's failure to conclude an agreement for the acquisition of Bosworth, Inc.

Zukor's being absent from the final negotiation with Garbutt is also interesting. It would seem that Jesse Lasky and Arthur Friend were the diplomats who finally put the deal across. Taking control of Garbutt's interests allowed the Famous Players-Lasky Corporation to formally take over Paramount Pictures Corporation in 1917 and to create the first fully integrated American film company with interests in production, distribution, and exhibition.

# 24

# Joan the Woman

Produced by Cardinal Film Corporation (Jesse L. Lasky Feature Play Company). Director: Cecil B. DeMille. Original story and scenario by Jeanie Macpherson. Art director: Wilfred Buckland. Photography: Alvin Wyckoff. Lighting: Howard Ewing. Musical score: William Furst

Picture started: June 19, 1916. Picture finished: October 7, 1916. Length: ten reels. Cost: $302,976.26. Released: January 15, 1917. Gross: $605,731.30

Cast: Geraldine Farrar (Joan of Arc), Wallace Reid (Eric Trent), Theodore Roberts (Cauchon), Charles Clary (George de la Tremoille, the Spider), Hobart Bosworth (General La Hire), Raymond Hatton (Charles VII of France), Tully Marshall (L'Oiseleur), Larry Peyton (Gaspard), Horace B. Carpenter (Jacques D'Arc), Lillian Leighton (Isambeau), Marjorie Daw (Katherine), Walter Long (executioner), Billy Elmer (Guy Townes), and Cleo Ridgely (the king's favorite)

I n 1915 D.W. Griffith's twelve-reel epic, *The Birth of a Nation*, took the country by storm and convinced filmmakers that audiences would pay advanced prices for big pictures in exclusive road-show engagements.[1] With production costs and road-show distribution expenses, *The Birth of a Nation* was a risky $110,000 investment for Griffith and his backers; but the film's success attracted investment capital to the picture business, and, in the best movieland tradition of "never a leader but a follower be," 1916 saw a number of productions designed to rival Griffith's success. Thomas Ince produced *Civilization*, Vitagraph brought out *The Battle Cry of Peace*, the Selig Polyscope Company had its own Civil War epic in *The Crisis*, and Griffith sought to top himself with *Intolerance*.

When the Famous Players-Lasky merger was announced on June 29, 1916, Cecil B. DeMille was nearly two weeks into production on his own contribution to the epic-film cycle. *Joan the Woman* was planned as a special production with a huge budget for the time, and it was clearly beyond the scope of the five-reel pictures that were the staple of the Paramount program. Adolph Zukor and Jesse Lasky agreed to treat

DeMille's epic as an issue apart from the merger, and Lasky created the Cardinal Film Corporation solely to produce and exploit the picture.

Bringing the life of Joan of Arc to the screen was an odd choice for 1916. The film opens in the midst of World War I with Eric Trent, a young British soldier, finding a long-buried sword on the eve of a great battle. Questioning his own courage in the face of heavy odds, he receives from the rusted sword a vision of another time—a time when a distant ancestor was part of an English force set on conquering France. The earlier Trent is wounded in battle and befriended by Joan. Though they are on different sides of the conflict, they fall in love.

Later, when Joan leads the French army to retake Orleans, she defeats Trent. During the Church-sponsored witch hunt, Trent betrays Joan to her accusers, and she is burned at the stake. Now, back in 1916, the same French fields are the scene of another fierce conflict. The spirit of Joan persuades Eric Trent to atone for the mistakes of his ancestor by fighting for the liberation of France.

The element of reincarnation had special appeal to Macpherson, according to DeMille, who also had an interest in the subject. Framing the story of Joan against the current world upheaval was designed to make modern audiences identify more closely with the long-ago fifteenth-century conflict. But France and Britain were allies in the First World War, and resurrecting the historical hostility between the countries was a clearly misguided result of America's naive and neutral sensibilities in 1916.

Although the foreign market was in upheaval because of the war, the United States did not enter the conflict until April 1917 and was supplying films to all the belligerent countries. Even though the sinking of the *Lusitania* in 1915 caused sympathy for Germany to decline, the majority of Americans were content to let the Europeans settle their own affairs, and a sizable segment of the American people were actually anti-British. And because *Joan the Woman* stirred up memories of ancient conflicts and religious witch hunts, it is doubtful that the British, French, Germans, or the Roman Catholic Church found much to embrace in the film.

*Joan the Woman*'s release several months after *Intolerance* has caused some to assume that DeMille was borrowing a page from Griffith in developing modern and historical stories in a single film, but in fact production of *Joan the Woman* was well underway before *Intolerance* was released; furthermore, given Griffith's great secrecy about his project, it is unlikely that *Intolerance* had any significant influence on DeMille.

What is more likely is that DeMille and Macpherson were inspired by Thomas Ince's *Civilization*, which was released in April 1916. *Civilization* was set in the world war and had Christ's spirit returning to show the king of the imaginary nation of Wredpryd (who bore a striking resemblance to Germany's own "Kaiser Bill") the error of his uncivilized ways.

The modern story with historical flashback also owed much to *The Road to Yesterday*, a 1906 play by Beulah Marie Dix and Evelyn Greenleaf Sutherland that pioneered the use of the technique. DeMille would use historical flashbacks in many of his pictures, including his own film version of *The Road to Yesterday*. Interestingly, *The Road to Yesterday*, which was so influential to both DeMille and Griffith, only came to the screen near the end of the "historic flashback" cycle that lasted roughly from 1916 to 1925.

Another influence on *Joan the Woman* was *The Personal Recollections of Joan of Arc*, Samuel L. Clemens's 1896 novel about the life of Joan.[2] Clemens's description of Joan makes readily apparent the character's great appeal for Macpherson and DeMille: "The contrast between her and her century is the contrast between day and night. She was truthful when lying was the common speech of men; she was honest when honesty was become a lost virtue; . . . she was a rock of convictions in a time when men believed in nothing and scoffed at all things; she was unfailingly true in an age that was false to the core; she maintained her personal dignity unimpaired in an age of fawnings and servilities. . . . " In his own way, of course, Clemens the social critic (whose most common voice was that of humorist Mark Twain) was writing of his own time, and his words gave Macpherson further inspiration for the framing story. The closing lines of Clemens's book read: "Love, Mercy, Charity, Fortitude, War, Peace, Poetry, Music—these may be symbolized as any shall prefer: by figures of either sex and of any age; but a slender girl in her first young bloom, with the martyr's crown upon her head, and in her hand the sword that severed her country's bonds—shall not this, and no other, stand for Patriotism through all the ages until time shall end?"

Given the success of the first three Geraldine Farrar pictures, her selection to play Joan was logical, although at age thirty-four she was well past creating the illusion of being a seventeen-year-old milkmaid. In the year after her first work for DeMille, she married Lou-Tellegen and gained several pounds. In July 1916, DeMille wrote Jesse Lasky that Farrar seemed "to have lost a little something of the great spark of genius that animated her last year. Although she is tremendously enthused over the story and says it is the greatest work of her life, at the same time, that little spark seems missing. She may get it as she goes on in the work."[3] According to DeMille's later recollections, Farrar was annoyed that Famous Players-Lasky could not find a spot on their payroll for Lou-Tellegen as a director. In fact, the dispute between Tellegen and Famous Players-Lasky was more complex. Paramount exhibitors were complaining that Tellegen as a leading man meant poison at the box office, and Jesse Lasky was desperately trying to find a way to terminate the company's contract with him. It was March 1917 before Famous Players-Lasky and Lou-Tellegen reached a settlement. On March 2 Jesse Lasky wired DeMille:

ON ACCOUNT OF COMPLAINTS OF EXHIBITORS WE ARE COMPELLED TO CANCEL TELLEGEN'S CONTRACT. IT HAS BEEN A DELICATE MATTER AND I HAVE ONLY SUCCEEDED IN DOING SO THROUGH FARRAR HERSELF. REMEMBERING THEIR TALK WITH YOU REGARDING TELLEGEN BECOMING A DIRECTOR, THEY HAVE AGREED TO COMPROMISE AS FOLLOWS IN AS MUCH AS WE OWE HIM SIX WEEK'S WORK WE HAVE AGREED TO GIVE TELLEGEN A TRIAL AS DIRECTOR AS QUICKLY AS YOU CAN ARRANGE A PLACE FOR HIM. I BELIEVE WITH YOU THAT TELLEGEN MAY MAKE AN OUTSTANDING DIRECTOR AND IT IS IMPORTANT THAT YOU ADVISE ME QUICKLY AS POSSIBLE BY WIRE WHERE YOU CAN USE TELLEGEN . . . HE IS ANXIOUS TO START AT ONCE AND I HAVE PROMISED TO GIVE HIM A TRIAL WITHOUT DELAY. HAVE AGREED HE IS TO DIRECT TWO PICTURES.

Tellegen did direct two Famous Players-Lasky productions: *What Money Can't Buy* (released July 16, 1917) and *The Thing We Love* (released February 11, 1918). Given the long-standing tension between Famous Players-Lasky and Tellegen, relations on the set of *Joan the Woman* became strained between DeMille and Farrar. In his autobiography, DeMille insists that Farrar regained that "spark of genius" as work on *Joan the Woman* progressed, but Farrar's performance as Joan differs from her earlier screen work, and the difference is worth noting because it offers a clue to DeMille's approach to costume drama. The lively and natural Geraldine Farrar of *Carmen* is replaced in *Joan the Woman* by a more formal and stylized screen persona. The other players also perform in a style that owes more to the historical pageant than to popular theater or motion pictures. Considering the naturalistic performances DeMille elicited in pictures like *The Golden Chance*, *The Cheat*, and *Maria Rosa*, we must assume that this departure represented a conscious directorial decision. DeMille continued to use this same conventional approach to acting in his later historical films.

Work on *Joan the Woman* progressed through the summer and into the fall. By August, DeMille and Lasky were considering who would compose the musical score to accompany the picture. DeMille suggested Melville Ellis, who made his mark in the world of musical comedy and had played mood music on the set of *Carmen*. Lasky wired DeMille:

REGARDING MELVILLE ELLIS. HAD INTERVIEW
WITH HIM AND AM CONVINCED THAT WE WOULD
NOT GET A PRACTICAL SCORE SUCH AS WE WOULD
GET FROM A TRAINED COMPOSER AND ARRANGER
. . . IF ELLIS WAS ALLOWED TO CARRY OUT HIS
PLAN OF IMPROVISING THE SCORE AND TAKING A
RECORD OF IT ON A RECORDING PHONOGRAPH
I AM SURE THAT WHOEVER ARRANGED AND
ORCHESTRATED ELLIS'S MUSIC WOULD HAVE
ENDLESS DIFFICULTIES WITH THE MUSIC ITSELF
AND ARGUMENTS WITH ELLIS IN FACT I SERIOUSLY
DOUBT IF ELLIS WOULD EVER FINISH WHAT HE
UNDERTAKES TO DO.

Ellis was either a madman or ahead of his time. It seems inconceivable that the primitive acoustical recording equipment of the day, which yielded a wax master and was capable of recording no more than four minutes of music on disc or cylinder, would provide a record of sufficient quality to enable Ellis's improvisations to be transcribed into a usable musical score. Certainly there was no practical way to accurately synchronize the tempo of such recordings to the running speed of the film, creating yet another nightmare for the arranger. Whether Ellis could have persuaded any producer to attempt such an approach in 1916 is doubtful. He died in 1917 at the age of forty-one without ever having a chance to test his ideas for film scoring.

Ultimately Lasky and DeMille settled on William Furst to compose and assemble the score for *Joan the Woman*. Furst began work on the picture while DeMille was still shooting, and on October 17, 1916, DeMille wired Lasky that "Furst's music for Joan is excellent, but I will need him for some time yet. What do you think of putting him on regular salary and sending me print of [latest] Pickford picture for him to do music?"[4]

Lasky replied:

DO NOT ADVISE PUTTING FURST ON REGULAR
SALARY. PICKFORD MUSIC SCORES HAVE TO BE
FINISHED WEEK AFTER DIRECTOR FINISHES
SHOOTING PICTURE, THEREFORE NO TIME TO SEND
PRINT TO COAST. WILL RE ENGAGE FURST WHEN
HE COMES EAST TO DO A PICKFORD SCORE AND
WILL TRY KEEP HIM BUSY UNTIL OPENING TO
JOAN.[5]

As production on *Joan the Woman* continued into its third month, D.W. Griffith's *Intolerance* opened at the Liberty Theatre in New York, and Jesse Lasky wired his initial reaction to DeMille:

GRIFFITH PICTURE INTOLERANCE OPENED LAST
NIGHT. IT IS BEING SEVERELY CRITICIZED ON ALL
SIDES AND OPINION EVERYWHERE IS THAT IT DOES
NOT COMPARE WITH BIRTH [OF A NATION]. THE
LACK OF CONSECUTIVE STORY IS THE PICTURE'S
WORST FAULT IN FACT IT PROVED A DISAPPOINT-
MENT AS FAR AS THE FIRST NIGHT AUDIENCE WAS
CONCERNED HOWEVER THE PART OF THE PRODUC-
TION WHICH DEALS WITH THE FALL OF BABYLON IS
WONDERFUL AND IN MY OPINION THE PICTURE
WILL BE A GENERAL SUCCESS. SINCE WATCHING
THE GRIFFITH PICTURE MR. ZUKOR AND I ARE
CONVINCED THAT YOU HAVE A WONDERFUL
CHANCE WITH THE FARRAR PICTURE. YOU WILL BE
COMING INTO NEW YORK AT JUST THE RIGHT
MOMENT, AND IF YOU HAVE A STORY YOU WILL BE
GIVING THE PUBLIC JUST WHAT THEY ARE CLAM-
ORING FOR.[6]

A month later, Lasky was anxious to see *Joan the Woman* completed.

... IT IS IMPORTANT YOU FINISH CUTTING THE BIG
PICTURE AS SOON AS POSSIBLE AND BRING IT TO
NEW YORK WITH YOU IMMEDIATELY IT IS FINISHED
... ADVISE AT EARLIEST POSSIBLE MOMENT PROB-
ABLE DATE OF YOUR DEPARTURE. I DOUBT IF I CAN
COME TO HOLLYWOOD TO SEE THE PICTURE AS
PLANNED, BUT GIVE ME SUFFICIENT NOTICE AND
WILL DO MY BEST TO JOIN YOU.[7]

DeMille's reply was oblique, referring to other business concerns to avoid coming to terms with his slow progress on the picture:

I HAVE JUST BEEN ELECTED PRESIDENT OF
MOROSCO COMPANY AND VICE PRESIDENT OF
BOSWORTH COMPANY, SO I AM FILLED WITH
HONOR AND HAVE LOST A GOOD DAY'S WORK.
HAVE DECIDED TO LET [director James] YOUNG GO
AFTER OLIVER TWIST [starring Marie Doro and released
December 6, 1916]. HE HAS SO CHANGED LOST AND
WON [also starring Doro, released January 16, 1917] AS TO
HAVE SERIOUSLY HURT IT. DO YOU KNOW GOOD
DIRECTOR TO REPLACE HIM?[8]

As *Joan The Woman* neared completion rumors began to circulate that William Fox was planning his own production based on the life of Joan, just as he had jumped in with a Theda Bara version of *Carmen* to compete with DeMille's and a *Romeo and Juliet* (1916), also starring Bara, to rival Metro's production with Francis X. Bushman and Beverly Bayne. Lasky moved quickly to reassure DeMille, "Just talked personally with Fox, who claims he does not know what west coast studio is doing and if they are doing production of Joan of Arc he will stop same. Wire me more details if possible how long Fox coast studio have been working on production."[9]

DeMille replied that "Fox production of Joan shrouded in mystery. [Oscar Apfel] who has just left Fox assures me no such production is being made and I cannot get any definite information excepting general denials but rumors have come from many sources."[10] The rumors turned out to be false alarms. There was no Fox version of Joan, but the studio did turn to French history for two of its biggest pictures of the year, *DuBarry*, featuring Theda Bara, and *A Tale of Two Cities*, starring William Farnum.

Because the Lasky pictures were released through Paramount there was concern that exhibitors would expect DeMille's expensive super-production to be included as a regular release on the Paramount program. For this reason it was felt that Jesse Lasky's name should not appear in the credits. Even the main title of DeMille's picture was in doubt to the last minute because the producer and director could not agree on what the picture should be called. On November 2, 1916, Lasky wired DeMille:

ALTHOUGH EVERY EFFORT HAS BEEN MADE . . . TO
AVOID GIVING TITLE OF FARRAR PICTURE, EVERY-
ONE INCLUDING THEATRICAL MANAGERS, NEWS-
PAPER MEN, MAGAZINE PUBLISHERS AND CRITICS
HAVE SO UNANIMOUSLY ASSUMED THE TITLE WILL
BE "JOAN OF ARC" THAT WE TOOK THE MATTER UP
HERE [in New York] AGAIN AND FOUND UNANIMITY
OF OPINION IN FAVOR OF THAT TITLE. IT SEEMS TO
US THAT WE WOULD BE THROWING AWAY ONE OF
THE PICTURE'S GREATEST ASSETS IF WE USED ANY
OTHER TITLE, EVEN IF THE TITLE YOU SUGGEST
[Joan the Woman] WOULD BETTER FIT THE VERSION.
HOPE YOU AGREE THIS VIEW. IF SO, MAIN TITLE
SHOULD READ:

GERALDINE FARRAR
IN CECIL B. DE MILLE'S CINEMA PRESENTATION OF
"JOAN OF ARC"
PRODUCED AND COPYRIGHTED 1916
BY CARDINAL FILM CORPORATION

CONFIRM SO WE CAN PROCEED WITH LITHOGRAPHS [post-
ers] AND ADVISE WHEN YOU WILL BE HERE WITH PRINT.
ABOUT TO CLOSE FOR LONG RUN AT LIBERTY [Theater] OPEN-
ING CHRISTMAS.[11]

DeMille replied, "I don't like the words cinema presentation on main title of Joan. It spoils the effects, and putting my name between that of Farrar and Joan of Arc spoils line up of title. If agreeable, I should prefer Cecil B. DeMille presents. Will be ready to leave here [Los Angeles] about first of December or possibly sooner. Picture is now thirteen thousand feet and am having some difficulty in getting out a thousand feet more."[12]

Lasky finally gave in. He wired DeMille:

> ... AFTER LONG DISCUSSION, HAVE CONCLUDED TO LEAVE FINAL SELECTION TITLE FARRAR PICTURE ENTIRELY TO YOU, STILL FEELING HOWEVER THAT TITLE SUGGESTED BY US IS PROPER. EQUALLY WELL CONVINCED HOWEVER THAT PICTURE WILL BE A SUCCESS UNDER EITHER TITLE AND WANT YOU TO KNOW THAT I WILL BE SATISFIED WITH ANY DECISION YOU MAKE. POLITICAL SITUATION WHICH LEADS US TO AVOID USE OF LASKY NAME HAS CLEARED TO SUCH AN EXTENT AS TO SATISFY US WE CAN NOW ENJOY FULL BENEFITS USE OF NAME AND THEREFORE YOU ARE TO USE IN MAIN TITLE THE WORDS: JESSE L. LASKY PRESENTS AT TOP, WITH PRODUCED AND COPYRIGHTED 1916 BY CARDINAL FILM CORPORATION AT BOTTOM. BALANCE OF TITLE TO BE WORKED OUT BY YOU SO THAT IT SETS UP PROPERLY AND TO YOUR OWN SATISFACTION.[13]

On-screen the final main title reads

JESSE L. LASKY PRESENTS
GERALDINE FARRAR
IN
JOAN THE WOMAN
BY JEANIE MACPHERSON
Produced and Copyrighted by Cardinal Film Corporation

DeMille's credit followed on a separate card after a dedicatory title to the spirit of Joan.

*Joan the Woman* is a prototype for DeMille's later spectacles. His handling of the large battle scenes (with the aid of seventeen cameras and a small army of assistant directors including William deMille, George Melford, and Donald Crisp) is exceptional—equal to Griffith's work in *The Birth of a Nation* and *Intolerance*. The real strength of the picture, however, is found in the director's provocatively compelling images:

- After the celebration of her victory at Orleans, Joan is left alone in the great hall with Eric Trent. He confesses his love. She tells him she loves France alone, and Eric walks through the empty, confetti-strewn hall as Joan, her back to the camera, watches him leave. Cut to mid-front shot of Joan framed by the throne and the symbols of the Church. She turns in despair to the symbols of her great love. . . .
- At Joan's trial by torture, officers of the Church are clad in white, hooded robes with black holes for eyes. DeMille frames his shot so that the top of Cauchon's mitre is out of frame and he looks not like a bishop of the Church, but like a black-clad grand dragon of the invisible empire surrounded by Klansmen and hiding behind a crucifix. . . .
- The empty town square on the morning of Joan's execution. An executioner drives a single horse cart piled with kindling to lay around the stake where Joan will meet her death. A lone dog is the only living thing barking a futile protest. . . .
- The weak king, reveling in debauchery as Joan is tried for witchcraft. In addition to wine and women, we see two male courtiers locked in embrace. Too late the king comes to his senses, only to find his most "loyal" supporters passed out at his feet. For all his wealth and position, the king is powerless. . . .
- As Joan is led to the stake, Bishop Cauchon seizes her ornate crucifix, and as the flames surround her Eric Trent hands Joan a handmade cross of simple twigs that she carries to her death. . . .

Unlike Griffith, DeMille shuns the use of florid agitprop subtitles to carry his message, weaving instead a tapestry of highly complex images that call on the audience to discover the symbolism and meaning without ever drawing attention away from the narrative.

For the first time DeMille and Wyckoff employed the elaborate stencil-color Handschiegl Process in addition to the usual tints and tones. The Handschiegl Process gave a full-color effect to portions of the film—notably on establishing shots and art titles that showed little movement on-screen. The process was also used to color the flames when Joan is burned at the stake.

Critical reaction to *Joan the Woman* was almost universally positive, and the picture did well at the box office—but not nearly well enough. It was clear almost from the time of its Christmas day opening that the picture was not going to perform to expectations. The twelve-reel picture was cut very early in the run, and on January 5, 1917, DeMille wired Jesse Lasky:

> . . . I WISH YOU WOULD MAKE EVERY EFFORT TO
> KEEP THE ADVERTISING FORCE TURNING EVERY
> POSSIBLE TRICK TO INCREASE THE BUSINESS OF
> JOAN. THERE IS ABSOLUTELY NO QUESTION IN
> MY MIND ABOUT THE SUCCESS OF THE PIECE
> BUT THIS IS A MOST CRITICAL TIME AND A LET-
> UP WOULD BE FATAL. DO NOT LET THEM KEEP
> PLUGGING THE FACT OF THE TERRIFIC ADVANCE
> SALE AS I HAVE SEEN TWO LETTERS TO PEOPLE
> [here in Hollywood] THAT THEY [the writers] WERE
> NOT GOING UNTIL LATER, AS THEY UNDER-
> STOOD ALL SEATS WERE SOLD FOR FOUR WEEKS
> OR MORE. DO NOT LET THE ENTHUSIASM
> SLACKEN AND THE MORE I THINK OF THE LAST
> [shortened version] CUT, THE LESS I LIKE IT. THE
> PRESENT LENGTH OF THE PICTURE HAS NOTHING
> TO DO WITH ITS RECEIPTS. I PLACE MY ENTIRE
> CONFIDENCE IN YOU TO LEND ALL YOUR
> WEIGHT AND ENTHUSIASM TOWARD PUSHING
> THE NEW YORK RUN INTO FINANCIAL SUCCESS
> IT CAN BE MADE.[14]

Film historian Russell Merritt tracked road-show engagements for *Joan the Woman* in the eleven leading American cities of the time, and his research offers an insight to the picture's performance at the box office:

| | | | |
|---|---|---|---|
| New York (*44th Street Theater*) | $2 top. | December 25, 1916 to April 14, 1917. | 16 weeks |
| Los Angeles (*Majestic Theater*) | $1.50 loges. | January 15 to March 18, 1917. | 8 weeks |
| Boston (*Colonial Theater*) | $.25 to $1.00. | March 20 to April 28, 1917. | 6 weeks |
| Chicago (*Colonial Theater*) | $1.00 top. | March 28 to May 5, 1917. | 7 weeks |
| San Francisco (*Cort Theater*) | $.25, $.50, $.75, $1.00. | April 6 to April 26, 1917. | 3 weeks |
| Philadelphia (*Chestnut Street Opera House*) | $1.00 top. | April 9 to May 12, 1917. | 5 weeks |
| Pittsburgh (*Pitt Theater*) | $2.00 top. | April 16 to May 5, 1917. | 3 weeks |
| Cleveland (*Stillman Theater*) | $1.50. | April 16 to May 5, 1917. | 3 weeks |
| Baltimore (*Auditorium Theater*) | $.75 to $1.50. | April 23 to May 5, 1917. | 2 weeks |
| Detroit (*Detroit Opera House*) | $2.00 top. | June 17 to July 8, 1917. | 3 weeks |
| St. Louis (*Royal Theater*) | | November 5 to November 17, 1917. | 2 weeks |

*Joan the Woman* played a total of fifty-eight first-run road-show weeks in these eleven major cities. By comparison, *Intolerance* played ninety-three first-run road-show weeks, and *Civilization* played sixty weeks, before going into general release.[15]

The eight-week run in Los Angeles was remarkable, considering that the city's population hovered around three hundred thousand in 1916. The sixteen-week New York run, on the other hand, was relatively modest because the city boasted a population of several million people. On March 13, 1917, Lasky reported that "JOAN is doing absolutely no business in New Jersey and indications are that state rights men will have difficulty in exhibiting JOAN at high prices. . . ."[16]

Although *Joan the Woman* grossed double its negative cost,[17] the picture did little more than break even by the time distribution costs were factored in, and Famous Players-Lasky did not seem inclined to repeat the experiment.

## 25

# A Romance of the Redwoods

An Artcraft Picture. Produced by the Mary Pickford Film Corporation. Director: Cecil B. DeMille. Original story by Cecil B. DeMille and Jeanie Macpherson. Scenario by Jeanie Macpherson. Art director: Wilfred Buckland. Photography: Alvin Wyckoff

Picture started: February 17, 1917. Picture finished: March 23, 1917. Length: 6,574 feet (seven reels). Cost: $134,831.65 (includes $96,666.67 in Mary Pickford's salary charged to the picture). Released: May 14, 1917. Gross: $424,718.52

Cast: Mary Pickford (Jenny Lawrence), Elliott Dexter ("Black" Brown), Charles Ogle (Jim Lyn), Tully Marshall (Sam Sparks, a gambler), Raymond Hatton (Dick Roland, a miner), Walter Long (the sheriff), and Winter Hall (John Lawrence, Jenny's uncle)

As Adolph Zukor negotiated the Famous Players-Lasky merger in mid-1916, he was also involved in negotiations to retain the services of his number one box-office star, Mary Pickford. On June 24, 1916, Zukor signed a contract with Pickford that called for Mary to receive a salary of $10,000 a week, with a $300,000 bonus for signing, 50 percent of the profits from her pictures produced under the contract, and an additional $40,000 for a month's layoff that resulted while she was renegotiating the terms of her employment. The contract also called for Pickford to be given her own studio in the East. If her pictures were made in California, Mary Pickford was to have the exclusive use of a stage on the Lasky lot in Hollywood.

The average Paramount release of the time cost about $20,000 to produce. Under her new contract the Pickford pictures cost five to six times that figure. Existing contracts with Paramount-affiliated theaters simply didn't allow the distributor to pass on the inflated production costs to exhibitors. To put it bluntly, Paramount couldn't afford Pickford. On September 2, 1916, a four-page advertising spread in *The Moving Picture World* announced the formation of the Mary Pickford Film Corporation and stated that Pickford's films would be released through a new company, Artcraft Pictures Corporation.

Artcraft was not bound by Paramount's block-booking contracts, and the Pickford pictures were offered on significantly higher guarantees and percentages than the standard program fare. Paramount exhibitors were understandably upset when they learned that they had lost Pickford and even more so when they noticed an odd coincidence. W.E. Greene and Al Lichtman, the president and general manager of Artcraft, were former Paramount employees.

Theater owners had little choice but to bite the bullet and pay the higher ante if they wanted future Pickford releases. Paramount pictures were generally conceded to be the best films available, and few wanted to terminate their Paramount contracts for less-desirable product. Besides, Fox Film Corporation was already contracted with its own theaters. The Mutual Film Corporation had Charlie Chaplin under contract, but the balance of the Mutual program was often second-rate. Universal offered quantity over quality, and Metro always seemed to be on shaky ground. The Triangle Film Corporation provided Paramount's stiffest competition, offering productions supervised by D.W. Griffith, Thomas H. Ince, and Mack Sennett and starring popular actors like Douglas Fairbanks, William S. Hart, Lillian and Dorothy Gish, and Roscoe "Fatty" Arbuckle. But despite the box-office value of its filmmakers and stars, the company's highly restrictive distribution policies brought Triangle to the brink of financial ruin.[1]

Just as theater owners became aware that Artcraft was merely a front created by Zukor to squeeze the highest possible dollar in film rentals, they had to face the fact that Zukor was moving behind the scenes to consolidate his position. Within a year the industry was rocked with a series of announcements: the Douglas Fairbanks Pictures Corporation was formed and would release through Artcraft; D.W. Griffith signed with Artcraft in March 1917; Thomas Ince signed in June 1917; and William S. Hart Productions, Inc., also announced its affiliation with Artcraft. To soften the blow, Zukor signed Mack Sennett to produce two-reel Paramount-Sennett Comedies, and picked up Roscoe Arbuckle's Comique Film Corporation comedies for Paramount release. With these additions to the Paramount and Artcraft rosters, Adolph Zukor controlled the filmmaking activities of nearly all the top stars in the movies, with the exception of Charlie Chaplin.

The first two pictures of the Mary Pickford Film Corporation were *Less Than the Dust* (Artcraft, 1916) directed by John Emerson, which was generally considered to be the worst picture the star ever made, and

*The Pride of the Clan* (Artcraft, 1917) directed by Maurice Tourneur, which did not perform to expectations.

According to DeMille, Adolph Zukor personally asked him to make two pictures with Pickford to help put an end to her downward skid at the box office. However, the grosses of DeMille's two Pickford films were far higher than any previous DeMille film except *Joan the Woman*, and higher than for any other picture he made before *Male and Female* in 1919. Clearly, Mary Pickford was the drawing card, and the director benefited at least as much from the teaming as the star.[2]

The pairing of Pickford and DeMille served Zukor's interests in a number of ways. By offering Pickford an opportunity to work with one of the industry's top directors, he convinced her to leave the East Coast and thus reduced studio overhead costs charged to her pictures. He also managed to beef up the star power of the DeMille pictures, helping establish the DeMille name itself as an attraction worthy of Artcraft release.

Jesse Lasky suggested Kate Douglas Wiggin's *Rebecca of Sunnybrook Farm* as the first DeMille-Pickford collaboration, but the director had no interest in the property.[3] DeMille proposed *The Little American* as his first Pickford project, but Jesse Lasky was nervous that a film dealing with German atrocities in the Great War would get the cold shoulder in the still-lucrative markets of Germany and Austria-Hungary. DeMille then suggested a Western as a compromise, and Lasky gave the green light.

The original story for *A Romance of the Redwoods* bears more than a little resemblance to *The Girl of the Golden West*—a girl falls in love with an outlaw and saves him from the hangman's noose—but DeMille and Macpherson gave the basic plot some fascinating twists.

Jenny Lawrence is sent to live with her last surviving relative—an uncle who lives in the West. During her long journey, the uncle is killed by Indians. An outlaw, "Black" Brown, comes across John Lawrence's body and switches clothes with the corpse so the pursuing posse will think Brown has been killed. Brown assumes the dead man's identity, and when Jenny arrives she threatens to expose the outlaw. But Strawberry Flats is a wide-open town and no place for an innocent young girl. Jenny has a choice between accepting the dubious hospitality of the outlaw impostor or working for bed and board in the local dance hall. Jenny and the outlaw eventually fall in love, and she persuades him to reform. Brown agrees to walk the straight and narrow but decides to pull one last stagecoach holdup to raise a stake for their future. He is captured and threatened with hanging. Jenny intervenes with the vigilantes and shows them some doll clothes, persuading them that she is pregnant with "Black" Brown's child. The sheriff agrees to let Brown go on condition that he marries Jenny and leaves the county. As the newlyweds head for the county line, the sheriff discovers Jenny's ruse, but he has a good laugh and lets them go on their way—better for the government to preserve the illusion of order than to admit its mistakes.

DeMille and Macpherson turned a relatively hackneyed basic plot into a subtle and fascinating exploration of human relationships. In the primitive environment of the West, Jenny is a sex object. Just as the outlaw offers the appearance of respectability, the "respectable" male citizens of the town who pay court would be just as content to pay for her favors at the dance hall. Although Jenny and "Black" Brown are genuinely in love, she symbolically traps him into marriage—and wedded bliss is presented as the only alternative to a necktie party.

For *A Romance of the Redwoods* DeMille took his company to Northern California redwood forests near Boulder Creek in Santa Cruz County. The rustic town sets used in the picture were actually leftovers built by the California Motion Picture Corporation of San Rafael for its productions of *Salomy Jane* (1914) and *The Lily of Poverty Flat* (1915).

# The Little American

An Artcraft Picture. Produced by the Mary Pickford Film Corporation. Director: Cecil B. DeMille. Original story and scenario by Jeanie Macpherson. Art director: Wilfred Buckland. Photography: Alvin Wyckoff. Assistant directors: Charles Whittaker, Walter N. Sherer, and Cullen B. "Hezie" Tate

Picture started: April 13, 1917. Picture completed: May 22, 1917. Length: 5,926 feet (six reels). Cost: $166,949.16 (includes Mary Pickford's salary of $86,666.66 charged to the picture). Released: July 1917. Gross: $446,236.88

Cast: Mary Pickford (Angela More), James Neill (Senator More), Ben Alexander (Bobby More), Guy Oliver (Frederick von Austreim), Edythe Chapman (his American wife), Jack Holt (Karl von Austreim, their son), Raymond Hatton (Count Jules de Destin), Hobart Bosworth (German colonel), Lillian Leighton (Angela's great aunt), Lila Lee (French maid), Horace B. Carpenter, Ramon Samaniegos [Novarro], and George Field (wounded French soldiers), Walter Long (a German captain), De Witt Jennings, and Robert Gordon

In a nation of immigrants, popular sentiment was divided as World War I raged on the European continent. Americans were outraged by reported German atrocities in Belgium and by the sinking of the *Lusitania*—but the issues were not clear-cut. Reports of atrocities were often exaggerated, and suspicion lingered (later confirmed) that the passenger ship *Lusitania* was also carrying munitions bound for Britain. A substantial segment of the population was hostile toward Britain, but most Americans looked on the war as a family squabble between blood-related monarchs and felt the world would be better off if monarchy were abolished as an institution among men.

As a neutral nation, the United States reserved its right to trade in nonmilitary goods with all the belligerents. The Germans, however, felt it was in their military interest to stem the flow of all supplies to Britain. Earlier in the war, the United States protested Great Britain's interference with American shipping in the British blockade of Germany; but when Germany launched a campaign of unrestricted submarine warfare against any and all ships bound for Britain, President Woodrow Wilson felt compelled to ask Congress for a declaration of war against Germany on April 2, 1917. When Congress passed the formal declaration on April 6, 1917, *The Little American* was ready to go before the cameras.

Rushed into release within six weeks of its completion, *The Little American* was one of the first films to deal seriously with American involvement in the conflict. Jeanie Macpherson's story is a strange blend of flag-waving, sadism, and divine intervention. Although clearly part of the "hate the Hun" cycle that became common for war films, *The Little American* retains a pre-war sense of American neutrality that later films ignore, and it presents a fair (if exaggerated) sense of the American psyche on the eve of the nation's entry into the "War to End All Wars."

Angela More is an American girl who is courted by Jules de Destin, a Frenchman, and Karl von Austreim, a German American. Both men are friends, but Angela's romantic interest centers on the German. On the eve of the European war, her great aunt, who lives in France, summons Angela for a visit. War breaks out, and Angela's French and German suitors return to Europe to enlist. Angela receives her aunt's letter and sails for France on the *Veritania*. En route, the ship is torpedoed and sinks. Angela is rescued and makes it to France, but on arriving at her aunt's chateau she finds that her relative has passed away and the German army is advancing on the village.

Angela attempts to leave, but the retreating French army asks to turn the chateau into a hospital, and she remains to care for the wounded. She also agrees to the French setting up a reconnaissance post at the house. Later, the Germans commandeer the chateau as a field headquarters, announcing their intention by firing a volley of rounds into the house.

On her first encounter with the German army, Angela resolutely, if naively, stands her ground, holding a small American flag and proclaiming her neutrality in subtitles like

> "Gentlemen, you are breaking
> into the home of an American
> citizen. I must ask you to leave."

During the occupation of the chateau, the Germans chase Angela into a darkened room. She is nearly raped by von Austreim, who, thinking she went down with the *Veritania,* does not recognize her in the dark. When the lights go on he realizes his mistake and is overcome with shame and regret.

Later, von Austreim refuses to stand up to his superiors in defense of

Angela, and she uses a telephone planted by the French to call in artillery fire on the German positions. Von Austreim discovers Angela's spying. When she is scheduled for execution, he finally comes to her aid and is also sentenced to death. As they stand before the firing squad, French artillery shells kill their executioners, and the lovers escape. During the battle that rages through the night, Angela and von Austreim take refuge in the ruins of a church. Even though bombs fall around them, the crucifix above the destroyed altar seems to guard their ragged sleep. In the morning they are found by the French. Von Austreim is sent to a detention camp, but in return for Angela's help the French arrange to release him to her custody.

The fascinating thing about *The Little American* is that the hero of the film is von Austreim, the German. The film clearly states early on that Austreim's father is German and his mother American. Although he is a German citizen, he returns to his country only on orders, rather than from any patriotic zeal. His attempted rape of Angela is blamed on hard drink and peer pressure from his fellow officers as well as his grief over Angela's presumed death at sea. But Austreim only belatedly comes to Angela's defense, raising no protest when French locals are executed and housemaids are gang-raped by order and acquiescence of the German high command. How is it that Angela finds anything attractive in this weak sister, and how can she forgive his actions? The final scene of *The Little American* shows America's Sweetheart kissing her German lover through the barbed wire fence of a POW camp. The image is an unsettling one, even for a present-day audience nearly a century removed from the political passions of the time.

Both Kevin Brownlow and William K. Everson have written that after negative audience reaction an alternate ending was prepared for *The Little American* in which Pickford returns home to marry the French count. If this is correct, the altered version must have been prepared for foreign release or at the behest of local censor boards. The trade press of the time offers no evidence that critics or audiences found anything particularly distasteful about the ending, strange as that may seem. Only the original ending is known to survive. *The Little American* performed handsomely at the box office and justified Mary Pickford's enormous salary.

*The Little American* was a transitional film for DeMille, notable for its combining spectacle with personal drama, and for its move toward a brighter and less stylized lighting design. In the July 21, 1917, issue of

*The Moving Picture World* DeMille and art director Wilfred Buckland contributed a pair of articles on the future of motion picture design.

"Much is being done," wrote DeMille,

> in following out the Rinehart idea of suggestive settings. The audience is made to feel the background rather than see it . . . but, of course, the idea cannot be used promiscuously.
>
> Another thing—we are beginning to place and regulate the action and movements of the incidents with consideration of their picture value. To be more explicit, we are beginning to pose our people in the settings as a painter would pose them in his painting, with consideration for the perfect balance of the scene, with more thought given to the lighting.[1]

Buckland carried the thought further in his article. "The present obvious method of photographing nature is lacking in the higher class of artistic expression and is not the ultimate end of motion picture possibilities," he wrote.

> Motion pictures are, or should be, pictorial art, so we cannot disregard the judgment of painters, the makers of real pictures. . . . The method which we are gradually introducing substitutes imaginative for realistic scenery, and depends for its effects on art lighting, which probably was the method Rinehardt so successfully applied to stage productions.
>
> In this method natural scenery does not help except as it is combined with painted drops. One does not need plains and mountains or the sun from which nothing escapes, for in any suggestive art more depends on what is left out than what is put in.[2]

Interestingly, DeMille and Buckland give a nod to German theatrical director Max Reinhardt at a time when the rest of America was hating the "Hun."[3] The striking thing about these articles, aside from the fact that neither DeMille nor Buckland seemed to know how to spell Reinhardt's name, is that both men appear poised for a change in their approach to screen art direction. Their knowledge of Reinhardt's work is secondhand, and they are responding to their understanding of his ideas rather than to his work, but these articles represent a manifesto for the controlled, studio-bound style that would become increasingly popular in Hollywood films during the 1920s. It has been broadly assumed that Hollywood was influenced by German Expressionist films, but these early articles by DeMille and Buckland suggest that the interest in German ideas about theatrical design predated the Expressionist films of the postwar era.

While *The Little American* was in production, DeMille received a wire from Jesse Lasky regarding the length of future Artcraft Pictures:

> . . . ARTCRAFT PICTURES IN THE FUTURE MUST NOT EXCEED FIFTY-FIVE HUNDRED FEET [in length]. THIS APPLIES TO [future] FARRAR AND PICKFORD [pictures] DO YOUR UTMOST TO HOLD PRESENT PICKFORD PICTURE TO AT LEAST SIX THOUSAND FEET. ARE GIVING YOU FIVE HUNDRED FEET LEEWAY ON ACCOUNT OF THIS INFORMATION REACHING YOU SO LATE.

By July 1917 Zukor and Lasky were even willing to let their names be associated with Artcraft. With Pickford, Fairbanks, Griffith, Ince, Hart, and DeMille under the Artcraft banner, they no longer felt the need to maintain any subterfuge. The deluxe Artcraft line was rapidly turned into just a slightly longer and higher-priced version of the Paramount program. DeMille took advantage of the extra footage allowed on his second Pickford picture, and the final cut of *The Little American* came to slightly over 5,900 feet.

# The Woman God Forgot

An Artcraft Picture. Director: Cecil B. DeMille. Original story and scenario by Jeanie Macpherson. Art director: Wilfred Buckland. Photography: Alvin Wyckoff. Assistant directors: Charles Whittaker and Cullen B. "Hezie" Tate

Picture started: July 2, 1917. Picture finished: August 10, 1917. Length: 5,292 feet (six reels). Cost: $115,420.32. Released: November 8, 1917. Gross: $340,504.98

Cast: Geraldine Farrar (Tezca), Wallace Reid (Alvarado), Theodore Kosloff (Guatemoc), Raymond Hatton (Montezuma), Hobart Bosworth (Hernando Cortes), Walter Long (Taloc), Charles B. Rogers (Cacamo), Olga Grey (Marina), and Julia Faye (lady in waiting)

The relative failure of *Joan the Woman* put Cecil B. DeMille in an awkward position. His agreement with Jesse Lasky allowed him to make lengthy "special productions" for road-show release, but it was clear that the market for twelve-reel epics was virtually nonexistent in 1917. As plans were being firmed for Geraldine Farrar's annual summer trek to the West Coast, DeMille received a less-than-subtle hint from the New York office. On March 10, 1917, Jesse Lasky wrote:

IN CONFERENCES ATTENDED BY [Hiram] ABRAHAMS [*sic*] AND [W.E.] GREEN IT WAS STRONGLY URGED THAT YOU PRODUCE TWO PICTURES WITH FARRAR SIX THOUSAND FEET EACH COSTING ABOUT SEV-ENTY-FIVE THOUSAND DOLLARS EACH INCLUDING HER SALARY INSTEAD OF ONE LONG EXPENSIVE PICTURE AS PLANNED ARGUMENT IS THAT WE COULD RELEASE THE PICTURES THROUGH ARTCRAFT AND GIVE THAT PROGRAM PRESTIGE AS WELL AS MAKE ASSURED PROFITS EQUIVALENT TO PROFITS THAT COULD BE MADE ON ONE BIG PIC-TURE GIVE THIS IMMEDIATE SERIOUS CONSIDER-ATION AND ADVISE YOUR OPINION DO YOU FEEL

Cecil B. DeMille in his office at the Burns and Revier Studio in 1914. (Unless otherwise noted, all photographs are from the author's collection.)

December 31, 1913, the first day of shooting on *The Squaw Man*. Cecil B. DeMille, Dustin Farnum, and Oscar C. Apfel are at right holding the loving cup. Cameraman Alfred Gandolfi (with mustache and dark suit) sits to DeMille's left and behind. Joseph Singleton (in headdress), Baby Carmen DeRue, and Red Wing are in front to the left. Standing prominently in the center, left to right, are Dick La Reno, Billy Elmer (in patterned shirt and white bandanna), and Fred Montague. (Hollywood Heritage Museum)

[Above] *The Squaw Man* troupe on location in early 1914. Cecil B. DeMille sits on the fender. Leading man Dustin Farnum stands in the center of the truck bed. Red Wing stands in front of him. To Farnum's right are Dick La Reno and Joseph Singleton. To his left and behind is Noble Johnson, a black man who had a long career as an actor and bit player and who often played Indians, Mexicans, and other ethnics. (Marc Wanamaker/Bison Archives) [Below] James Wynnegate tells Nat-U-Rich to keep quiet as he intends to shoulder the blame for her killing of Cash Hawkins. Dustin Farnum, Red Wing, and Billy Elmer in the saloon set built beside the train tracks in the San Fernando Valley north of Hollywood.

Jesse L. Lasky surveys his Hollywood studio in 1914.

Cecil B. DeMille, seated on breadbox at right, directs a scene from *The Virginian* with Dustin Farnum, face partially obscured, at left. Note the white tape on the stage floor marking the camera's viewing range.

[Left] Cecil B. DeMille (left) and Oscar C. Apfel during their days as co-directors for the Jesse L. Lasky Feature Play Company. Apfel's career as a director faltered in the 1920s, and he became a character actor and bit player. He appeared in several of DeMille's later films. (Marc Wanamaker/Bison Archives)

[Below] Alvin Wyckoff, who would be Cecil B. DeMille's principal cinematographer from *The Virginian* (1914) through *Adam's Rib* (1923). A former Chicago area actor, Wyckoff came to California as a cameraman for the Chicago-based Selig Polyscope Company in 1909.

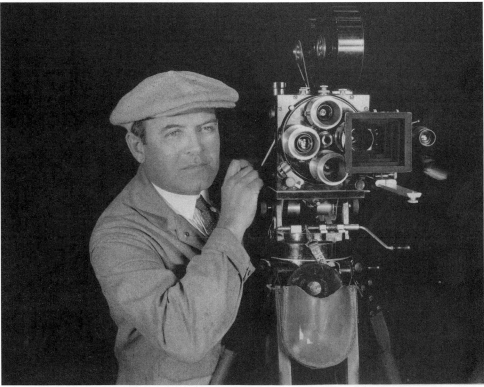

[*Above*] Cecil B. DeMille (at left), Robert Edeson (third from left), Theodore Roberts (fourth from left), and the Lasky troupe on location in Big Bear, California, for *The Call of the North*. [*Below*] (Standing, left to right) director Oscar C. Apfel, actors Max Figman and Charles Richman, art director Wilfred Buckland, actors Theodore Roberts, Robert Edeson (in costume for *Where the Trail Divides,* released October 12, 1914), Edward Abeles, and Cecil B. DeMille. (Seated, left to right) actress Lolita Robertson (wife of Max Figman), studio head Jesse L. Lasky, and actress Bessie Barriscale on a set for *The Making of Bobby Burnit* (released September 17, 1914).

[*Above*] Nellie calls Fairfax's attention to her wedding ring. Lolita Robertson points to her third finger, left hand, as Fred Montague registers shock in *What's-His-Name*. The necessary story information in the close-up detail was lost in the overall action. [*Below*] The original Broadway production of *The Rose of the Rancho* opened November 27, 1906, at the Belasco Theatre and ran 480 performances. Frances Starr (seated center) played Juanita. Ernest M. Gros and Wilfred Buckland were the scenic designers.

[*Above*] Monroe Salisbury and Bessie Barriscale (foreground) in *The Rose of the Rancho*. Wilfred Buckland's impressive hacienda patio set for DeMille's film was a near dupli-cate of the set he designed for David Belasco's original stage production. [*Below*] Bit players gather on the side of a hill to watch the climactic storming of the hacienda. Alvin Wyckoff mans the Pathé camera in the background.

[*Above*] Wilfred Buckland built the hacienda rooftop against the side of a hill to create the illusion that the whole house had been built. Note the head of the bit player in the right foreground. [*Below*] House Peters and Mabel Van Buren in *The Girl of the Golden West*. Alvin Wyckoff's foreground lighting is rather flat. However, the background falls into shadow, and the rim lighting around Mabel Van Buren's hands gives a real suggestion that they are backlit by the fire in the fireplace.

[*Above*] Cecil B. DeMille and his brother, William C. deMille, at the Lasky studio about 1916. [*Below*] (Left to right) House Peters, Page Peters, James Neill, Mabel Van Buren, and Blanche Sweet in a tense moment from *The Warrens of Virginia*. Theatrical "spot-lighting" separates the main action from the background action.

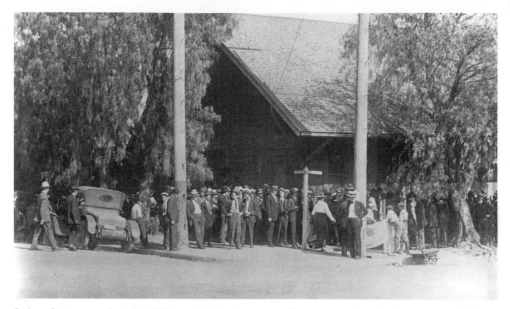

[*Above*] Any work today? Hopeful bit players and extras gather at the corner of Selma Avenue and Vine Street outside the Lasky studio in 1915. Before the motion picture industry created Central Casting, this sort of scene was common at the front gates of every Hollywood studio. [*Below*] The Lasky studio circa 1915. From the roof of the barn on Vine Street looking east. Note the square, concrete film vault on the left and the new glass-covered stage at the far end of the lot. On the long open-air stage the sets are covered with tarps to protect them from the elements. The long, low buildings on the right are dressing rooms and offices. (Marc Wanamaker/Bison Archives)

Jeanie Macpherson, who first worked with Cecil as a bit player in *The Rose of the Rancho*, began her career as DeMille's favorite screenwriter on *The Captive*. She and DeMille were also lovers—a situation tolerated by Constance deMille, who was advised by her doctors against having more children after the birth of Cecilia deMille.

Cecil B. DeMille offers Ina Claire instructions on where to focus her sight line for a close-up during production of *The Wild Goose Chase*. Alvin Wyckoff sets the Pathé camera, as Mr. Horowitz (first name not known) looks on holding script. (Courtesy Academy of Motion Picture Arts and Sciences)

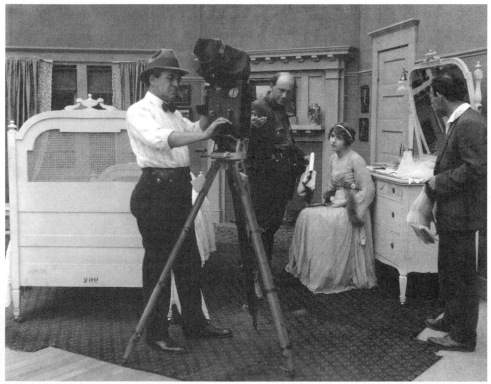

[*Above*] April 20, 1915. Sharing a laugh on the harem set during production of *The Arab*. (Left to right) Cecil B. DeMille, Ruth Wilcox (Mrs. Edgar Selwyn), and Edgar Selwyn. Based on Edgar Selwyn's play, *The Arab* weaves a complex love story between a missionary's daughter (played by Gertrude Robinson), the Turkish governor of Syria (played by Theodore Roberts), and the Bedouin Jamil (played by Selwyn). (Courtesy Academy of Motion Picture Arts and Sciences) [*Below*] Shooting a scene for *The Arab* on the Lasky lot. Edgar Selwyn, Ruth Wilcox, and Gertrude Robinson are seated in costume at left. Alvin Wyckoff stands between the two cameras on the platform. DeMille is on the platform at right. The second camera was for protection and for creating a negative for foreign release. (Courtesy Academy of Motion Picture Arts and Sciences)

Heine Schultz (Thomas Meighan) tells his wife (Charlotte Walker), "I'd rather kill a child of ours the day it is born than send it up against a life like that." DeMille pictured tenement life as grim and unrelenting in his screen adaptation of Charles Kenyon's *Kindling*.

In an obviously staged publicity shot, Geraldine Farrar finishes dressing on the front lawn of her rented Hollywood home with rose in mouth à la Carmen.

[*Above*] Ramon (Pedro de Cordoba, left) and Andreas (Wallace Reid) vie for the hand of Maria Rosa (Geraldine Farrar). Wilfred Buckland's "little Spanish town" seems to have been built to three-quarter scale. [*Below*] Ever the diva, Geraldine Farrar plays to the still camera as Cecil B. DeMille shows Wallace Reid how to kill Carmen. (Marc Wanamaker/Bison Archives)

Jesse L. Lasky
(by arrangement with Morris Gest)
presents
Geraldine Farrar in
"Carmen"

Carmen and Frasquita fight.

[*Above*] "A fight between two dames." Geraldine Farrar and Jeanie Macpherson go at it in the cigarette factory. This element of Prosper Merimée's original story had been eliminated from the operatic adaptation, but became a part of most productions after Farrar added it as a gag during a later stage performance. [*Below*] Shall we dance? Bowery tough Chimmie Fadden (Victor Moore) holds his own against a couple of hard hombres out west. Behind the hotel registration desk are future director Tom Forman (with mustache and grey hat) and Henry Bergman (in white shirt and tie), who would become closely associated with comic Charlie Chaplin. Billy Elmer stands behind Bergman (with mustache and black hat).

Hector Turnbull, soon to be Jesse Lasky's brother-in-law, wrote *The Cheat*. The lurid, racially charged melodrama was a great critical and commercial success, but the black-hearted Tori was not the sort of villain that appealed to DeMille. (Marc Wanamaker/Bison Archives)

Edith Hardy (Fannie Ward) attempts to cover her theft of charity funds by borrowing from Tori (Sessue Hayakawa). His price? She must come voluntarily to his bed. When Tori enforces the bargain by branding Edith with his mark of ownership, she shoots him, and the scandal she sought to avoid blows wide open.

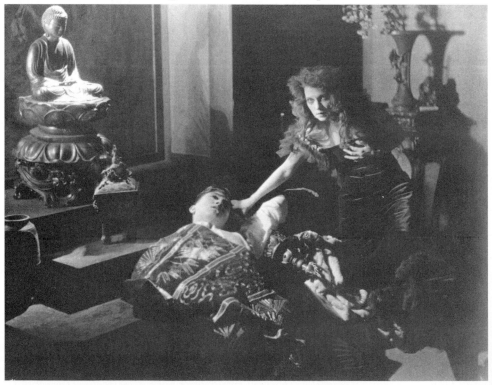

YOU CAN FIND TWO SUITABLE SUBJECTS FOR TWO SIX-REEL FARRAR PICTURES.[1]

DeMille was wary—afraid that his status with Famous Players-Lasky was being eroded. "Before answering your suggestion of doing two Farrar pictures instead of one, there is strong rumor here that [D.W.] Griffith has joined us," DeMille replied. "While I assume this would have no bearing on my doing single big picture, I should like word from you that his joining us is not a factor in the matter."[2]

Lasky was able to give his old friend and associate some assurance:

GRIFFITH IS ABOUT TO SIGN WITH ARTCRAFT FOR ONE YEAR TO DO SIX PICTURES OF SIX REELS EACH WITHOUT STARS[.] SINCE INTOLERANCE HE IS CONVINCED THERE IS NO MONEY IN BIG PICTURES AND WILL NOT DO A BIG PICTURE FOR AT LEAST ANOTHER YEAR HOWEVER, GRIFFITH HAS ABSO-LUTELY NO BEARING ON YOUR DOING A BIG PIC-TURE. . . .

WE WOULD PROBABLY NOT BE ABLE TO PROFIT-ABLY DISPOSE OF ANOTHER LONG PICTURE WITH FARRAR AS THE STAR[.] ON THE OTHER HAND TWO SIX-REEL PICTURES WOULD CAUSE A SENSATION BOOKED THROUGH ARTCRAFT AND WE WOULD BE ASSURED OF HANDSOME PROFITS WITH MUCH SMALLER INVESTMENT THIS IS OUR ONLY MOTIVE IN SUGGESTING CHANGE IN PLANS YOU SHOULD KNOW THAT I PERSONALLY WOULD NOT STAND FOR AN ALLIANCE WITH GRIFFITH INTERFERING WITH ANY OF YOUR PLANS[.][3]

*The Woman God Forgot* deals with the Spanish conquest of Mexico and seems to have been planned as a "big" picture. One indication that DeMille was forced to limit the scope of *The Woman God Forgot* is that the $115,000 negative cost was far in excess of Lasky's $75,000 recommendation. Costumes and settings must have been in preparation before the cost-cutting measures were suggested. Despite the appearance of grandeur, however, the tighter budget is evident in the settings. For example, the exterior of the great Aztec pyramid was built against the side of a hill and shot from a carefully selected angle, eliminating the need to build a freestanding set.

The picture bears much in common with *Joan the Woman*. Again Wallace Reid plays a soldier from an invading army who falls in love with a daughter of the enemy. Tezca, daughter of Montezuma, defies the gods of the Aztecs by refusing to permit the sacrifice of her handmaiden, Marina. Taloc threatens that the gods will forget her. Later, when Alvarado comes to Montezuma as a representative of Cortes, he is wounded by the Aztecs. Tezca hides the wounded Alvarado from his Aztec assailants, and Alvarado tells her that he comes to conquer Mexico in the name of the Cross. As she embraces Alvarado, Tezca is discovered by Guatemoc. He tells Montezuma, who threatens to kill his daughter for harboring the stranger. Guatemoc offers to marry the tainted Tezca on condition that Alvarado be offered for sacrifice on the wedding day, and Montezuma agrees. Tezca sends one of her servants to Cortes's camp with Alvarado's crucifix, and the Spanish army marches against the Aztecs. In saving her love, Tezca seals the doom of her people.

*The Woman God Forgot* seems a radical departure for DeMille, who, although never championing organized religion in his work, is noted for religious themes. Both civilizations in the film distort religious values to their own ends: the Aztecs use the appeasement of their gods as pretext for human sacrifice; the Christians conquer in the name of the Cross. For DeMille, the institutions of men are corrupt. He may revel in the glory of pageantry and ceremony, but he always sees through the hypocrisy of invoking the name of God to conquer or subjugate an enemy. His imagery in *The Woman God Forgot* is especially savage; for example, Cortes and his army raise a Christian banner as they climb a pyramid littered with Aztec dead. D.W. Griffith used similar scenes in the French story of *Intolerance*, but he tempered the scene of the St. Bartholomew's Day Massacre by showing a sympathetic priest hide a Huguenot child from French troops. Griffith condemned hypocrisy, but he did not condemn the institution of the Church. For DeMille, however, God could be known only on the most personal level. In later years he would go out of his way to avoid outwardly offending organized religion, but the fact remains that one almost never finds a sympathetic clergyman of any belief as a major character in DeMille's work.

At the end of *The Woman God Forgot*, Tezca lives in exile—the last of the Aztecs. Alvarado finds her in a beautiful, untouched valley.[4] She tells him, "Leave me—for in my heart is only hate!" But he responds,

"There is one thing stronger than hate and that is—*love!*" Tezca softens, and lip-readers can see her say, "Yes, yes."

The intent may have been to return to DeMille's favorite recurring theme—the character who loses everything when he turns away from his place in life; still, it is difficult to justify the destruction of a civilization as the basis for consummating a love affair—even in a work of romantic fiction. Ultimately, *The Woman God Forgot* is a disturbing film, though audiences of the time responded well, apparently ignoring the wider issues.

*The Woman God Forgot* is notable for several elements that would become more or less common in later DeMille pictures. It contains DeMille's first bath scene (Tezca's maids are seen bathing as they attend the Aztec princess), and the costumes Geraldine Farrar wears in the picture are more revealing than in any previous DeMille film. In 1915 and 1916, nudity seemed to be everywhere on the screen. Artist's model Audrey Munson, who was known as "the girl with the perfect figure," posed for statuary at the Panama-Pacific Exposition in 1915 and went on to star in two films, *Inspiration* (Thanhouser, 1915) and *Purity* (American, 1916), which revealed all of her charms. Griffith included scenes of nude handmaidens in *Intolerance. The House of a Thousand Scandals* (American, 1915) featured naked "living statues," serial star Grace Cunard even posed nude in an episode of *The Purple Mask* (Universal, 1916), and there were dozens of other examples. Although such scenes were usually done in "good taste," the various state and local censors were not often impressed with the artistic aspirations of the filmmakers. A star of Farrar's magnitude and reputation certainly would not have bared all for the camera in 1917, but DeMille was learning how to tweak the nose of the censors without openly challenging them.

28

# The Devil Stone

An Artcraft Picture. Director: Cecil B. DeMille. Scenario by Jeanie Macpherson, from a story by Beatrice A. deMille and Leighton Osmun. Art director: Wilfred Buckland. Photography: Alvin Wyckoff

Picture started: August 18, 1917. Picture finished: September 14, 1917. Length: 5,720 feet (six reels). Cost: $67,413.36. Released: December 31, 1917. Gross: $296,031.58

Cast: Geraldine Farrar (Marcia Manot), Wallace Reid (Guy Sterling), Tully Marshall (Silas Martin), Hobart Bosworth (Robert Judson), Lillian Leighton (Berthe), Horace B. Carpenter (fisherman), Burwell Mamrick (Pierre), Mary Wilkinson (grandmother), William Carroll, Mabel Van Buren, Ernest Joy, James Neill, and Gustav von Seyffertitz

*The Devil Stone*, based on a story by DeMille's mother and Leighton Osmun, was the last picture the director made with Geraldine Farrar. It is a story of mysticism and fate surrounding an emerald that once belonged to a Viking queen and bears a curse for subsequent owners. The Viking angle provided ample excuse for an historical flashback, but some of the elements of the picture—especially the characterization of Tully Marshall as a greedy and seedy old man who marries Farrar only to gain possession of the Devil Stone—seem to anticipate the work of Erich von Stroheim.[1]

As if to make up for the high budget of *The Woman God Forgot*, *The Devil Stone* was completed for less than $68,000. It did not do as well at the box office as the previous Farrar picture, but the difference in gross rentals was virtually equal to the difference in production cost for the two films, and since costs for prints and advertising were probably identical, *The Devil Stone* was almost certainly a more profitable picture for Paramount than *The Woman God Forgot*.

Geraldine Farrar was a great asset for the Famous Players-Lasky Corporation, but the strained relations between the company and Lou-Tellegen caused Farrar to sever her connection with Lasky and DeMille. "[T]he picture [Tellegen] directed was not satisfactory to the officials [of

Famous Players-Lasky]—which is no crime or reflection on either party," wrote Farrar. "However, Tellegen chose to get very upset about the whole matter. Naturally, my interest and support were his, and, whether right or wrong, I did not renew a further engagement with Lasky on his account, though my personal relations were . . . without rancor. In this instance, wifely loyalty prevailed over professional discretion."[2]

At Goldwyn Pictures, Sam Goldfish tried to duplicate Farrar's success by signing opera star Mary Garden to appear in an adaptation of the opera *Thaïs*. Garden made virtually no impression on film audiences, however, and when Farrar failed to renew her contract with Famous Players-Lasky, Goldfish moved quickly to sign her. To help grease the deal, Goldfish also signed Lou-Tellegen to co-star with his wife. Farrar's name brought instant distinction to the Goldwyn program, but the producer and star were destined to clash over what she considered to be poor stories and Goldfish's lack of consideration. Her pictures slipped at the box office, and with them the fortunes of the Goldwyn company.

When Goldfish asked Farrar for concessions on her long-term contract, she obliged him by tearing it up and returning to the opera and concert stage. Goldfish was grateful—Farrar's gesture saved him a lot of money; but Hollywood lost one of its most exciting screen personalities.

Unfortunately, only two of the original six reels of *The Devil Stone* are known to survive in the American Film Institute Collection in the Library of Congress.

# 29

# The Whispering Chorus

An Artcraft Picture. Director: Cecil B. DeMille. Scenario by Jeanie Macpherson, from a story by Perley Poore Sheehan. Art director: Wilfred Buckland. Photography: Alvin Wyckoff

Picture started: December 10, 1917. Picture finished: January 31, 1918. Length: 6,555 feet (seven reels). Cost: $72,499.55. Released: March 28, 1918. Gross. $242,109.27

Cast: Raymond Hatton (John Tremble), Kathlyn Williams (Jane, his wife), Edythe Chapman (his mother), Elliott Dexter (George Coggeswell), Noah Beery (Tremble's friend), Guy Oliver (Chief McFarland), Tully Marshall (F.P. Clumley), Gustav von Seyffertitz (mocking face), Walter Lynch (evil face), Edna Mae Cooper (good face), Julia Faye (girl in Shanghai dive), and James Neill (Channing)

A legend persists that Cecil B. DeMille was an artist betrayed by his audience; thus, the failure of *The Whispering Chorus* is said to have led him to cynically put commercialism above artistic integrity in making his pictures. It makes a good story—it is also untrue.

Criticized in some quarters as being overly morbid, *The Whispering Chorus* did not perform as well as DeMille's four previous star vehicles with Geraldine Farrar and Mary Pickford, but it was far from a commercial disaster. Besides, *The Whispering Chorus* hardly represents an artistic dead end for DeMille. In fact the film develops elements that would become familiar in his work in the early 1920s.

DeMille had planned to make a film version of Richard Walton Tully's stage success *Bird of Paradise*, but Lasky was unable to secure rights to the property. Instead, DeMille was offered *The Whispering Chorus* by Perley Poore Sheehan, which Famous Players-Lasky acquired in advance of its January 1918 serialization in *All-Story Weekly*. Sheehan's narrative tells of John Tremble, a desperate accountant pushed to the wall by debt, who embezzles his employer's funds and stages his own death by trading clothes with the corpse of a tramp he finds in the woods. Later, in his new identity, he is arrested and tried for his own murder. The whispering chorus of the title refers to the voices of his conscience, portrayed by DeMille as ghostly images of superimposed faces, as Tremble engages in a moral tug-of-war over his decisions.

The use of parallel action and montage as cinematic devices in *The Whispering Chorus* represents a distinct departure from DeMille's earlier editorial technique. During the wedding of the supposed widow of John Tremble, DeMille intercuts the sacred rite with the assignation of the still-very-much-alive Tremble and a Shanghai whore. Later, when Tremble is executed, the death house sequence is assembled from sharply etched details. Tremble's hand is strapped to the chair. He fingers the petals of a rose. The electric switch is thrown. The petals fall to the floor.

*The Whispering Chorus* was an elaborate production. Wilfred Buckland redressed a section of Selma Avenue outside the Famous Players-Lasky studio to double for a night street scene in Shanghai, China. DeMille remembered that during a daylight dress rehearsal one of the Chinese extras touched off the fireworks strung around the street for the night shoot. As the director's temper erupted, the extra ran for the hills.[1]

For the wedding of Jane Tremble and George Coggeswell, DeMille took his company to a local Los Angeles church. Elliott Dexter recalled:

> The wedding [scene] took place in Christ Episcopal Church . . . and the Rev. Baker P. Lee the rector of that church, directed. Mr. DeMille sent invitations to the affair and the church was crowded. A list of those present was published in the society column of the Los Angeles papers. There were famous players from all the studios and a number of distinguished people from Los Angeles and Pasadena. Charlie Eyton [the husband of Kathlyn Williams in real life] was the best man [in the scene], and I had to use his wife's real wedding ring for the scene. [Charles Eyton] kicked a little at this but finally gave in. We even had the little choir boys—nothing was missing to make it look like a real wedding.[2]

The belief held by many critics that DeMille was unable to deal effectively with actors is based on a misunderstanding of his conscious decision to play many of his pictures in a "grand manner." One need only compare the overwrought, arm-flailing style of Kathlyn Williams in *The Girl at the Cupola* (Selig, 1912) or *The Spoilers* (Selig, 1914) to appreciate the restraint and subtlety of performance that DeMille managed to achieve with her in *The Whispering Chorus*.

One measure of DeMille's commercial success as a filmmaker was a commensurate decrease in the amount of money Famous Players-Lasky spent to promote his productions. The director was not pleased by this dubious honor. "Regarding *Whispering Chorus* advertising," he wired Jesse Lasky. "I have not seen in print one piece of the special stuff sent on from here. I have seen however two pages of *Bluebird* advertising to one page of *Whispering Chorus* stuff. I cannot do it all from this end and I should like to be assured that [my next picture] *Old Wives for New* will receive better and more publicity than my previous pictures."[3]

# Old Wives for New

An Artcraft Picture. Director: Cecil B. DeMille. Scenario by Jeanie Macpherson, based on the book by David Graham Phillips. Art director: Wilfred Buckland. Photography: Alvin Wyckoff

Picture started: March 2, 1918. Picture completed: April 9, 1918. Length: 6,251 feet (seven reels). Cost: $66,241.31. Released: May 19, 1918. Gross: $286,504.11

Cast: Elliott Dexter (Charles Murdock), Sylvia Ashton (Sophy, his wife), Wanda Hawley (Sophy in flashback), Florence Vidor (Juliet Raeburn), Theodore Roberts (Berkeley), Helen Jerome Eddy (Norma Murdock), Marcia Manon (Viola), Julia Faye (Jessie), J. Parke Jones (Charlie Murdock Jr.), Edna Mae Cooper (Bertha), Gustav Seyffertitz (Blagden), Tully Marshall (Simcox, Murdock's butler), Lillian Leighton (maid), Mayme Kelso (housekeeper), Guy Oliver (Berkeley's butler), Edythe Chapman (Mrs. Berkeley), Raymond Hatton, Charles Ogle, Alice Terry, and Madame Sul-Te-Wan

"C ostume stuff" was out in 1918, and the Famous Players-Lasky company insisted that the public pulse was quickened by "modern stuff with plenty of clothes, rich sets, and action."[1] As DeMille was in production on *The Whispering Chorus*, Jesse Lasky advised the director: "We are holding *Old Wives For New* which we paid $6,500 for until we get some word from you as to whether or not you think you can make a picture out of it. Personally, I would like to see you become commercial to the extent of agreeing to produce this novel. It will do twice as much business as *The Woman God Forgot* or *The Devil Stone*." Later Lasky further urged DeMille to "get away from the spectacle stuff for one or two pictures and try to do modern stories of great human interest."[2] DeMille, deeming it unwise to ignore Lasky's advice, submitted to the studio's suggestion.

The plot of *Old Wives for New* is convoluted and propelled by coincidence. Charles Murdock is a middle-aged business man. His wife, Sophy, is an overweight hypochondriac who sits in bed all day and refuses to clean up after herself. In a flashback we see the beautiful young girl Sophy was when she first met Charles. Now he feels unloved and tells

Sophy he wants out of the marriage. To get away from the house, Charles takes a month-long hunting trip in the company of Blagden, his male secretary. In the woods Charles meets Juliet Raeburn, a dress designer who is also on a hunting vacation. As Charles and Juliet come to know each other they fall in love, but Charles is an honorable man: he tells her that he is married. Juliet is an honorable woman: she refuses to have anything to do with him. Back in the city, Blagden informs Sophy Murdock about her husband's interest in Juliet.

Murdock takes his daughter clothes shopping and runs into his friend Berkeley, a wealthy middle-aged roué who is shopping for Jessie, his latest conquest. By chance this is the store where Juliet Raeburn works. Charles and Juliet meet. He tries to explain; she refuses to listen.

Berkeley persuades Charles to go nightclubbing with him and Jessie and her friend, Viola. As luck would have it, Viola used to work with Juliet. At the club, Berkeley flirts with another girl, and when Jessie makes a public scene, Berkeley sends her packing. He goes to the girl's apartment. Jessie intrudes, roughs up the new girlfriend, and shoots Berkeley. Mortally wounded, Berkeley calls Murdock and asks him to cover up the circumstances of his death so there won't be any scandal. Murdock manages to make the world believe that Berkeley died of a heart attack.

In yet another coincidence, Sophy Murdock goes shopping for widow's weeds with Berkeley's widow at Juliet Raeburn's store. Mrs. Berkeley tells Sophy the truth about her husband's death—that he was shot in a woman's apartment, and when Sophy learns that her husband and Berkeley were both in the store on the morning of the murder she jumps to the conclusion that the murder took place in Juliet's apartment. She sues Charles for divorce and names Juliet as co-respondent.

To save Juliet from scandal Charles makes a public show of going to Europe with Viola, and the newspapers back off Juliet. Sometime later, Juliet and Charles meet in Venice, Italy. After explanations, they wed. Sophy marries Blagden, and the two Murdock children both find romance.

Little wonder Cecil B. DeMille hesitated before agreeing to make *Old Wives for New*. Despite his reluctance, he decided to expend his best efforts in bringing the story to the screen. The film has an uncompromising realism despite the melodramatic turns in the story. In scene after scene *Old Wives for New* must have been startling for 1918 audiences. Sophy Murdock pops chocolate candy and reads the Bible while ignoring her family. Old Berkeley leaves his own wife at home while he dallies with young gold diggers. Jessie and Viola take the most casual attitude to their unconventional lifestyles, and Blagden openly courts his boss's wife, hoping to live on her divorce settlement.

Juliet Raeburn is no sweet, innocent ingenue seduced by a lecherous villain; she is a successful, independent business woman. Charles Murdock is a middle-aged married man trapped in a decaying relationship. The anguish of these reluctant lovers is played in counterpoint to the casual philandering of Murdock's friend, Berkeley.

The scenes of Juliet as a camper and hunter, which may seem a convenient but rather strained way of introducing the lovers, are actually drawn, at least in part, from Jeanie Macpherson's own experiences as an outdoorswoman. Because Macpherson was a liberated woman, her female screen characters never wallow in cliché, though an audience used to more conventional characterizations sometimes find them difficult to comprehend.

Berkeley's murder is especially disturbing. Jessie shoots. Berkeley stands his ground, more in shock than pain. As he starts to move toward Jessie, the realization that he has been shot finally sinks in. As he goes to a nearby chair, his limbs become weak. He sits, and the stain grows as blood seeps through his white starched shirt. His life literally ebbs away. DeMille's restrained staging gives the scene a strong sense of realism.

What really made *Old Wives for New* startling, however, was the suggestion that divorce could be a solution to the "irreconcilable differences" that might infect a marriage. When Adolph Zukor saw the picture he was shocked and seriously considered withholding the film from distribution. The picture opened in May for special engagements, but general release was delayed. *Motion Picture News* finally reported that "*Old Wives for New*, produced for Artcraft by Cecil B. DeMille, has been set for release on June 16, instead of in May, as originally announced. Pre-release showings were booked by the Rivoli theatre, New York, and the Kinema theatre, Los Angeles, and it is reported the picture played to record-breaking business at both houses and was acclaimed by local newspaper critics as one of the most notable productions ever made."[3] Following his own maxim that "the public is never wrong," Zukor relented when the test engagements proved successful.

Despite Lasky's assurance to the contrary, *Old Wives for New* did not do twice as much business as *The Woman God Forgot* and *The Devil*

*Stone*; in fact, it did not do quite as well as either of them, but the film created a sensation and led directly to the social comedies with which DeMille would be identified into the early 1920s. With this film Cecil B. DeMille closed the door on the "age of innocence" and ushered in the Jazz Age.

# 31

# We Can't Have Everything

An Artcraft Picture. A Cecil B. DeMille Production. Director: Cecil B. DeMille. Scenario by William C. deMille, from a novel by Rupert Hughes. Photography: Alvin Wyckoff. Film editor: Anne Bauchens

Picture started: April 16, 1918. Picture finished: May 24, 1918. Length: 5,611 feet (six reels). Cost: $61,267.83. Released: July 15, 1918. Gross: $207,890.42

Cast: Kathlyn Williams (Charity Cheever), Thurston Hall (Peter Cheever), Elliott Dexter (James Dyckman), Sylvia Breamer (Zada l'Etoile), Wanda Hawley (Kedzie Thropp), Sylvia Ashton (her mother), Charles Ogle (her father), Tully Marshall (the director), Theodore Roberts (the "sultan"), Ernest Joy (the heavy), Billy Elmer (the prop man), James Neill (a detective), and Raymond Hatton (Marquis of Strathdene)

Of all the lost DeMille films, *We Can't Have Everything* is the most intriguing. The story was a rather mixed-up tale of star-crossed lovers who must endure a succession of mis-matings before finally coming together with action ranging from the back lots of Hollywood to the battlefields of the Great War. Much of the action took place in a movie studio and offered a rare behind-the-scenes look at the Famous Players-Lasky studio. DeMille even incorporated documentary footage of a fire that broke out at the studio during production.

Tully Marshall based his characterization of the movie director on two real-life directors he knew first hand. "It was a sort of composite," Marshall remembered. "Partly Mr. DeMille and partly D.W. Griffith. I didn't tell anyone what I intended doing and when the time came I could see Mr. DeMille smiling covertly. But I went on unconcernedly as if I had no thought in the world of caricaturing anyone."[1] Although Cecil B. DeMille portrayed himself in any number of later promotional films and cameo roles, it would be fun to see Marshall's impersonation to observe another, perhaps more objective portrait of the director at this early stage of his career. Ward Bond patterned his role of John Dodge after director John Ford in Ford's *Wings of Eagles* (M-G-M, 1957) to create a fascinating portrait—one can only imagine how Marshall captured the essence of DeMille. Alvin Wyckoff and other members of the DeMille unit also played bits in *We Can't Have Everything*. Oddly, the director did not think to keep a print for his film library. No prints of the film are known to survive in any archive or private collection.

## 32

# Till I Come Back to You

An Artcraft Picture. A Cecil B. DeMille Production. Director: Cecil B. DeMille. Scenario: Jeanie Macpherson. Art director: Wilfred Buckland. Photography: Alvin Wyckoff and Charles Rosher. Film editor: Anne Bauchens

Picture started: June 25, 1918. Picture finished: July 22, 1918. Length: 6,499 feet (seven reels). Cost: $52,646.56. Released: September 1, 1918. Gross: $183,834.23

Cast: Bryant Washburn (Capt. Jefferson Strong, U.S.A.), Florence Vidor (Yvonne von Krutz), G. Butler Clonbough [Gustav von Seyffertitz] (Karl von Krutz), Winter Hall (King Albert of Belgium), Clarence Geldart (U.S. colonel), George E. Stone (Jacques), Julia Faye (Susette), Lillian Leighton (Margot), Frank Butterworth (German boy), May Giraci (Rosa), C. Rohfeld (her father), W.J. Irving (Stroheim), Monte Blue (an American doughboy), Guy Oliver, Wallace Beery, Clarence Burton, and Tully Marshall

*Till I Come Back to You* is a blatant piece of wartime propaganda full of stiff-upper-lip heroics and totally improbable situations designed to buoy up spirits on the home front.

Jeanie Macpherson's perverse sense of drama is again in evidence. Yvonne, the Belgian heroine played by Florence Vidor, is married to a hateful Hun. While von Krutz is at the front, King Albert of Belgium stops near the von Krutz home and sees Yvonne's young brother, Jacques, playing soldier. The kindly king gives the boy an ivy cutting to symbolize the Belgian motto—"I die where I cling"—and asks the boy to protect Belgium "Till I Come Back to You."

As the German army advances, von Krutz returns home and finds Jacques saluting a portrait of King Albert. Against the protests of his wife, he sends the boy to a German-controlled orphanage to learn respect for the kaiser.

Later, von Krutz is captured in battle. American officer Jefferson Strong is sent behind German lines to find and destroy a cache of "liquid fire" (a napalm-like weapon). He takes Krutz's identity and forges a letter to Yvonne that leads her to believe that he is a friend of her husband acting with his knowledge and approval.

In the orphanage Jacques is punished for defending King Albert's name. He is brought home to be disciplined and is surprised to see that Strong has taken his uncle's place. Strong pretends to punish the boy for the benefit of the German gatekeeper, and the boy subsequently returns to the institution.

Yvonne tells Strong that he is like no other German she's met and reveals that she is Belgian. Taking a chance, Strong reveals his identity. With Yvonne's support he finds the store of liquid fire and directs the American army to tunnel from the allied trenches, under the Krutz home, to a position directly beneath the deadly storage depot. The plan is to blow up the jellied gasoline at the precise moment of an American charge "over the top."

In the meantime, the children are scheduled to be sent to a German munitions factory, and von Krutz escapes from an Allied prison camp. Jacques helps the children break out of the orphanage and leads them to his home. They have just enough time to take the tunnel to the American lines before the big blast. Krutz returns. The children take the wrong tunnel. Strong escapes the German's clutches, realizes the children are in danger, cuts the wires just as the switch is thrown, and single-handedly defends the tunnel against a German attack led by von Krutz.

The children arrive in the American trench just as the attack is to begin. Soldiers are sent to save Strong, and von Krutz is killed in action. Now, despite the fact that he acted to save the lives of war orphans, Strong faces court martial for interfering with the American attack. Fortunately, Jacques locates King Albert and asks the monarch to personally intervene on Strong's behalf. Strong is acquitted, and the king tells Jacques that he will come back when the Americans have rid Belgium of the hated Hun. DeMille gave the film his usual polished effort, but *Till I Come Back to You* is not one of his mightier achievements.

King Albert's cameo appearance at the beginning of the film is not particularly unusual for a wartime drama, but his direct intervention as a character at the climactic court martial is virtually without precedent. In DeMille's defense it should be said that Albert did lead Belgian troops in the field during the war, and his fictional action on Strong's behalf is at least plausible, if highly improbable.

Amusingly, the evil von Krutz is played by would-be Britisher "G. Butler Clonbough." In reality, Clonbough was German actor Gustav von Seyffertitz. Once the United States entered the war, anti-German sentiment reached a fever pitch.[1] Seyffertitz dropped the "von" from his name for *Old Wives for New*, but it wasn't enough. Typical of the tenor of the times is a handwritten note to DeMille from actor Arthur Allardt:

> I would like to call your attention to Mr. Robert Ries of 5519 B Sierra Vista Ave. (my neighbor) a German who came from San Francisco (Chicago and Milwaukee) in January. At that time they complained of his not being able to find employment and has found none to date yet live well and never Hooverize.[2]
>
> His wife spoke to my wife of the German soldiers as "our boys" also said "the officials at Washington were not doing the right thing in going into this war." "We should have kept out of it."
>
> Altho he has no imployment he leaves every day at all hours and returns at all hours.
>
> I believe his son Robt. Ries (or Reese) is known to you and Miss Macpherson.
>
> Miss [Gladys] Rosson [DeMille's secretary] told me that Gustav von Seyffertitz told her he was Dutch-Swiss whereas Robert Ries told me (and he is von Seyffertitz's best and most intimate friend) that he was German born, and brought up in Germany and was not a citizen of this country. Mrs. Ries Jr. told my wife he said "The poor United States is having such a hard time of it."
>
> P.S. Mrs. Ries also said Mr. von Seyffertitz spent money like water.[3]

In the face of such attack by innuendo, one can easily understand why Seyffertitz chose to change his name for the duration.

Leading lady Florence Vidor was one of the finest actresses of the silent screen. At the time of her two pictures with DeMille, she was married to director King Vidor, though at this point in their careers she was enjoying greater success. Leading man Bryant Washburn was primarily known as a light comedian in such films as *Skinner's Dress Suit* (Essanay, 1917). Popular throughout the early and mid-1920s, Washburn continued to play supporting roles well into the 1940s.

One of the doughboys who rescues Captain Jefferson, U.S.A., is Monte Blue, who got his start as an extra in *The Birth of a Nation* (1915) and who soon became a major star for Warner Bros. Blue is probably best remembered for the Ernst Lubitsch production *So This Is Paris* (1926).

For the first time Alvin Wyckoff shared screen credit as cameraman with Charles Rosher, who had worked as second cameraman on several DeMille pictures, including *Carmen* and *Joan the Woman*. In an interview with Kevin Brownlow, Rosher recalled that "Alvin Wyckoff, an excellent photographer and a very easygoing man, was the head cameraman. DeMille used to shout at him, but he took it lying down. Wyckoff wrecked himself with DeMille when he founded the cameraman's union."[4]

Wyckoff was active in trying to organize cinematographers in the late 1920s, and his career went into eclipse as a result of a not-so-subtle studio blacklist. However, his association with DeMille ended in 1923, and it is clear from DeMille's comments and his experiments with other cameramen between 1918 and 1923 that the director was seeking to change the look of his pictures long before he formally broke with Wyckoff. *Till I Come Back to You* has a softer look than previous DeMille pictures, and there is a greater reliance on back rim-lighting to separate actors from the background.

The New York office objected to the title *Till I Come Back to You* and suggested *Paths of Glory* as a substitute. "There is absolutely no action in the picture on which such a title could be hinged," DeMille wrote Jesse Lasky, "but if you think it good business [to use that title] I am willing. I still think Till I Come Back to You is a good commercial title."[5] DeMille had his way. The title remained unchanged.

# The Squaw Man

## (first remake)

An Artcraft Picture. A Cecil B. DeMille Production. Director: Cecil B. DeMille. Scenario by Beulah Marie Dix, from the play by Edwin Milton Royle. Photography: Alvin Wyckoff and King D. Gray

Picture started: August 19, 1918. Picture completed: September 12, 1918. Length: 6,141 feet (six reels). Cost: $43,858.96. Released: December 15, 1918. Gross: $283,556.56

Cast: Elliott Dexter (Jim Wynnegate), Thurston Hall (his cousin, Henry), Katherine MacDonald (Diana, Henry's wife), Helen Dunbar (Henry's mother), Winter Hall (Petrie), Ernest Joy (Fletcher), Herbert Standing (the bishop), Julia Faye (Lady Mable), Theodore Roberts (Big Bill), Noah Beery (Tabywana), Ann Little (Naturich), Raymond Hatton (Shorty), Jack Holt (Cash Hawkins), Monte Blue (Happy), Edwin Stevens (the sheriff), Guy Oliver (the deputy), Jack Herbert (the barkeeper), James Mason (Grouchy), and Pat Moore (Little Hal)

B eginning with *We Can't Have Everything* DeMille was elevated to equal footing with Mary Pickford, Douglas Fairbanks, and William S. Hart. The words "A Cecil B. DeMille Production" were added to the main titles and his films were offered as a separate Artcraft series. This new arrangement brought him great status, but little else. Making DeMille the "star" of his own productions meant a reduction in the budget for name acting talent, and while DeMille could suggest properties to the New York office, he had no real power to pick and choose his projects.

DeMille wanted to follow *Till I Come Back to You* with a production based on the exploits of Sir Henry Morgan, the British buccaneer, but Famous Players-Lasky would not hear of it. On June 24, 1918, DeMille received a wire from Jesse Lasky that spelled out the studio's attitude:

REGARDING MORGAN BUCCANEER NO ONE HERE
[in New York] AGREES WITH ME THIS WOULD BE

GOOD SUBJECT FOR YOU AT PRESENT TIME SUC-
CESS OF NEXT DE MILLE SERIES DEPENDS ON POPU-
LARITY OF FIRST FEW PICTURES AND OUR
ASSOCIATES FEEL YOU OUGHT NOT TO TAKE
CHANCES WITH THIS SUBJECT ON ACCOUNT OF IT
BEING UNDOUBTEDLY COSTUME PLAY WHICH
EXHIBITORS WILL RESENT AND PUBLIC MIGHT BE
SLOW IN RESPONDING TO IN SPITE OF UNDOUBTED
MERIT OF PRODUCTION STOP WE ADVISE LAYING
ASIDE AND RECONSIDERING IT FOR FIFTH OR SIXTH
OF DE MILLE SERIES NEXT SEASON[1]

Not quite three weeks later, Lasky reached a decision on DeMille's
next project:

WOULD LIKE YOU TO DO THE SQUAW MAN WITH
WILLIAM FAVERSHAM AS STAR FAVERSHAM
LOOKS SPLENDID . . . CONFIRM BY WIRE IF THIS IS
AGREEABLE TO YOU SO CAN IMMEDIATELY CLOSE
WITH FAVERSHAM AND MILTON ROYLE FOR
RIGHTS OF PLAY THIS WOULD BE FIRST DE MILLE
SPECIAL FOR NEXT SEASON ADVISE DATE
FAVERSHAM SHOULD ARRIVE IN HOLLYWOOD . . .[2]

DeMille replied with enthusiasm and some reservation: "I think
Squaw Man idea excellent and will consider it closed as my next feature
provided you give me your personal word that Faversham's appearance
is in your opinion Okay. Remember you cannot make a hero out of an old
man. . . ."[3]

For Lasky the appeal of remaking *The Squaw Man* was based on the
availability of William Faversham, who originated the role on stage. For
DeMille it meant something more. Despite all of his subsequent successes, Cecil B. DeMille's standing in the industry was based on the
original 1914 production of *The Squaw Man*, yet it was not really his
picture. The proposed remake offered him an opportunity to show what
he could do with Edwin Milton Royle's play on his own. Or perhaps he
felt that going along with Lasky's suggestion was simply politically
astute.

The project was nearly stillborn, however. On July 16 Lasky wired:

REGRET INFORM YOU SUDDEN CHANGE IN
FAVERSHAM'S PLANS MAKES IT IMPERATIVE WE
POSTPONE UNTIL LATE NEXT SEASON PROPOSED
PRODUCTION OF SQUAW MAN IF WORK HAS BEEN
COMMENCED ON SCENARIO SAME SHOULD BE
STOPPED IMMEDIATELY AND LAID ASIDE UNTIL
LATER STOP SILVIA BREMER AND WANDA PAWLEY
ALSO [Elliott] DEXTER HAVE CREATED VERY FAVOR-
ABLE IMPRESSION IN WE CAN'T HAVE EVERYTHING
THIS PICTURE SEEMS TO BE POPULAR SUCCESS
PLAN IS NOW TO FEATURE EITHER OF THESE GIRLS
OR BOTH WITH DEXTER IN FORTHCOMING SERIES
OF DE MILLE PRODUCTIONS HAVE YOU ANY SUG-
GESTION OR IDEAS ON MATERIAL SUITABLE FOR
THIS COMBINATION ADVISE

DeMille would not be swayed. "I do not want Faversham for Squaw Man," he wrote. "Was much relieved when you wired me did not have to use him. . . . I understand Old Wives and Can't Have Everything are giving excellent satisfaction—that is another reason why I prefer to proceed as originally outlined and neither do I wish to be burdened with additional Faversham salary. I sincerely trust you will not insist upon my using Faversham."[4]

With his newfound popularity in the wake of *Old Wives for New*, Elliott Dexter was selected to play the Squaw Man. Katherine MacDonald, who was known as "the American Beauty," played Diana, and the part of Naturich was given to Ann Little.

Little had a background in musical comedy, but she made her mark in the movies as a Western heroine at the Ince-KayBee and Flying "A" studios. She got plenty of practice riding horses. When she worked at Inceville in the early 1910s, the studio was so remote that just to get to work she rode a streetcar to the end of the line, took a stagecoach to the outskirts of the studio property, and rode horseback the rest of the way. When William S. Hart visited the Ince studio for the first time in 1914 he toured the lot, and he saw Ann Little playing the part of an Indian princess riding her pinto pony bareback over the Santa Monica hills. Between takes she rode over to meet the visitor. When her pony reared up and knocked the hat off his head, Hart had his first introduction to the horse that became his beloved Fritz. Little retired from the screen in 1923 to become a Christian Science practitioner, and for years she was also the manager of the Chateau Marmont hotel in Hollywood.

With most of the action taking place outdoors and no big box-office names in the cast, DeMille turned out *The Squaw Man* remake in less than four weeks on an economical budget. Again Alvin Wyckoff shared screen credit with another cinematographer, King D. Gray. It was Gray's first significant credit, and provides another suggestion that DeMille was increasingly anxious to find a new look on the screen.

Popular with audiences, *The Squaw Man* grossed nearly as well as *Old Wives for New*. Assessing the picture's success on an artistic level is difficult, however, because only the final reel of the 1918 version is known to survive. Judging from this fragmentary evidence, the picture offers little to distinguish itself from the flock of run-of-the-mill Westerns that were a mainstay of Hollywood production at the time. Thematic elements of the play were brushed aside to favor action, and the footage has a slap-dash feeling that is not typical of DeMille's work.

During 1918 much of DeMille's attention was directed toward the war in Europe. He desperately wanted to go "Over There," but the army said he was too old, the flying corps told him he was too inexperienced, and Adolph Zukor felt he was too valuable to Famous Players-Lasky. In his frustration, DeMille took command of the Fifty-first Company of the California Home Guard, a largely ceremonial militia of studio personnel. He also actively sold war bonds and raised funds for the Red Cross. DeMille took his war work seriously, but he still wanted to be closer to the action. In 1918 the War Department asked him to shoot films at the front. DeMille was enthusiastic, but Zukor was still unwilling to let his top director go to France.

Fate intervened. A deadly epidemic of Spanish influenza caused public health officials to close theaters throughout the United States, and Adolph Zukor was gripped with a sudden patriotic fervor. He gave DeMille permission to take a leave—without salary. Both men were let down when armistice was declared on November 11, 1918.

*The Squaw Man* remake proved to be a tremendous financial success. This, as much as anything else, prompted DeMille to turn one more time to the venerable Edwin Milton Royle play in the early days of sound when he was haunted by self-doubt and lack of inspiration.

# 34

# Don't Change Your Husband

An Artcraft Picture. A Cecil B. DeMille Production. Director: Cecil B. DeMille. Original scenario by Jeanie Macpherson. Art director: Wilfred Buckland. Technical director: Howard Higgin. Photography: Alvin Wyckoff. Film editor: Anne Bauchens

Picture started: October 12, 1918. Picture finished: November 29, 1918. Length: 6,420 feet (seven reels). Cost: $73,922.14. Released: January 26, 1919. Gross: $292,394.10

Cast: Elliott Dexter (James Denby Porter), Gloria Swanson (Leila, his wife), Lew Cody (Schuyler Van Sutphen), Sylvia Ashton (Mrs. Huckney), Theodore Roberts (the bishop), Julia Faye (Nanette, the maid), James Neill (butler), Ted Shawn (Faun), Sam Wood, Raymond Hatton, and Jack Mulhall

The Triangle Film Corporation was on shaky financial ground even before Adolph Zukor lured Griffith, Ince, Fairbanks, and Hart to Artcraft, but the loss of these talents precipitated the company's collapse. Forced to improvise, Triangle made an effort to develop new stars, and one of their discoveries was nineteen-year-old Gloria Swanson.

Swanson entered pictures in 1914 with the Essanay Film Mfg. Co. in Chicago. Later she signed with Mack Sennett and co-starred in such Triangle-Keystone two-reelers as *The Danger Girl* (1916) and *Teddy at the Throttle* (1917). Clarence Badger, her director on *The Danger Girl*, remembered Gloria and recommended her to fellow director Jack Conway. Swanson starred in two pictures for Conway and began to attract industry attention. Triangle raised her salary by fifteen dollars a week but didn't offer Swanson a formal contract.

She received a call from Famous Players-Lasky casting director Oscar Goodstadt asking her to meet Cecil B. DeMille. DeMille had seen her work and offered her the lead in his next picture. She was elated and assured DeMille that she was under no contractual obligation. However, when Swanson informed Triangle, the company argued that since Swanson accepted the raise, a tacit contract was in force. Famous Players-Lasky took the dispute to arbitration and lost, and Swanson was forced to sign with Triangle in mid-1918.[1]

Triangle quickly ground out a picture a month with their new star, but bankruptcy was looming and the studio was in no position to capitalize on Swanson's popularity. It became evident that Triangle had not offered a contract earlier because the company did not want to carry her still-modest weekly salary as an obligation in its books. H.O. Davis, Triangle's vice-president and general manager, asked Swanson if she would be willing to be released from her contract. Feeling that she had been blackmailed into signing it in the first place, Swanson refused. Davis told Swanson that DeMille had tried to borrow her for another picture, and he offered to contact Famous Players-Lasky on her behalf to see if something could be worked out.[2] Davis called Oscar Goodstadt, and arrangements were made to loan Gloria Swanson to Famous Players-Lasky for *Don't Change Your Husband*.[3]

Swanson's recollection of her first day working with DeMille offers insight into his technique with actors. After she was costumed, a Pinkerton detective arrived in her dressing room with a tray full of jewels. Swanson was to select her own accessories to complement her dress. Shortly before 10:00 A.M. she heard the strains of a violin and was escorted to the stage by an assistant director. DeMille greeted her and led her to the set. "This is your home," he explained. "Take all the time you need to get acquainted with it. If anything seems wrong, we'll talk about it."[4]

After she had an opportunity to become familiar with the room, DeMille "In a voice not much louder than a whisper . . . said we would begin with a simple scene. . . . He pointed to the closet where the trunk would be, and to another closet where he said I should select things I wanted to pack. . . . That was all. He didn't tell me why I was packing or where I was going . . . he never gave specific instructions or directions."[5] Perhaps because Swanson was a late addition to the cast she received no background on her role. DeMille was noted for his preproduction script readings during which he told the story of the film to the assembled players. Often in casting, DeMille related the story from the perspective of the character he wished an actor to play, treating the role as if it were the most important in the film.[6]

On the surface, *Don't Change Your Husband* seems like a reworking of *Old Wives for New* with the genders of the leading characters reversed, but what makes the film unique and so much fun is that DeMille and

Macpherson created a truly sophisticated comedy, discarding the feeble dramatic conventions that propelled the earlier film.

Leila Porter is disappointed with her careless, onion-eating husband and openly pleased at the attentions of the suave sophisticate Schuyler Van Sutphen. She divorces and remarries. In *Old Wives for New*, the romance between the married man and the young woman develops by chance, and the plot is propelled by a melodramatic contrivance—the hero's desire to save the reputations of his friend and his lover. In *Don't Change Your Husband*, Leila actively encourages a lover who is fully aware that she is married, and she leaves her husband without giving a thought to what society might think. Her union with Van Sutphen proves no better than her first, and Leila just as eagerly allows her now reformed ex-husband to woo her again.

Leila discovers that Van Sutphen is having an affair with Nanette, the maid, whose pet name is Toodles. When Toodles threatens to raise a scandal over her own illicit relationship with Van Sutphen, Leila agrees to pay her off—not for her silence, but because Leila sees no point in their both being cheated. The lesson is practical rather than moral, and this casual approach to sexual liaisons made the film remarkable in its time.

Surprisingly, *Don't Change Your Husband* did not provoke demands for censorship. Critics found the film to be "clean and interesting," even "clean and wholesome."[7] Zukor's threatened suppression of *Old Wives for New* had its effect, and DeMille developed a scheme for presenting lurid themes without raising the hackles of censors. The formula can be stated in a single sentence: In order to promote reform, it is first necessary to show the wages of sin. As demands for censorship increased in the 1920s, DeMille's pictures seemed immune from challenge, even when they consistently flaunted accepted standards with outrageous imagery and situations.

The sense of "loss through love" so evident in earlier collaborations between DeMille and Macpherson seems to be missing from *Don't Change Your Husband*, but in fact James and Leila Porter discover that new lovers simply bring new problems, and they lose their illusions about romantic love—perhaps the greatest loss of all.

# For Better, For Worse

An Artcraft Picture. A Cecil B. DeMille Production. Director: Cecil B. DeMille. Scenario by Edgar Selwyn and Jeanie Macpherson (DeMille's records indicate that William C. deMille wrote the scenario), from a story by Edgar Selwyn. Art director: Wilfred Buckland. Production manager: Howard Higgin. Photography: Alvin Wyckoff

Picture started: January 27, 1919. Picture finished: March 24, 1919. Length: 6,939 feet (seven reels). Cost: $111,260.93. Released: April 27, 1919. Gross: $256,072.97

Cast: Gloria Swanson (Sylvia Norcross), Sylvia Ashton (her aunt), James Neill (her uncle), Elliott Dexter (Dr. Edward Meade), Tom Forman (Dick Burton), Wanda Hawley (Betty Hoyt), Theodore Roberts (Dr. Roland), Raymond Hatton (Bud), Spotiswoode Aitken and Winter Hall (doctors), Jack Holt (crusader), Monte Blue and Fred Huntley (colonial militiamen), Edythe Chapman, and May Giraci

After the completion of *Don't Change Your Husband*, DeMille offered Gloria Swanson a contract on behalf of Famous Players-Lasky. He was not above using his personal charm in the interests of the studio. Swanson was arguably naive. She almost certainly thought that DeMille was looking out for her best interests when in fact he was only concerned with signing her at a bargain-basement salary. The agreement, dated December 30, 1918, paid Swanson the munificent sum of $150 a week for the first four months and $200 a week thereafter. With the usual options to be exercised at the discretion of the company, Gloria Swanson would be earning $350 a week in two years.[1] Considering that Tom Mix was making $350 a week as a star-director of two-reel comedies for the Fox Film Corporation in 1917, and that Mary Pickford received $10,000 a week that same year, Gloria Swanson was clearly being exploited.

Swanson's second DeMille picture is a strange, overwrought drama of a doctor who had the courage to stay at home and minister to sick children when the nation and the woman he loved were urging him to take up arms and go to war. Just as DeMille had been one of the first filmmakers to deal with American involvement in the Great War, he was also the first to address the issues of life on the home front, during and immediately after the conflict. Armistice was declared on November 11, 1918, and little more than two months later *For Better, For Worse* was ready to go into production.

During the war Americans came to despise slackers and draft dodgers.[2] Patriotic posters urged young men to enlist, and Hollywood joined forces with the government by producing films like *Draft 258* (Rolfe-Metro, 1917), *The Yellow Dog* (Universal-Jewel, 1918), *The Slacker* (Metro, 1917), *The Slacker's Heart* (Emerald, 1917), and *Mrs. Slacker* (Astra-Pathé, 1918). *For Better, For Worse* attempted to smooth over the ill feeling Americans had for slackers. No doubt some of DeMille's interest in the project derived from his own inability to get "Over There." Still, the film is basically a moralistic melodrama, notable primarily for its production values and the performance of Gloria Swanson. Swanson is excellent as the frigid and vindictive Sylvia Norcross, so much so that it is difficult to see what Elliott Dexter's character sees in her.

When war is declared, both Edward Meade and Dick Burton are in love with Sylvia and set to go to France with the American Expeditionary Force. Sylvia favors Dr. Meade, but he doubts her love; she shies at his touch and is unready for any romantic commitment. The war presents a convenient excuse for her to stay romantically uninvolved. She tells Meade:

> "I'm glad you and Dick
> are both going, Ned—a
> girl never forgives a man
> who stays home when
> he's needed 'over there'!"

At St. Agnes Hospital Dr. Roland persuades Meade that his talents are more necessary in the children's ward. Reluctantly, Meade refuses his military commission. When he tells Sylvia of his decision she scolds him:

> "Ned, you've always been
> my hero, but I couldn't
> love a man who stayed
> home—when brave men
> are going out to die!"

She waves under Meade's nose a newspaper article about German sharpshooters killing military doctors. When this attempt at shaming him into the army fails, she wraps herself in the flag and appeals to his sense of patriotism. Meade sadly returns to his young patients.

As troops march off to war, Dick Burton asks Sylvia to marry him. She tenses, and shakes her head "No." But Dick is persistent:

> "Since the world began, dear—
> men have needed some woman
> to fight for! Do you think 'Harald
> the Dane' would have burned
> the ships of half the world if
> 'Gyda' hadn't whispered—
> 'Dear, I love you.'"

A series of flashbacks follows: a Viking scene, then an episode set in the time of King Arthur, and finally a vignette from the American Revolution. Gloria Swanson in each age sends a different hero off to battle. Still Sylvia refuses Burton's proposal, but he pushes on:

> "Nothing ever changes, dear
> —Men are the same now, as then!
> And if you'll marry me
> tomorrow, before I leave—I
> won't claim you till I've earned
> the right in France!"

The prospect of a long-delayed honeymoon sways Sylvia to accept Burton's proposal. Added to this strange triangle is Betty Hoyt, who has loved Dick Burton since she was a young girl.

Burton goes to France, and Sylvia aids families affected by the war. Her chauffeur accidentally hits a young orphan whose father was killed in France and whose mother died in the flu epidemic. Sylvia searches for a doctor only to find that all qualified surgeons are off to war. In desperation she turns to Dr. Meade.

In France Dick Burton is wounded in battle—his arm lost, his face shattered. Horrified by his appearance he sends word through a friend that he has been killed. Meanwhile, Dr. Meade saves the young girl and offers to adopt her.[3] In her gratitude Sylvia agrees to marry him. But army surgeons reconstruct Burton's face and give him a prosthetic arm. He decides to return home, arriving on the night of his wife's engagement party.

The remedy for all this intrigue is inherent in the basic character relationships. Dr. Ned Meade tells Sylvia to stay with her husband; Sylvia tells Dick Burton that she loves Ned; Betty tells Dick of her love and offers herself as a solution. Dick comes to his senses, and when Ned tells the returned soldier that he will not come between husband and wife, Dick assures his friend that everything is all right. He lays the moral on with a trowel:

> "You're doing this, Ned, because I'm
> in uniform. If you think I'm a soldier—
> what about You—and the 30 million
> more like you who stayed home? Not
> because they didn't want to fight—but
> because their work was here!
> "Somebody had to feed us and had to
> buy our guns—and somebody had to
> raise the billions it took to win this war.
> And that somebody was the Man who
> Stayed at Home!
> "You're as much of a soldier as I am,
> Ned, and you'll get an even break."

There are some fine moments in *For Better, For Worse*, but not nearly enough of them to sustain the film's seven-reel length. The performances of Swanson and Tom Forman are compelling, but Elliott Dexter is stolid, and the story is much too contrived and predictable. DeMille's visual treatment, however, is interesting. He uses rooms and doors as symbols throughout the picture. In critical moments the characters are shown on opposite sides of a door. After the party on the night of Dick's return, each of the characters seems trapped in a different room, alone and unable to connect with the others.

The strange sexual tension inherent in Sylvia's relationships is never fully resolved. She refuses to be touched by Meade early in the film, or by Burton after he returns from France. In the end she professes her love for Meade, but one can't escape the symbolism of the adopted daughter. With a ready-made family, Sylvia's ultimate exercise of her wifely duties is moot at best. Could DeMille and his writers have etched Sylvia in such detail without being consciously aware of her perversion? It is doubtful. Why they decided to cast the character in such a mold is a mystery, however.

DeMille wanted to call the picture *Repent at Leisure*, but Lasky didn't like the title. "None of titles submitted for [Edgar] Selwyn picture satisfactory," Lasky telegraphed. "While I like *Man Who Stayed At Home*, [the Artcraft] distributing department is absolutely opposed to this title on account of its suggesting that story has to do with the war. Please submit new titles."[4]

DeMille replied, "I am astonished you do not like title REPENT AT LEISURE. [Adolph] Zukor and all here [in Hollywood] like it very much. Please reconsider this title, also the following: THE THUNDERBOLT [and] FOR BETTER, FOR WORSE. If none of these take your fancy have [Edgar] Selwyn suggest title."[5]

After years of experimenting with moody lighting and deep shadows, in *For Better, For Worse* DeMille moved even further toward the brighter, more evenly-lit approach that marks his later work. In several scenes the shadows have a "milky" look that suggest Wyckoff underexposed the shots and the laboratory compensated by force developing the negative. These lapses give the picture an uneven look.

Pressure was applied to complete the film quickly to meet an early release date, but DeMille resisted. In 1915 he made two pictures simultaneously because other directors on the Lasky lot "were beginning to want six, seven, and eight weeks to make a picture and were complaining about this, that, and the other thing, and I felt that the complaints were not valid. They were all staggering around from the amount of work they were doing, so I decided to make . . . two pictures at once . . . in four weeks or five weeks, and I did."[6]

However, in 1919 he pleaded,

Think it very serious mistake to try [to] make me finish this picture for March release. I am having same trouble with it that I have had with all of them and the additional worry of trying to meet early release date is serious handicap. . . . My request is that all my productions be moved forward at least one month and even then the dates will be difficult to meet. If you want me to make good pictures I absolutely cannot be rushed in my work. If our policy is to really make good pictures and fewer of them let's start now. I cannot possibly make more than five pictures in a year and have them of the kind we all want. I realize that these pictures have been sold [in advance] and am willing to make every effort if you all think the risk is worth it. . . .[7]

What a difference a few years made!

DeMille kept a fascinating souvenir of *For Better, For Worse* in his collection of offstage film footage. It shows DeMille and Gloria Swanson dancing on the set with Tom Forman and others looking on. Gloria is secure in Cecil's arms. He has his jacket wrapped tightly around her, partially hiding her from the camera in a teasing sort of way, strongly suggesting that their relationship was something more than merely professional at the time.

*For Better, For Worse* was DeMille's most expensive film since *The Woman God Forgot*, but for all the timeliness of its theme, it was only a modest box-office success. His next picture was even more costly, and it is doubtful that Famous Players-Lasky would have approved the higher expenditure if all the returns on *For Better, For Worse* were in. Fortunately for DeMille and the studio, the decision was made without benefit of hindsight.

# 36

# Male and Female

A Famous Players-Lasky Super Production. A Paramount-Artcraft Picture. A Cecil B. DeMille Production. Director: Cecil B. DeMille. Scenario by Jeanie Macpherson, from the play *The Admirable Crichton* by Sir James M. Barrie. Photography: Alvin Wyckoff. Art director: Wilfred Buckland. Production manager: Howard Higgin. Film editor: Anne Bauchens

Picture started: June 15, 1919. Picture finished: July 30, 1919. Length: 8,952 feet (nine reels). Cost: $168,619.28. Released: November 16, 1919. Gross: $1,256,226.59

Cast: Gloria Swanson (Lady Mary Lasenby), Thomas Meighan (William Crichton), Lila Lee ("Tweeny"), Theodore Roberts (earl of Loam), Raymond Hatton (Hon. Ernest Woolley), Mildred Reardon (Lady Agatha Lasenby), Bebe Daniels (Babylonian king's favorite), Julia Faye (Susan), Wesley Barry ("Buttons"), Robert Cain (Lord Brockelhurst), and Rhy Darby (Lady Eileen Dun Craigie), Edward Burns (Treherne)

Adolph Zukor's stranglehold on star talent in the film industry ended almost as quickly as it began. Angry exhibitors pooled their resources to create the Associated First National Exhibitors Circuit in April 1917. Several months elapsed before First National mounted an effective assault against the Famous Players-Lasky and Paramount/Artcraft interests, but the new cooperative venture quickly signed Charlie Chaplin and made overtures to Mary Pickford.

As early as December 1917, Lasky wrote DeMille:

Zukor had a talk with Pickford in California regarding new contract with which I believe you are familiar. She was to decide whether she preferred to continue present contract until its expiration next June [1918] or to make a new contract January first for two years along the lines of our contract with Fairbanks. Mr. Zukor is under the impression that if she preferred Fairbanks style of contract she would forward same to us for approval before end of year. We have not heard from her and think it best not to communicate with her direct but would like to know whether her idea is that she is going to make the next picture under the old contract or under a new one. We deem it best that you sound her out without arousing her suspicions as to your purpose so that you can advise us what her intentions are. . . . Have a talk with her as if you were acting on your own responsibility.[1]

Pickford did not sign the revised contract. She entered into a three-picture deal with First National for the 1919 season and then joined with Charlie Chaplin, Douglas Fairbanks, and D.W. Griffith to form the United Artists Corporation.[2]

To make up for the fading glory of the Artcraft line, Zukor created the Realart company to complement the Paramount program. However, stars like Mary Miles Minter, Constance Binney, and Alice Brady were not in the same league with Pickford and Fairbanks, and the Realart brand never carried quite the prestige of the Artcraft line.

Under the Famous Players-Lasky merger agreement, Lasky was in charge of all production for the company. However, Adolph Zukor began to take a more active role in production decisions, and to keep peace in the company Lasky agreed to share production oversight credits with his partner. Titles of East Coast productions were to read "Adolph Zukor presents," and pictures made in the West would credit "Jesse L. Lasky presents." On films of special interest or prestige, Zukor, at his discretion, could opt for the dual credit "Adolph Zukor and Jesse L. Lasky present." The only problem with this detente was that the lion's share of Famous Players-Lasky pictures were made in Hollywood. To increase Eastern production, the decision was made to abandon the old Famous Players studio in Fort Lee, New Jersey, and build a new plant at Astoria, Long Island. Lasky wired DeMille:

WILL YOU KINDLY GIVE US YOUR ADVICE ON
QUESTION OF WHETHER OR NOT THE BIG STUDIO
WE ARE BUILDING IN LONG ISLAND SHOULD HAVE
A SOLID ROOF OR A GLASS ROOF DO YOU THINK WE
WILL GET BETTER PHOTOGRAPHY IF YOU USE
NATURAL LIGHT DIFFUSED THROUGH A GLASS
ROOF IN CONJUNCTION WITH ARTIFICIAL LIGHT OR
DO YOU RECOMMEND DEPENDING ENTIRELY ON

ARTIFICIAL LIGHT THE STUDIO PLANS ALSO CALL
FOR A SEPARATE DARK STAGE SIMILAR TO ONE WE
ARE NOW BUILDING IN HOLLYWOOD . . . THIS POINT
MUST BE DECIDED IMMEDIATELY AND THERE ARE
DECIDED DIFFERENCE OF OPINION HERE A GLASS
ROOF WOULD COST SEVENTY FIVE THOUSAND
MORE THAN A SOLID ROOF[3]

"Regarding studio," DeMille replied, "the use of natural light through a glass roof with diffusers underneath will give you a much finer photographic effect than a solid roof. On that point there is no question. Of course, what drawback a glass roof may have for an eastern winter I do not know."[4] Zukor opted for economy, and the Astoria studio was built with a solid roof.

On January 22, 1919, DeMille received word that Lasky had bought the screen rights to Sir James M. Barrie's 1902 play *The Admirable Crichton*. The play is a fable of class consciousness. Crichton is household butler to Lord Loam and his indolent family. He loves his master's daughter from afar and in turn is loved by "Tweeny" a young maid in the lord's house. On a vacation cruise the family and staff are shipwrecked on a deserted island. In the wild they find that social standing counts for nothing. Through his leadership and skill in conquering their primitive surroundings, Crichton becomes "king" of the island. He is about to take the lord's daughter as his wife when a passing ship stops and rescues the castaways. Back in England, master and servant revert to type. Lord Loam brags of his exploits in the wild, and Crichton diplomatically confirms his master's tall tales.

To Barrie's play, DeMille and Jeanie Macpherson added an historical "back story." Mary Lasenby takes pleasure in lording it over Crichton because of a long-ago incident that occurred many lives in the past. The dimly remembered connection finds expression in their mutual interest in the poem "Or Ever the Knightly Years," by William Ernest Henley:

Or ever the knightly years were gone
With the old world to the grave,
I was a King in Babylon
And you were a Christian Slave.

I saw, I took, I cast you by,
I bent and broke your pride.
You loved me well, or I heard them lie,
but your longing was denied.
Surely I knew that by and by
You cursed your gods and died.

And a myriad suns have set and shone
Since then upon the grave
Decreed by the King of Babylon
To her that had been his Slave.

The pride I trampled is now my scathe,
For it tramples me again.
The old resentment lasts like death,
For you love, yet you refrain.
I break my heart on your hard unfaith,
And I break my heart in vain.

Yet not for an hour do I wish undone
The deed beyond the grave,
When I was a King in Babylon
And you were a Virgin Slave.[5]

Henley's verse provides inspiration for the historical flashback. Crichton tells Mary a tale of ancient Babylon. A slave is brought to the king. He makes her a courtesan, and she falls in love with him. In an exercise of power he sends the slave to meet her death in a lion's den. The slave vows that the king will pay for his misdeed throughout time. DeMille staged the slave's death as a living recreation of a famed Victorian painting titled "The Lion's Bride."

Today, eighty years after the production of *Male and Female*, DeMille's reliance on mid-Victorian models for inspiration may seem odd, but it should not come as a surprise. In our own time, a director like Oliver Stone shows an obsession with the 1960s. The late 1980s saw a wave of nostalgia for the 1950s. If one goes back to the 1950s, while rock 'n' roll was sweeping the country there was also a revival of interest in the Roaring Twenties. In the late 1930s and early 1940s, dozens of films dealt with life in the 1910s, and the early 1930s witnessed a fascination with the Gay Nineties. It seems there is a "thirty-year syndrome" of nostalgia that affects art and society. In 1919, William Ernest Henley's 1888 poem was about thirty years old, and Gloria Swanson remembered that her grandmother had a print of "The Lion's Bride" hanging on the wall.[6] 1919 audiences were familiar with the literary and artistic sources of DeMille's inspiration.

Because an operator at the Postal Telegraph-Cable Company confused the word "admirable" with "admiral," DeMille became convinced that others would make the same transformation in their heads of *The Admirable Crichton* and expect a war picture.[7] "Crichton" (pronounced Cry-ton) was considered beyond anyone's level of understanding. The inspiration for a new title came from Henry C. deMille and David Belasco's 1890 play about a bank fraud and family honor, which they called *Men and Women*. Cecil took the cue, added a biblical reference, and suggested *Male and Female (Created He Them)* as an alternative to *The Admirable Crichton*. The New York office lopped off the parenthetical phrase, and Jesse Lasky gained J.M. Barrie's approval for the change.

Elliott Dexter was scheduled to play Crichton, but just as DeMille was about to start shooting he reported, "Elliott Dexter quite sick in hospital. This will delay me probably two weeks either until he is well enough or until William de Mille finishes with [Thomas] Meighan. You had better change release dates accordingly postponing Crichton four weeks to play safe and not counting on extra de Mille special until November."[8]

As a special production, *Male and Female* was allowed to run nearly nine thousand feet in length. The simple story didn't necessarily justify the footage, but DeMille filled the picture with sly observational details. The character introductions common in features of the 1910s are more clearly integrated into the film as houseboy "Buttons" peeks through keyholes to reveal Lord Loam and his family. The famous bathtub scene is purely gratuitous and plays like an ad for American-Standard plunked into the middle of the action, although it does serve to contrast with the primitive island conditions later in the film. The Babylonian flashback is an opulent blend of archaeological realism and *Vanity Fair* fantasy. Mitchell Leisen, who would become DeMille's right-hand man in the late 1920s, did his first costume sketches for the director on this sequence. The flashback also features Bebe Daniels, fresh from a four-year stint as Harold Lloyd's leading lady in dozens of one and two-reel comedies, in her first appearance for DeMille.

The script for *Male and Female* features two slim but cunning sub-plots. Mary Lasenby's fiancé, Lord Brockelhurst, takes up with one of Lord Loam's maids while the family is away and suffers no consequences, while Mary's best friend, Lady Eileen, finds nothing but social ostracism when she marries her chauffeur. Jeanie Macpherson would later use these elements to create the script for *Saturday Night*.

Like Frank Capra in the 1930s, DeMille was able to shroud his social criticism in a celebration of traditional values. DeMille and Macpherson added a coda to Barrie's tale. Crichton and Tweeny wed, move to America, and take up farming. The final scene of idyllic farm life borrows from *Kindling*, and is hardly in keeping with the tone of *Male and Female*, but one of the popular songs of 1919 was "Let the Rest of the World Go By," and the promise of a "little nest somewhere out in the west" was compelling at the time.

*Male and Female* was the first DeMille picture since *Joan the Woman* to be released as a separate picture on its own merits apart from any series or program, and the results were staggering. The film performed as well as the previous five DeMille pictures put together and created a sensation. Just why *Male and Female* was so successful is something of a mystery, however, because it is one of DeMille's weaker social comedies.

Audiences of the time were accustomed to seeing "artistic" nudity on-screen, so the famous bathtub scene cannot account for the film's great popularity, and though DeMille was faithful to J.M. Barrie's plot, the charm that marked the playwright's style is missing in the DeMille version. Still, the figures speak for themselves: *Male and Female* was DeMille's biggest hit to date. Perhaps the explanation can be found in the context of the times. Having made the world safe for democracy, Americans were sympathetic to the themes of equality and the folly of class distinctions presented in the film. The war was over, the flu epidemic was past, and there was a brief commercial boom before a severe economic downturn in the early 1920s. Also, because of their new affiliation with United Artists, Mary Pickford and Douglas Fairbanks had far fewer pictures in release, making DeMille's film all the more valuable in the marketplace.

# Why Change Your Wife?

A Famous Players-Lasky Super Production. A Paramount-Artcraft Picture. A Cecil B. DeMille Production. Director: Cecil B. DeMille. Scenario by Sada Cowan and Olga Printzlau, from a story by William C. deMille. Art director: Wilfred Buckland. Production manager: Howard Higgin. Photography: Alvin Wyckoff. Film editor: Anne Bauchens

Picture started: September 2, 1919. Picture finished: October 22, 1919. Length: 7,613 feet (eight reels). Cost: $129,349.31. Released: May 2, 1920. Gross: $1,016,245.87

Cast: Thomas Meighan (Robert Gordon), Gloria Swanson (Beth, his wife), Bebe Daniels (Sally Clark), Theodore Kosloff (Radinoff), Sylvia Ashton (Aunt Kate), Clarence Geldart (doctor), Maym Kelso (Harriette), Lucien Littlefield (butler), Edna Mae Cooper (maid), and Jane Wolfe (a woman client)

*Why Change Your Wife?* was never intended to be a Cecil B. DeMille production. The story was developed by William deMille, who was also supposed to direct, but circumstances led Cecil to take over the property.

His first choice for a follow-up to *Male and Female* was an adaptation of the novel *Susan Lenox, Her Fall and Rise* by David Graham Phillips, author of *Old Wives for New*. Negotiations for the novel bogged down over price, and Jesse Lasky was concerned that DeMille could not "picturize the story so that it might not stir up grat [*sic*] censorship agitation."[1]

DeMille's second choice was Walter Browne's 1911 allegorical play, *Everywoman*. He and Macpherson were also developing a story with the working title *Mother-in-Law*. However, dollars and sense intervened as Jesse Lasky looked to Cecil B. DeMille's box-office reputation. "We are all of the opinion, that it is a mistake for you to do Every Woman," Lasky wrote on May 9, 1919. "Our idea being that we can sell Every Woman produced by a less important director at a big profit and that we can get as much for another DeMille special with a less expensive story built along the lines of your great successes. . . . We are very short on special pictures for next season and the above plan would allow us one extra special—Every Woman—in addition to the DeMille special."[2]

DeMille was disappointed but philosophical about the company's decision. "I had already started preparation for Everywoman," he replied. "Have engaged [Theodore] Kosloff for [the character of] Passion and one or two girls for smaller parts. However, I agree with your business judgment in the matter and will do Mother-in-Law after Crichton. This change will take at least a month longer as it is more difficult to prepare script of an original for which I haven't even a story than it would have taken to prepare script for Everywoman."[3]

The reason DeMille was so accommodating was that Jesse Lasky offered a plum prize that DeMille was most anxious to make, a biblical spectacle called *The Wanderer*. Lasky wired:

> PROVIDED YOU WOULD LIKE TO PRODUCE IT WE
> CAN CLOSE IMMEDIATELY WITH MORRIS GEST AND
> DAVID BELASCO FOR THE WANDERER WOULD
> WANT YOU TO PRODUCE THE PICTURE NEXT SEA-
> SON TO BE SHOWN IN TWO DOLLAR THEATRES THE
> SAME ELABORATE PRODUCTION AND CAST AS
> JOAN THE WOMAN PLEASE GIVE THIS YOUR MOST
> SERIOUS CONSIDERATION . . . AS WE WOULD NOT
> CLOSE FOR PLAY UNLESS YOU ARE CONVINCED
> YOU CAN MAKE GREAT SPECTACULAR TWO DOL-
> LAR PICTURE [4]

The prospect of having a crack at another big production fired DeMille's imagination. "Think your idea of doing Wanderer excellent," he answered.

> The story has much more physical appeal than Joan. I could take the high spots from half the great Biblical stories of the world such as great chariot race and other smashing incidents of the kind. The sensuous life of a great ancient eastern city has never been, in my mind, touched and the story has stood the test of eighteen hundred years. [Scenario editor] Frank [Woods], Jeanie [Macpherson] and Bill [deMille] agree that it has wonderful possibilities.[5] . . . Have started already preparing, assuming that it is closed. Will you send on manuscript

and any material Gest may have. . . . I can do WANDERER immediately after Crichton which would have it ready for you for a New Years opening. Whereas if I do MOTHER-IN-LAW first you could not get WANDERER before March. You must figure twelve weeks to shoot WANDERER. This . . . arrangement would be more satisfactory to me but I am prepared to do either you desire.[6]

By May 14, Jesse Lasky could report:

WANDERER CLOSED AND ALL MATERIAL BEING MAILED IT IS REALLY MOST IMPORTANT TO GET ONE DE MILLE SPECIAL TO SELL ON ITS MERITS UNDER NEW PLAN TO BE RELEASED IN OCTOBER TO BE POSITIVELY FOLLOWED BY THE WANDERER FOR WHICH YOU CAN START PREPARATIONS WHEN-EVER YOU PLEASE WE PLAN TO OPEN THE WAN-DERER IN NEW YORK ABOUT FIRST OF APRIL ON ACCOUNT OF DIFFICULTIES AND TIME NECESSARY TO PREPARE MOTHER-IN-LAW THEME WE SUGGEST NOVEL 'THE GUARDED FLAME' BY W.B. MAXWELL AND SATURDAY EVENING POST SERIAL 'A WOMAN'S WOMAN' BY NALBRO BATLEY. . . .[7]

Lasky's suggested story alternatives did not thrill the director. "I read Woman's Woman in synopsis form," DeMille wrote, "and I did not care for it. May get more out of the story [itself]. Will also read The Guarded Flame. If I do not care for either of these believe it would be best to take extra three or four weeks and do Mother-in-Law. Could still deliver you Wanderer plenty of time for April release. Unless I hear from you to the contrary will consider this the plan until I have read the two novels mentioned."[8]

But *Mother-in-Law* never came together, and DeMille suggested the possibility of taking over a property William deMille was developing called *Don't Change Your Wife*. William's film was clearly designed to cash in on the trend pioneered by Cecil; so it seemed appropriate that Cecil should do it. He also proposed changing the title to *Why Change Your Wife?* and hiring Milton Sills to play the male lead. Lasky was enthusiastic about the property, but not about the actor. "Think your plan excellent of producing Don't Change Your Wife immediately after Crichton," he wired.

> Think new title suggested Why Change Your Wife? better than former title. Your whole plan very satisfactory except am not sure about Milton Sills. Advise you hold question of engaging him for Why Change Your Wife? in abeyance for few days until I can advise you more definitely about his popularity. Suppose of course you only want Sills for this one picture and that you don't expect to use him in Wanderer. Think we can probably get you leading man of more pleasing personality for Wife story. If that is all you want. How about David Powell? He will be available in time as we just put him under year's contract. In my opinion he is ideal type. Can play anything that Dexter plays. You can see his work in His Parisian Wife [Famous Players-Lasky, 1919] with [Elsie] Ferguson or The Better Half [Select Pictures, 1918] with Alice Brady.[9]

DeMille wanted Milton Sills because of Elliott Dexter's continuing illness and a growing tension with Thomas Meighan. Meighan had been with the Lasky Company since 1915, but was considered to be only a pleasant leading man. However, when he took one of the four leading roles in *The Miracle Man* (Mayflower Photoplay Corp./Paramount-Artcraft, 1919) and fell heir to the lead in *Male and Female*, Meighan began to develop a new sense of his value to the studio. The actor's contract with Famous Players-Lasky was up for renewal just before the two pictures were scheduled for release, and he took a calculated risk that the company would be forced to gamble on his future box-office potential.

"Am having difficulty making [Thomas] Meighan see anything reasonable," DeMille wrote on August 30, 1919. "He wishes to wait until [attorney Nathan] Burkan gets here [to Hollywood] before talking. He is at present asking twelve [hundred and] fifty [dollars a week] for first year, two thousand for second year and one thousand dollar raises for each additional year. His head is quite turned with The Miracle Man. Meighan has given his word he will not talk business with anyone else until we definitely fail to reach an agreement."[10]

Famous Players-Lasky and Meighan reached an understanding, and the spectacular success of *The Miracle Man* (released September 4, 1919) virtually dictated that he should play the lead in the new DeMille special. The big returns generated by *Male and Female* (released November 16, 1919) further confirmed the studio's wisdom in renewing Meighan's contract. Although the director resented Meighan's inflated sense of self-worth, the fact remains that *Male and Female*, *Why Change Your Wife?*, and *Manslaughter*, which also starred Meighan, were DeMille's most successful pictures in the late 1910s and early 1920s. Only *The Affairs of Anatol* matched the performance of the Meighan pictures, and it featured the equally popular Wallace Reid. Box-office returns on DeMille's pictures with Elliott Dexter, Conrad Nagel, and Milton Sills, although substantial, simply did not compare.

Although *Why Change Your Wife?* is little more than a simple reversal on the theme of *Don't Change Your Husband*, it represents a distinct advance on DeMille's earlier social comedies. The humor is observant, pointed, and beautifully played, especially by Gloria Swanson, and the scenario by Sada Cowan and Olga Printzlau has a subtlety lacking in Jeanie Macpherson's work. For once the humor comes not only from the situations and the subtitles, but also from a delightful sense of visual wit that adds a dimension lacking in the earlier pictures.

Each scene in *Why Change Your Wife?* contrasts with another. A shot of the husband, Thomas Meighan, and his girlfriend, Bebe Daniels, huddled on the couch at an illicit midnight rendezvous is juxtaposed with a shot of the demanding wife, Gloria Swanson, turning down the twin beds at home. Bebe Daniels doffs her slip as she models a negligee, while Gloria Swanson puts her slip on when she wears the same diaphanous nightgown. Thomas Meighan has perilous adventures in shaving with both Swanson and Daniels, and in a brilliant comic reversal of melodramatic convention, ex-wife Swanson locks herself in a room with current wife Daniels to fight over the privilege of whose bed the concussion-befuddled Meighan will go to. Despite the fact that DeMille took on the project as a matter of convenience, *Why Change Your Wife?* turned out to be an outstanding artistic and commercial success.

# Something to Think About

A Famous Players-Lasky Super Production. A Paramount-Artcraft Picture. A Cecil B. DeMille Production. Director: Cecil B. DeMille. Original story and scenario by Jeanie Macpherson. Art director: Wilfred Buckland. Production manager: Howard Higgin. Photography: Alvin Wyckoff and Karl Struss. Film editor: Anne Bauchens

Picture started: January 20, 1920. Picture finished: March 30, 1920. Length: 7,140 feet (seven reels). Cost: $169,330.00. Released: October 3, 1920. Gross: $915,848.51

Cast: Elliott Dexter (David Markley), Claire McDowell (his housekeeper), Theodore Roberts (Luke Anderson), Gloria Swanson (his daughter, Ruth), Monte Blue (Jim Dirk), Theodore Kosloff (jester, at the circus), Julia Faye (Alice Blair), Mickey Moore (Bobby), James Mason (a masher), Togo Yammamoto (a servant), Guy Oliver, and Agnes Ayres

In addition to *The Wanderer*, Cecil B. DeMille also had his eye on Richard Walton Tully's *Bird of Paradise* as a future picture property. As he went into production on *Why Change Your Wife?*, DeMille heard that George Loane Tucker, director of *The Miracle Man,* was planning to make a film of Tully's play. He complained to Lasky and was told to "PAY NO ATTENTION TO TUCKER'S STATEMENTS YOU WILL POSITIVELY GET BIRD OF PARADISE PROVIDED WE ARE ABLE TO ACQUIRE IT."[1]

*Bird of Paradise* remained an elusive property, and plans to produce *The Wanderer* evaporated with Paramount's need for more and cheaper specials. Instead Jeanie Macpherson and DeMille concocted *Something to Think About*, a confused allegorical tale that is long on symbolism and short on substance.

Again, the scenario borrows elements from several sources. The central symbol of Life being tested in God's forge comes from a passage in Henry Wadsworth Longfellow's poem "The Village Blacksmith," and there is a reasonable possibility that F.N. Westcott's 1916 novel *Dabney Todd*, which centers around a blacksmith and his daughter, provided some inspiration as well. The Greek legend of Pygmalion also added to the mix.[2]

Even *The Wanderer* was used in framing *Something to Think About*. The biblical play is a retelling of the parable of the prodigal son. In Macpherson's scenario, Ruth Anderson is the prodigal who is never turned away by her Heavenly Father because she never denies God—as does her father, Luke Anderson—and never worships false idols—as does her suitor, David Markley.[3]

The box-office success of *The Miracle Man* was a consideration in developing a modern story with a religious theme, and Claire McDowell's upturned heavenly gazes in *Something to Think About* are reminiscent of Joseph J. Dowling's similar poses in George Loane Tucker's picture.

Elliott Dexter was sufficiently recovered to resume his screen career, but in the best nineteenth-century tradition of tailoring a vehicle to the talents and limitations of a starring player, DeMille and Macpherson incorporated the actor's condition into their story. "Elliott Dexter was . . . slightly lamed after his illness," wrote DeMille, "and Jeanie Macpherson wrote the scenario around a lame man's frustrated and embittered but finally victorious search for love."[4]

As with many of the later DeMille-Macpherson religious stories, fate and redemption strike an uneasy balance, but in *Something to Think About* the issue seems especially muddled. The central conflict develops when Ruth Anderson elopes with the man she loves, leaving her father and handicapped fiancé-benefactor behind. Both men are embittered, and the father is blinded in an accident. Although Ruth is the catalyst for all the misery that befalls the characters, she is not the one to receive the religious conversion. One could say that her actions are inspired by love, whereas Markley and her father are motivated by a desire to exert control over her, and therefore she is not touched by the hatred that withers their souls. However, such a reading cannot account for other elements in the story.

A carnival clown serves as a stand-in for the devil, offering misleading prophesies. A thieving derelict serves as an inspirational motivator, even as he picks Ruth Anderson's pocket. Markley's housekeeper is the instrument of divine intervention, although she has no active role in the story, and Markley's worship of idols (he collects the religious art of vanished cultures) is more benign than sacrilegious. The only message in *Something to Think About* that can be gleaned with any degree of certainty is that the Lord works in mysterious ways.

In her autobiography Gloria Swanson claims that she and Elliott Dexter had little regard for the script, but this was a latter-day assessment. The story offered Swanson a real star turn in which she goes from school girl, to young woman, to social outcast, to society matron. The part definitely had range, even if it was lacking in dramatic consistency, and Swanson clearly enjoyed the opportunity to show off her talents in the multifaceted role.

What is striking about *Something to Think About* is the look of the picture. Wilfred Buckland's sets are economical, yet eye-filling, and DeMille made greater use of exterior locations than he had in several years. The photography has an almost three-dimensional quality, due largely to the contribution of Karl Struss. Originally hired in 1919 to shoot stills, Struss quickly proved himself to be a capable cinematographer, and Alvin Wyckoff was again forced to share screen credit.

At seven reels, *Something to Think About* is much shorter than *Male and Female* and *Why Change Your Wife?*, but even with less footage the movie feels padded. Audiences didn't seem to mind, however. Despite costing more than *Why Change Your Wife?* and grossing less, the picture was still highly successful. It seemed as if DeMille could do no wrong.

# 39

# Forbidden Fruit

A Famous Players-Lasky Super Production. A Paramount-Artcraft Picture. A Cecil B. DeMille Production. Director: Cecil B. DeMille. Original story and scenario by Jeanie Macpherson. Art director: Wilfred Buckland. Photography: Alvin Wyckoff and Karl Struss. Production manager: Howard Higgin. Costumes: Claire West (department head), Mitchell Leisen, and Natasha Rambova

Picture started: July 13, 1920. Picture completed: October 2, 1920. Cost: $339,752.00. Length: 7,941 feet (eight reels). Released: February 13, 1921. Gross: $848,121.87

Cast: Agnes Ayres (Mary Maddock), Clarence Burton (Steve Maddock), Forrest Stanley (Nelson Rogers), Theodore Roberts (Mr. Mallory), Kathlyn Williams (Mrs. Mallory), Theodore Kosloff (Giuseppe, the butler), Winter Hall (the bishop), Shannon Day (Nadia Craig), Bertram Johns (John Craig), and Julia Faye (maid)

F amous Players-Lasky was reluctant to give DeMille the green light on a big picture and anxious to break up the director's winning team of leading players. Gloria Swanson and Bebe Daniels demonstrated enough box-office appeal to be handed over to less-expensive directors, and the studio felt that the market for historical spectacles was still unpredictable. Searching for his next picture in this atmosphere, DeMille returned to one of his earlier successes.

While *Forbidden Fruit* has many virtues, it lacks the intensity and simplicity of its predecessor, *The Golden Chance*. Jeanie Macpherson's basic scenario remains intact, but there are significant alterations: A fantasy sequence added by DeMille and Macpherson points up the parallels to Cinderella and pares down the wretched details of the heroine's home life. The hard-edged original was further embellished with a happy ending designed to meet audience expectations and downplay the moral ambiguity of the tale. These changes contribute little, although the Cinderella sequences (scattered throughout the picture rather than isolated in a single flashback episode) are extraordinary in design.

*Forbidden Fruit* demonstrates DeMille's use of visual motifs to convey character. The meddling Mrs. Mallory is seen manipulating tiny paper-doll cutouts of a dinner-party seating planner—she manipulates people's lives as well. Mary Maddock's predicament is visualized by the wedding ring that traps her in a frustrating relationship and a wild orchid offered by her new love. Mary also owns a caged bird that only wants to sing, but her husband tries to silence its song. These illustrative metaphors are far from subtle, but they are used with effect.

The standout sequence in *Forbidden Fruit* is Maddock's burglary of the Mallory home. Unaware that his wife is a weekend houseguest, Maddock enters a bedroom in the middle of the night to steal Mrs. Mallory's jewels. In the dim glow of his flashlight, Maddock approaches the bed. Just as he realizes he is about to rape his own wife, Mary wakes up to see Maddock's half-lit face hovering inches above her head. The scene at the bed in *The Golden Chance* is dramatic and disturbing, but it is mostly played in a single shot that takes in all the action. In *Forbidden Fruit* DeMille pulled out all the stops, carefully building a sequence of shots that blend suspense, sexual voyeurism, and terror in a cinematic tour de force.

DeMille also managed to make a sly and biting comment on Prohibition. With the nation preoccupied by World War I and under pressure from the Anti-Saloon League, the Women's Christian Temperance Union, and other special interest groups, Congress voted to submit a constitutional amendment to the states in December 1917. The amendment read: "After one year from the ratification of this article the manufacture, sale, or transportation of intoxicating liquors within, the importation thereof into, or the exportation thereof from the United States and all territory subject to the jurisdiction thereof for beverage purposes is hereby prohibited." With the approval of forty-six of the forty-eight states, Prohibition became the law of the land on January 16, 1920. Contempt for the law was not universal, but it was immediately apparent the nation's elected representatives had voted with their campaign contributors rather than with the majority view on the issue. The muddle-headed amendment failed to prohibit the purchase or consumption of alcohol, and it also ignored basic human nature. With Prohibition came increased desire for the new forbidden fruit, and a bootleg industry in rum-running and bathtub gin sprang up to supply the demand.[1]

Surprisingly, Hollywood paid Prohibition little attention, either ignoring the subject entirely or picturing it as a mere inconvenience. Booze was glorified on-screen in the guise of stock characters like the witty and urbane drunk, the go-getter with a silver hip flask, or the friendly boot-legger with a satchel full of illicit brew. Invariably the satchel was dropped, or run over by a car, or mistaken for a lady's overnight bag. Occasionally a fatal glass of beer would lead to dire consequences on-screen, but more often than not Hollywood treated the consumption of John Barleycorn in a humorous vein throughout the 1920s.

DeMille showed the hypocrisy inherent in the law by contrasting the consumption of alcohol in different social strata. At a skid-row "social club," frequented by Maddock and the conniving Giuiseppe, alcohol is scarce and kept hidden behind the counter, while at the affluent Mallory home, liquor is openly served at a dinner party and even the visiting church bishop has a cocktail in hand.

Just as DeMille was forced to replace Edna Goodrich in *The Golden Chance*, he also encountered casting problems making *Forbidden Fruit*. King Baggot, a screen idol from the early 1910s, and Ann Forrest were originally slated to play leading roles, but both were replaced. Baggot was too mature looking and too well established as a screen hero to be truly effective in the part of the villainous Steve Maddock. He later became a director, but alcohol was his downfall; he ended his career in the 1940s working as an extra. Baggot was replaced by Clarence Burton, who became one of DeMille's favorite character actors. Ann Forrest was another Triangle Film Corporation alumna. She received several choice roles at Famous Players-Lasky, including the female lead in *The Faith Healer* (1921), but her screen career came to an end in the mid-1920s. Agnes Ayres, who gained a certain fame as Rudolph Valentino's leading lady in *The Sheik* (Famous Players-Lasky, 1921), took over the role of Mary Maddock.

Karl Struss again shared photography credit with Alvin Wyckoff. An article titled "What the Cameraman Needs to Advance in His Profession," published under Wyckoff's byline in the January 22, 1921, issue of *Motion Picture News*, offers some insight into his attitude about the role of the cinematographer. At the time, fellow cinematographer Phil Rosen was making a name for himself as a director, and former camera-man Irvin Willat was highly regarded as the director of *Behind the Door* (Ince-Paramount-Artcraft, 1919) and *Below the Surface* (Ince-Paramount-Artcraft, 1920). Wyckoff had the itch to follow suit.

"When a film corporation looks around for a new director the most logical man to fill that position should be a cameraman . . . ," wrote Wyckoff. "Logically, a good cameraman should be promoted and should be able to advance, either to the position of assistant to a very successful director or producer, or to the position of director when he could first be entrusted with a small picture until he is able to build himself higher. A good cameraman who has become a director could thus be in a position to supervise the work of a cameraman who is not so successful and through his knowledge and cooperation, build up the latter until he, in turn, is ready to advance."[2]

Wyckoff was obviously fishing for a move up, but neither DeMille nor Paramount acted on his thinly veiled piece of self-promotion.

Although *Forbidden Fruit* was thought to be a film that could be made quickly and inexpensively, it proved to be a costly production. The elaborate Cinderella fantasy sequences and the casting changes contributed to budget overruns, and the shooting schedule stretched to two and a half months. The added costs did nothing to enhance the picture's market potential. *Forbidden Fruit* did respectable box-office business, but the returns were disappointing after the astronomical grosses generated by *Why Change Your Wife?* and *Male and Female.*

# 40

# The Affairs of Anatol

A Famous Players-Lasky Super Production. A Paramount Picture. A Cecil B. DeMille Production. Director: Cecil B. DeMille. Scenario by Jeanie Macpherson, Beulah Marie Dix, Lorna Moon, and Elmer Harris, suggested by the play *Anatol* by Arthur Schnitzler and the paraphrase thereof by Granville Barker. Art director: Paul Iribe. Photography: Alvin Wyckoff and Karl Struss. Film editor: Anne Bauchens

Picture started: December 2, 1920. Picture finished: January 25, 1921. Length: 9,002 feet (later cut to 8,813 feet) (nine reels). Cost: $176,508.08. Released: September 25, 1921. Gross: $1,191,789.19

Cast: Wallace Reid (Anatol DeWitt Spencer), Elliott Dexter (Max Runyon), Gloria Swanson (Vivian, Anatol's wife), Wanda Hawley (Emilie Dixon, a jazz girl), Theodore Roberts (Gordon Bronson), Theodore Kosloff (Nazzer Singh, a Hindu), Agnes Ayres (Annie Elliott, a country girl), Monte Blue (Abner, her husband), Bebe Daniels (Satan Synne, the wickedest woman in New York), Polly Moran (orchestra leader), Raymond Hatton (Hoffmeier), Julia Faye (Tibra), Winter Hall (Dr. Johnson), Charles Ogle (Dr. Bowles), Guy Oliver (butler), Ruth Miller (maid), Lucien Littlefield (valet), Zelma Maja (nurse), Shannon Day (chorus girl), Elinor Glyn and Lady Parker (bridge players), William Boyd, Maud Wayne, Fred Huntley, and Alma Bennett

Jesse Lasky arranged to acquire Arthur Schnitzler's play *Anatol* and recommended it to DeMille, suggesting that it serve as "a sort of sentimental farewell appearance of [Gloria] Swanson, [Bebe] Daniels, [Wanda] Hawley, and [Agnes] Ayres" as members of the DeMille stock company. DeMille couldn't have been happy that the studio wanted to break up his unit, and he complained that Schnitzler's play of revolving romances would be difficult to bring to the screen. He lost the battle. Lasky recommended that the title be changed to *Five Kisses* (for Anatol's five affairs of the heart) and announced it as the next Cecil B. DeMille special production.[1]

DeMille's adaptation of *Anatol* was twice removed from the original, for it was freely adapted from Granville Barker's English "paraphrase" of the German-language play and owed more to Jeanie

Macpherson and Beulah Marie Dix than to Arthur Schnitzler. But if it lacks some of Schnitzler's effervescent bite, the picture is still an engaging entertainment and a fitting climax to DeMille's cycle of films with Gloria Swanson and Bebe Daniels.

With a long-suppressed desire to direct and a dissatisfaction over the modest salary Famous Players-Lasky paid him, Wilfred Buckland quit the studio to join director Allan Dwan's independent company.[2] With the cost overruns on *Forbidden Fruit*, Famous Players-Lasky was probably relieved to see him leave.

Buckland's association with Allan Dwan led to his selection as art director on *Douglas Fairbanks in Robin Hood* (Fairbanks/United Artists, 1922), which Dwan directed. Dwan signed with Famous Players-Lasky after completing *Robin Hood*, and Buckland's career went into virtual eclipse. DeMille brought Buckland back to Famous Players-Lasky to design a primeval forest for *Adam's Rib*. He also hired Buckland when he set up his own studio in 1925, and brought him to M-G-M in 1928. However, despite some co-credits as art director on two DeMille Studio productions in 1927, Buckland worked largely as a production illustrator after 1923.[3]

The French art nouveau stylist Paul Iribe was selected to replace Buckland. A multifaceted talent, Iribe was an illustrator, fashion designer, interior decorator, and furniture maker. His work came to the attention of Jesse Lasky, who introduced the artist to DeMille. Iribe created one of Gloria Swanson's costumes for *Male and Female*, and served as art director on the George Fitzmaurice production *The Right to Love* (Famous Players-Lasky, 1920) before joining the DeMille unit on *The Affairs of Anatol*. The artist became a valued member of DeMille's staff, although costumer Mitchell Leisen accused Iribe of taking the glory and leaving much of the real work to others.[4]

DeMille thought highly of Iribe's work, even though the two men clashed on numerous occasions. Perhaps because Buckland had been denied a real opportunity to direct, DeMille even sponsored Paul Iribe as a director—although he kept the Frenchman on a short leash. As a filmmaker Iribe was invariably partnered with co-director Frank Urson; the pair became known as the "U and I team."

Iribe's contribution to the look of DeMille's films was a subtle one. In many ways he simply followed the style and approach Buckland established in *Don't Change Your Husband*, *Male and Female*, and *Why Change Your Wife?* The difference was that Buckland was merely influenced by art nouveau, while Iribe was one of its leading practitioners.

Throughout the silent era DeMille experimented with color effects for his black-and-white pictures. The earliest films were tinted (amber for interiors, blue for night, etc.), but beginning with *Joan the Woman*, DeMille also employed an elaborate, stencil color process to create the impression of full color photography. In original prints of *The Affairs of Anatol*, the subtitle art and many of the more-or-less static establishing shots took on the lovely purple, yellow, green, and pink hues familiar in hand-colored photographs, adding greatly to the mood and artistic effect.[5]

Considering the high cost of *Forbidden Fruit*, *The Affairs of Anatol* came in for a modest $176,500. The figure is deceptive, however. When DeMille and Anne Bauchens assembled *Five Kisses*, the picture was deemed too long. They deleted one of the "kisses," and changed the title of the shortened picture to *The Affairs of Anatol*. The deleted sequence featured three of the studio's top stars, and it seemed a shame to waste the footage, so Famous Players-Lasky "bought back" the deleted sequence from Cecil B. DeMille Productions, considerably reducing the final audited production cost of *The Affairs of Anatol*. With the aid of new subtitles, a revised storyline by Lorna Moon, and additional footage directed by former DeMille assistant Sam Wood, the episode was transformed into a five-reel program feature titled *Don't Tell Everything*. The cut-and-paste effort received a less than grand premiere in Des Moines, Iowa, but the test engagement proved successful enough, and *Don't Tell Everything* went into general release in December 1921.

After the relatively disappointing performance of the costly *Forbidden Fruit*, *The Affairs of Anatol* proved to be another box-office bonanza.

# 41

# Fool's Paradise

Famous Players-Lasky Super Production for Paramount release. A Cecil B. DeMille Production. Director: Cecil B. DeMille. Scenario by Beulah Marie Dix and Sada Cowan, from the story "The Laurels and the Lady" by Leonard Merrick. Photography: Alvin Wyckoff and Karl Struss. Film editor: Anne Bauchens

Picture started: April 4, 1921. Picture finished: June 2, 1921. Length: 8,847 feet (nine reels). Cost: $291,367.56. Released: December 9, 1921. Gross: $906,937.79

Cast: Dorothy Dalton (Poll Patchouli), Conrad Nagel (Arthur Phelps), Mildred Harris (Rosa Duchene), Theodore Kosloff (John Rodriguez), Clarence Burton (Manuel), John Davidson (Prince Talaat-Ni), Julia Faye (Samaran, his chief wife), Guy Oliver (Briggs), Jacqueline Logan (Girda), and Kamuela Searle (Kay)

Novelist Francis Marion Crawford once said, "In art of all kinds the moral lesson is a mistake." Cecil B. DeMille would have disagreed. The filmmaker delighted in building screen stories that offered a liaison with a lesson, and he would have embraced critic George Jean Nathan's comment that "Great art is as irrational as great music. It is mad with its own loveliness." While one could argue whether or not *Fool's Paradise* is great art, there is no question that it is "irrational" and "mad with its own loveliness"—it is also highly entertaining.

Wounded in the Great War, Arthur Phelps is nursed to health by a volunteer nurse, Rosa Duchene. Phelps falls in love with Rosa, not realizing that she cares only for the "finer things in life." Returning to his work in the oil fields on the Mexican border, Phelps rescues Poll Patchouli, a fiery Mexican saloon dancer, from the homicidal intentions of Rodriguez. Poll falls in love with Phelps, but he spurns her attentions. The dancer gives the oil engineer an exploding cigar. With eyes already weakened by his war wound, Phelps is blinded. He curses Poll and refuses to have anything to do with her. Later, however, he hears the dancer imitate Rosa's French accent, and thinks the love of his life has come to look after him again. Reluctantly, Poll keeps up the impersonation to be close to Phelps. Learning of an operation that might cure Phelps's blindness, Poll makes the supreme sacrifice. She pays for the operation that will destroy Phelps's illusions. When Phelps regains his sight, he leaves Poll in search of Rosa and finds her living as a kept woman in the court of a Siamese prince. Unable to decide between the two men, Rosa tosses her glove into a crocodile pit and promises to go with the man who retrieves it. The prince enters the pit and is nearly killed by the reptiles. Phelps rescues his rival, and realizing Rosa's selfish nature, he returns to Texas and Poll's true love. The plotting is extravagant and improbable, but the premise is fascinating—not unlike the underlying theme of Alfred Hitchcock's *Vertigo* (Paramount, 1958).[1]

The screenplay for *Fool's Paradise* was adapted by Sada Cowan and Beulah Marie Dix from a short story by Leonard Merrick. Dix, a friend and former client of the DeMille Play Agency, came to Los Angeles for a four-month visit in 1916 at the invitation of Cecil's mother, Beatrice. The four-month vacation turned into a twenty-year stay, and Dix became a successful screenwriter, working first with William deMille. She shared Cecil B. DeMille's enthusiasm for historical detail and clearly influenced the development of the director's dramatic tastes.[2]

DeMille's skills as a director are often overlooked in the trappings of melodrama and decor that are so much a part of his work, but Mitchell Leisen remembered that "He directed the actors well. He had very positive ideas about what he wanted, and he wasn't satisfied until he got it."[3] Dorothy Dalton, the star of *Fool's Paradise*, was an actress of uneven talent. She came to the studio in the deal that brought Thomas H. Ince to Paramount-Artcraft in 1917. Dalton was a personal favorite of Ince (they were said to be lovers), and Zukor had no interest in picking up her contract. Her performance in director George Melford's *Moran of the Lady Letty* (Famous Players-Lasky, 1922) is virtually catatonic, while under DeMille's guidance she becomes a full-blooded, even exciting, screen personality. At the end of her Paramount contract, Dorothy Dalton retired and married producer Arthur Hammerstein in 1924.

Mildred Harris, who had been in films from age nine, was Charlie Chaplin's first wife, and they were only recently divorced when she made *Fool's Paradise*. Harris was one of many players DeMille helped through the years. She had a small part in *The Warrens of Virginia* in 1915 and was still doing bits in DeMille films into the 1940s when no one else in Hollywood had a part to offer.

The year 1921 saw dramatic developments in the motion picture industry. The public again became interested in large-scale historical pictures like *Orphans of the Storm* (Griffith-United Artists, 1921), *The Three Musketeers* (Fairbanks-United Artists, 1921), and *The Queen of Sheba* (Fox Film Corporation, 1921). The American product was bolstered by the release of several German spectacles, including *Madame Du Barry* (released in the United States as *Passion*), *Carmen* (released as *Gypsy Blood*), and *Anna Boleyn* (released as *Deception*). At the same time, the United States experienced a severe economic downturn that resulted in cutbacks at the studios.

While conditions improved relatively quickly, executives at Famous Players-Lasky were understandably concerned over expenses. DeMille was asked to trim his production costs, but the director complained that budget restraints would result in reduced quality, and he couldn't help being upset that others in the industry were being given the opportunity to make the sort of big pictures he longed to produce. Through his attorney, Neil McCarthy, DeMille urged Jesse Lasky to increase the budget for *Fool's Paradise*. Lasky took the request to the studio finance committee and succeeded in raising the budget, but at great political cost. He telegraphed DeMille on Friday afternoon, May 27, 1921:

WIRED YOU LAST NIGHT AFTER FINANCE
COMMITTEE MEETING APPROVING ADDITIONAL
EXPENDITURE FOR [Fool's Paradise]. . . . TONE OF
YOUR WIRES WHICH [are] APPARENTLY DICTATED
BY [attorney Neil] MC CARTHY ARE CREATING
SITUATION WHICH I DO NOT LIKE. MR. ZUKOR AND I
AFTER LONG AND SERIOUS TALK URGE THAT YOU
LEAVE FOR NEW YORK DAY AFTER YOU FINISH
SHOOTING IF POSSIBLE. REST ON TRAIN WILL DO
YOU GOOD AND WE FEEL YOUR PRESENCE
ABSOLUTELY NECESSARY TO BRING ABOUT
BETTER UNDERSTANDING [on] BOTH SIDES. ALSO
NECESSARY [to] PLAN AND DISCUSS FUTURE
POLICY [on] DE MILLE PRODUCTIONS AND
ARRANGE AMOUNT EXPENDITURES. PLEASE BE
ADVISED BY ME THERE CAN BE NOTHING MORE
IMPORTANT THAN YOUR COMING HERE FOR ONLY
TWO OR THREE DAYS CONFERENCE SOON AS

POSSIBLE. EXTRAORDINARY CONDITIONS ARE
DEVELOPING IN INDUSTRY WHICH YOU SHOULD
STUDY AT FIRST HAND. FOR YOUR INFORMATION [it
is] ABSOLUTELY NECESSARY WE CLOSE NEW YORK
STUDIO IMMEDIATELY MAKING ALL PRODUCTIONS
IN HOLLYWOOD. IMPERATIVE WE REDUCE COST OF
ALL OUR PRODUCT. I LEAVE HERE JUNE ELEVENTH
AND EXPECT [to] ACCOMPLISH IMMEDIATE
REDUCTION ALL THROUGH STUDIO
ORGANIZATION. . . . MY RELATION WITH COMPANY
VERY HAPPY. I FULLY APPROVE ALL POLICIES AND
EXECUTIVE AND FINANCE COMMITTEES [are]
WORKING AS HARMONIOUS WHOLE. FEEL FEW
DAYS HERE WOULD CHANGE YOUR WHOLE
ATTITUDE TOWARD COMPANY AND YOU SIMPLY
CANNOT AFFORD TO LET MISUNDERSTANDING
GROW.[4]

As DeMille's Famous Players-Lasky contract came up for renewal
in 1921, several companies approached the filmmaker with tantalizing
propositions. United Artists offered a salary of $300,000 per picture, and
First National proposed a deal that would give DeMille a total of $1
million per picture to cover salary and production costs. DeMille felt a
certain loyalty to Famous Players-Lasky, but wrote Jesse Lasky, "I do
believe that I should share somewhat more in the success of my [pic-
tures]. . . . Having avowed my intention and desire to remain with the
company I want to let the matter rest with you and Mr. Zukor and I feel
sure I can abide by your decision. I know of no other way to show where
my heart is."[5]

Famous Players-Lasky offered a salary of $6,500 a week to be ad-
vanced against a gross production budget of $290,000 per picture. In
addition, DeMille was to receive a percentage of gross revenues from
worldwide distribution of his future pictures based on a sliding scale.[6]
The contract was generous. Adolph Zukor could not afford to lose DeMille,
but he wasn't certain he could afford to keep him either.

# Saturday Night

Famous Players-Lasky for Paramount release. A Cecil B. DeMille Production. Director: Cecil B. DeMille. Original story and scenario by Jeanie Macpherson. Art director: Paul Iribe. Photography: Alvin Wyckoff. Film editor: Anne Bauchens

Picture started: September 26, 1921. Picture finished: January 2, 1922. Length: 8,597 feet (nine reels). Cost: $224,635.05. Released: February 5, 1922. Gross: $753,807.83

Cast: Edith Roberts (Shamrock O'Day), Sylvia Ashton (her mother), Jack Mower (Tom McGuire), Leatrice Joy (Iris Van Suydam), Conrad Nagel (Richard Prentiss), Edythe Chapman (his mother), Julia Faye (Elsie Prentiss), Theodore Roberts (uncle), John Davidson (the count), James Neill (Tompkins), and Winter Hall (the professor)

W ith the recession at its height, and past budgetary indiscretions to be accounted for, DeMille was under pressure from Famous Players-Lasky to limit the cost of his next picture to $150,000. *Saturday Night* was designed to be produced inexpensively. There was no historic flashback or dream sequence, and the actors (with the exception of Conrad Nagel) were selected for economy rather than star power. Jack Mower and Edith Roberts were both moderately popular players who spent the better part of their careers in Universal program pictures. Leatrice Joy was "at liberty" after an engagement with the struggling Goldwyn Company. Even with the drive for economy, however, DeMille found it impossible to make the picture for the budgeted figure. Lasky again interceded, and the budget was increased 50 percent.

*Saturday Night* turned into an impressive production. Though the settings lack some of the conscious style of earlier DeMille pictures, the film offers an uninhibited Halloween pool party, a spectacular tenement fire, and a brightly lit Coney Island midway.

"Paul Iribe was DeMille's French art director," recalled Mitchell Leisen, Iribe's assistant on *Saturday Night*.

I used to have knock-down drag-out fights with him and he'd

fire me. . . . At the end of the day, Iribe would suddenly drop everything on my shoulders and go home. I remember one time I worked all night long trying to get a set for a big carnival sort of thing [the Coney Island set for *Saturday Night*]. At 6:00 in the morning, I decided that I would go home and take a bath, and then come back and finish up what had to be done. I fell asleep on the bathroom floor and I didn't wake up until 10:00. I tore back to the studio and Iribe was in flames because he had to go back in there and finish this thing up. That was one of the times I got fired; maybe it was the last, I can't remember. Eventually I heard Douglas Fairbanks needed somebody to do costumes [on *Robin Hood*], so I took that job instead of trying to get back in Iribe's good graces.[1]

At the time *Saturday Night* was in production, Leatrice Joy was married to actor John Gilbert. According to their daughter, Joy's work with DeMille led to the breakup of their marriage. Gilbert was jealous of his wife's success and accused her of having an affair with the director, and the arguments between husband and wife began to affect her work in the picture. DeMille threatened to replace the actress, telling her, "Miss Joy, your work must come first. If it doesn't, then you and I will have no reason to continue together. Is that perfectly clear?" Leatrice Joy, not about to throw away her opportunity to be seen in a DeMille picture, left her husband to pursue her career.[2] She became one of Cecil B. DeMille's favorite players. Like Gloria Swanson, Joy graduated from two-reel comedies, bit parts, and leads in modest features.

The real star of *Saturday Night*, however, is Edith Roberts. Born in 1901 (or 1899 according to some sources), Roberts was on stage from the age of six. Her first screen work came with Al Christie's Nestor brand comedies, and by 1917 she was starring in Bluebird brand features for Universal. In *Saturday Night* she shows a vivacious charm, and it is pity she never worked again with DeMille. Her career lasted to the end of the silent era, but she never became a top box-office attraction. Edith Roberts died in 1935 from complications of childbirth.

For all the compromise that went into its creation, *Saturday Night* turned out to be one of DeMille's very best films—genuinely funny, and at the same time touching, thrilling, and even tragic. The characters are vividly etched, the counterpoint between the two doomed relationships neatly handled, and the film's visual touches deftly applied.

The story essentially picks up where *Male and Female* leaves off. Tom McGuire, a chauffeur, rescues and marries Iris Van Suydam, a society girl. Her fiancé, Richard Prentiss, falls head-over-heels for Shamrock O'Day, a laundry maid, and, breaking his engagement, marries the tenement girl. The consequences are devastating. The once-poor girl feels ill at ease in society, and the rich girl can't get used to living in a one-room flat perched next to the "el" tracks. The couples eventually change partners. As in *The Golden Chance*, DeMille and Macpherson end *Saturday Night* on an ambiguous and downbeat note. Shamrock O'Day and Tom McGuire find happiness together, while Richard Prentiss and Iris Van Suydam become resigned that they should marry—even if they aren't really in love.

Though DeMille relied on many of his favorite story devices, they take on a new depth in *Saturday Night*. Even the "trial by fire" (an element of *Joan the Woman*, *Triumph*, *The Road to Yesterday*, and *The Godless Girl*) was given a complex dramatic edge. Leatrice Joy's character prefers death in the tenement fire to life without her great love, even though she knows they can never be happy together.

Ultimately, *Saturday Night* is a subversive film. It dares to suggest that "they" may not live happily ever after. DeMille flirted with this theme in *Don't Change Your Husband* and *Why Change Your Wife?*, but in those pictures the would-be rovers come to the realization that things at home aren't so bad after all. Here, the message is that an alliance based on romantic expectations can be a living hell. Little wonder that the picture did not attain the popularity of DeMille's previous social comedies.

# 43

# Manslaughter

Famous Players-Lasky for Paramount release. A Cecil B. DeMille Production. Director: Cecil B. DeMille. Scenario by Jeanie Macpherson, from the
novel by Alice Duer Miller. Art director: Paul Iribe. Choreography: Theodore
Kosloff. Photography: Alvin Wyckoff and L. Guy Wilky. Film editor: Anne
Bauchens

Picture started: May 2, 1922. Picture finished: June 17, 1922. Length: 9,680
feet (later cut to 9,218 feet) (ten reels). Cost: $384,111.14. Released: Sep-
tember 25, 1922. Gross: $1,206,014.65

Cast: Leatrice Joy (Lydia Thorne), Thomas Meighan (Daniel O'Bannon), Jack
Mower (Officer Drummond), Julia Faye (his wife), George Fawcett (Judge
Homans), Jack Miltern (Governor Albee), Dorothy Cumming (Eleanor), Edythe
Chapman (Adeline Bennett), Lois Wilson (Evans, Lydia's maid), Casson
Ferguson (Bobby Dorset), James Neill (butler), Mickey Moore (Dicky Evans),
Sylvia Ashton (prison matron), Raymond Hatton (Brown), Lucien Littlefield
(witness), Shannon Day (Miss Santa Claus), Guy Oliver (musician), Charles
Ogle (doctor), Edward Martindel (Wiley), Mabel Van Buren, Ethel Wales,
Dale Fuller (prisoners), Louise Lester, and George Field

How does one explain *Manslaughter*? On one hand it was an important picture for DeMille—his most expensive and one of his most
successful films to date, with thematic elements that reverberated through
his later work. On the other hand, the script was weak, the staging inept,
and the settings lackluster. *Manslaughter* exhibits all of the excesses and
none of the virtues evident in the director's other work.

After completing *Saturday Night*, DeMille went on a European vacation accompanied by his Japanese valet, Yamabe, and art director Paul
Iribe. While in Paris he contracted rheumatic fever. Although not considered fatal, the disease is highly debilitating. Severely swollen joints robbed
DeMille of his ability to move. Confined to bed, and unable to keep food
down, the director felt sure he was at death's door. When he was finally
well enough to make the ocean voyage home, rough seas and mal de mer
contributed to his discomfort. By the time he got back to Hollywood,
DeMille was a physical wreck. It was April 1922 before he was able to

walk around the grounds of his Hollywood home, and *Manslaughter* went before the cameras on May 2.[1]

DeMille's illness may explain many of the picture's shortcomings. Alice Duer Miller's novel offers strong melodramatic action with a dose of social consciousness. Lydia Thorne is a rich, orphaned playgirl. She bribes a speed cop with a diamond bracelet to ignore her wild driving. Lydia's maid needs money to pay for her child's medical expenses. The rich girl ignores the maid's pleas for a loan and prosecutes when the desperate servant steals her jewels. The district attorney, Dan O'Bannon, loves Lydia but cannot accept her wanton ways. When the speed cop is killed as a result of Lydia's recklessness, O'Bannon vows to send her to jail "for her own good."

While DeMille's dramas are often extravagant, they are usually well constructed. In *Manslaughter*, however, Lydia's expected conversion in prison (with the aid of her former maid) is given the most perfunctory treatment, and O'Bannon's guilt-ridden fall into alcoholic desperation also receives short shrift. The basic plot is strong enough, but Macpherson's script is unfocused, and DeMille's treatment lacks visual finesse. Evelyn F. Scott, daughter of screenwriter Beulah Marie Dix, wrote that her mother "never really thought of . . . [Macpherson] as a writer, but as an exceptional collaborator for an exceptional man. . . . Cecil, with his past experience in writing and acting, knew not only what he required in every story he directed, but in every scene. Jeanie had a genius . . . for putting this on paper."[2] If one accepts Dix's assessment, Macpherson's script must have suffered from DeMille's weakened state.

Through a friend in Detroit Macpherson arranged to have herself anonymously arrested for shoplifting and sent to jail for three days. DeMille claimed that she was doing research—but the arrest and imprisonment had more to do with publicity than perspicacity. Only months earlier Bebe Daniels was arrested for speeding in Orange County and spent time in the county jail. The arrest made headlines, and her crime was glorified with publicity photos of Bebe sitting for a mug shot. Only the cynical believed the star's plight was connected with the release of her picture *The Speed Girl* (Realart, 1921); only the simpleminded presumed that it wasn't. Macpherson's exploit showed the fine hand of the Paramount publicity department.

The driving and motorcycle sequences in *Manslaughter* were largely accomplished through trick photography using the Williams Process. Leatrice Joy and Jack Mower were photographed in the studio against a black velvet drop. The background action plates were shot on location. A high-contrast print was made of the studio footage to create a crude, traveling holdback matte. Then the original negative, the high contrast matte, and the background plate were tri-packed in a step printer, allowing the background to be printed onto the original negative of the foreground action. The illusion could be effective or ludicrous depending on proper exposure and perspective in the backgrounds. The results in *Manslaughter* are decidedly uneven, contributing to the overall slipshod look of the picture.

Although there are no on-screen technical credits, photography on *Manslaughter* was divided between Alvin Wyckoff and L. Guy Wilky.[3] Wilky was an excellent cinematographer who began his career with the Lubin Mfg. Co. southwest unit in 1913. After working at the American Film Company in Santa Barbara and at the Ince-Triangle studio, Wilky joined Famous Players-Lasky and was closely associated with William deMille. Both Wyckoff and Wilky were active in trying to unionize Hollywood cameramen, and both were blacklisted in the late 1920s. Wyckoff found some work in Poverty Row quickies in the 1930s, while Wilky was essentially forced out of the business until the 1950s when the International Photographers Union helped him find work as an assistant cameraman in television production to activate his pension benefits.

*Manslaughter* shows early evidence of DeMille's penchant for giving roles to players who had seen better days. George Field and Louise Lester, who were stars in the nickelodeon era with the American Film Company, and Mabel Van Buren, the star of DeMille's *Girl of the Golden West*, appear in bit parts.

# 44

# Adam's Rib

Famous Players-Lasky for Paramount release. A Cecil B. DeMille Production. Director: Cecil B. DeMille. Original story and scenario by Jeanie Macpherson. Art director: Paul Iribe. Photography: Alvin Wyckoff and L. Guy Wilky. Film editor: Anne Bauchens

Picture started: September 26, 1922. Picture finished: November 27, 1922. Length: 9,530 feet (ten reels). Cost: $408,432.64. Released: February 4, 1923 (Los Angeles premiere). Gross: $881,206.75

Cast: Anna Q. Nilsson (Marian Ramsay), Milton Sills (Michael Ramsay), Pauline Garon (Mathilda "Tillie" Ramsay), Theodore Kosloff (M. Jaromir, king of Moravia), Elliott Dexter (Professor Reade), Julia Faye (the mischievous one), Clarence Geldart (James Kilkenna), George Field (minister to Moravia), Robert Brower (Hugo Kermaier), Forrest Robinson (Kramer), Gino Corrado (Lt. Braschek), Wedgewood Nowell (secretary to the minister), and Clarence Burton (caveman)

DeMille returned to top form with *Adam's Rib*. The picture has a rich, well-made look, and there are many fine moments. Ultimately, however, the film suffers from a reliance on creaky, melodramatic plot devices that dim its overall effect.

The premise is simple: the wild young flapper of today is not so different from the wild young cave girl of several eons ago. Deep down she has heart, soul, and a willingness to sacrifice her own happiness for the happiness of others. The plot devised by Macpherson and DeMille concerns a middle-aged couple and their daughter. Michael Ramsay is a Chicago commodities trader trying to corner the market in wheat. After nineteen years of marriage, Marian Ramsay suffers "the wife's dilemma—a grown daughter and a lost romance." Their teenager, Tillie, "like most children today is left to shift for herself."

Tillie is in love with Professor Reade, a gifted but socially backward paleontologist.[1] Meanwhile, Tillie's mother is being courted by Jaromir, deposed king of Moravia. At the risk of losing her scientist "caveman," Tillie saves her mother's reputation by pretending to cozy up to Jaromir to keep her father from discovering that his wife and the monarch are planning to run off together. When Professor Reade becomes disenchanted over the girl's seeming interest in Jaromir, she explains her actions by telling him a domestic tale of primitive men. One of the better motivated flashbacks in DeMille's work, the prehistoric sequence is visually stunning and serves not only as a vague parallel to modern life, but also foreshadows the action to come in the film. Although Paul Iribe was the primary art director on *Adam's Rib*, Wilfred Buckland returned to create the primitive setting for the flashback. Idealized and realistic at the same time, Buckland's stage-bound forest of ancient redwoods is a fine example of the "imaginative" scenery he sought to bring to the screen.

Where *Manslaughter* is devoid of any visual distinction, *Adam's Rib* amply demonstrates DeMille's visual wit. In the museum after hours Tillie (the modern Eve) pursues Professor Reade (the reluctant Adam) around the skeletons of long-extinct dinosaurs. The scene plays on biblical associations between the first two people and all their ancestors with subtle charm. Later, at a party, Mrs. Ramsay expects to meet Jaromir in the garden. Michael Ramsay suspects his wife and manages to head off the deposed king. Ramsay approaches his wife from behind and puts his hands on her shoulders. Unaware that the man is not Jaromir, Marian Ramsay confesses her love and with closed eyes kisses her devastated husband. She turns away and goes back to the party without realizing the substitution. While the scene might be improbable, DeMille stages the action convincingly, and the impact is much greater than if Ramsay had merely discovered Marian in Jaromir's embrace.

Where *Adam's Rib* fails to be believable, however, is in the resolution of the dramatic situation. As Marian is about to leave with Jaromir, Tillie comes to stop her mother. Michael Ramsay arrives to buy off the king, and both women hide in his apartment. Just as Ramsay is about to discover his wife, Tillie reveals herself as being Jaromir's hidden love. Ramsay is even more devastated—certain that no decent man will marry his daughter now that she has spoiled herself with the likes of Jaromir. This is exactly the sort of moralistic claptrap that DeMille avoided in most of his earlier social comedies, and the melodramatic turn drags *Adam's Rib* down in its final act. What starts out as a defense of the "flapper" turns into a muddled "women's drama."

One problem with the film is the casting. Pauline Garon was a pleasant, nondescript screen personality. DeMille touted her as a major discovery, but Garon had none of the charisma of Gloria Swanson, Bebe

Daniels, or Leatrice Joy. *Adam's Rib* is supposed to be Tillie's story, but attention shifts to the characters played by Anna Q. Nilsson and Milton Sills. Garon simply was not strong enough to carry the picture.

While critics were relatively kind toward *Manslaughter*, they roasted *Adam's Rib* with phrases like "The Ornate DeMille's latest—and worst" and "A silly, piffling screenplay." The last word was written by playwright-critic Robert E. Sherwood in old *Life* magazine: *"Adam's Rib* is somewhat above the usual DeMille standard—which statement may be added to the Dictionary of Faint Praise." 1923 audiences agreed with the critics. While *Manslaughter* piled up huge grosses, returns on *Adam's Rib* fell by a third. With distribution fees and costs for prints and advertising, the picture barely broke even. After five years and ten pictures the DeMille "bedroom" cycle was threadbare.

Buster Keaton offered a devastating parody of the DeMille flashbacks in his first feature, *The Three Ages* (Keaton-Metro, 1923). What had passed for art in 1919 was becoming pretension in 1923.

One factor that contributed to the modest box-office performance of *Adam's Rib* was the growth of Christian fundamentalism in the 1920s. From the founding of the first colonies, Americans have always exhibited strong religious inclinations, but there is a cyclical ebb and flow to the public expression of religious belief. The 1880s saw the growth of camp meetings and religious revivals. In the 1980s the televangelist rose quickly and then fell from favor. While the 1920s are remembered as the Jazz Age, it was also a decade of religious fundamentalism. Evangelists like Billy Sunday and Aimee Semple McPherson were well-known national figures, and the debate pitting creationism against Darwinism raged. The 1925 Dayton, Tennessee, "Monkey" trial of John T. Scopes brought the issue to national attention. Tennessee passed a law forbidding the teaching of evolution, and biology teacher Scopes set out to test the law. Chicago attorney Clarence Darrow came south to handle Scopes's defense; William Jennings Bryan (Democratic presidential candidate in 1896, 1900, and 1908) volunteered his services as assistant to the prosecution. Ultimately Scopes lost, and the Tennessee law was upheld. Given the atmosphere of the time, the scenes of apelike cave people in the *Adam's Rib* flashback were anathema to a sizeable segment of the audience. The relative failure of the picture contributed to the anxiety of Paramount executives as costs began to mount on DeMille's next film, *The Ten Commandments*.

# 45

# The Ten Commandments

Famous Players-Lasky for Paramount release. A Cecil B. DeMille Production. Directed by Cecil B. DeMille. Scenario by Jeanie Macpherson, from a suggestion received through a contest in the *Los Angeles Times*. Art directors: Paul Iribe and Francis McComas. Assistant director: Cullen B. "Hezie" Tate. Photography: Bert Glennon, Edward S. Curtis, J.F. Westerberg, J. Peverell Marley, Archie Stout, and Donald Biddle Keyes. Technicolor photography: Ray Rennahan. Technical director: Roy Pomeroy. Film editor: Anne Bauchens

Picture started: May 21, 1923. Picture finished: August 16, 1923. Length: 11,756 feet (fourteen reels). Cost: $1,475,836.93. Released: December 4, 1923 (Hollywood premiere). Gross: $4,169,798.38

Cast: Prologue—Theodore Roberts (Moses), Charles deRoche (Rameses), Estelle Taylor (Miriam, sister of Moses), Julia Faye (Pharaoh's wife), Terrence Moore (Pharaoh's son), James Neill (Aaron, brother of Moses), Lawson Butt (Dathan, the Discontented), Clarence Burton (taskmaster), Noble Johnson (The Bronze Man). Modern story—Edythe Chapman (Mrs. McTavish), Richard Dix (John McTavish), Rod LaRocque (Dan McTavish), Leatrice Joy (Mary Leigh), Nita Naldi (Sally Lung), Robert Edeson (Reading, an inspector), Charles Ogle (doctor), and Agnes Ayres (The Outcast)

A three-page ad for Paramount Pictures in the December 8, 1923, issue of *Motion Picture News* proclaimed:

RICHES, RICHES, RICHES—Never before in the history of Famous Players-Lasky Corporation has Paramount offered to exhibitors a greater line-up of pictures than the ten that are now coming: *To the Ladies, The Call of the Canyon, Big Brother, West of the Water Tower, Don't Call It Love, Flaming Barriers, The Humming Bird, Pied Piper Malone, Shadows of Paris, The Next Corner.*

Nearly all of these pictures have been completed, and all of them have been screened sufficiently to allow us to promise, in the name of Paramount, that each one of them contains every element for tremendous box-office success.

What makes the ad remarkable is what it doesn't say. Cecil B. DeMille's production of *The Ten Commandments* premiered at Grauman's Egyptian Theater in Los Angeles on December 4, 1923, and was scheduled to open at the George M. Cohan Theatre in New York on December 21 in its first engagements. With a final negative cost of nearly a million and a half dollars, *The Ten Commandments* was the most expensive picture ever produced by Famous Players-Lasky—it may have been the most expensive picture produced by anyone up to that time. Cecil B. DeMille was the studio's number one box-office director. His nearly unbroken string of hits made Paramount Pictures the envy of the industry. Yet there was no mention of *The Ten Commandments* in the Paramount trade ad.

DeMille's picture was featured in an ad on the inside back cover of the December 22 issue of *Motion Picture News*, but the space was taken by the Precision Machine Company to announce:

THE TEN COMMANDMENTS
a Paramount Production
opens at the
COHAN THEATRE
New York City
with
SIMPLEX
Projectors

If the makers of Simplex projectors thought *The Ten Commandments* was worth a cross-plug, why didn't Paramount find the picture worthy of a mention in any of its trade ads during the entire month of December 1923? *Motion Picture News* didn't even review the film until late-January 1924.

It is true that *The Ten Commandments* was a road-show attraction and not scheduled to play regular engagements for weeks or months to come. It might be argued that trade advertising was of little value during the early stages of the film's release. Still, one might expect Paramount to prime the publicity pump for the general release to follow. Why did the company virtually ignore the 1923 DeMille special? To put it simply, Cecil B. DeMille was in the doghouse.

Although DeMille had been promised the opportunity to make another large-scale production ever since *Joan the Woman*, by 1923 the goal seemed further away than ever. Elsewhere, big pictures were again meeting with box-office success. Even economy-minded Universal announced *The Hunchback of Notre Dame* (1923) as a big-budget Super Jewel, and (if publicity was to be believed) allowed Erich von Stroheim a virtually unlimited budget on his "million dollar picture" *Foolish Wives* (1922). All of these movies owed a great deal to Cecil B. DeMille's pioneering efforts, but at Famous Players-Lasky, DeMille himself felt constrained by studio limitations on subject matter and budget.

Paramount was slow to join the big parade, but Jesse Lasky found an opportunity in Emerson Hough's *Saturday Evening Post* serial, "The Covered Wagon." The story was purely pedestrian Western stuff, but Lasky envisioned an epic semi-documentary of pioneer life. Going against the studio sales force, the producer raised the projected budget from $110,000 to $500,000, and selected James Cruze to direct.[1]

At first glance, Cruze was an odd choice. He was noted for light-hearted, small-scale comedy-dramas. But his parents crossed the plains in a covered wagon, and as a boy in Ogden, Utah, he experienced the fading days of the Old West. What Cruze lacked in large-scale filmmaking experience, he made up in feeling for the subject matter.

Five hundred thousand was more than DeMille had ever been allotted on a picture, but the budget went out the window as *The Covered Wagon* unit spent months on location. The cost grew to a staggering $782,000.[2] Critical and box-office success ultimately justified the overwhelming expense, but Cecil B. DeMille was vexed by Adolph Zukor's continued harping about his own production costs in the face of Cruze's profligacy.

Even before the critical and financial drubbing encountered by *Adam's Rib*, DeMille decided to ask the public to suggest the idea for his next picture. The contest, which was announced locally in the *Los Angeles Times*, offered a thousand-dollar prize to the winner and attracted entries from all over the country. The winning suggestion came from F.C. Nelson of Lansing, Michigan. The opening line of his story suggestion read: "You cannot break the Ten Commandments—they will break you."[3]

When Jesse Lasky presented the Ten Commandments concept to Adolph Zukor and Sidney R. Kent, he "succeeded [in] arousing considerable enthusiasm . . . over Commandments idea."[4] However, all DeMille had was a theme without a story. Jeanie Macpherson tried several treatments before she and the director came up with a workable script. "My first thought," recalled Macpherson, was to interpret the Commandments in episodic form. We would have illustrated the Commandments one at a time, or perhaps in pairs.

I worked for several weeks along these lines with growing dissatisfaction. Something was wrong. In episodic form the story didn't have the right "feel." It was bumpy. It started and stopped, ran and limped. The thread or theme of it seemed subtly broken every time we commenced a new episode.[5]

DeMille recalled that "After considering the possibility of constructing *The Ten Commandments* as a series of episodes, each written by a different author, I decided against that. Few, if any, episodic pictures have ever succeeded: the audience's instinct is, rightly, for dramatic unity of construction. The only writer who worked with me on this film was Jeanie Macpherson."[6]

Finally, DeMille and Macpherson settled on an awkward two-part structure. A biblical prologue recreating the major episodes of the Book of Exodus, and a modern allegorical story addressing F.C. Nelson's original suggestion—"You cannot break the Ten Commandments—they will break you."

"There are four people in the modern story of *The Ten Commandments*," wrote Macpherson in a treatment for the film,

and they view these Commandments in four different ways. There is Mrs. McTavish, the mother, who keeps the Commandments the wrong way. She is narrow. She is bigoted. She is bound with ritual. She is a representative of orthodoxy, yet withal she is a fine, clean, strong woman just like dozens we all know.

There is a girl, Mary Leigh, who doesn't bother about the Ten Commandments at all. She is a good kid, but she has spent so much time working that she hasn't learned the Ten Commandments. . . .

Dan McTavish knows the Ten Commandments, but defies them.

John McTavish is the garden variety of human being, which believes the Ten Commandments as unchanging, immutable laws of the universe. He is not a sissy or a goody-goody, he is a regular fellow, an ideal type of man of high and steadfast principals, who believes the Commandments are as practicable in 1923 as they were in the time of Moses.[7]

Macpherson's description of the principal characters is fascinating because it suggests a strong negative attitude toward brassbound Bible thumpers. DeMille chose not to dwell on the mother's fundamentalism, however, and played up the "fine, clean, strong" qualities of the woman.

In Macpherson's treatment, as Dan feels driven to leave home, John McTavish's suggested dialogue title reads: "You yourself are breaking the Third Commandment, mother, by preaching narrowness and intolerance in the name of God, you are taking the name of the Lord in vain."[8]

By the time the scene was in script form, John McTavish's dialogue title was only slightly less inflammatory: "You can't make people love God with fire and brimstone, Mother! You're trying to make Dan fear God—not love him!"[9]

However, in the completed film, the dialogue for the scene was further diluted:

"You're holding a Cross in your hand, Mom—
but you're using it like a whip."

In her treatment, Jeanie Macpherson clearly noted that "Dan is not vicious. He is just modern." Rod LaRocque played the role very much after the writer's intention, but downplaying the mother's religious intolerance had the effect of turning the character of Dan McTavish into a more villainous character than Macpherson intended. DeMille's treatment of the mother made sense in an era of fundamentalist revival and mother worship in the popular arts, but Macpherson held to her conception of the character even after the film's release. In her article for *The Ten Commandments* souvenir program she asked herself rhetorically

what the mother of two such boys would be like—and an old lady I had known all my life came to mind. A thoroughly good and honest woman, who believed everybody should believe as she did, or else they were all wrong. A woman who kept the Ten Commandments, it is true, but who kept them the wrong way. A woman who was so busy interpreting the letter of the Bible she had forgotten its spirit.

And so in *The Ten Commandments* it is this woman's

stern and unreasonable attitude of "hammering" religion home, which causes one of her sons to swing off to the other extreme, an atheistic tangent. This is a logical reaction from what the boy calls his mother's eternally "harping on one string."

Despite Macpherson's vivid description, the character of Mrs. McTavish that emerges in the film seems genuinely pious rather than irrationally rigid in her beliefs. It was not until *The Godless Girl* that DeMille brought Macpherson's antifundamentalist notions to the screen with full force.

After the false start, the final script for *The Ten Commandments* was written very quickly through March and April 1923. With the script completed, Famous Players-Lasky allotted $750,000 to bring the picture to the screen—a figure comparable to the final cost of *The Covered Wagon*.

The discovery of Tutankhamen's tomb in 1922 brought a wave of interest in things Egyptian. In Hollywood, Grauman's Egyptian Theater became the first deluxe movie house on the boulevard, complete with Arabs in flowing robes calling the faithful—not to prayer, but to the start of the next show. For a time the Spanish-style residential architecture of Southern California gave way to Egyptian-influenced curiosities decorated with fluted columns and images of Ibis and Ra.

Paul Iribe's Egyptian settings for *The Ten Commandments* were spectacular and based on solid archaeological research. The city of Ramses was built in the Guadalupe sand dunes in northern Santa Barbara County. A tent city, called Camp DeMille, sprang up to accommodate cast and crew. According to production statistics published at the time, 500 carpenters, 400 painters, and 380 decorators were employed in building Iribe's designs. Such figures tend to be inflated for publicity value, but photos taken during construction of the sets seem to bear out the studio's statistics. As many as 2,500 extras were used in the Exodus, with costumes and meals required for all. *The Ten Commandments* was a huge undertaking.

Shooting in late spring, DeMille found typical California coastal weather—night and morning low clouds and fog clearing by midday. A reporter visiting the location in early June wrote, "There is much fog and little sunshine. . . . Though the scenes were supposed to take place in intense heat, the wind was so bitter that the cast and extras had to huddle in blankets to keep warm before a scene began."[10]

As weather and the sheer complexity of the production took their toll, costs began to spiral exponentially. Even before DeMille started shooting the modern story, Paramount wanted out of the picture. "Have had to ride Cecil pretty hard last few weeks [on] account of *Ten Commandments* going so far over his estimate," Lasky wired Zukor on July 5, 1923.

> On two or three occasions Cecil said if we could not finance [the] picture he would have no trouble taking it off our hands. Finally today he came from meeting of his bank and advised me he believes he is in position to take picture off our hands, reimburse us for our investment, and finance completion of the picture, in which event he would make arrangement with us to distribute it for [a] small percentage of [the] profits after parties financing picture have recouped its cost. As our financial position does not [permit] making such [a] tremendous investment as we are forced by circumstances to make, [I] suggest you immediately give serious consideration [to] Cecil's proposition, and if interested advise me what percentage of profits we should try to get for distribution, taking into consideration what we have given production in way of time, studio facilities, actors, etc.[11]

DeMille managed to raise a pledge of $500,000 from A.P. Giannini of the Bank of Italy (later Bank of America) and $250,000 each from producer Joseph M. Schenck and Jules Brulatour, the West Coast franchisee for Eastman motion picture films.[12] Zukor was eager to be rid of the picture, but Frank Garbutt offered a piece of unsolicited advice by long-distance telephone: "Don't sell what you haven't seen." Zukor backed off, and Famous Players-Lasky reluctantly financed the picture to completion.[13]

For the first time since *The Virginian* in 1914, Alvin Wyckoff was not behind a camera on a DeMille picture. In a 1971 interview director Irvin Willat suggested the reason for the final split:

> I was a photographer [before I became a director], and that made my pictures look better even if they weren't better [as films]. I had good photography, I'd see to it.
>     I remember one instance very well. C.B. DeMille had

made a picture in the snow, and the film came back from the Paramount lab, and DeMille was hollerin' like hell because everything was too contrasty—all whites and blacks. I went up to Truckee [California] in the snow to make a picture [titled] *The Siren Call* (Famous Players-Lasky, 1922), and I didn't send any exposed film back from location. The studio wired, they phoned, they complained:

"We're getting no film!"

And I said, "You're not going to get any, either—I'm not going to let the [studio film] lab take care of my film as they did DeMille's."

It was growing into a real feud—they were ready to send up some studio officials. My attitude was: "I don't give a damn, you won't get the film!" (It wasn't true, I was very concerned.) I knew the man in the laboratory, and I knew he wasn't a good lab man—and I couldn't say anything, because he worked with DeMille's cameraman.

When we returned . . . I brought all the film with me and locked it in a vault. The next day I went in the lab and I made tests, gave them the development time, and asked them to develop it that way. And they did.

As I was going to the projection room later, I saw DeMille walking out. It got all over the studio—DeMille was raising hell:

"Why are Willat's snow scenes so beautiful, and ours so bad?" [DeMille asked].[14]

It is difficult to know what snow scenes DeMille might have shot in 1922; there are none in the final release versions of his films that year. Perhaps Willat was misremembering the film of his that DeMille saw, or perhaps DeMille was simply remarking on the quality of Willat's snow scenes without reference to any of his own footage. But Willat's story jibes with DeMille's own statements about Wyckoff's work—"DeMille was hollerin' like hell because everything was too contrasty—all whites and blacks." Willat's ability to achieve scenes of pictorial beauty in a difficult "white-on-white" snow-covered environment caused DeMille to question the veteran cameraman's work and ultimately led the director to replace him.

For *The Ten Commandments* DeMille selected George Melford's cinematographer, Bert Glennon, to head the photographic crew. Glennon's work on Melford's *Burning Sands* (Famous Players-Lasky, 1922) suggested that he was ideal to shoot the Egyptian desert scenes. Glennon was joined by a small army of cameramen, including J. Peverell Marley, who quickly became one of DeMille's favorite cinematographers, and Archie Stout, who was noted for his outdoor work. Studio portrait photographer Donald Biddle Keyes brought his sense of lighting to the picture, and DeMille even utilized the talents of famed ethnographer Edward S. Curtis to shoot documentary-like details of the action.[15]

Ray Rennahan of the Technicolor Motion Picture Corporation went on location to shoot color footage of the Exodus. Although Technicolor had produced several pictures on its own to show off its two-color system, including a highly successful feature, *The Toll of the Sea* (Technicolor-Metro, 1922), the major Hollywood studios showed little interest in the fledgling company. Early Technicolor was costly and unreliable. A special camera exposed two black-and-white frames simultaneously through red and green filters; separate prints were struck from each color record and toned in complementary red and green dyes. Finally, the toned prints were cemented together to achieve a color image. The process doubled the amount of film exposed, the double-thick prints made holding focus on-screen difficult, and the prints often buckled in the projector.[16]

Laboratory services for Technicolor were headed by Carl A. "Doc" Willat, older brother of Paramount director Irvin Willat. With an entrée to the studio, Technicolor offered to shoot for free. If DeMille liked the footage, he could use it in the finished film. If he didn't, Technicolor agreed to destroy the color material. With his own long-standing interest in using color to enhance dramatic impact, the proposal appealed to DeMille.

Rennahan's scenes met with the director's approval and were used in the picture. However, the color footage of the Exodus did not duplicate every setup of the black-and-white cameras; so DeMille was forced to integrate the Technicolor scenes with tinted and toned monochrome footage. As odd as this may seem, the warm red and green tones of the Technicolor footage blended almost imperceptibly with the sepia-tinted scenes. DeMille also employed the Handschiegl stencil color system in several sequences to augment the natural color footage.[17]

The task of recreating the parting of the Red Sea fell to DeMille's multitalented technical director, Roy Pomeroy. Dapper, and sporting a waxed moustache, Pomeroy had a certain arrogance that found full flower in the late 1920s when he was made head of Paramount's sound department, and became the prototype for the overbearing sound "expert" who ruled briefly during Hollywood's transition from silence to "All Talking, All Singing, All Dancing!"

The Red Sea sequence offered a challenge to Pomeroy, who was noted for his clever miniature work. He utilized the Williams Process to combine footage of fleeing Israelites shot at Guadalupe Sand Dunes with reverse-printed slow motion footage of a flood of water cascading over gelatin mounds that represented the walls of the Red Sea. Although it was simple in execution, Pomeroy's work is still impressive. Equally striking are the visual effects as Moses receives the Law from God in a dazzling shower of spark and explosion. The sheer eye-filling audacity of the biblical prologue makes the modern story seem anticlimactic, although DeMille and Macpherson managed to work the collapse of a cathedral and a storm at sea into their allegorical melodrama.

Macpherson wrote that "There was nothing of spontaneous generation in building the story of *The Ten Commandments*."[18] She saw this as a positive thing, and in her "well-made" screenplay the character of Dan McTavish breaks all Ten Commandments within a single convoluted storyline that strains dramatic sensibilities.

Audiences today might find Macpherson's modern story contrived and difficult to embrace. Yet on its release, *The Ten Commandments* was seen as a towering artistic achievement. On October 5, 1923, Jesse L. Lasky wrote Adolph Zukor:

Although twenty-four hours have passed since I saw *Ten Commandments* last night, I am still under the spell of greatest motion picture that has ever been produced since very beginning of the feature photoplay. Cecil has created a masterpiece that will live long after other famous pictures are forgotten. Picture teaches a lesson that is so big and yet so simple it will be endorsed by every fair minded individual, church, society and sect. You will be amazed at the sincerity with which Cecil has handled this tremendous subject, it is almost as if he were inspired, a new and much bigger Cecil DeMille. I do not believe we can measure possible earning power of *Ten Commandments*. It will make new motion picture industry, make new records and show power and possibilities of the screen in a way that has never been approached. I have never heard a sermon, read a book, nor seen a play that has effected me as has *The Ten Commandments* and I sincerely believe that picture will do more good than combined pulpit of America and it is not a sermon but sheer entertainment of most gripping kind. [Paramount sales manager Sidney R.] Kent feels as I do and I understand he wired you his own opinion this morning but I waited on purpose to study my own reactions, and the longer I wait the bigger this remarkable picture becomes. I feel I want to see it again and again. I wish it were possible for you to get on the train with [Hugo] Riesenfeld [musical director of the Rialto and Rivoli Theaters in New York] and see the picture for yourself. I think we have the greatest property in this picture that the world has ever seen and I doubt if it will be surpassed in our time. Spread the good news.[19]

Jesse Lasky was not an unbiased observer, and his overstatement was to be expected, but the producer was not alone in his praise for DeMille's film. James R. Quirk, editor of *Photoplay* magazine, wrote that *The Ten Commandments* was "The best photoplay ever made. The greatest theatrical spectacle in history . . . it will last as long as the film on which it is recorded."[20]

Despite the enthusiasm of Lasky and Quirk, Adolph Zukor had no love for DeMille. The road-show release schedule for *The Ten Commandments* was deliberately protracted. After the December 4, 1923, opening in Los Angeles, and the New York premiere on December 21, DeMille's picture did not play Chicago and Philadelphia until February 1924. The Boston and London openings were delayed until March 1924. Despite the lack of support from Paramount, however, *The Ten Commandments* fulfilled Jesse Lasky's prediction, and proved to be a potent box-office attraction.[21]

In spite of its length, DeMille made only two relatively minor cuts after the Los Angeles premiere. The first was a 319-foot scene in which Mary McTavish comes to the apartment of her husband's mistress. As Jeanie Macpherson described the episode, "The scene is very different from the usual triangular meeting. There is no, 'My God, the wife!'—no shouting, just a very tense situation, and the measuring of woman against woman, as Sally [the mistress] asks Mary very suavely if she won't sit down and join them at tea. Mary pays no attention to Sally, but briefly states to Dan the situation about the [sub-standard] concrete. And Dan, alarmed by the events, leaves with Mary."[22]

The "civilized" meeting between the two women had parallels in Macpherson's own relations with Constance DeMille, but Los Angeles audiences found the scene lacking in dramatic credibility and it was eliminated. The second cut was a 35½-shot in the final sequence. The studio continuity described the action: "City showing sunrise—head of Christ dissolves into scene, raises hands, dissolves out leaving scene of sunrise." Because Jews, Christians, and Moslems all recognize the Old Testament of the Bible, the image of Christ limited the universal appeal of *The Ten Commandments*, and deleting this visual reference to Christ seemed reasonable.[23]

*The Ten Commandments* left an indelible impression on at least two filmmakers. The images of snapping curtain rings as the Eurasian leper is killed and the construction elevator point-of-view racing toward the heavens were to be quoted by Alfred Hitchcock in *Psycho* (Hitchcock-Paramount, 1960) and King Vidor in *The Fountainhead* (Warner Bros., 1949).

# 46

# Triumph

Famous Players-Lasky for Paramount release. A Cecil B. DeMille Production. Director: Cecil B. DeMille. Scenario by Jeanie Macpherson, from a story by May Edginton. Assistant director: Frank Urson. Photography: Peverell Marley. Editor: Anne Bauchens

Picture started: January 10, 1924. Picture finished: February 22, 1924. Length: 8,383 feet (nine reels). Cost: $265,012.53. Released: April 20, 1924. Gross: $678,526.14

Cast: Leatrice Joy (Anna Land), Rod LaRocque (King Garnet), Victor Varconi (Silver), Theodore Kosloff (Varinoff), Charles Ogle (Jim, the foreman), Robert Edeson (Overton, the lawyer), George Fawcett (King Garnet's father), Julia Faye (Countess Rika), Spotiswoode Aitken (Torrini), ZaSu Pitts (factory girl), Raymond Hatton (a tramp), Alma Bennett (a flower girl), Jimmie Adams (a painter), Mervyn LeRoy (factory worker), Roscoe Karns (butler), William Boyd (chauffeur), and Eugene Pallette

As DeMille finished editing *The Ten Commandments*, Famous Players-Lasky offered him a new three-film contract. It wasn't stated in so many words, but the director was expected to turn out several relatively inexpensive pictures to compensate the studio for indulging his whims on the biblical spectacle.

*Triumph*, the first film under the new contract, was based on a short story by May Edginton and augmented with a Romeo and Juliet flashback. In 1922 DeMille suggested making a screen version of Shakespeare's romantic tragedy with Rudolph Valentino and Leatrice Joy in the title roles. The New York office was apoplectic. "[I would] lock you up rather than let you make such a terrible mistake," Lasky wired.[1] With the benefit of hindsight, DeMille's proposal seems far more interesting than many of the films he was allowed to make, but *Romeo and Juliet* was not to be. DeMille was forced to confine his illusions of grandeur to a brief flashback, as he had so many times in the past.

*Triumph* offers all of the allegorical elements that by 1924 had become synonymous with the director's work. Even the names of the characters are evocative—Anna Land (solid, steadfast), King Garnet (only semiprecious, not a real gem), William Silver (silver, but not gold). DeMille and Macpherson also managed to work in a "trial by fire"—a favorite device from *Joan the Woman* that was reworked in *Something to Think About* and *Saturday Night* and had its finest treatment in *The Godless Girl*.

In fact, *Triumph* is replete with all of DeMille's thematic concerns. King Garnet is a playboy idler who rarely visits the canning factory he inherited. Garnet's half-brother, William Silver (illegitimate issue of a European fling), is foreman of the factory and a rabble rouser who spouts off about workers controlling the means of production. Unaware of their father's indiscretion, the brothers do not know that they are related. Anna Land works in the factory but dreams of a career as a star of grand opera, and both men are attracted to her.

By terms of a secret will, if King Garnet does not take direct management responsibility for the canning factory within two years of his father's death, his inheritance will revert to William Silver. The playboy Garnet is content to "live on dead man's legs" and has no interest in work. Just as Silver is about to incite the factory workers to strike, he learns that he is now the owner—and with the sudden reversal of fortune, he quickly comes to see management's point of view.

Anna loves King Garnet but refuses his attentions because he is a wastrel. She also spurns William Silver. However, when she receives an opportunity to make her concert debut on condition that she wear a proper gown, Anna succumbs to Silver's conditional proposal—he will provide the gown if she agrees to marry him.

If the characters' relationships seem incredible and the circular narrative too convenient, DeMille's social observation and visual wit lift *Triumph* out of the ordinary. For example, as Anna Land escorts King Garnet through his factory she points out a woman on the assembly line and offers the comment:

> "You think you're a great financier,
> Mr. Garnet! Yet that woman supports
> an old mother and two children on
> $18.00 a week!"

Also, both Garnet and Silver wait after work for the privilege of driving Anna home—Garnet in his fancy Packard, Silver in his rattling Tin Lizzie.

With roles reversed, Silver the Bolshevik is now Silver the Plutocrat. To save Anna from marrying Silver, the now-destitute Garnet robs from his rich brother to give to the poor Anna and tells Silver:

> "Not one cent of this coin is for me!
> Besides, you always said if you had
> money you'd DIVIDE it—and I'm taking
> you at your word!"

The position of women in society also comes under scrutiny. Though she loves King Garnet, Anna Land chooses to marry William Silver, telling her lover:

> "King, he wants to marry me—and I want
> a career. A woman, today, can't always
> listen to her heart if she is to win success!"

The film ends with a comic touch. King Garnet regains his factory and also wins Anna's hand. William Silver is back where he began as factory foreman. A long-suffering factory girl (ZaSu Pitts), who has loved Silver from afar, offers him a "hopeful geranium" as he stares into space contemplating his strange fate.

Despite ZaSu Pitts's extraordinary dramatic work in Erich von Stroheim's *Greed* (finally released in January 1925 after over a year in production and editing), in *Triumph* she was relegated to her familiar role as well-placed comic relief. Hollywood never shared Stroheim's enthusiasm for Pitts as a leading lady, and though she did find a few starring roles—most notably in *Pretty Ladies* (M-G-M, 1925)—she soon became typecast as a reliable character actress. Perhaps this was for the best, because she outdistanced many of her contemporaries in career longevity and lasting (if modest) fame.

Knuckling under to studio pressure, DeMille managed to produce *Triumph* on a relatively modest budget. However, with a cost in excess of $250,000, the picture was still budgeted well above the average Paramount program picture of the time. DeMille's use of a practical canning factory was no doubt necessitated by budgetary considerations, but it adds an element of realism to an otherwise preposterous story, and is worth noting because DeMille, of all Hollywood directors, seemed most content to remain in the controlled environment of the studio.

Triumph appears to have exerted some influence over Clarence Brown's extraordinary *Smoldering Fires* (Universal-Jewel, 1925). Although Brown's film about an older woman in love with a younger man received a much more realistic treatment than DeMille's, the story revolves around life in a factory and offers a view of liberated women in the work place. The screenplay for *Smoldering Fires* was written by Sada Cowan and her husband, long-time DeMille assistant Howard Higgin.

Critical reaction to *Triumph* was generally favorable, and the picture performed well enough at the box office. However, the film was released just as *The Ten Commandments* started playing in cities outside New York and Los Angeles, and it offered no real competition to DeMille's spectacular epic.

# 47

# Feet of Clay

Famous Players-Lasky for Paramount release. A Cecil B. DeMille Production. Director: Cecil B. DeMille. Scenario by Beulah Marie Dix and Bertram Milhauser, from the novel by Margaretta Tuttle and the one-act play *Across the Border* by Beulah Marie Dix. Art director: Paul Iribe. Technical director: Roy Pomeroy. Assistant director: Frank Urson. Photography: J. Peverell Marley and Archie Stout. Film editor: Anne Bauchens

Picture started: May 12, 1924. Picture finished: July 12, 1924. Length: 9,665 feet (ten reels). Cost: $513,636.27. Released: September 22, 1924. Gross: $904,383.90

Cast: Vera Reynolds (Amy Loring), Rod LaRocque (Kerry Harlan), Julia Faye (Bertha Lansell), Ricardo Cortez (Tony Channing), Robert Edeson (Dr. Lansell), Theodore Kosloff (Bendix), Victor Varconi (The Keeper), and William Boyd

For the second picture under DeMille's new contract, Famous Players-Lasky suggested a magazine serial called "Feet of Clay." The director showed no interest in the project and suggested that Lasky purchase Sutton Vane's then-current hit play, *Outward Bound*, a stylized drama about a ship full of passengers who have no idea where they are going, only to discover that they are all dead and being transported to the "other side." It was the director's idea to combine elements of Vane's play with Beulah Marie Dix's one-act play *Across the Border* (1914), which had a similar theme. Lasky made little effort to acquire *Outward Bound* and suggested:

ADVISE YOU STRONGLY YOU DO COMBINATION OF
FEET OF CLAY AND ACROSS THE BORDER SO THAT
WE DO NOT GET INTO TROUBLE LATER BECAUSE OF
ANY SIMILARITY WITH OUTWARD BOUND.[1]

Margaretta Tuttle's "Feet of Clay" is about a soldier who loses the toes of one foot in battle. Dix's play is about a soldier who has an out-of-body experience after being mortally wounded. Under DeMille's guidance the final screen story emerged as a tale about a young millionaire whose foot is ravaged in a shark attack while he attempts to rescue Amy Loring from a boating accident.

The injured Kerry Harlan marries Amy; but her sister, who is also the wife of Kerry's doctor, tries to force herself on Kerry. Hiding on the ledge outside Kerry's apartment when her own husband arrives, the sister falls to her death, and in the resulting scandal Kerry and Amy attempt suicide by turning on the gas. Ultimately, their spirits are cast out by "The Keeper," and they return to the world to be rescued and resume their lives.

*Feet of Clay* gained some notoriety from Charles Higham's assertion that it represented the most vivid on-screen example of DeMille's penchant for foot fetishism.[2] Well, maybe, maybe not. Although DeMille ordered a print of *Feet of Clay* for his personal collection in 1925, the print was lost many years before Higham began his biography on the filmmaker.[3] Other examples of "foot fetishism" in DeMille's work— Mary Pickford cleaning the boots of the hated Hun in *The Little American*; or Forrest Stanley slipping a shoe onto the foot of Agnes Ayres in the Cinderella-themed *Forbidden Fruit*; or the maid painting Gloria Swanson's toes in *The Affairs of Anatol*, for instance—seem more symbolic devices than expressions of any latent perversion. The fact that *Feet of Clay* was imposed on the director by the studio further suggests that he had little enthusiasm for the underlying material.

What did interest DeMille was the supernatural element of Dix's play because it corresponded to the picture he really wanted to make— *Outward Bound*.[4] In fact, DeMille and his screenwriters tried to hew as closely to the basic premise of *Outward Bound* as they could, while relying on the similar situation in *Across the Border* to protect their newly fabricated property. Sutton Vane was not impressed with DeMille's literary carpentry. He felt that *Feet of Clay* clearly borrowed elements from *Outward Bound*, and he sued Famous Players-Lasky for plagiarism. Despite a carefully prepared defense, Paramount attorneys entered into an out-of-court settlement with Vane.[5]

As DeMille completed *Feet of Clay*, Famous Players-Lasky signed D.W. Griffith to a three-picture contract. DeMille's fear of 1918 was returning to haunt him. Zukor was still outraged over the cost of *The Ten Commandments* and the expense of maintaining DeMille's separate unit between pictures. The success of DeMille's pictures was also an issue. The director's contract called for an advance of production costs against a sliding percentage of gross box-office receipts. Zukor felt this arrangement put too much of Paramount's money in DeMille's pocket, and he proposed that the director receive 50 percent of the net profits from his films in his next Paramount contract, and he used D.W. Griffith as a bargaining chip. If DeMille didn't buckle under to the studio's demand, Zukor was prepared to have Griffith direct all future Paramount specials.[6]

DeMille was rankled because, despite its cost, *The Ten Commandments* was proving extremely popular and, with the exceptions of *Joan the Woman* and *Adam's Rib,* his box-office track record was outstanding. He felt that Zukor's position in the industry was due in no small part to the Lasky-DeMille pictures that cemented the Paramount program in the early days of the Famous Players-Lasky merger, and he resented Zukor's efforts to alter his standing within the company.

# 48

# The Golden Bed

Famous Players-Lasky for Paramount release. A Cecil B. DeMille Production. Director: Cecil B. DeMille. Scenario by Jeanie Macpherson, from the novel *Tomorrow's Bread* by Wallace Irwin. Art director: Paul Iribe. Photography: J. Peverell Marley. Film editor: Anne Bauchens

Length: 8,584 feet (nine reels). Cost: $437,900.66. Released: January 19, 1925. Gross: $816,487.88

Cast: Lillian Rich (Flora Lee Peake), Vera Reynolds (Margaret Peake), Henry B. Walthall (Colonel Peake), Rod LaRocque (Admah Holtz), Theodore Kosloff (Marquis de San Pilar), Warner Baxter (Bunny), Robert Cain (Duc de Savarac), Julia Faye (Mrs. Amos Thompson), Robert Edeson (Amos Thompson), Jacqueline Wells [Julie Bishop] (Flora as a child), and Charles Clary (James Gordon)

DeMille's last film for Paramount before he set up his own studio, *The Golden Bed,* is best remembered for the perhaps apocryphal story about a bit player who came to the director in later years and said, "Mr. DeMille, you probably don't remember me. I was a harlot in your *Golden Bed*."[1]

The plot is full of the kind of "red-earth-of-Tara" stuff about doing anything and everything to save the old family homestead, represented by the infamous golden bed. Flora Lee Peake manages to maintain her exotic lifestyle for a time on money her blindly adoring husband has pilfered from company funds. Finally, she gets her comeuppance, and hubby sees the light and marries the sister who has loved him long and from afar. The highlight of the film is the "candy ball," one of DeMille's most erotic sequences, with doting young men biting strategically placed marshmallows from the glittering gowns of Flora Lee's beautiful girl-friends; but beyond all of the melodramatic and glitzy trappings, *The Golden Bed* has a haunting quality that is ultimately quite affecting.

Henry B. Walthall, who plays the aging Colonel Peake, gained lasting fame as the "Little Colonel" in D.W. Griffith's *The Birth of a Nation* (Epoch Producing Corporation, 1915). A fondness for the bottle led him quickly to the world of bit parts and character roles. In *The Golden Bed* and films like *One Clear Call* (Louis B. Mayer-First National, 1922) and *Judge Priest* (Fox, 1934), Walthall's later parts often drew heavily on the audience's association with his characterization in *The Birth of a Nation*.

Warner Baxter, who plays Bunny, had been in films for eight years when he made *The Golden Bed*. He had a checkered career in silent films, starring in the first screen versions of *The Awful Truth* (Peninsula-P.D.C., 1924) and *The Great Gatsby* (Famous Players-Lasky,1926), as well as numerous program pictures. His greatest success came with talking pictures when he won an Oscar for his role as the Cisco Kid in *In Old Arizona* (Fox, 1929) and created the quintessential stage director, Julian Marsh, in *42nd Street* (Warner Bros., 1933).

For his next picture, DeMille wanted to make a screen adaptation of Marie Corelli's 1895 novel *The Sorrows of Satan; or The Strange Experience of One Geoffrey Tempest, Millionaire*. Famous Players-Lasky acquired the property for him, and DeMille planned to shoot the picture in Europe.

On December 2, 1924, Adolph Zukor asked Jesse Lasky to open negotiations with DeMille on a new contract; then on December 18, DeMille received what he called an "ultimatum" from Paramount sales head Sidney R. Kent. "It is not your [cash] advance that we object to so much as the added expense caused by your separate unit from which we feel you get no return commensurate with the expense it costs us," Kent wired from New York. "Mr. Zukor feels that this must be taken off our backs. . . . Zukor's [position] must be the general basis on which we meet. . . . Appreciate position you placed in by sailing without definite plans . . . but if you would not be interested in any proposal after you reached here, very likely you would not desire sail anyway."[2]

Despite their differences, DeMille was confident enough that a deal would be worked out that at the end of December he started east by train with his wife, Jeanie Macpherson and her mother, Mitchell Leisen, and cameraman J. Peverell Marley on what was intended to be the first leg of a working vacation in Europe to prepare for making *The Sorrows of Satan*. But negotiations did not go well, and on January 9, 1925, DeMille's contract with Famous Players-Lasky was terminated with sixty-days' notice.[3]

In his autobiography DeMille stated, "I have never understood why professional or business differences need necessarily affect friendships. My continued good personal relations with Adolph Zukor and Jesse Lasky proved the point, for they felt the same way."[4] But DeMille remained bitter to his dying day over the treatment he received from Zukor, Lasky, and Kent. He diplomatically omitted the names of the offenders in his book, but he could not resist recounting the incidents: "[M]y long life has had few bitterer moments than when one of those gentlemen said to me, and the other two heard it in unprotesting silence: 'Cecil, you have never been one of us.'" It was Adolph Zukor who said these words, and perhaps DeMille silently understood why many Paramount employees referred to Zukor behind his back as "creeping Jesus" or "the little creep."[5]

But equally hurtful was a perhaps unintentional slight by Jesse Lasky. "One of the New York executives had been quite ill," DeMille wrote, "and during his convalescence I invited him to come out [to California] and spend a month on [my yacht] the *Seaward* and at [my rural hideaway] Paradise, fishing and resting, regaining his strength." At the completion of his visit, DeMille asked if Lasky would send him some chestnuts for roasting. "When I was a little boy in New York, there used to be Italian chestnut vendors on the street corners in the wintertime," he remembered. "The chestnuts cost a nickel a bag. They roasted them right there and sold them hot out of the roaster, and you'd hold the bag to keep your hands warm while you ate the chestnuts." Lasky promised to send DeMille "the biggest bag of chestnuts in the world," and true to his word a bag of raw chestnuts arrived—accompanied by a bill. DeMille recalled that he roasted the last of this bitter fruit at Paradise in 1952.[6]

# 49

# The Road to Yesterday

Cecil B. DeMille Pictures for Producers Distributing Corporation release. Produced and directed by Cecil B. DeMille. Scenario by Jeanie Macpherson and Beulah Marie Dix, from a play by Beulah Marie Dix and Evelyn Greenleaf Sutherland. Art directors: Paul Iribe, Mitchell Leisen, and Anton Grot. Photography: J. Peverell Marley. Film editor: Anne Bauchens

Picture started: June 22, 1925. Picture finished: August 19, 1925. Length: 9,980 feet (ten reels). Cost: $477,479.29. Released: November 15, 1925. Gross: $522,665.77

Cast: Joseph Schildkraut (Kenneth Paulton, the bridegroom), Jetta Goudal (Malena, his bride), William Boyd (Rev. Jack Moreland), Vera Reynolds (Bess Tyrell), Trixie Friganza (Aunt Harriet), Casson Ferguson (Adrian Tompkins), Julia Faye (Dolly Foules), Charles Clary (doctor), Clarence Burton, Charles West, and Sally Rand

While in New York pondering his future, DeMille was approached by Henry Creange, an executive with Cheney Silks. Acting in a semiofficial capacity for the French government, Creange proposed that DeMille, and perhaps other American filmmakers, make pictures in Europe. The films would be made with an American director and star, and the rest of the cast and the production facilities would be European, allowing exploitation as European product on the Continent and American product in the States.

But DeMille put consideration of this proposition aside when he received a report from his business manager, John Fisher, about financier Jeremiah Milbank, who had recently taken over W.W. Hodkinson, Inc., the struggling distribution company that Hodkinson had established after his ouster from Paramount. The newly reorganized company was known as Producers Distributing Corporation. DeMille met with Milbank in New York, and, according to the director, they came to an understanding only when he outlined his plans to make a film about the life of Christ to the deeply religious Milbank. DeMille somewhat idealized his memory of the situation. The inspiration for *The King of Kings* would not emerge for another year, but Milbank and DeMille found much in common. Producers Distributing Corporation needed product, and DeMille needed an organization that could finance his future productions.

DeMille and Milbank came to an agreement that created the Cinema Corporation of America as a holding company for Producers Distributing Corporation (P.D.C.) and a new entity, Cecil B. DeMille Pictures, Inc., which would be controlled by DeMille and Milbank's Realty and Securities Company. After the agreement was set, DeMille arranged to purchase the Thomas H. Ince Studio in Culver City, which was for sale after Ince's untimely death at age forty-four.[1]

After the shock of being fired, DeMille made a relatively amicable exit from Famous Players-Lasky, but his departure was complex enough to require a separate contract covering various details. Famous Players-Lasky agreed to release Leatrice Joy and Rod LaRocque from their contracts, if they chose, so that they could sign with DeMille Pictures. The two companies agreed to a "favored nation" status with regard to cooperation, and Famous Players-Lasky also agreed to give DeMille $50,000 worth of camera and lighting equipment and to release certain key personnel should they also choose to make the move. On February 1, 1925, DeMille wrote Jesse Lasky:

> There are a number of people in the Coast studios who have been associated with me for many years, even before the formation of the Lasky Company, who may desire to continue their association with me personally. While these people have not expressed themselves, the situation may arise, and I should like to know your attitude in regard to them:
>
> George Dixon, the stage manager, who has been with me for almost eighteen years. Bessie McGaffey, head of the Research Department. Hattie, the hairdresser, who has a contract with you, but who has been regarded as one of my organization.[2] There is also a carpenter named Lee Moran, who was not associated with my unit in any way, but whom I would like to take in place of [George] Dixon, if you decide that you do not wish to release Dixon. Our contract gives us the right to take a designer, wardrobe woman and draper and I will take two women that I placed in the wardrobe myself, unless they prefer to remain with Famous. The man from [Roy] Pomeroy's [trick effects] department and the man from

the prop making department I will select after I get on the
Coast and discuss the matter with [Famous Players-Lasky
studio manager Victor H.] Clark[e] and the heads of those two
departments, so that I will in no way cripple those departments.[3]

DeMille told Lasky that the camera equipment he was taking was
valued at $29,000, and he requested some Cooper-Hewitt mercury vapor
lamps, prints of his personal productions, and some miscellaneous furniture to make up the $21,000 difference. On February 4, Lasky replied
that it was already his understanding that DeMille would take the lights
and that this would settle the equipment issue. Lasky wrote:

We are quite willing to turn over to you, not by way of any
trade, but as a courtesy which we are glad to show you, the
library of prints of your own subjects. . . .
     We forwarded you yesterday original contracts of Leatrice
Joy, Rod LaRocque, Lillian Rich and Vera Reynolds. While
you only requested the first two, you will want the others
sooner or later.[4]

DeMille's departure, it seems, afforded Famous Players-Lasky an
opportunity to trim the payroll of some DeMille players who were perceived to have limited prospects. However, it took several more days
before Lasky came to a decision on some of DeMille's other personnel
requests. Finally on February 13 Lasky allowed that "We are willing to
let you have George Dixon, Lee Moran, also Hattie, the hairdresser,
although we are sorry to lose her. We want, and expect to keep, Bessie
McGaffey, so I hope you will refrain from talking business with her. We
will turn over the magnavox [public address system] outfit to you with
the understanding that you will agree to lend it to us whenever we need
it. As we would not use it often, this will be no inconvenience to you I am
sure. . . ."[5]
     With much pomp and civic display the Ince lot was formally rechris-
tened DeMille Studio on March 2, 1925. DeMille's connection with
Famous Players-Lasky officially ended a few days later with a telegram
from Jesse Lasky to Victor H. Clarke:

Regarding deMille weekly advances we served notice on

deMille January ninth and his sixty days brings termination of contract to March eleventh. Contract provides that as an advance producer shall be entitled to receive on account of percentages on Saturday November seventeenth, 1923, sum of $6,731.00 and on Saturday of each and every week thereafter during term of this agreement same amount. Therefore check on March seventh which is last Saturday of term is last one DeMille is entitled to receive. . . .[6]

One issue that became a sore point with DeMille was whether his new company had a contract with actress Bebe Daniels. In January 1925, just before DeMille arrived in New York on the first leg of his aborted European vacation, Jesse Lasky had been negotiating with Daniels over a new contract. "However we could not agree on terms," wrote Lasky, "and when she told me she could get more money and better conditions from other producers than I was offering her I advised her frankly that she was a free agent and she could go and negotiate elsewhere without any hard feelings on my part."[7] Lasky advised DeMille that he was free to negotiate with Daniels.

Mr. Lasky approved my negotiating with Bebe Daniels for a contract to extend from the termination of her employment with Famous Players. . . . I started negotiations with her and same were carried to satisfactory conclusion on or about February ninth at which time [P.D.C. executive John] Flinn and I made definite agreement with Daniels . . . she agreeing to give us option on her services on such terms until February twenty first. On or about February nineteenth she was asked for an extension of one week's time which she granted and on February twenty sixth I notified her through her New York office that we elected to exercise our option.[8]

Everything was set, but in early March Daniels began raising issues over what DeMille called "four minor points." On March 16 he offered to take care of her fan-mail expenses up to fifty dollars per week, if she would concede the other points. But Daniels still wouldn't sign the formal contract. Ten days later DeMille learned that Robert T. Kane, acting as her representative, approached Jesse Lasky and asked "what the differences were between Famous Players and Bebe. After a discussion he informed me if I would make one concession she would rather work for Famous Players as conditions had arisen which made it almost imperative she live in east."

DeMille was incredulous because throughout his negotiations with Daniels and her attorney she had stressed her need to return to California for her health. DeMille was blunt in expressing his disappointment in Robert Kane. "For your private information," DeMille wired Lasky, "Robert Kane was endeavoring to make a connection with me which did not materialize and I assume he is endeavoring to sell Daniels elsewhere as a result of this although I am rather surprised at this action as I financed his last picture without compensation of any kind."[9]

To attorney Nathan Burkan in New York, DeMille reported, "At that time [when I was negotiating for Daniels's services] a certain gentleman expected to be working in the west for the coming year but a recent change in business plans has made it necessary for him to work in the east and this is the sole reason in my opinion for Daniels trying to break her contract."[10]

DeMille advised Burkan that he was "very anxious" to secure the services of comedian Raymond Griffith, and that if Famous Players-Lasky wanted Daniels, he would be willing to trade Daniels for Griffith. On April 4, 1925, Burkan wired DeMille with details of a meeting he held with Adolph Zukor: "He states . . . that she has changed her mind and wants to continue with the Famous Players. That while terms of a contract between her and Famous Players have been agreed upon it has not yet been signed and in view of your claim that you have a contract with her they will suspend doing anything further. . . . If she is willing to work for you Famous will give her up. Zukor said he would not exchange [Raymond] Griffith for Daniels as he thot Griffith had greater potentialities."[11]

DeMille continued to push for an acceptable trade with Famous Players-Lasky for another actor, but on April 8, 1925, Nathan Burkan advised DeMille: "Am of the opinion you have no valid claim upon Daniels services. . . . My opinion is based upon the fact that the contract could not be performed within one year from the date it was made and accordingly is void under the statute of frauds."[12]

DeMille's disappointment was mollified somewhat when he was advised by his distribution people that "Bebe Daniels has fair box office strength in the smaller towns but means very little in the cities,"[13] but he and Milbank were attempting to establish a major studio that could compete with Famous Players-Lasky and Metro-Goldwyn-Mayer, and to attract attention they needed more star power than Rod LaRocque and Leatrice Joy could provide.

Consideration was given to signing Elinor Glyn as a "supervisor" for a series of pictures. Glyn was best known as the author of such lurid novels as *Three Weeks* (1907) and *His Hour* (1910), which became the basis for some highly popular screen adaptations in the 1920s. She managed to parlay her success into a lucrative contract with Metro Pictures. Nathan Burkan outlined her deal to DeMille:

> Under Metro contract Glyn receives one third of their profits of each picture with a guarantee that such share of the profits will not be less than forty thousand dollars within twenty-four months from date of release. In addition she receives forty two hundred sixty dollars for writing scenario and three hundred dollars [per week] for supervision during making of pictures. Guarantee and payment aggregate approximately fifty thousand dollars per picture. Three Weeks grossed in the United States approximately six hundred thousand dollars. His Hour four hundred ten thousand dollars. Reliably informed that Glyn one of the very best draws on Metro program and world gross per Glyn program picture should be approximately seven hundred fifty thousand dollars. [Glyn] Should like a proposition whereby she has a percentage participating interest in the picture with a very substantial guarantee. Suggest you formulate very best possible proposition having in mind compensation now being paid by Metro and their desire to continue her services at a substantial increase. Her idea is to make three or four specials.[14]

DeMille decided to pass on making an offer to Glyn because he believed "her best paying material were her well known books and from now on [I] feel she would be making originals."[15]

The Producers Distributing Corporation–DeMille Pictures combination was on shaky ground from day one. Following its founder's original design for Paramount Pictures, the old W.W. Hodkinson company had acted as a distributor for various producers but never established its own production arm or theater chain. Hodkinson's ham-handed tactics also alienated a number of potentially lucrative customers.

"As you probably know," P.D.C. president Frederick C. Munroe advised DeMille,

> Cincinnati is completely controlled by Ike Libson and in the past our company has sold him practically nothing. Some years ago he had a disagreement with Hodkinson which he never got over and on that account also because of the fact that our product was not anything very great, he has never had a friendly feeling toward us—quite the contrary. Last year we sold him six or eight pictures for Cincinnati and he went along month after month refusing to give us play dates until we threatened him with the Film Board of Trade and he then gave us play dates. In addition to Cincinnati, Libson has houses in Indianapolis, Louisville, Dayton, Ohio, Akron, Ohio, and Columbus, Ohio. In some of these other towns we have played a few pictures with him but never have sold him anything like the majority of our product.[16]

William H. Morgan, hired away from First National Pictures to serve as P.D.C.'s new sales manager, was able to patch up the old wounds with Libson; he obtained a contract for twenty-three pictures in Cincinnati and thirty-two pictures for Dayton. But while P.D.C. was making some headway pushing the forthcoming DeMille Pictures product to theaters in midsized cities like Buffalo and Syracuse, the company was still without a first-run outlet in Chicago.

Still, DeMille was enthusiastic about the prospects of his new company, and with a touch of self-satisfaction he reported to Jesse Lasky, "I am not only up to my ears in work, but my ears have entirely disappeared, and even the shock of new hair upon the top of my head is not discernible when I get behind the pile of papers upon my desk. However, it is all terribly interesting work and I have much the same feel as I had when our shoulders were to the same wheel in the little old studio."[17]

The plan for DeMille Pictures was to produce a series of program pictures at a cost of around $200,000 each and for Cecil B. DeMille to produce one or two special productions a year. The rest of the P.D.C. program was to be filled out with pictures from Metropolitan Studios, another subsidiary of Cinema Corporation of America, as well as a few additional features from comedy producer Al Christie and other independent companies.[18]

From the beginning DeMille Pictures had trouble with its series of programmers. With the expense of a large studio and staff, as well as star salaries, the overhead costs were high, and in the first season the company only produced eleven films. One of the studio's first pictures, *The Coming of Amos*, a tongue-in-cheek modern day romantic adventure, cost some $238,000, and DeMille explained that the $38,000 overage was "due to week of bad weather on location and carrying part of initial cost of opening studio."[19]

When a proposed deal with producer Sam E. Rork failed to pan out, DeMille begged to take up the slack, asking Frederick C. Munroe to "give some consideration to the possibility of my doing two extra pictures at this Studio as this would be of great assistance to me in the distribution of overhead which is of necessity very heavy for twelve pictures to carry, and yet it would be dangerous to reduce the burden and still produce the quality of production that we must maintain to compete with Paramount and Metro."[20]

The limits of cooperation between Famous Players-Lasky and DeMille were tested on several occasions. On matters of mercy there was some agreement, but not always on matters of business. On June 15, 1925, DeMille advised Jesse Lasky that the mortgage on Theodore Roberts's house was due on the coming Wednesday. The character actor who had appeared in so many pictures for Lasky was ill and unable to work. DeMille suggested to Lasky that they go in fifty-fifty and pay off the mortgage. The following day Lasky replied, "Have arranged with company to continue paying Theodore Roberts same sum he now receives as long as he lives and is unable to work. Beyond this can do nothing."[21]

But DeMille found that his old company was not always willing to live up to its contractual obligations. On July 3, 1925, DeMille wired Nathan Burkan that he had reviewed ad clippings from several Chicago papers regarding *The Ten Commandments* and noted, "[M]y name appears in very small type reading quote DeMille's Triumph unquote and in two instances my full name in very small type and no mention what ever of picture being a Cecil B. DeMille Production." DeMille asked Burkan to advise Famous Players-Lasky that they were in violation of his contract:

The advertising clause in my contract dated November sixteenth nineteen hundred twenty-three with Famous Players-

Lasky Corporation refers to and incorporates the advertising clause contained in my previous contract dated August sixteenth nineteen hundred twenty . . . which latter clause reads as follows: "Each and every of the pictures delivered under the terms of this contract shall be advertised and publicized by the distributor to the same extent and in the same general manner as is indicated by the advertising and publicity given to the photoplay entitled Male and Female directed by Cecil B. DeMille, and in all publicity and advertising the name of Cecil B. DeMille shall receive such attention and prominence as was given to it in the advertising and publicity of Male and Female and each and every of the said pictures shall be announced as a Cecil B. DeMille production."[22]

Famous Players-Lasky, it would seem, did not want the public to confuse the phrase "a Cecil B. DeMille Production" with Cecil B. DeMille Pictures, Inc., and create the false impression that *The Ten Commandments* was anything but a Paramount Picture.

DeMille was also irked at an internal promotional film made for the 1925 Paramount sales convention. In the film actor Ford Sterling showed returning director Marshall Neilan the current glories of Paramount. At one point they came upon an empty chair with Cecil B. DeMille's name printed on it and a funeral wreath on the seat. "Whatever became of him," Neilan is said to have asked via subtitle. "Oh, he's gone down the road to yesterday," Sterling replied. The rather nasty joke outraged many Paramount exhibitors at the convention, and there was a minor scandal until some ten days later when Marshall Neilan took credit for the film, apologized for any unintended insult, and assured the industry that Adolph Zukor and Sidney R. Kent had no prior knowledge of the film's contents before it was shown at the convention.[23]

*The Road to Yesterday* was DeMille's first special production for the new company. The story involves two couples, newlyweds Kenneth and Malena Paulton and the spoiled Bess Tyrell who is first attracted to and then spurns Jack Moreland, a poor minister. Kenneth has a disfigured arm and Malena cannot stand to be touched by him—elements DeMille had used previously in *For Better, For Worse* and *Feet of Clay*. While the four are en route to Chicago, they are involved in a train crash and are catapulted back in time to seventeenth-century England, where they learn

[*Above*] Edna Goodrich and Horace B. Carpenter in the aborted first version of *The Golden Chance*. (Unless otherwise noted, all photographs are from the author's collection.) [*Below*] The ambiguous and haunting ending of *The Golden Chance* shows the lovers, Roger Manning (Wallace Reid) and Mary Denby (Cleo Ridgely), lost in thought over the tragic consequences of their romance.

[*Above*] "I love him more than home, more than my people, more than God." June Tolliver (Charlotte Walker) pleads with "Devil" Judd Tolliver (Theodore Roberts) for the life of her lover in *The Trail of the Lonesome Pine*. [*Below*] DeMille was involved in the production of a number of films that for one reason or another he declined to include in his personal filmography. Here he directs a sequence from *Nan of Music Mountain* (Famous Players-Lasky, 1917). George Melford received screen credit for directing the film.

[*Above*] On July 19, 1916, Adolph Zukor (left) and Jesse L. Lasky signed a merger agreement creating the Famous Players-Lasky Corporation. Here a cameraman shoots some promotional footage of the partners in the 1920s.

[*Right*] Oil man Frank A. Garbutt (circa 1930), the least known of the principals in the formation of Paramount. Although he was actively involved in the picture business for many years, Garbutt shunned publicity. (Courtesy Frank G. Hathaway)

[Above] DeMille calls, "Action!" as he shoots the trial sequence for *Joan the Woman* on the open-air stage at the Lasky studio. Geraldine Farrar requested mood musicians on the set to aid her performance, and set musicians soon became obligatory on the sets of Hollywood films until the end of the silent era. [Below] A moment between takes on *Joan the Woman.* Cecil B. DeMille chats with Geraldine Farrar and Sam Goldfish (seated in straw hat). A dispute over the status of her husband, actor Lou-Tellegen, led Farrar to quit Famous Players-Lasky in 1917, and Goldfish rushed in to sign her for his newly formed Goldwyn Pictures. (Marc Wanamaker/Bison Archives)

[*Above*] On the glass-covered stage at the Lasky studio, Cecil B. DeMille goes over his list of shots for the day with Mary Pickford and the assistant director. (Marc Wanamaker/Bison Archives) [*Below*] Cecil B. DeMille and Adolph Zukor sit down to tea in Hollywood with Mary Pickford (pouring) and her close friend, screenwriter Francis Marion, in Mary's Japanese-themed studio dressing room in 1917.

[*Above*] Silas Martin (Tully Marshall) attempts to gain the Devil Stone by marrying its current owner, fishermaid Marcia Manot (Geraldine Farrar). The depraved character played by Tully Marshall foreshadows similar characters that would appear later in the films of Erich von Stroheim. [*Below*] A Viking queen (played by Geraldine Farrar) holds the giant emerald known as *The Devil Stone*—which brings a curse on those who possess it. DeMille's flashbacks to historical periods offered the filmmaker an opportunity to add spectacle while keeping production costs in check.

[*Above*] Cecil B. DeMille consults with Famous Players-Lasky studio manager Milton Hoffman between takes. [*Below*] Jeanie Macpherson circa 1918. Macpherson's experience as an outdoorswoman brought added dimension to the character played by Florence Vidor in *Old Wives for New.*

[*Above*] The most intriguing of the seven lost DeMille films is *We Can't Have Everything*, with its depiction of studio life and a send-up of DeMille's directing persona by Tully Marshall (right). Theodore Roberts played the sultan, and cinematographer Alvin Wyckoff did a cameo behind the camera. [*Below*] Although DeMille wanted to go "Over There" as a soldier or flyer during the First World War, he was forced by circumstances to remain in Hollywood and make films about the conflict. He did organize a branch of the California Home Guard, a largely ceremonial unit recruited from the ranks of studio employees. Here DeMille marches his troops down Vine Street.

264-68

[*Above*] Elliott Dexter, Ann Little, and Jack Holt. Dexter took the role of James Wynnegate, the "squaw man" of the title. Jesse Lasky originally intended the remake to feature William Faversham, who originated the role on stage. Judging from stills, DeMille's staging of the action in the saloon bore a striking resemblance to the 1914 original. All but the last reel of the 1918 *Squaw Man* are lost. [*Below*] Shooting a close-up of Edward Burns for *Male and Female* aboard a yacht off Catalina Island. Seated behind DeMille in the white hat is assistant cameraman Jimmy Howe, who would become known as James Wong Howe in his later career as one of Hollywood's top cinematographers. (Courtesy Hollywood Heritage Museum)

[*Above*] Cecil B. DeMille and Gloria Swanson share a moment away from cast and crew during production of *Male and Female*. (Courtesy Hollywood Heritage Museum) [*Below*] Gloria Swanson and Cecil B. DeMille enjoy a box of Cracker Jack during production of *Something to Think About*. Assistant cameraman and future cinematographer James Wong Howe is background right. Editor and continuity secretary Anne Bauchens is seated front with her back to the camera.

*[Above]* Between takes on the outdoor stage at the Lasky studio. DeMille is at left. Cinematographer Alvin Wyckoff stands with hands on hips. The two side-by-side cameras—a Bell & Howell Model 2709 and a Pathé Studio Camera (foreground)—were used to shoot domestic and foreign negatives simultaneously. The Pathé was largely obsolete by 1920, but DeMille had a sentimental attachment for the camera he used on *The Squaw Man* and shot at least one setup with the camera on each of his films through the end of the silent era. (Marc Wanamaker/Bison Archives) *[Below]* Cecil B. DeMille meets with Agnes Ayres, star of *Forbidden Fruit*, in his office at the Famous Players-Lasky studio. (Marc Wanamaker/Bison Archives)

[*Above*] Cecil B. DeMille surrounded by his actors between takes on the Famous Players-Lasky glass stage during production of *The Affairs of Anatol*. (Standing, left to right) Theodore Kosloff, Gloria Swanson, Elliott Dexter, Agnes Ayres, Julia Faye, and Wallace Reid. (Marc Wanamaker/Bison Archives) [*Below*] (Left to right) William C. deMille, Jeanie Macpherson, British novelist Elinor Glynn, and Cecil B. DeMille. Madame Glynn had a bit part in *The Affairs of Anatol* but was best known as the arbiter of "It." (Marc Wanamaker/Bison Archives)

[*Above*] DeMille offers instructions for the *Saturday Night* scene in which Tom McGuire (Jack Mower) rescues Iris Van Suydam (Leatrice Joy). The rescue will lead to a doomed romance between the young society woman and the working man. [*Below*] Cecil B. DeMille, appearing as if he has just returned from an airplane flight, shares a box lunch with Mildred Harris in the Siamese palace set for *Fool's Paradise*. Harris was the first wife of comedian Charlie Chaplin. DeMille would use her in roles of varying importance from *The Warrens of Virginia* in 1915 up to her death at age forty-three in 1944. (Marc Wanamaker/Bison Archives)

[Above] The deMille family in the early 1920s. (Left to right) Cecilia, Cecil, adopted daughter Katherine, and Constance. The deMilles would adopt two more children, Richard and John deMille. Richard deMille was actually the son of William C. deMille and writer Lorna Moon. (Marc Wanamaker/Bison Archives)  [Below] Will H. Hays, former postmaster general and newly appointed president of the Motion Picture Producers and Distributors of America, offers his thoughts on the state of the industry he has been hired to clean up, as Cecil B. DeMille and other Famous Players-Lasky personnel turn out to greet him. The Roscoe "Fatty" Arbuckle scandal in 1921, the murder of director William Desmond Taylor in 1922, and the death of actor Wallace Reid from the effects of morphine addiction in 1923 all involved Paramount employees.

[*Above*] A scene from *Hollywood* (Famous Players-Lasky/Paramount, 1923), shot in DeMille's studio office. Shown here are Jeanie Macpherson, actor Luke Cosgrave, and Cecil B. DeMille. The carved wooden paneling and the cathedral windows were patterned after the taste in decor once exhibited by David Belasco in his Broadway office. [*Below*] What the well-dressed cave girl might have worn. Cecil B. DeMille and Jeanie Macpherson check out costume materials for the prehistoric flashback in *Adam's Rib*.

Two photos from the set of *Adam's Rib*: *[Above]* What the well-dressed flapper will wear. Pauline Garon models her modern-day costumes for DeMille and costume designer Claire West. (Marc Wanamaker/Bison Archives) *[Below]* Cecil B. DeMille directs Elliott Dexter while cameraman Alvin Wyckoff and camera assistant J. Peverell Marley look on. William deMille's cinematographer L. Guy Wilky shared screen credit with Wyckoff, who was turning the crank on his last Cecil B. DeMille film. (Marc Wanamaker/Bison Archives)

that their current troubles have been simmering for many generations. DeMille had long been attracted to the themes of mysticism and reincarnation that were the basis of the source play, but he attributed these elements to Christian rather than occult forces. The film contains many of his favorite elements—trial by fire, love and sacrifice at great personal loss, and the spectacular wreck (which owes much to the "realistic" stage craft of late-nineteenth-century American theater)—however these elements were blended somewhat arbitrarily, and little effort was made to smooth the transitions between the first- and third-act modern story and the second-act flashback.

Reaction to the New York trade showing of *The Road to Yesterday* was positive, but the film did not find an audience. Perhaps because the new Producers Distributing Corporation could not market the picture properly, or perhaps because audiences were tired of historical flashbacks, film rentals on *The Road to Yesterday* were decidedly meager, and DeMille bid farewell to the flashback as a story device.[24]

# The Volga Boatman

Cecil B. DeMille Pictures for Producers Distributing Corporation release. Director: Cecil B. DeMille. Scenario by Lenore Coffee, from the novel by Konrad Bercovici. Art directors: Max Parker, Mitchell Leisen, and Anton Grot. Assistant director: Frank Urson. Costumes: Adrian. Photography: Arthur Miller, J. Peverell Marley, and Fred Westerberg. Film editor: Anne Bauchens

Picture started: November 9, 1925. Picture finished: January 8, 1926. Length: 9,596 feet (eleven reels). Cost: $479,356.99. Released: April 13, 1926 (New York premiere). Gross: $1,275,374.78

Cast: William Boyd (Feodor, a Volga boatman), Elinor Fair (Vera, a princess of Russia), Robert Edeson (Prince Nikita, her father), Victor Varconi (Prince Dimitri, an officer in the White Army), Julia Faye (Mariusha, a Tartar camp-follower), Theodore Kosloff (Stephan, a mute blacksmith), and Arthur Rankin (Vasili, a boatman)

For his second personal production DeMille was urged to make a film with a Russian theme by his long-time associate, actor and ballet choreographer Theodore Kosloff. DeMille Pictures paid $9,000 for the screen rights to Konrad Bercovici's novel *The Volga Boatman*. But if the director was able to acquire this property at a relatively modest fee, in general DeMille Pictures was finding it tough going in the literary market place. On November 7, 1925, DeMille wrote his story editor Ella K. Adams, "Deem it advisable you return [to Los Angeles from New York] immediately for conference on material . . . it being evident we cannot purchase New York stage plays account prices. Believe magazines, originals and old novels rather than new best sellers at fancy prices will be source from which we must draw supply."[1]

It seems odd that a conservative Republican like Cecil B. DeMille should make a film dealing with the Russian Revolution, but in 1925 the world was still excited about the overthrow of the Czar, and Soviet films and art, though not widely circulated in the West, were admired in critical circles. Even so, DeMille carefully constructed his script in a manner that insured no segment of the audience would be offended.

The story revolves around two men, Prince Dimitri, an officer in the White Russian army, and Feodor, a barge hauler on the Volga River. Both men are in love with the princess Vera. The Russian Revolution tips the scales of romance first to one man and then the other, while Vera's life is threatened at every turn. Feodor sacrifices his love and escorts Dimitri and Vera safely to the border, but in the best romantic tradition, she elects to remain with Feodor.

Although he had been featured in *The Road to Yesterday* and played smaller bits in several earlier DeMille films, *The Volga Boatman* marked William Boyd's first starring role. The actor came to DeMille's attention when the director was shooting a swimming scene for *Saturday Night*. Working as an extra, Boyd managed to cover (quite literally) for actress Julia Faye when her patent leather bathing suit split at the seams as she hit the water. Later, DeMille asked Boyd to come to his office. He motioned the aspiring actor to a chair, but the afternoon sun glared through the window behind DeMille's desk and blinded him. Sensing that DeMille was attempting to intimidate him, Boyd got up, turned over a wastepaper basket beside the desk, and sat down on it so he could see the director's face. DeMille was delighted with Boyd's bravado and they became fast friends.

As *The Volga Boatman* neared production *The Road to Yesterday* had not yet opened, and the new studio had only released one picture, *The Coming of Amos*. Through his attorney, Neil McCarthy, DeMille urged his New York finance committee to approve a budget of $400,000 for his second personal production, but the company was reluctant to increase its commitment.

"I appreciate keenly your desire to make biggest picture possible of *Volga Boatman* and need not tell you how desirous we are in every way to support you in whatever you feel best to do in production," wrote F.C. Munroe. "At the same time strongly urge that you reconsider budget and endeavor to figure out way by which you can produce *Volga Boatman* for three hundred fifty thousand. . . . It will help us all here very much if you and John [Flinn] can figure out a way of keeping within total figure for financing as expressed in Motion Picture Capital contract."[2]

On November 7, two days before the first day of principal photography on *The Volga Boatman*, DeMille appointed William Sistrom as general manager of both the DeMille and Metropolitan studios to relieve himself of some of the administrative chores for which he had little patience.

Shooting *The Volga Boatman* was an ordeal. Weather on the Sacramento River delta location was bitterly cold, and cloud cover severely restricted shooting opportunities. DeMille had only thirty-five minutes of usable light on November 16. In addition to the physical problems, DeMille was working with a new cameraman. Cinematographer Arthur Miller was a brilliant visual stylist later noted for such 20th Century-Fox films as *The Rains Came* (1939), *The Mark of Zorro* (1940), and *How Green Was My Valley* (1941). There was no question of Miller's talent, but apparently he was slower than DeMille was used to in setting up shots. DeMille and Miller were also experimenting with newly perfected panchromatic film. "Pan" film offered great advantages over orthochromatic film. Both are black-and-white stocks, but they respond to the visual color spectrum in quite different ways. Ortho sees the color red as black or dark shades of grey, and requires white actors to wear heavy compensating makeup to keep them from appearing dark-skinned on-screen. Ortho also tends to wash out blue light, making it difficult to capture cloud detail in outdoor scenes. Panchromatic film solves many of these problems, but requires different makeup techniques and the use of contrast filters outdoors to obtain optimal results. Using a yellow contrast filter when shooting outdoors enhances cloud detail. A green filter can create dramatic effects by darkening skin tones. A red filter will produce a black sky, which is ideal for creating credible "day for night" scenes without having to resort to blue tinting in release prints, but the red filter causes faces to appear ghostly white unless compensating makeup is used.

Miller and DeMille agreed before shooting to use panchromatic film where it would enhance the overall photographic effect, but during production DeMille became increasingly impatient with Miller's lack of confidence in using the new panchromatic stock. "I didn't know anything about panchromatic film, other than the fact that I'd shot a roll in Rome, on THE ETERNAL CITY," Miller recalled in a 1970 interview with Leonard Maltin.

> I'd been shooting down the river. . . . I was down low with the camera . . . with the sun in back of me, with the blue sky up above. I wanted a lot of blue sky. Now I wanted the reverse . . . going away, so all I had to do was turn the camera around and look up the river, and I was looking into the sun, so I'd get the streak on the water. I didn't know what the hell I'd get with panchromatic film; I'd never tried it and I didn't want to take

a chance. It would only have taken me a minute and a half to change the magazine . . . the old man looked down and said, "I don't understand this; first you want this film, then you want another film. Just what do you want?" I looked up at him and I said, "All I want right now, for Christ's sake, is for you to let me alone so I can get the film on the camera, get the camera set, and get the boat going up the river before the sun drops down into the picture!" Well, nobody ever talked to Mr. DeMille like that, I'm sure.[3]

DeMille could be a tyrant on the set. Some who only knew him in a working environment, with the pressure of schedule and budget ever looming, found him to be disagreeable at best and downright nasty at other times. His family would quaintly say, "He had all the patience God gave him, because he never used any of it," and he was known to take out his frustrations on his crew and the army of extras he often employed, though he rarely turned his temper on his leading players.[4]

Losing DeMille's confidence, Miller seemed to feel that his every move was being questioned by the director. The cameraman eventually walked off the set and asked to be released from his contract. DeMille told *The Volga Boatman* company that Miller had been taken ill, and the cinematographer was reassigned to work with other directors. Miller retained his first position screen credit as cinematographer on *The Volga Boatman,* though he shared credit with J. Peverell Marley, who took over as first cameraman.

A month into production, DeMille was feeling expansive about his latest production. Revised budget estimates for *The Volga Boatman* projected the final negative cost to be $484,000—a figure that included $50,000 in contingency set-asides. On December 7, DeMille suggested to F.C. Munroe that the company spend an additional $50,000—above and beyond the $484,000—and turn *The Volga Boatman* into a road-show attraction. "In my opinion this is exceptional production," DeMille wired, "and by spending fifty thousand in addition to estimated cost . . . believe it could be road showed and gross conservatively two million. I suggest you have J.J. McCarthy [who handled the road-show releases of *Ben-Hur* and *The Big Parade* (both M-G-M, 1925)] come to Los Angeles immediately to view production in its present condition and discuss matter with me . . . provided [John] Flinn can withdraw picture from regular program release."[5]

214 / Cecil B. DeMille's Hollywood

Due to ill health and his ongoing business with M-G-M, J.J. McCarthy could not come to Los Angeles, and Munroe sought "further information as to what you have in mind for augmenting story or production before definitely deciding here what can be done in arranging additional finance to cover your recommendations."[6] DeMille advised that the "Purpose of additional funds is to add certain scenes of epic quality which would assist in road showing values. This however could be added after the picture is completed but important we make decision on matter at earliest possible moment as it will effect somewhat the treatment for balance of story as to tempo and length."[7]

The prospect of road showing *The Volga Boatman* was made more attractive, in DeMille's mind at least, because Samuel Goldwyn had leased George White's Apollo Theatre in New York and another house in Chicago in which to play his production of *Stella Dallas* (Goldwyn-United Artists, 1925), and he was looking to unload his excess lease time after *Stella Dallas* closed. This ensured the availability of road-show venues in the two largest cities. On December 15 DeMille advised Munroe, "I am convinced picture is too big to get best results without either road showing or arranging for extended runs in eight or ten big cities. . . . I will discuss picture fully with Sam Goldwyn, show him some of the film and get his reaction as to its roadshowing possibilities as I hesitate to take the responsibility of making this decision alone on one of my own productions."[8]

Two days later, DeMille told Munroe he had arranged to screen the work in progress for Goldwyn, "but as I am putting in twenty hours a day work on the production and must continue to do so until it is finished, I do not want to take time to confer over road showing it unless [P.D.C. executive] John Flinn thinks he can get theatres to release it."[9]

Munroe responded both with good news and some decidedly bad news. "Our opinion in view of existing contracts for *Volga Boatman* in twenty-three hundred eighty-three theatres precludes policy of handling picture as road show in strictest sense of term," he stated. But while the total number of contracted theaters was impressive, they must have all been in tank towns, because Munroe's list of cities that had not yet contracted to play the picture included virtually every major population center in the country: Atlanta, Baltimore, Chicago, Denver, Des Moines, Detroit, Kansas City, Los Angeles, Minneapolis, New York, Pittsburgh, San Francisco, and Seattle. Mentioning that as many as sixty "smaller key points" were up for grabs, Munroe also noted, "Exhibitors are meeting with disappointment in box office receipts of Road to Yesterday, which reason further prompt us in decision not to attempt to disturb existing contracts." He went on to say that there would be no approval for a budget increase.[10]

DeMille reported that Sam Goldwyn, after seeing an assembly of the unfinished film, was encouraging about the picture's road-show potential, but the director also gave up his expansive plans and promised that the final cost would not exceed $485,000.

Without the added expenditure, *The Volga Boatman* turned out to be the epic on a budget that DeMille warned about. Settings were often suggestive rather than realistic, as in scenes of the boatmen hauling loaded barges up the Volga River, where the far bank is implied by silhouettes of trees and buildings. Although there are some impressive moments, the picture seems padded at times with footage that could have been trimmed with little loss in overall dramatic impact.

Still, despite its disappointing pre-release contracts, *The Volga Boatman* rang up some formidable film rentals and helped keep DeMille Pictures afloat after the failure of *The Road to Yesterday* and the generally dismal performance of the studio's slate of program pictures. It also spawned a short cycle of films dealing with the Russian revolution and its aftermath, including *Mockery* (M-G-M, 1927), *The Red Dance* (Fox, 1928), *Tempest* (United Artists, 1928), *The Scarlet Lady* (Columbia, 1928), and *The Last Command* (Paramount-Famous-Lasky, 1928).

*The Volga Boatman* also inspired a lasting offscreen romance. A thirteen year-old school girl named Grace Bradley fell madly in love with William Boyd when she saw the film and dreamed of becoming his wife. Several years later, and working in pictures herself, the starlet met her dream lover of the silent screen. They were married in 1937.

# The King of Kings

Cecil B. DeMille Pictures for Producers Distributing Corporation release. Director: Cecil B. DeMille. Scenario by Jeanie Macpherson. Assistant director: Frank Urson. Art direction: Mitchell Leisen, Dan Sayre Groesbeck, and Anton Grot. Photography: J. Peverell Marley, Fred Westerberg, and J.A. Badaracco. Film editors: Anne Bauchens and Harold McLernon. Musical setting: Hugo Riesenfeld

Picture started: August 24, 1926. Picture finished: January 10, 1927. Length: 14,200 feet (eighteen reels) (later cut to 10,391 feet [twelve reels] for 1928 general release). Cost: $1,265,283.95 (approximate). Released: April 19, 1927 (New York premiere). Gross: $2,641,687.21

Cast: H.B. Warner (Jesus, the Christ), Ernest Torrence (Peter), Joseph Schildkraut (Judas), James Neill (James), Joseph Striker (John), Robert Edeson (Matthew), Sidney D'Albrook (Thomas), David Imboden (Andrew), Charles Belcher (Philip), Clayton Packard (Bartholomew), Robert Ellsworth (Simon), Charles Requa (James, the Less), John T. Prince (Thaddeus), Jacqueline Logan (Mary Magdalene), Rudolph Schildkraut (Caiaphas), Victor Varconi (Pontius Pilate), William Boyd (Simon of Cyrene), Montagu Love (Roman centurion), and Dorothy Cumming (Mary, the mother)

In his autobiography Cecil B. DeMille chose to remember *The King of Kings* as the film that made his studio possible, but scant evidence exists to suggest that he actually pitched the idea of filming the life of Christ during his initial meetings with financier Jeremiah Milbank. It would be more accurate to say that the film allowed DeMille's faltering company to continue in operation as picture after picture in the studio's regular program failed at the box office.[1]

DeMille originally planned to make *The Deluge*, based on the Old Testament story of Noah and the Flood, as his next personal production; but it was abandoned when he learned that Warner Bros. intended to produce *Noah's Ark* (1928). The Warner project could have been a DeMille film—it featured a modern story, a train wreck, characters catapulted back through time, and a cataclysm of epic proportion. DeMille had little reason to shoot his own version, especially given P.D.C.'s weak distribution capabilities.

On May 20, 1926, after learning that *The Deluge* was being abandoned, DeMille Pictures contract writer Denison Clift suggested another biblical story.[2] He wrote:

> Why skirt around the one great single subject of all time and all ages—the commanding, majestic and most sublime thing that any man can ever put upon the screen: the Life, Trial, Crucifixion, Resurrection and Ascension of Christ: in other words, the LIFE OF CHRIST, with its awe-inspiring power, its simplicity and its unutterable tragedy. There are only one or two men who could possibly have within themselves the power and the understanding to do this thing. Certainly, to my mind, you are the one to do it.
>
> The title of the picture would be:
>
> THE KING OF KINGS[3]

The idea appealed to DeMille. More important, it appealed to Jeremiah Milbank, who was apparently willing to back such a film no matter what the cost. Milbank's commitment would become crucial, as money grew scarce at the DeMille studio.

If DeMille had the same enthusiasm for his new company as he had with Lasky in 1914, he also had many of the same headaches—but without the benefit of a string of box-office hits. By August 5, 1926, the situation was desperate. Even as company comptroller G.M. Davidson was turning off the cash spigot, DeMille pleaded with F.C. Munroe:

> Need for working capital at DeMille studio imperative. [G.M.] Davidson's recent adjustment simply wiped out capital furnished last year and leaves not one dollar other than production funds. The need for capital is for exactly the same purpose as at Metropolitan [Studio] and is about in proportion to production program. DeMille plant handling more than four million [dollars] and Metropolitan less than two million. You have seen the need for and actually furnished two hundred thousand [dollars] capital at Metropolitan. The following items must be covered: first, last year's plant improvements, equipment purchases and payments on [Ince] studio purchase contract [amounting to] one hundred thirty thousand [dollars];

second, this year's improvements, equipment purchases, necessary advance production work, supplies necessarily carried in stock, [amounting to] three hundred thousand. Against this if the one hundred thousand [dollars] furnished last year is considered withdrawn we can only figure depreciation reserves and accounts payable, a total of about two hundred thousand. Therefore a minimum working capital of two hundred thousand is essential and should be provided at the rate of not less than ten thousand [dollars a week]. . . . Only by providing capital can we avoid last year's situation of having spent production funds without having made the productions. Situation will be extremely acute from September on and will be impossible at end of production year because we will not have the funds to make the productions on which we will have already received advances . . . no settlement will meet situation other than furnishing actual money.[4]

Ultimately DeMille received the cash his studio needed by means of a shrewd conspiracy with Jeremiah Milbank. *The King of Kings* would cost approximately $1,265,283.95 in direct costs, but the final cost was actually carried on the books as $2,265,283.95, with the extra million used to bury the "cost of studio building and stock company [of contract actors] carried for other productions."[5] This deception hid some of the real costs of the company's other product and allowed Milbank and DeMille, who retained ownership of *The King of Kings* after the company was sold to other interests, to show a loss on an otherwise successful film.

Although Denison Clift proposed the idea for *The King of Kings*, DeMille turned to Jeanie Macpherson to adapt the Gospels into a scenario. "I became aware of the slavery that attached to the office of an author in Hollywood," wrote Daniel A. Lord, S.J., who served as the official advisor for the Catholic Church on the film during production. "Jeanie Macpherson was the scenarist, swiftly killing herself with an intensity of work and a passion for precise detail that kept her on a sixteen-hour-a-day schedule during the long months of production. In a welded devotion to her work she had no time for anything—friendship, correspondence, hobbies, or care for her health."[6]

According to Lord, based on the success of *The Ten Command-*

*ments*, DeMille and Macpherson originally intended *The King of Kings* to have a similar two-part structure with a modern story dealing with a man who tries to walk in the footsteps of Christ; but they gave up on this idea early on. However, DeMille was insistent on developing a love story between Judas and Mary Magdalene, which was derived "out of some ancient and little-known German legend of the Middle Ages."[7]

Casting proceeded as the script was being prepared. By July 21, 1926, DeMille had decided on H.B. Warner to play the Christ. He seemed an odd choice for the role. The son of famed British stage star Charles Warner, Henry Byron Warner had achieved his greatest success on-screen in the late 1910s. By 1926, he was fifty years old and nearly forgotten in Hollywood. His relative anonymity was certainly a plus, for he did not have to shed an already established screen image. Of course, a newcomer could have been used, but for DeMille, who had a great deal of appreciation for proven talent, the fact that Warner brought some forty years of stage and screen experience to the role must have been decisive.

Among those tested for the role of Mary Magdalene were Jetta Goudal, Evelyn Brent, Mildred Harris, Julia Faye, Phyllis Haver, Paulette Duval, Barbara Bedford, Gretchen Thomas, May Allison, Lila Lee, Estelle Taylor, Seena Owen, Virginia Valli, Ruth Clifford, Kathleen Key, Anne McKay, Margueritte de la Motte, and Selina Royle. All would receive a form letter from DeMille stating that the part was destined for another:

My dear Miss _____,

Allow me to express to you my thanks and appreciation of your interest in making the tests of the Magdalene for THE KING OF KINGS.

Your tests were excellent and in them you look beautiful and show unquestionably that you have the talent and ability necessary to portray this difficult role; but the Committee, composed of Mr. Jesse L. Lasky, Mr. Sam Goldwyn, Mr. Bruce Barton, Mr. Sid Grauman, Mrs. Lasky and Mrs. Barton have chosen Miss Jacqueline Logan, not because they feel her ability is any greater than yours, but because of type.[8]

With kind personal regards,

Very truly yours,[9]

On August 23, 1926, DeMille invited his cast and technical staff to his home for the now traditional reading of the script. With an intermission for lunch and a discussion afterword, the session took six and a half hours. Before detailing the narrative, DeMille offered some of his thoughts and concerns about the project and the audience with an odd mix of reverence and ballyhoo, which in some ways was a dry run for his 1956 *Ten Commandments* curtain speech:

> Our story, ladies and gentlemen, has to do with Jesus Christ, His life, His ideals, and what he stood for.
>
> The story has to do with bringing to the public an understanding of the Greatest Man who ever lived—an understanding that is not as general as it should be. It is an unfolding of the greatest love story of the ages.
>
> The story will present to the coming generation who now fill our schools and colleges a picturization of the life and particularly the ideals of this Man of Galilee—Jesus of Nazareth.
>
> And, speaking of schools and colleges a recent examination of over nine thousand college students brought forth this result concerning their understanding of the Bible and the life and ideals of Jesus Christ. Sixteen percent did not know where Christ was born. Seventeen percent did not know of the Sermon on the Mount; Sixty percent did not know what Christ meant by, "Love thy neighbor as thyself." Sixty-five percent did not know the Golden Rule; forty percent thought that Saint Paul was only a book in the Bible. Thirty percent thought that Jesus was the name of a river; three percent thought that Herod was an apostle; twelve percent thought that Peter was a king and nine percent thought that Peter was a priest; some of them thought the Revelations was a Province and many thought that Martha was a book of the Bible; some thought that the Elders were some kind of a bush and that the Scribes were bad men and the Tithes were something with which you fastened things together; nine percent thought that "Sin" meant debt.
>
> Of course it is this class that we have to combat and interest, this class that does not know what it is all about. We must interest this class as well as to satisfy them and hold

them interested in the story. We must interest this class and hold them, as well as the other class, born with a Bible in their hand, who will criticize and hurl curses if we change an "if" or fail to dot an "i."

We have to protect all classes of people, especially the Jew. The purpose of the story is to treat all classes fairly and particularly the Jew, because the Jew is put in the most unfortunate place of any race in the Bible, because it was not really a matter of the Jew having persecuted Jesus, it was Rome, Rome with her politics and graft.

The difficult thing of course is to tell the story so as not to offend any religion or sect, to attack certain usages of ancient Rome, and show the crucifixion of Christ, His persecution, not by the Jewish people, but by a group of Roman politicians who saw that the ideals of Jesus, accepted by the people, would sweep away the power of Rome, who saw their power being taken away by the man from Galilee. They saw their great system of graft being swept away, a system comparable to our Boss system of today.

In the discussion that followed, Cecil sought suggestions for cuts in the script.

C.B. DeMille: My particular interest is in taking out rather than putting in. I now have about 36 reels and that is altogether too long. Bill, how do you feel about the feeding of the five thousand?

W.C. de Mille: My own idea is that it should come out. Also I think we have too much Caiaphas and Pilate after the crucifixion. That is the way it struck me. It drags. There is too much anti-climax and it extends over too long a period. The audience wants that resurrection and what it stands for, but they are pretty tired afterwards. That crucifixion is going to be a pretty hard thing to sit through.

CB: Don't you think it is necessary to give some little something, to let it sink in that he is dead.

WC: You get it all, from the disciples in the room of the last supper.

CB: Yes, but you don't get it until afterwards. Of course it could be advanced.

WC: Yes, it could be.

CB: Then too, there is that point that always used to bother me in reading the scriptures. I said to myself a hundred times, "Well, maybe the disciples did steal Him away." If we could see that answered, I think that is a point many people have thought about.

WC: That is a point some people believe and some people don't believe. I don't think I would try to prove it. They are not going to believe in it anyway just because they see it on the screen.

CB: Yes they are. If you printed seventy five million Bibles, their idea of the life of Jesus Christ is going to be formed by what we give them. This next generation will get its idea of Jesus Christ from this picture.[10]

If Cecil seemed presumptuous in promoting the importance of his film, there is no question that he was sincere in his desire to tell the story of Jesus of Nazareth without consciously offending believers. On the first day of production, August 31, 1926, he spoke to his assembled company before the cameras started to turn:

You cannot take a picture of a character the whole world is praying to every day . . . and do anything that will show the slightest disrespect. The world gets down on its knees and prays to these figures. . . . You cannot take the figure of Jesus Christ and say, "Well, look. Here comes Holy jumping Jesus Christ himself." That thing will jar and shock, and it will do immeasurable damage to the great work you have undertaken. . . . I am going to ask for your very sincere cooperation along those lines. It is so very, very important. . . . They will be watching us all the time we are making the picture and they are very easily shocked by the things that we might very innocently and very easily do. You cannot see the figure of Jesus Christ sitting on a stump smoking a large cigar without immediately associating that with what he stands for. It would hurt you. It will hurt many who are a great deal more sensitive than we are. We must treat these characters while they are in makeup as if they were the original characters of the Bible. May I have your cooperation on that?[11]

Much of the action was shot on Catalina Island to avoid gawking visitors; but even on so reverential a subject the practicalities of film-making received due consideration. On August 17, 1926, DeMille advised art director Paul Iribe to "Make the carpenter shop location right near or the same as the feeding of the FIVE THOUSAND—so as to save having to transport the people to two places." On September 7, DeMille wrote Iribe, "to suggest that you utilize the miniature backing used on the Mary of Magdala set, which can be added to and made to be the City of Jerusalem for the background shooting away from the cross on Calvary." The same day DeMille proclaimed, "The final title of our picture will be AMEN—not The End." He ordered that the final visual effect with the closing title be shot in French, Italian, German, and Scandinavian versions so that the visual integrity of the closing could be maintained for most audiences, and he insisted that appropriate language Bible translations be used for foreign subtitles, not simply free translations from English.[12]

Observing DeMille during the making of *The King of Kings*, Daniel Lord described him as "a strange and fascinating blend of absolute monarch and charming gentleman, of excellent host and exacting taskmaster, of ruthless drive on the set and complete letdown the moment that the day's shooting had come to an end; a Renaissance prince who had the instincts of a Barnum and a magnified Belasco; frankly in love with hokum (which he liked to discuss and reduce to terms of understandable basic emotion)."[13]

Lord was disturbed, if not horrified, by some of DeMille's "improvements" to the Gospels, but as the production went on, he said, "a strange thing had begun to happen. . . . Christ began to take over. It was a motion-picture Christ. It was a Christ of synthetic whiskers and grease paint. H.B. Warner was a good actor but by no means a great one. . . . He moved about in his public life, quietly, effectively, miraculously, without too much emphasis on the divine nature (this was not eliminated but never underlined), and yet compellingly, Christ was doing to the film what Christ does to all life, once He has been given a chance. He was so dominating that no one else mattered."[14]

During the screening of rushes one evening DeMille reached out and touched Daniel Lord's hand:

"He is great, isn't He?" DeMille said.

"Warner?" Lord responded.

"Jesus. He is great." Then after a pause, "I doubt if we shall need the story of Mary Magdalene and Judas."[15]

224 / Cecil B. DeMille's Hollywood

Because of concern that any hint of scandal could ruin box-office prospects for *The King of Kings*, the players were required to sign a clause requiring exemplary behavior on and off the set. Publicist Barrett Kiesling told film czar Will H. Hays that "Dorothy Cumming [who played Mary, Mother of Jesus] agreed to let DeMille approve any role she might take for a period of five years. . . . Warner, [who is] under contract, was not forced to sign such an agreement, but it was understood."[16] No hint of scandal marred the production, but several years later a bit player who portrayed Mary Magdalene's maid would gain a degree of notoriety for her fan dance at the Chicago World's Fair. Her name was Sally Rand.

On March 9, 1927, not long after shooting was completed, DeMille Studio staffer W.G. Crothers reminded DeMille:

It is customary at the close of each picture, to quote to the Producers Association, the salaries paid artists in that picture.

In the "King of Kings," so many people were willing and anxious to cut their salaries to work in the picture with you, it seems unfair to me that we should hurt these actors and actresses, by making it possible for other studios to find out what salaries they received.

For example: Ernest Torrence's salary is $3500; he worked for $300. Dorothy Cumming's salary is $600; she worked for $400. Casson Fergusson's salary is $500; he worked for $250. Jacqueline Logan's salary is $3,000; she worked for $500, and so on. Practically everyone in the cast cut their salary some.[17]

In a handwritten note on Crothers's letter DeMille stated: "I instructed Crothers not to submit salaries."

Despite DeMille's best intentions, reaction to *The King of Kings* in the Jewish community was mixed. Soon after the New York premiere at the Gaiety Theatre, Rabbi Edgar F. Magnin wired DeMille from Los Angeles: "Delighted to receive your telegram. Knew The King of Kings would be a success. Hearty congratulations to you and Miss Macpherson. I believe this picture will exercise a spiritual and wholesome effect upon all who will have the privilege of witnessing it. Kindest Regards."

But others in the Jewish community took great exception to the film, and a committee consisting of Rabbi Stephen S. Wise; Senator Alfred M. Cohen; Dr. Boris D. Bogan, president and executive secretary of the

B'nai B'rith; and composer-conductor Hugo Riesenfeld was appointed
to review the film and suggest changes. The committee looked at the
picture, but Rabbi Wise backed out of any further participation.

Changes were made. A foreword was added before the main title:

> The Events portrayed by this picture
> occurred in Palestine nineteen centuries
> ago, when the Jews were under the
> complete subjugation of Rome—Even
> their own High Priest being appointed by
> the Roman procurator.

And subtitles were changed. The title introducing the character
Caiaphas originally read:

> The High Priest CAIAPHAS—who cared
> more for Revenue than for Religion—and saw
> in Jesus a menace to his rich profits from the Temple.

It was replaced by:

> The High Priest CAIAPHAS—an appointee
> of the Roman government, and arch-enemy of Jesus.
> Upon him rests the responsibility for the world's supreme
> tragedy.

Some changes were subtle. A title in reel 7 originally read:

> The TEMPLE . . . to the faithful of Israel,
> the dwelling place of Jehovah.
> But to the High Priest, Caiaphas,
> a corrupt and profitable market-place.

The revised text read:

> The TEMPLE . . . to the Jewish people a
> cherished sanctuary.
> But to the High Priest, Caiaphas,
> a profitable market-place.

Also, intercuts of Caiaphas and the Pharisees with images of Jesus on the Cross were ordered removed. In all, there were minor changes to ten of the eighteen reels. But these concessions did not solve the problem. Out of the blue, on December 4, 1927, over seven months after the film's initial release, Rabbi Stephen S. Wise delivered a sermon at Carnegie Hall, condemning the film and publicly taking Rabbi Edgar F. Magnin to task for his support of DeMille. Rabbi Magnin was sufficiently concerned about the potential damage to his reputation that he consulted with DeMille and obtained a copy of his congratulatory telegram so that he could frame a response. The dispute eventually blew over with little damage to Magnin or the film.

After the initial road-show engagements, and after Pathé had taken over the P.D.C. interests, *The King of Kings* was recut for general release. A little over 3,800 feet, or some forty-two minutes of running time, were eliminated. Major cuts included scenes in which Judas attempts to heal a retarded child, Peter finds a gold coin in the mouth of a fish he has caught, and Peter betrays Jesus three times before dawn. But beyond the cuts, the film was dramatically restructured with scenes moved around and some titles changed. To accompany the shortened general release, Hugo Riesenfeld's New York premiere score was adapted by Pathé music director Josiah Zuro and recorded by the RCA-Photophone process. Although the long version of *The King of Kings* survives, it is the short version that has been in general circulation since 1928.

*The King of Kings* has become Cecil B. DeMille's most enduring film. What makes the film so moving is the simplicity and sincerity with which it was made. In a radio address broadcast over Los Angeles station KNX on July 11, 1927, DeMille concluded by saying: "I am only the humble and thankful instrument through which the screen . . . is carrying the greatest of all messages to hundreds of thousands of fellow human beings."[18]

After its theatrical run DeMille supplied the picture at reduced rentals to any organization that wanted to show it. In 1961, after DeMille's death, *The King of Kings* was sold to Modern Sound Pictures, which continued DeMille's policy of making the film widely available.

# The Godless Girl

Cecil B. DeMille Pictures for Pathé Exchange, Inc., release. Director: Cecil B. DeMille. Original story and scenario by Jeanie Macpherson. Additional writing: Ernest Pascal. Titles: Beulah Marie Dix. Art direction: Mitchell Leisen. Photography: J. Peverell Marley. Assistant director: Frank Urson. Costumes: Adrian. Film editor: Anne Bauchens

Picture started: January 3, 1928. Picture completed: March 24, 1928. Length: 9,129 feet (twelve reels). Cost: $722,315.17. Premiere: August 20, 1928, at Biltmore Theatre, Los Angeles. General release: March 31, 1929. Gross: $489,095.49

Cast: Lina Basquette (The Godless Girl), George Duryea (Bob, the Boy), Marie Prevost (Mame), Eddie Quillan (Bozo, the goat), Noah Beery (head guard), Clarence Burton (guard), Mary Jane Irving (the victim), Gertrude Quality, Kate Price, and Hedwig Reicher (matrons), and Julia Faye, Emily Barrye, and Jacqueline Dyris (inmates)

On May 11, 1927, during the early research stages of *The Godless Girl*, DeMille wired Charles Beahan, East Coast story editor for DeMille Pictures, that he wanted to close a deal for screen rights to the play *Chicago*, as he had received assurances that Will Hays and the Motion Picture Producers and Distributors Association would not object to bringing the story to the screen. *Chicago* is about a two-timing wife who kills her boyfriend and becomes a flash-in-the-pan celebrity during the ensuing "Trial of the Century."[1]

The resulting film was controversial enough that DeMille Pictures attached a special title to the front of the picture especially for censor board screenings. It read:

Chicago attacks a great evil in our time—the hysterical tendency
to make a vulgar criminal an heroic figure in a public circus.
Since the force of the story comes from the biting truth
with which it is presented we ask you to consider very earnestly
before suggesting changes which may weaken its effect.

In production from September 30 through November 20, 1927, *Chicago* was credited to Frank Urson as director but in every other respect it bears the stamp of a Cecil B. DeMille personal production—photography by J. Peverell Marley, art direction by Mitchell Leisen, assistant director Roy Burns, costumes by Adrian, film edited by Anne Bauchens. In the January 1928 issue of *Picture Play Magazine*, Edwin and Elza Schallert wrote:

> It has been done with much secrecy, but facts will out. Cecil B. DeMille is directing "Chicago," the film based on the famous stage satire on the farcical way in which murder trials are sometimes conducted. DeMille's name, however, probably won't be mentioned on the screen when the picture is released, except as general supervisor.
> He became so interested in the story during its preparation that he couldn't resist the temptation to make it himself. So, when "Chicago" comes to the screen, you will know the reason if it seems to be replete with the famous DeMille touches.

The Schallerts apparently had the inside scoop. DeMille kept a record of *Chicago* in his list of personal productions compiled by his secretaries—although only with the credit "Supervision by: Cecil B. DeMille." He also kept a print of *Chicago* at home in his personal vault—something he did with none of his other DeMille Pictures supervised productions. There may have been reason to not associate his name with the film. On December 21, 1927, DeMille urged Sid Grauman to book *Chicago* into his Chinese Theatre, but the showman replied on December 30:

> Dear Mr. DeMille
> . . . I want you to know that I deeply appreciate that you gave me an opportunity to see this great picture. I am sure it is going to be an absolute clean up, but do not feel it is the kind of production for this house at this time so close to the "King of Kings" and on that I would not deem it best to play.

But if *Chicago* was considered too hot to follow *King of Kings*, *The Godless Girl*, with its seemingly improbable story of atheism in public school and sadism in reform school, seems a curious substitute. The film could easily be dismissed as ludicrous exploitation fare designed with a cynical eye toward the box office, but in fact the two major background elements—the high school "Godless Society" and the unrelenting brutality against underage inmates—were based on fact.

The idea for the picture first took shape after DeMille inquired about the screen rights to T.E. Lawrence's *Revolt in the Desert*, and was informed by Charles Beahan that publisher George H. Doran & Co. wanted $75,000 dollars for the screen rights and the scenario had to be approved by Lawrence's agents. Such an expense was prohibitive for the shaky company, and on May 27, 1927, DeMille wired Beahan:

> Am much interested in story dealing with boy's and girl's reformatories and [need] some inside information on conduct of these places stop Not what one would get from superintendents or officers but facts from boys and girls recently released whose confidence you may be able to obtain and whom you may be able to get to talk to you stop Please get on this yourself immediately or put someone on it and see if you can have something for me . . . stop Understand the inmates of these institutions use sign language, that they are not allowed to speak to each other except at certain times, that there is no beauty whatsoever inside the walls, that they are taught to spy on each other etc stop Secure as much data as possible and if you think advisable register idea with Hays office although I have as yet no title for story stop Am interested in this personally stop

Beahan made some preliminary inquiries and obtained permission to visit several East Coast reformatories. On June 9 he wired DeMille that he had registered the reformatory idea with the Motion Picture Producers and Distributors of America under the tentative title *The World against Them*.

Elizabeth McGaffey headed research efforts and received affidavits from former inmates attesting to the use of electrified fences and bloodhounds in Nebraska. In other states she also confirmed incidents of girls being tied and whipped with straps. Sometimes, teenage female prisoners were also confined in straitjackets or shackles during solitary confinement, and boys were being chained to bars in solitary. McGaffey received thirteen affidavits and four letters from those who had experienced water torture firsthand during their incarcerations.

While this research proceeded, a flyer distributed by the American Association for the Advancement of Atheism created a stir when it was found in student lockers at Hollywood High School:

ATHEISTS! ATTENTION! THE AAAA ANNOUNCES
THAT ON FRIDAY, JUNE 10, 1927, AT 8:00 P.M.
FRANK CASSIDY
WILL LECTURE IN CLEVELAND HALL
4th FLOOR OF THE WALKER AUDITORIUM BLDG.
730 SOUTH GRAND AVENUE
SUBJECT: RELIGION IN THE SCHOOLS
ADMISSION FREE

Jeanie Macpherson wove these elements into a script that was part outrageous melodrama, part social comedy, part prison reform propaganda, and part religious parable. And, as if aware that *The Godless Girl* would be his farewell to the silent screen, DeMille pulled out all the stops to create an extravagantly visual work of irrational yet compelling power.[2]

DeMille's larger-than-life treatment of these subjects is again allegorical rather than realistic. A meeting of the "Godless Society" at a high school campus is attacked by a group of well-meaning students. In the ensuing riot a young girl is killed, and the ringleaders are sent to an isolated coed prison with the recreation yard divided by an electrified barbed-wire fence. After living through hell as the reformatory burns to the ground in another DeMille "trial by fire," the Godless Girl concedes the possibility that God exists, while Bob, the religious zealot, becomes more accepting of the girl's lack of formal religion. In the end, *The Godless Girl* is a plea for tolerance.

The mother in the modern story of *The Ten Commandments* (1923) was intended to embody the evils of religious zealotry, but that aspect of her character became diluted in the finished film. There can be no misreading of the character of the boy in *The Godless Girl,* however. His brassbound ideology leads him to attempt the conversion of the Godless Society by force, leading directly to the death of one of his classmates.

In September 1927, as DeMille prepared to cast *The Godless Girl*, Charles Beahan suggested that Sylvia Sidney, who gained attention on Broadway in *Crime*, might be "ideal for young girl role in your new picture. . . . Miss Sidney is small dark seventeen years old and a splendid actress."[3] DeMille had seen *Crime* during an April visit to New York, but now he wanted to see film: "If possible Mr deMille would like very much to see the test of Miss Sylvia Sydney, (who is now playing in A.H. Woods' production, CRIME, in Chicago) that was made by D.W. Griffith showing the entire last act of her part in CRIME."[4] However, on October 25, 1927, in a memo to West Coast scenario editor Ella K. Adams, Gladys Rosson wrote: "In your wire to Mr. Beahan tonight, will you just include the following line: 'Mr. deMille and [casting director] Mr. Goodstadt have seen the test of Sylvia Sidney made by Griffith and are not interested.'"[5]

Sidney would gain screen fame in the early 1930s, but if her test did not ignite DeMille's interest, the role of Bob was cast based solely on test footage shot by a maker of industrial, scientific, and educational films. George Duryea appeared in a film directed by W. Allen Lucey for the National Safety Council, and, unsolicited, Lucey sent DeMille tests he had shot. The Hollywood director was impressed with what he saw. On November 12 L.M. Goodstadt sent Charles Beahan a telegram demanding immediate attention:

> Mr. DeMille has just seen test of GEORGE DURYEA STOP Duryea may be reached either at Actor's Equity or in care of W. Allen Lucey, Worccster Film Corporation, one thirty-West Forty-Sixth Street. STOP Please see Duryea your earliest moment and discuss deal on basis of one picture at a salary of one to two hundred per week and options covering period five years; these options for six month periods, increasing fifty dollars per week each period. STOP Try negotiating contract at slightly less than salary paid for single picture. STOP Please wire me giving your impression of Duryea and result of negotiations. Don't close without my instructions. Regards.[6]

Three days later, George Duryea was under contract to DeMille Pictures at a starting salary of $150 per week for his work on *The Godless Girl.* The contract included an option to be exercised within thirty days after completion of the picture or before each option period that would keep him on salary at $125 per week for the first six months and $150 for the next six months, with $50.00 increases at each semiannual option pickup for a period of five years. Duryea proved to be an actor of modest charm who, in his early years on-screen, seemingly always sported a toothy, but bewildered, grin. He would come to be known as cowboy star Tom Keene and character actor Richard Powers as his Hollywood career slowly ebbed through the 1930s and 1940s.

Lina Basquette was apparently cast when DeMille saw pre-release footage of her work with Richard Barthelmess in *The Noose* (First National, 1928). Under the name Lina Baskette she had worked in films as a child in the teens and early 1920s. She resumed her career as an actress after the sudden death of her husband Sam Warner, the brother responsible for bringing the Vitaphone sound system to Warner Bros.

Rounding out the cast were former Mack Sennett comic performers Eddie Quillan and Marie Prevost. This despite a warning DeMille received from E. Jason Temple that he had overheard a conversation by Marie Prevost, "in which she claims she always holds up production to get more money and that the producers love it."[7]

In shooting *The Godless Girl*, DeMille did not scrimp on film. According to a June 1, 1928, report he exposed 408,060 feet of negative in making the picture—an incredibly high shooting ratio of nearly forty-five feet shot for every foot seen on the screen. This figure is mitigated by the fact that two negatives—a domestic and foreign version—were shot simultaneously—but even with a shooting ratio of twenty-two to one, DeMille has to be considered among the most extravagant directors in his use of raw film. Despite the fact that he was no longer associated with Paramount, DeMille insisted that all the footage for his personal productions be developed at the Paramount-Famous-Lasky Corporation laboratories.[8]

The coming of sound and DeMille's departure from his own studio conspired to make *The Godless Girl* a box-office flop. The release of Warner Bros.' *The Jazz Singer* in October 1927 created a true panic in the motion picture industry. Although *The Godless Girl* opened as a silent in its first engagements in August 1928, by the time of its scheduled general release it was determined the picture needed sound to compete in the market place. Two "goat gland" talking sequences were written, and on November 23, 1928, Pathé executive Benjamin "Barney" Glazer wrote DeMille asking for his approval to shoot the sequences.[9] Apparently DeMille did not object, but he did not care to participate. The cast was reassembled under the direction of Fritz Feld on Sunday, November 25, to make the talking sequences. Feld would become a familiar character actor, noted for bringing his hand up to his mouth to make a funny popping sound, and mostly consigned to bit parts as a comic waiter. His talents were never fully utilized in Hollywood, but in Germany he had been an assistant to Max Reinhardt, and he had some credentials as a director.

"I was selected to direct the talking scenes in *The Godless Girl*," he later said, "because I was the only one in Hollywood brave enough—or stupid enough—to take over a Cecil B. DeMille production."[10]

# Dynamite

Produced and distributed by Metro-Goldwyn-Mayer. A Cecil B. DeMille Production. Director: Cecil B. DeMille. Story by Jeanie Macpherson. Dialogue by Gladys Unger, John Howard Lawson, and Jeanie Macpherson. Art directors: Cedric Gibbons and J. Mitchell Leisen. Photography: J. Peverell Marley. Gowns: Adrian. Film editor: Anne Bauchens

Picture started (sound version): January 22, 1929. Picture completed: April 13, 1929. Reshoots for silent version: May 28 to June 5, 1929. Length (sound version): 11,540 feet (fourteen reels). Length (silent version): 10,667 feet. Negative cost: $661,123.32. Released: July 25, 1929 (premiere engagement at Carthay Circle Theater in Los Angeles). General release: December 13, 1929. Gross: $1,182,869.03

Cast: Kay Johnson (Cynthia), Charles Bickford (Derk), Conrad Nagel (Roger), Julia Faye (Marcia), Muriel McCormac (Katie), and Joel McCrea (Marcia's boyfriend)

With a string of box-office flops and pressure from his New York financiers, Cecil B. DeMille grew tired of running a studio. He sold his stock in Pathé to Joseph P. Kennedy and signed a three-picture contract with Metro-Goldwyn-Mayer on August 2, 1928. Like DeMille Pictures, M-G-M was the product of Wall Street maneuvering, combining the interests of theater chain Loew's, Inc., and Metro Pictures with those of the Goldwyn Company and Louis B. Mayer Productions. But unlike the DeMille-Metropolitan-P.D.C.-Pathé combine, M-G-M became a company that was much stronger than the sum of the rather anemic predecessor companies that had come together in 1924. Boasting "More stars than there are in Heaven," M-G-M specialized in producing glossy star vehicles. In some ways, Louis B. Mayer's interest in signing DeMille was odd. Although several high-powered filmmakers—like Fred Niblo, King Vidor, and Clarence Brown—were under contract to M-G-M, it was not known as a "director's studio," and the company seemed to favor directors like Jack Conway, W.S. Van Dyke, and William Nigh—men who cut their teeth making low-budget fare and who could be depended upon to toe the mark for the front office. Over the years, strong and individualistic directors like Erich von Stroheim, Josef von Sternberg, John Ford, and Howard Hawks flirted with M-G-M but never found a comfortable home there. Initially, however, Cecil B. DeMille received a royal welcome as he moved his office the few blocks west from the DeMille-Pathé Studio to the M-G-M lot.

For all its success, M-G-M was the slowest among the major studios to embrace talking pictures. Still, by the time Cecil B. DeMille was signed, the handwriting was on the wall. In big city theaters silent pictures had virtually disappeared from the screen in the ten months since the premiere of *The Jazz Singer*, and it was clear that DeMille's first film for his new employers would be a "100% All Talking Picture."

By November 20, 1929, Jeanie Macpherson delivered a massive 219-page "story and continuity" containing some 1,097 lines of dialogue. Although screenwriters Gladys Unger and John Howard Lawson would share screen credit with Macpherson for writing the dialogue, the November 20 script, on which only Macpherson is credited, contains virtually all the dialogue that would be heard in the finished film. In his autobiography, Charles Bickford states that he objected to much of the dialogue during DeMille's reading of the script and that DeMille then invited Bickford to sit with the writers as they reluctantly made revisions based on his suggestions. If this occurred as Bickford described, it certainly had little or no effect on the finished product. Only minor cuts and revisions were made in the November 20 draft as *Dynamite* went from script to screen.[1]

The story is about a young heiress who learns she will lose her fortune if she is unmarried on her twenty-third birthday. The good news is that she's in love—the bad news is that the light of her life is already married, and though a divorce is in the offing it won't occur before the deadline. The heiress marries a condemned murderer the evening before his scheduled execution, but a last-minute confession by the real murderer throws a monkey wrench into her best-laid plans.

The script for *Dynamite* was written relatively quickly, but apparently the idea had been in preparation for some time. According to DeMille:

As far back as 1926 I read an account of the marriage in a prison in Tokio of a man and woman, both of whom were sentenced to death.
In 1927, I happened to read of a woman who married a

man the day before his execution. I read this item aloud and
made some comment about what would happen if the Governor reprieved the man at the last moment. This idea so intrigued me that I communicated with various wardens
throughout the country on the subject and obtained some very
interesting replies. For instance, Warden Lewis P. Lawes, of
Sing Sing, wrote me that a woman had married a condemned
prisoner five minutes before his death, thereby becoming a
wife and a widow within five minutes.

It was while at the DeMille Studio, late in 1927, that I first
put an author to work on this subject. I told the situation to
Clara Beranger, who worked for practically three months on
the story. I then told the situation and the story to Jane Murfin,
who did considerable work on it, but unsatisfactorily.

I then told the story to Miss Macpherson and put her to
work on it.[2]

To speak the lines, DeMille required actors whose voices would
record well on the primitive and terrifying sound equipment. By Decem-
ber 18, 1928, Mitchell Leisen had supervised sound screen tests of Monte
Blue, Buck Jones, Bob Custer, Gordon Elliott, Tom Tyler, Ricardo Cortez,
Jason Robards (Sr.), Guinn "Big Boy" Williams, Randolph Scott, Dean
Jagger, Kast Sanderson, and Harold Goodwin for the role of the condemned man. Among the women tested for the role of the heiress were
Carmelita Geraghty, Katherine Crawford, Ann Cornwall, Merna Kennedy,
Leila Hyams, Dorothy Burgess, and Sally Blane. Aside from Monte Blue
and Ricardo Cortez, who were genuine stars and had worked with DeMille
before, the rest of the male list is a curious collection of cowboy actors
and, at the time, minor character players; the women were lesser leading
ladies. It can only be speculated whether DeMille was looking to save
money or hoping to establish future stars.

He ultimately chose two stage actors for the roles of Derk and
Cynthia—Charles Bickford and Kay Johnson. Bickford had appeared in
the original Broadway production of *Chicago* and had a critical success
in *Gods of the Lightning*. Kay Johnson was starring in *The Silver Cord* at
a Los Angeles theater when she was signed for the picture. As the third
part of the romantic triangle, DeMille cast Conrad Nagel, who, after a
long and successful career in silents, suddenly became the busiest actor
in Hollywood during the first days of sound. His voice registered per-

fectly in the new medium of talking pictures—remarkably so. Even as the early microphones often rendered other actors voices as muffled or scratchy, Nagel's voice always recorded clearly.

*Dynamite* marked the screen debut of Joel McCrea, who had been a classmate of DeMille's daughter Cecilia. He played the lover of Roger's estranged wife, Marcia, and registered pleasantly if not memorably. Carole Lombard was initially scheduled to play Marcia. The former Jane Peters began her movie career as a Mack Sennett bathing beauty, bouncing around the beach with a bevy of swimsuit-clad lovelies who provided S.A. in the B.G. while comics like Billy Bevan supplied the laughs.[3]

Lombard was soon starring in Sennett-Color two-reel specials, but even as leading lady in comedies like *Run, Girl, Run* or *The Campus Vamp* (both Sennett-Pathé, 1928) she was required to do little but wear skimpy costumes and jiggle nicely. Still, Lombard's striking beauty and her lively offscreen personality attracted attention, and she was seen around Hollywood as a young lady with screen potential. However, she failed to impress Cecil B. DeMille, who replaced her with his longtime associate Julia Faye. One might accuse DeMille of dumping Lombard to make a job for his sometime mistress, but in truth Lombard's early talkie performances for other directors are often flat and colorless, and Julia Faye gives a delightful performance in *Dynamite*. Unfortunately, it would be the last time Faye would have a real opportunity to demonstrate her acting talents in anything but bits and walk-ons.

Lombard would soon develop into one of Hollywood's brightest comediennes, but being fired by DeMille just as her career was getting off the ground was a blow. DeMille had been an actor himself and had known his own share of disappointments in the theater, and he apparently was able to soften the blow somewhat—or maybe Lombard felt compelled to salvage some dignity as she wrote:

My dear Mr. DeMille,

Regardless of my disappointment and unhappiness caused because of that disappointment, I feel that I must thank you for what you have done for me. To be associated with you and to learn of the inimitable way of your genius in its expression is in itself a schooling. But to have you hold up the mirror before my face of unschooled dramatic action showing me every weakness is to insure my success in the future, for in knowing them I can and will correct them—first by daring to look at them—then erasing them through hard work and study.

You know, hope dies hard and thank God it ever springs anew in the human breast.

You have proven yourself to be a very real friend and I thank you heartily.

Carole Lombard[4]

Originally scheduled for fifty-four shooting days at an estimated cost of $575,220, DeMille spent fifty-eight days in production over an eighty-two day period as costs ballooned by $86,000. Production was held up when Kay Johnson had an attack of appendicitis. On March 4, 1929, M-G-M casting director Fred C. Beers advised DeMille that "Dr. Willis who operated on Miss Kay Johnson reports that Miss Johnson should be able to report to work in two weeks."[5] Another delay was caused when mining equipment set to be used as props in the climactic mine cave-in sequence was diverted to a real-life mine disaster in Parnassus, Pennsylvania. DeMille managed to save money on the pickup shots needed to create the silent version of the picture, which occupied another seven shooting days. The silent version was necessary to supply the majority of smaller town theaters that had not yet wired for sound. Ultimately, *Dynamite* came in about $11,000 under the combined budget for the silent and sound versions.

A third version of *Dynamite* was created for foreign territories. On August 9, 1929, DeMille wrote his production manager Roy Burns:

I understand that a foreign negative on Dynamite is to be cut from whatever may be left over from the sound and silent negatives, and that this cut is to be made by the laboratory.

If a third negative is desired, I should prefer to have it cut by my own cutters as I regard the European negative of extreme importance.

If, however, there is some important reason why Metro-Goldwyn-Mayer wishes to make their own cut on the foreign negative, then the sample print from same must be submitted to me prior to its release.[6]

To appreciate DeMille's skill in adapting to sound one need only compare *Dynamite* with some of its 1929 competition—films like Alexander Korda's *The Squall,* Lionel Barrymore's would-be tearjerker *Madame X,* Rouben Mamoulian's celebrated *Applause,* William deMille's *The Idle Rich,* or M-G-M's Oscar-winning musical *The Broadway Melody.*

*Dynamite* looks like a movie, not a photographed stage play. The shots are well composed, the editing is purposeful instead of merely functional, the dialogue, while stylized, is not stilted, and the performances are quite good. The actors play in the extravagant DeMille tradition, to be sure, but while they may never equal the poignancy of Helen Morgan's aging burlesque queen in *Applause* neither do they sink to the absolutely unwatchable excesses of the two young lovers in Mamoulian's film.

From the opening scene of *Dynamite* it is evident that DeMille immediately grasped the potential of sound to heighten the film experience. As described in Macpherson's script the courtroom scene was to open with a closeup of the judge's gavel in the best silent film tradition where sound effects had to seen because they couldn't be heard. In the finished film, DeMille opens on a wide shot of the courtroom with the sound of the gavel hitting the bench. Other innovative uses of sound include the jail scene with the dialogue of the wedding ceremony overlaid with hammering on the gallows and blending with a convict's song; the stylized ticking of the clock as the real murderer is persuaded to confess; and the offscreen sound of an approaching car as anxious miners await the arrival of a doctor—all may seem dated today, but were startling (if largely unsung) innovations in 1929.

For all of its strengths, however, *Dynamite* is the kind of improbable melodrama that appealed to DeMille and his audience, but never to the critics. With the addition of sound it would become increasingly difficult for many to judge whether the director was being serious or satiric in his films. This unresolved tension between realism and hokum would lead to a critical double standard that would dog DeMille to the end of his career. Nearly always his technical skill and his ability to please an audience were acknowledged, while his choice of subject matter and theme were decried.

*Dynamite* opened as a road-show attraction at the Carthay Circle Theater in Los Angeles on July 25, 1929, grossing $106,649.32 during its eight-week run. The day after the premiere, Harold B. Franklin of Fox West Coast Theaters wrote DeMille, asking that he cut the picture to 8,000 feet, losing nearly forty minutes of running time, so that smaller houses could get in more screenings per day in general release. DeMille replied on July 27 that he had cut some sixty feet of footage that very day and said that he would do everything he could to reduce the length when it went to smaller cities. Whether a shorter version was made before general release is not known. DeMille's fourteen-reel cut is the version that survives.

# 54

# Madam Satan

A Metro-Goldwyn-Mayer Picture. Produced and directed by Cecil B. DeMille. Story by Jeanie Macpherson. Dialogue by Gladys Unger and Elsie Janis (additional, uncredited dialogue by John Howard Lawson). Assistant director: Mitchell Leisen. Costumes: Adrian. Art director: Wilfred Buckland. Music and lyrics by Clifford Grey, Herbert Stothart, Elsie Janis, and Jack King. Dance director: LeRoy Prinz. Recording engineer: J.K. Brock. Photography: Harold Rosson. Film editor: Anne Bauchens

Reading of script: February 17, 1930. Rehearsal started: February 24, 1930. Picture started: March 3, 1930. Picture finished: May 2, 1930. Length: 10,472 feet (thirteen reels). Cost: $979,933.07. Released: September 24, 1930 (Los Angeles premiere). Gross: $853,404.69 (This figure is taken from DeMille's records. M-G-M studio records show a worldwide gross of $1,015,000 and a net loss of $390,000.)

Cast: Kay Johnson (Angela Brooks), Reginald Denny (Bob Brooks), Lillian Roth (Trixie), Roland Young (Jimmy Wade), Elsa Peterson (Martha), Irwin Boyd (Captain), Wallace MacDonald (first mate). At the party: Theodore Kosloff (Electricity), Wilfred Lucas (Roman Senator), Tyler Brooke (Romeo), Martha Sleeper (fish girl), Julanne Johnston (Miss Conning Tower), Jack King (Herman), Edward Prinz (Biff), Allan Lane, Mary Carlisle, Katherine DeMille, Ella Hall, Lorimer Johnston, and Abe Lyman and His Band

In 1929 M-G-M produced *The Broadway Melody* for $379,000 and reaped a box-office bonanza of $1,604,000 in profits. *The Hollywood Revue of 1929* cost the studio $426,000 and returned a profit of $1,135,000. "All Talking, All Singing All Dancing" was the order of the day, and it is little wonder that Louis B. Mayer suggested Cecil B. DeMille make a musical. The result was one of DeMille's strangest films, a social comedy incorporating elements of operetta and avant garde ballet set aboard a captive dirigible—at least it's captive until an electrical storm separates the airship from its mooring mast.

DeMille's initial instincts were interesting and ambitious. He wanted Cole Porter to write the song score for *Madam Satan*, but was advised in September 1929 that the songwriter would not be available for another two months. He also considered lyricist Oscar Hammerstein II and operetta composers Rudolf Friml and Sigmund Romberg, but lost enthusiasm when he was told they would demand a percentage of the film's profits. Another interesting prospective choice was English composer Albert Ketelbey, who wrote the evocative concert piece "In a Persian Market," but the music department warned that Ketelbey was difficult to work with and had refused an assignment to write music for the Warner Bros. production *Honky Tonk*. On October 29, 1929, DeMille advised M-G-M's London office that he was no longer interested in Ketelbey.

The two songwriting teams finally assigned, while perhaps not as well known today, were nevertheless first-rate. Lyricist Clifford Grey wrote "If You Were the Only Girl in the World," and supplied lyrics for Jerome Kern, Rudolf Friml, and Sigmund Romberg shows. He also worked on *The Love Parade* (Paramount, 1929). Herbert Stothart went from writing college shows at the University of Wisconsin to being musical director for Arthur Hammerstein on Broadway before coming to Hollywood in 1929. Jack King, who teamed with Elsie Janis, was a child prodigy who played piano concerts in North America and Europe until 1921 and was assistant director of the University of California glee club before trying his hand at vaudeville. He composed the theme song "How Am I to Know?" for DeMille's *Dynamite*.

The original screen story for *Madam Satan* was written by Jeanie Macpherson, but DeMille clearly wanted a certain sophistication in the dialogue, and on November 9, 1929, he wrote Dorothy Parker, who had penned the lyrics for "How Am I to Know?," asking if she was available to do additional writing on the picture. Learning that Parker was in France, he finally signed a letter of agreement with Broadway and vaudeville headliner Elsie Janis on December 7, 1929. Janis was to receive $1,500 per week starting on December 2, 1929, but agreed to take half salary until she advised DeMille she was available full-time. The agreement for Janis's services could be terminated at any time by either party, and it was further agreed that if she and DeMille could not agree on a phrase to describe her contribution to the script that was satisfactory to both parties, her name would not be used in the film's credits. Eventually the film's main title credit read:

Metro-Goldwyn-Mayer
presents
Cecil B. DeMille's
MADAM SATAN
by
Jeanie Macpherson
Gladys Unger & Elsie Janis

The first "final" script was dated January 11, 1930, but was followed by another "final" script dated February 12, 1930. But "final" was a relative term, and there were rewrites throughout production. Apparently at a loss for new words, Elsie Janis finally bowed out six weeks into principal photography with a note to DeMille on March 24, 1930:

> Dear Mr. DeMille
> Because it is a matter of form, I want to ask you to allow me to quit your gracious presence in two weeks, I won't say why, because "The pen is stiller than the word" and anyway I'm sure you are way ahead of me! I would like to add, however, that if you would care to save a little money, I would be glad to "kick out" at once before the Zeppelin sequence destroys all of the charming memories that I hope to retain, of de Mille of the Gods, B.M.S. (before mob scenes) It has been a great joy to know you, and I hope to be a friend long after Madam Satan has gone the way of all "Talkies"
>
> Devotedly,
> Elsie[1]

Even with the departure of Janis, DeMille was handwriting notes for revisions as late as April 1, and John Howard Lawson supplied additional dialogue for the picture.

DeMille campaigned heavily to have Gloria Swanson play Madam Satan, but his best efforts met with resistance from Swanson's lover and business partner Joseph P. Kennedy. Just after Christmas 1929 Kennedy wired the director:

> Gloria told me last night of her talk with you previous to this time As the suggestion had come through agent I have given it no consideration As you know Gloria is under contract to deliver three more pictures to United Artists and she must finish [Queen] Kelly which should be finished some time in February I doubt the possibility of getting a release from United Artists until she has completed contract. If however you think this idea to be of great benefit to her I would go to work on it immediately. Very kindest regards and best wishes for the new year.
>
> Joe Kennedy

DeMille replied with a passionate pitch for the role but offered little detail about remuneration:

The part of Madam Satan is perhaps the best woman's part that has ever come under my direction. It is the type of story that I used to make with Gloria, but done with some light music stop I am spending one million dollars on the production and it is all centered around this one character which has the brilliance and dash that she responds to so splendidly and needs so much at the present time stop I suggest you advise me by wire or phone what the financial requirements would be and if these can be arranged we can then go to work on the other obstacles to be removed stop I know you had a joyous Christmas and hope the new year fulfills your fondest desires. Cecil

Swanson was Paramount's biggest female star when she left to start her own production company under the United Artists banner in 1927. Suddenly it seemed as if everything turned to brass for golden Gloria. Her pictures did not perform as expected, and she became embroiled in making *Queen Kelly*, written and directed by Erich von Stroheim, which turned out to be a costly debacle that would never receive a domestic release. Still, Joe Kennedy felt it was to Gloria's advantage to make her own pictures and not accept outside offers. He replied on December 31:

Dear CB I had a long talk with [your attorney] Neil McCarthy today re Swanson situation Three difficulties offered themselves One I advanced other day about United Artists contract Second having established price value which will get us over two million dollars gross on The Trespasser. I am afraid these prices might be sacrificed by another company Third the money she might get out of picture would be so small in proportion to amount she could possibly get out of one made by herself I question whether it would be possible to get together on any terms. . . .[2]

In addition to being turned down by Swanson, DeMille found no enthusiasm for two of his former stars who were seeking parts in the picture. On November 12, 1929, DeMille wired Thomas Meighan's agent

Frank Joyce of Myron Selznick, Ltd: "Replying your wire Have highest regard for Tommy Meighan's ability but he is not suitable for this part stop Part is similar to Donald Brian in MERRY WIDOW but very modern. Kindest regards."[3] Dorothy Dalton came to DeMille's M-G-M office to audition, but on February 13, 1930, he replied with a gracious but definite "No": "Many thanks for your interest in coming to the studio and singing for me, and although I have the highest regard for your singing and acting ability, at the same time I do not believe this part is the right one for you to make your reappearance on the screen, and you are much too fine an artist to make the mistake of returning to the films in any but the most suitable part. stop. It was very nice to see you again. With kindest personal regards."[4]

DeMille looked at a screen test of Dorothy McNulty, who would later be known as Penny Singleton, but he was not impressed. Then, a month before *Madam Satan* started shooting, he asked to see footage from the yet-to-be-released *Let's Go Native* (Paramount, 1930) hoping to see his vision of Madam Satan in Jeanette MacDonald. He wrote: "I have seen her performance in [Ernst Lubitsch's] LOVE PARADE but would like to see something of her that calls for a little more fire and color and in which she plays in a more seductive mood. Part of Madam Satan calls for perfect abandon."[5]

But if Jeanette MacDonald didn't quite pass DeMille's muster, *The Love Parade* did bring another performer to DeMille's attention. He initially favored former silent comedienne Martha Sleeper for the part of the girlfriend, Trixie, but Lillian Roth's bubbly personality in the Lubitsch film earned her the role, and Martha Sleeper was relegated to a speaking bit as "fish girl" in the charity auction sequence. Roth proved to be a real delight in *Madam Satan*. Her bubbly and natural screen presence steals the show, especially when she belts out the song "Low Down" ("I love all the gin that puts the sin in syn-copation") with a hip-churning bump and grind. She is joined in the number by composer Jack King and dancer Edward Prinz, brother of dance director LeRoy Prinz. Unfortunately, the role proved to be the high point of Roth's movie career, which soon evaporated in an alcoholic haze.[6]

DeMille saw a test of Lynne Overman and very much wanted him for the part of Jimmy Wade, but Overman's test had not interested the rest of Hollywood at the time, and he returned to the stage before DeMille's call. The director would remember Overman, however, and he would become a member of DeMille's stock company in the late 1930s.

Reginald Denny was finally cast in the leading male role on January 9, 1930, for $1,500 per week and a ten-week guarantee with a start date to be designated, but not later than February 10, 1930. Denny built his silent screen reputation as an all-American boy-next-door in a series of popular comedies at Universal Pictures in the 1920s. Audiences were surprised to hear that he spoke with a British accent, and his days as a major star were numbered. Denny's accent suggested that his on-screen drinking companion ought to be English as well, and the droll Roland Young landed the role of Jimmy. DeMille finally settled for Kay Johnson in the title role, though she never quite displayed the "perfect abandon" he said he was seeking.

Originally budgeted at $1,011,609.00 with a seventy-day shooting schedule, *Madam Satan* was completed in fifty-nine days, this despite the fact that Reginald Denny was ill for a week and Kay Johnson missed two shooting days. DeMille expressed his pleasure in a note to M-G-M production manager J.J. Cohn: "We have closed MADAM SATAN, finishing the picture considerably under our budget due largely to the very splendid co-operation we have received from all of the departments on the lot. . . ."[7]

*Madam Satan* was previewed in San Bernardino, California, on July 29, 1930, and publicist Barrett Kiesling offered the opinion that "It was very evident . . . that extreme length was the only thing that kept the picture from being an absolutely unbroken succession of laughs." A second preview was held at the Alexander Theater in Glendale on August 19, and Kiesling reported that M-G-M executive Irving Thalberg hated the "Maid's Song" and wanted someone else to reshoot the scene, but that overall audience reaction was positive. "By actual count picture clocked 239 laughs at Glendale," wrote Kiesling, "as against 221 at San Bernardino and 139 at the studio. . . . Every cut made since San Bernardino definitely stepped up the pace of the picture and increased its value as a laugh getter."[8]

Thalberg didn't get his way—the maid's song was not reshot—but the strong initial audience reaction had no impact on the ultimate success of the picture. Released after a flood of movie musicals—at least seventy-five were produced in 1929—*Madam Satan* failed to ignite a spark at the box office. The picture suffered somewhat from the very different styles of the two songwriting teams. The first half of the film features isolated song numbers, while the second half makes an abrupt turn toward operetta with involved ensemble recitatives often carrying the plot.

However, from a technical standpoint, it is hard to imagine a more accomplished film in 1930. While many other filmmakers were still struggling with how to adapt to talking pictures, DeMille demonstrated complete mastery of the new medium.

# 55

# The Squaw Man
## (second remake)

A Metro-Goldwyn-Mayer Picture. Produced and directed by Cecil B. DeMille. Continuity by Gladys Unger, Josephine Lovett, Lucien Hubbard, and Lenore Coffee. Dialogue by Elsie Janis. (Additional, uncredited writing by Jeanie Macpherson.) From the play by Edwin Milton Royle. Assistant director: J. Mitchell Leisen. Photography: Hal Rosson. Film editor: Anne Bauchens. Incidental music: Herbert Stothart

Picture started: February 9, 1931. Picture finished: March 26, 1931. Length: 9,792 (twelve reels). Cost: $722,811.93. Released: July 1931. Gross: $584,630.60

Cast: Warner Baxter (James Wyngate, the Squaw Man), Eleanor Boardman (Diana, countess of Kerhill), Paul Cavanagh (Henry, Lord Kerhill), Roland Young (Sir John Applegate), Julia Faye (Mrs. Chichester-Jones), Lawrence Grant (General Stafford), Eve Dennison (dowager), Desmond Roberts (Hardwick), Lillian Bond (Babs Barrington), Harry Northrup (silly ass), Lupe Velez (Naturich), Mitchell Lewis (Tabywana), Charles Bickford (Cash Hawkins), J. Farrell McDonald (Big Bill), Dickie Moore (Hal), DeWitt Jennings (Sheriff Hardy), Raymond Hatton (Shorty), Ed Brady (McSorley), Victor Potel (Andy), Frank Rice (Grouchy), Frank Hagney (Clark), and Chris "Pin" Martin (Pete, a half-breed)

In the wake of a cycle of big-budget Westerns like *In Old Arizona* (Fox, 1929), *Billy the Kid* (M-G-M, 1930), *The Big Trail* (Fox, 1930), and *Cimarron* (RKO, 1931), it must have seemed a good idea for Cecil B. DeMille to undertake a sound version of *The Squaw Man*. In order to clear the rights, Metro-Goldwyn-Mayer was forced to deal with two rival studios: Paramount-Famous-Lasky controlled the silent motion picture rights to Edwin Milton Royle's play; but Warner Bros. acquired the talking picture and television rights on March 12, 1930, only to turn them over to M-G-M for a quick profit on June 18, 1930.

The new *Squaw Man* had a high-powered—and highly priced—cast. In the leading roles, Warner Baxter signed for $5,000 per week, and Lupe

Velez for $2,500. Even the character actors were in for a fair piece of change, with Roland Young pulling down $2,000 a week and J. Farrell McDonald earning $1,000. As the country plunged desperately into economic depression, Nicholas Schenck, president of Loew's, Inc., parent company of M-G-M, tried to stop production due to the heavy costs. He relented only when he was convinced that the cost of shutting down would equal the projected losses. DeMille started *The Squaw Man* knowing that he had another failure on his hands.

As had become his custom, DeMille began production with a reading of the script for the principal players and technical crew on February 5, 1931. A second reading for the British cast members took place on February 7, and rehearsals also began that day. The camera started rolling on February 9, and DeMille's records indicate the production consumed forty days and six hours of shooting time. The 171,380 feet of negative that was shot made for a relatively modest shooting ratio, by DeMille's standards, of seventeen and a half to one.

Despite the sense of gloom that pervaded the production, *The Squaw Man* turned out quite well and proved to be one of DeMille's most interesting sound films. Just as D.W. Griffith had demonstrated the power of the old-fashioned theatrical warhorse *Way Down East* in 1920, here DeMille pulled together all the surefire melodramatic contrivances and played them with sincere conviction, and one can finally understand the reasons for *The Squaw Man*'s enduring appeal. Writing in the *New York Times* of September 19, 1931, Mordaunt Hall noted the film was "Skillfully acted by a dozen good players, handsomely produced as to scenery and technical excellence it makes an interesting entertainment—one that is too somber in its story to be called amusing and too neatly carpentered in its plot to be called a genuine tragedy."

*The Squaw Man*'s Arizona locations were a big plus, and a rarity for a director who generally preferred to work in the controlled environment of the studio. Also remarkable is the seemingly authentic treatment of Southwestern Indian culture—with the exception that the principal Native American roles were played by non-Indians.

Edwin Milton Royle's play, written just after the turn of the century, was meant to be contemporary. DeMille updated the action to 1931, striking an odd note. Still it allowed DeMille another of his subtle swipes at Prohibition—the signs outside the saloon promise soft drinks, but firewater seems to be the only liquid available on the inside.

Regrettably, DeMille did not make more of Eleanor Boardman's role. One of the finest actresses of the silent screen, her career was waning by 1931. Frank McGrath, who worked as Warner Baxter's double on *The Squaw Man*, would not gain wide public recognition for another twenty-five years, when he took on the role of the bearded and grizzled chuck-wagon cook on TV's *Wagon Train*.

DeMille's contract with M-G-M was not renewed and, after completing *The Squaw Man*, he closed up his production office, laid off many of his staff, and embarked on a trip to Europe. He and his wife stopped in New York from June 10 to June 24, waiting for the *Ile de France* to sail. On his first day in the city he met with Jesse Lasky and paved the way for what he hoped might be a future reconciliation with Paramount.

While abroad, DeMille received offers from several British companies and from the Soviet government to make films—but these offers were contingent on his being able to obtain guarantees of U.S. distribution. Unable to deliver such pledges, DeMille watched his prospects as a filmmaker dim as the deals evaporated.

Back in Hollywood, DeMille tried to start a new company to be called The Directors Guild with fellow filmmakers King Vidor, Lewis Milestone, and Frank Borzage. He approached Sidney R. Kent, former head of sales for Paramount, with the idea, describing a company that would service independent theaters. DeMille felt certain that film manufacturer DuPont and Consolidated Film Industries laboratories would go along with the plan. But Kent had other commitments, and the growing economic depression made it impossible to arrange financing.[1]

DeMille's once-proud staff also fell on hard times. His longtime film editor, Anne Bauchens, reported that work was hard to come by. "Dear Chief," she wrote, "I have run across a temporary job. A private party with a lot of film on their hands that I may be able to help them with. It will possibly keep me busy four or five weeks at the most."[2]

# 56

# The Sign of the Cross

Paramount Publix Corporation. Produced and directed by Cecil B. DeMille. Screenplay by Waldemar Young and Sidney Buchman, from the play by Wilson Barrett (additional, uncredited writing by Nick Barrows). Art director: Mitchell Leisen. Music: Rudolph Kopp (also Milan Roder, Paul Marquardt, and Jay Chernis [uncredited]). Assistant director: James Dugan. Photography: Karl Struss. Film editor: Anne Bauchens

Picture started: July 25, 1932. Picture finished: September 29, 1932. Length: 11,262 feet (14 reels). Cost: $694,064.67. Released: November 30, 1932 (New York premiere). Gross: $2,738,993.35. Net profit: $627,207.38 (gross and profit figures to 1937)

Cast: Fredric March (Marcus Superbus), Elissa Landi (Mercia), Claudette Colbert (Poppaea), Charles Laughton (Nero), Ian Keith (Tigellinus), Vivian Tobin (Dacia), Harry Beresford (Favius), Ferdinand Gottschalk (Glabrio), Arthur Hohl (Titus), Joyzelle Joyner (Ancaria), Tommy Conlon (Stephanus), Nat Pendleton (Strabo), Clarence Burton (Servilius), William V. Mong (Licinius), Harold Healy (Tibal), Richard Alexander (Viturius), Robert Manning (Philodemus), Joe Bonomo (the mute giant), and Charles Middleton (Tyras)

At the lowest point in his film career DeMille turned to Wilson Barrett's *The Sign of the Cross*, a popular play of 1895, as the source for his next film. He saw the project as the third part of a religious trilogy that began with *The Ten Commandments* and *The King of Kings*. During his extended vacation DeMille arranged for attorney Neil McCarthy to secure the rights. A film version had been made by the Famous Players Film Company in 1914, but in the intervening years the property had been acquired by Mary Pickford, who was now on the verge of retirement and had no plans to produce it.

With nearly all doors in Hollywood closed, DeMille and Neil McCarthy swallowed hard and approached Jesse Lasky and West Coast production head B.P. Schulberg at Paramount with what amounted to a deal for a co-production. Paramount would provide studio services and half the budget; Cecil B. DeMille Productions, Inc., was to provide the other half of the money. *The Sign of the Cross*, an epic spectacle, would be produced for a mere $650,000. DeMille was to receive a salary of nearly $24,000, but only $14,322 would be paid in cash, with the rest being deferred. The salary would be paid out of a $50,000 advance against future royalties that would not be charged to the negative cost. The deal was inked over the reservations of Adolph Zukor, with Paramount insisting that DeMille keep his personal staff to a minimum. He was not allowed to employ Jeanie Macpherson in writing the film, nor would he be allowed to use Anne Bauchens as his editor; the studio would assign Alexander Hall to cut the picture. Only art director Mitchell Leisen and production manager Roy Burns were allowed to come on board, and both took greatly reduced salaries. Jesse Lasky did agree to DeMille's request that Charles Laughton be hired for the role of Nero, but he caught hell from the New York office for doing so.

The Paramount of 1932 was a far cry from the studio DeMille left in 1925. Paramount Pictures once dominated the box office, but now the company looked to be an economic train wreck waiting to happen, with only four of the twenty-three pictures released in the first half of the year projected to turn a profit—and only modest profits at that. A November 1932 estimated gross statement ticked off the bad news.[1] Josef von Sternberg's *Shanghai Express* would turn a modest profit of $33,000 on an $851,000 investment, but the prestigious Ernst Lubitsch productions of *Broken Lullaby* and *One Hour with You* promised a combined loss of nearly $800,000. The overall release slate for the first half of 1932 was predicted to lose a then-staggering $2,560,000, and as DeMille and writer Waldemar Young set about adapting *The Sign of the Cross* for the screen, the Paramount board of directors, spearheaded by theater man Sam Katz, moved to tighten the reins in Hollywood.

On April 25, 1932, just as the ink was drying on DeMille's new contract, Jesse L. Lasky was asked to take a three-month leave of absence subject to recall on two-weeks' notice. At the end of the three months, Lasky was asked to take an additional two-weeks' leave as the details of his contract settlement were worked out.

Then in May, B.P. Schulberg went on a trip, and Emanuel Cohen, who had been working in the executive ranks at the studio for several months, was selected to fill in for Schulberg as head of production. A banty rooster in physical stature, Cohen came to the job after careers as a writer on politics and economics and as editor first of Pathé and then Paramount newsreels. He also oversaw Paramount's short subjects department. Cohen's interim appointment was brief. Schulberg was fired in

June, and Cohen took over his job. The appointment of Cohen signaled that budgets would be tighter at Paramount in the future.

Cohen quickly established himself in his newly won position. In a memo dated May 26, 1932, he informed DeMille that *The Sign of the Cross* would not be charged for the use of already standing sets, but that the production would be charged for set dressing, and he also noted that costumes left over from *The Ten Commandments* would be available at no charge except for cleaning and altering. But with this helping hand, Cohen also berated DeMille for casting Nat Pendleton in the role of Strabo, somehow thinking that Pendleton was a football coach with no screen experience. DeMille sent Cohen a list of some thirty-nine talkie credits plus mention of three years in silents to persuade Cohen of the actor's credentials. Cohen also asked about DeMille's using Macpherson against studio orders. The director replied he had only asked her to read the 1907 novelization of *The Sign of the Cross* before production and had spoken to her one day about another proposed project, *No Bed of Her Own*, which was eventually made as *No Man of Her Own* (Paramount, 1932) and directed by Wesley Ruggles.[2]

*The Sign of the Cross,* originally scheduled to start shooting on July 11, 1932, was delayed for a week to allow Paramount leading man Fredric March to complete *Smilin' Through* on loan-out to Metro-Goldwyn-Mayer. But by July 18, the Metro picture was running behind schedule. DeMille was forced to delay the start of *The Sign of the Cross* for another week, and M-G-M paid Paramount $7,459.00 to cover the cost of talent and crew left waiting to start. The extra time allowed for last-minute script revisions that were carried out by writers Sidney Buchman and Nick Barrows.

As the cameras started to turn, DeMille was also delayed by his own studio. Claudette Colbert was tied up shooting another picture and was not available when her provocative milk-bath scene was scheduled to shoot. On August 11, 1932, production manager Roy Burns was advised: "We should not be charged with the cost of POPPAEA'S set, as the studio had to strike the set on account of lack of stage space before we were able to shoot it. The fact that it was our second set on our schedule; but on account of putting Miss Colbert in THE PHANTOM PRESI-DENT, we agreed not to use her [at that time] although the set was built and the studio had to strike it before it was used."[3] Shooting on this sequence was postponed from Wednesday, August 3, to Tuesday, August 16. Legend has it that DeMille insisted on using real milk in the bath scene and that by the second day of shooting the milk was curdling under the hot lights and turning into a rather smelly cheese; but according to the shooting schedule the six script pages of the bath scene were completed in one day.

Even with these complications, DeMille was obsessed with remaining on schedule and budget to prove to Paramount that their shaky faith in him was well placed. By August 19, 1932, he had made up the delay caused by *The Phantom President*, and Emanuel Cohen was quick to acknowledge the accomplishment. "I note on the production report today," Cohen wrote, "that you have caught up on your schedule. Congratulations. I can well appreciate what an effort this has been on your part."[4]

As often happens when high-powered talents come together, conflicts over billing erupted. Claudette Colbert's February 16, 1931, contract with Paramount was clear that "no name can be announced more prominently." However, Paramount's agreement with Fox covering the loan-out of Elissa Landi stated that "no other feminine player shall precede or appear in type larger than" Landi's name on the screen, and "only the male lead may precede or appear in type larger." Colbert's role as Poppaea, "the wickedest woman in the world," was a plum that would lift her above the somewhat lifeless roles she'd been playing for Paramount up to that time, and on July 21, 1932, she finally agreed to allow Fredric March and Elissa Landi's names to appear before hers in the main title credits.

The star salaries for *The Sign of the Cross* wouldn't even cover a week of a lead actor's paycheck today. Fredric March received $2,101.91 per week for the eight weeks the picture was in production. Elissa Landi, on loan from Fox, received $1,500 weekly. Claudette Colbert received a flat $15,000 for her work on the picture, and Charles Laughton $1,250 per week. On the other end of the scale, extras in the crowd scenes generally received $10 per day.

With the economy in a slump, those ten-dollar checks took on great importance for Hollywood's legion of bit players and extras, and Cecil B. DeMille received hundreds of heartbreaking letters from actors looking for work. DeMille took it as a point of personal responsibility to see that, if possible, he would offer work to these underemployed actors, and even though he was on probation with Paramount, he was adamant that his casting promises be kept by the studio. On September 8, as he was shooting the first day in the Coliseum arena, DeMille became aware that a number of those he had promised work had not been called, and he quickly dictated a pair of notes to the studio casting department: "A week or so ago, I told Joseph Sasso that he would work in the arena sequence, but he informed me tonight that he has not been called and that Mr. Weaver did not have his name on the list. Will you please see that he is called for work tomorrow?" and "Kindly make certain that every request name that I have sent through for work in the arena crowd sequence have been called and on the set tomorrow or else I will not shoot."[5]

Several days later this issue was still not completely solved. DeMille noted that Will Geer had been promised work on the picture but had not had a call. His secretary also informed casting that Gertrude Robinson, a minor leading lady in the silent era, should be put on the list, as "Mr. deMille positively wishes her called."[6]

As he had done earlier on *The Volga Boatman*, DeMille spent his budget with great prudence and skill. Art Director Mitchell Leisen and his staff were able to build what appeared to be a good portion of ancient Rome, including a full-sized replica of the Coliseum, for a mere $44,900 in labor and materials, with an additional $9,150 spent on set dressing. *The Sign of the Cross* was a huge production with fifteen different sets and locations, thousands of extras, and lots of special photographic effects, but it was also meticulously pre-planned, and only those portions of the settings that would show on-screen were constructed. It is nothing short of amazing that DeMille was able to make the film for under $700,000, while, across the lot, Ernst Lubitsch spent over $1 million on the four-character musical comedy *One Hour with You*, which was staged largely in one somewhat-lavish townhouse.

For all the power a director of DeMille's stature is supposed to exert over his films, sometimes control over all the elements can be elusive. In the middle of shooting, Rudolph Kopp and the studio orchestra were set to record the background music for Ancaria's lesbian dance, one of the more sensational elements of *The Sign of the Cross*. DeMille intended to have actors playing Romanesque instruments on camera and dub in the music during postproduction. Kopp's music for the sequence did not please DeMille, however. On August 16, he wrote Fred Leahy, head of the music department:

> Approximately six weeks ago, I informed the Music Department of the musical requirements for Ancaria's dancing scene. I explained at great length to the Department that this

was not a "musical number," but a most dramatic scene; that I showed the Roman orchestra which was playing the accompaniment, and that anything suggesting a modern symphony orchestra, or modern combination of instruments would not do; that it must be a musical part of the scene, and I was informed on Saturday, August 13th, that they were using twenty pieces in the orchestra. I objected on the grounds that it could not possibly give the result of a barbaric group of some ten instruments. I was assured by Mr. Kopp that the effect I desired would be there.

We were prepared to make sound track on Monday night, and the twenty-two piece orchestra and orchestration was such that you would hear any night at the Biltmore Hotel. There was not even a suggestion of cymbals, or any of the instruments necessary to give the required character, and we were forced to spend an hour and a half on the set endeavoring to correct the orchestra and orchestration after we had lost three hours of rehearsing time with the symphony orchestra. This, in my opinion, is a needless and careless waste of money. I have been most insistent on several occasions to explain again and again to the Music Department that I did not want a "musical number" but an orchestration that would suggest the semi-barbaric instruments of a Roman orchestra.

On Sunday night, I again objected to the twenty instruments and was told that was necessary to give the effect that I wanted. No endeavor apparently was made to give the effect I desired, and no attention whatsoever paid to my request for the type of orchestration needed. This blunder has cost practically a full day's shooting time.[7]

In the completed film, the final result is not particularly satisfying. DeMille was forced to compromise, and Joyzelle Joyner's heavily accented song is nearly drowned out by a cacophonous musical din, in part because several executives found her dialogue and vocal performance to be "terribly bad."[8]

As *The Sign of the Cross* neared completion, production manager Roy Burns is said to have come to the set to tell DeMille that the budgeted $650,000 had been spent, and the director, unwilling to expend another nickel, stopped production in the middle of a take. A great story, but somewhat unlikely. The picture did run somewhat over budget, with some of the additional costs occurring during postproduction. The final cost was tagged at just over $694,000.

Theater man Sam Katz, new head of Paramount Publix, the parent of the production arm, was especially anxious to see *The Sign of the Cross* even before DeMille was finished shooting. On September 19 the director wrote Katz:

> My cutter tells me you want to see THE SIGN OF THE CROSS tomorrow or the next day.
> The picture is not in condition to run at all; it is merely assembled film with many scenes incomplete awaiting work by the trick and technical departments. Unless it is imperative for you to see it in this unsatisfactory form, I would consider it a favor if you can wait until I can spend some time on the cutting, as it is very unfair to the picture to see it in its present form. You can imagine what showing THE TEN COMMANDMENTS would be without the opening and closing of the Red Sea, etc.[9]

Katz agreed to wait, but he didn't wait long, and DeMille was enraged when he learned that the picture was screened for Katz without his knowledge. On October 7 Katz wrote a letter of apology, noting:

> I am extremely sorry to have heard from Al [Kaufman] that you were disturbed about the procedure I employed in connection with looking at the rough cut of "SIGN OF THE CROSS."
> All I had in mind, C.B., was to make certain that when I did talk with you about it I could talk with you intelligently and offer some constructive suggestions. . . .
> I am sure that when we get together you will be satisfied with the procedure. If a mistake was made it was a mistake of judgment, not of intent. . . .[10]

DeMille offered a conciliatory response to Katz:

> Firstly, I am for Paramount, you and all the new management, one hundred and one per cent. The attitude of the whole plant toward me has been one that would warm the cockles of any

man's heart. With the exception of one or two, perhaps justifiable little spasms of nervousness on the part of one or two executives, this association has been a very delightful one, and your letter gives me assurance that it will continue so.

Perhaps, as we grow older, our skin, instead of toughening, becomes a little thinner, and our nerves perhaps a trifle more sensitive. In this instance, I sent for George M. Arthur and had a talk with him in my office relative to cutting THE SIGN OF THE CROSS and asked his advice on the subject, and asked that as soon as I had completed my first cutting he sit down with me and look at the picture in order that I might have his ideas. He was very gracious and consented to this. I was, perhaps a little unjustifiably, startled later when I heard he was running the picture with you before I could even make my first cutting.

However, I should have known that what you do, you do constructively, and I want to assure you that I prize your opinion and views most highly and that you can, in addition to your production and showmanship knowledge, give me the exhibitor's angle which is so valuable.[11]

In the wake of this dispute, the studio allowed DeMille to replace Alexander Hall, who was just beginning his own career as a director after years as an actor and editor, with his longtime film editor Anne Bauchens.

For a film filled with suggestive and sensational elements, *The Sign of the Cross* had very little trouble with industry censors—at first. The most questionable moment in the film was the lesbian dance performed by Joyzelle Joyner in an effort to provoke the Christian, Mercia. Colbert's milk bath was also considered potentially censorable. DeMille decided to take his case directly to James Wingate of the Motion Picture Producers and Distributors of America before giving the picture a wider viewing among industry and state censor boards.

On November 14, Wingate was invited to a private screening at the studio. In a memo sometime afterward, Wingate offered, "In my opinion the Roman Holiday sequence and the indecent movement of the hips . . . were a violation of the Code. Mr. DeMille did not think so and believed that it was necessary to use this dance to show the sensuousness of the pagan as contrasted with the purity of the Christian." DeMille went east to plead his case before the New York State censor board, and Wingate was surprised to note: "[S]trange to say, none of the official censors made deletions in either [sequence]."[12]

However, an enterprising Paramount advertising man named A.L. Selig sent a copy of the script to the Rev. Christian F. Reisner, a Methodist minister, in hope of obtaining an endorsement for the film. Reisner had shown a certain affinity for business when, in the economic boom of the 1920s, he'd posted a billboard proclaiming: "Come to Church. Christian Worship Increases Your Efficiency. Christian F. Reisner, Pastor." But no one was prepared for Reisner's scathing opinion of *The Sign of the Cross*. On October 5, 1932, he responded to Selig's request, in part: "The picture . . . as shown in the script sent to me is repellent and nauseating to every thinking Christian. It endeavors to get a lot of lewd scenes and sex appeal exhibitions on the screen and then dresses the whole with a cheap and unhistorical hodge-podge of hymns and vignettes from sacred Christian martyrdom. Only an ignoramus concerning Christian history, feelings and facts would compose such a script. . . . I confess I feel chagrined to think that you had such a cheap notion of me as to think I would in any way commend it."[13]

Martin Quigley, publisher of the *Motion Picture Herald* trade magazine and a Catholic who would help establish the Legion of Decency in 1934 to clean up Hollywood movies, demanded that film czar Will H. Hays intervene to have the lesbian dance eliminated. DeMille flatly refused, and *The Sign of the Cross* was released as the director intended.

Audiences flocked to see the picture, in part for the spectacle and the racy elements, but also because they found the message of hope in the face of oppression a welcome one in the Depression-torn 1930s. Despite a "Bank Holiday" that coincided with its general release, *The Sign of the Cross* proved to be one of Paramount's few hits in the 1932–33 season and reestablished DeMille as a power in the industry.

Even Adolph Zukor, who had been delighted to be rid of DeMille in 1925, was now moved to write: "Words cannot express my deep appreciation of the wonderful treatment you have given Sign of the Cross. Although it is a most marvelous spectacle it still retains all of the spiritual values and this in my estimation is an achievement which has never been equaled. Congratulations."[14]

The censors almost had the last laugh, however. When the picture was reissued in 1938, 760 feet were cut to conform with the revised and strengthened 1934 production code. In 1944 DeMille added a World

War II prologue for a second reissue, and the picture was trimmed by another 800 feet.[15] It was in this final shortened form that *The Sign of the Cross* was seen on television. The original 1932 cut survived only as a single nitrate print in DeMille's personal vault until it was recently restored by the UCLA Film and Television Archive.

Samuel Goldwyn, now an independent producer releasing through United Artists, remained friendly with Cecil, although he didn't allow friendship to get in the way of a little friendly competition. Before their pictures were released Goldwyn bet DeMille one hundred dollars that his production *The Kid from Spain*, starring Broadway comic Eddie Cantor, would outgross *The Sign of the Cross* by at least 30 percent after the pictures had been in release for a year. In November 1933 DeMille proudly informed Goldwyn that *The Sign of the Cross* had gross film rentals of $819,000 to date, but he dutifully wrote out a check for $100 when Goldwyn executive Abe Lehr informed him that *The Kid from Spain* grossed $1,352,769 in its first forty-nine weeks of release.

# 57

# This Day and Age

A Paramount Picture. Director: Cecil B. DeMille. Screenplay by Bartlett Cormack, from the story "Boys in Office" by Sam Mintz. Assistant director: Cullen B. "Hezie" Tate. Photography: Peverell Marley. Art director: Roland Anderson. Music: Howard Jackson, also L. Wolfe Gilbert and Abel Baer

Picture started: May 17, 1933. Picture finished: June 21, 1933. Length: 7,481 feet (nine reels). Cost: $279,811.24. Released: August 25, 1933. Gross film rentals: $661,069.34 (to 1937)

Cast: Charles Bickford (Louis Garrett), Judith Allen (Gay Merrick), Richard Cromwell (Steve Smith), Harry Green (Herman), Eddie Nugent (Don Merrick), Ben Alexander (Morry Dover), Bradley Page (Toledo), Harry C. Bradley (Mr. Smith), Louise Carter (Mrs. Smith), George Barbier (Judge Maguire), Charles B. Middleton (district attorney), Warner Richmond (defense attorney), Samuel S. Hinds (mayor), Fuzzy Knight (Max), Guy Usher (chief of police), Billy Gilbert (nightclub manager), Oscar Rudolph (Gus), John Carradine, Donald Barry, and Junior Coghlan

Cecil B. DeMille believed that his return to Paramount would be short-lived. On September 22, 1932, he wrote a job seeker that he expected to make only one picture at Paramount and had no openings to offer. But the studio seemed pleased with his work on *The Sign of the Cross*, and on November 14, DeMille told his special publicity representative, John Flinn, "They are asking me to start a small picture in January."[1] The film would be produced on a budget that was reminiscent of DeMille's expenditures in the late 1910s, but he felt he could not reject the offer. The same day he also wrote a note to Adolph Zukor expressing gratitude and seeking to patch up old differences. "It is inspiring to be working under the old Paramount banner again," he wrote, "and to renew an association under your vital and constructive leadership which proved so pleasant and profitable for us both for so many years."[2]

In *This Day and Age* high school students take advantage of their "career week" positions as chief of police and district attorney to kidnap a public enemy and force his confession to a murder in a horrifying sequence that has some parallel to the kangaroo court in Fritz Lang's

1930 German film, *M*. Lang, of course, was preaching against vigilantism; DeMille, on the other hand, is making a case for community involvement and declaring that apathy in the face of terrorism can only lead to the breakdown of society.

Not surprisingly, *This Day and Age* has been branded a fascist tract. But DeMille was not advocating mob rule; rather, he was offering an allegory (represented by youth versus adults) about the necessity for society to renew and maintain the will to defend itself from totalitarian forces (the gangsters).

At a time when growing anti-Semitism was largely ignored, DeMille pointedly showed the students to be friends of Herman, the Jewish tailor, and it is their outrage at his murder that is the catalyst for their actions. Also, as they set their kidnapping plan into action the students enlist the aid of a well-dressed and well-spoken black classmate to masquerade as a stereotypical shoeshine boy. This acknowledgment of black role-playing as a mode of survival within the predominant white society is virtually unique in pre-1960s American film.

The theme of the justice system being balanced in favor of the rights of criminals is familiar in films like *Dirty Harry* (Warner Bros., 1971) and its many sequels and derivatives, but is quite unexpected in a film from the 1930s, a decade that produced films like *Scarface* (Caddo-United Artists, 1932) and *Little Caesar* (Warner Bros., 1930) in which the government and police relentlessly pursue organized crime. In DeMille's film a corrupt society looks the other way as racketeers bleed the community dry, accepting the illusion that these are "respectable" businessmen because doing so is easy and advantageous. In this light, the students' actions against organized crime are more correctly cast in the populist tradition.

To adapt the screenplay from Sam Mintz's story "Boys in Office," DeMille turned to Bartlett Cormack, whose 1927 play, *The Racket*, was one of the models for the Hollywood gangster cycle of the early 1930s. On April 18, 1933, DeMille sent out a rough-draft script for review noting that he thought it was sixty pages too long. Three weeks later the script had been pruned, but even with Cormack's knack for the vernacular, DeMille wasn't sure the writer had a sense of current slang, and he asked Los Angeles High School student Horace Hahn to read Cormack's script and comment.

Today we often laugh at the "Gee, that's swell" dialogue of early 1930s films but, according to Hahn at least, this was the way he and his fellow students talked. He wrote DeMille that the majority of the dialogue in Cormack's script was "really not typical of high school students. [It] Should be interspersed with a few exclamations like, 'heck'—'gosh'—'gee,' etc." Hahn also suggested that in Steve's speech about the murdered tailor the writer add: "Gosh, he was swell to us fellows."[3] Despite seeking Hahn's advice, however, DeMille and Cormack did not take up his suggestions.

While preparing *This Day and Age* and receiving the first encouraging box-office returns on *The Sign of the Cross*, DeMille devoted much of his attention to what he hoped would be his next "big picture," a disaster epic to be called *The End of the World*. Although the screenplay was to be an original, DeMille had Paramount buy the screen rights to Philip Wylie and Edwin Balmer's novel *When Worlds Collide* for $7,500. He also sought to purchase the 1930 French film *Le Fin du Monde,* directed by Abel Gance.

*The End of the World* was to be rushed into production according to a May 4, 1933, memo from A.M. Botsford, with production to begin July 1 on a sixteen-week shooting schedule—just days after *This Day and Age* was to wrap. The proposed start date was clearly unrealistic. Since there was no script as yet, it was impossible even to budget or build sets. Undoubtedly the start date would have been pushed, but other factors caused the project to be put on indefinite hold. Just as Warner Bros.' plans for *Noah's Ark* put a halt to DeMille's proposed film *The Deluge* in 1927, a new, unrelated, and cheaply made independent film coincidentally also titled *The Deluge* (K.B.S.-RKO, 1933) put the kibosh on *The End of the World*. DeMille eventually allowed Paramount to sell *When Worlds Collide* to George Pal, who produced a film version in 1951.

Initially, seventeen-year-old Junior Durkin was DeMille's choice for the role of Steve Smith, leader of the students in *This Day and Age*, but on February 6, 1933, Cormack suggested that twenty-two-year-old Columbia Pictures contract player Richard Cromwell would be a better choice. DeMille toyed with the idea of casting Franchot Tone in the role, but even at a youthful twenty-seven, Tone was well beyond the capability of playing a convincing high school student.

On April 4, 1933, Paramount casting director Fred Datig notified DeMille that "Richard Cromwell will be available on May 8th according to present indications, but in borrowing anyone from Columbia, it is always necessary that we in turn promise them one of our players of like calibre."[4] But by April 19, casting reported that Columbia would let

Paramount have Cromwell for *This Day and Age* with no strings attached, provided they paid his $200-per-week salary starting May 1.

For the role of gangster Louis Garrett, DeMille had his eye on *Scarface* star Paul Muni, and even when he was informed that the actor was impossible to get, DeMille did an end run around Paramount's casting department. On April 22, 1933, he sent a personal wire to Muni at the Cass Theater in Detroit, asking if he'd be available as of May 15. The answer was no.

Chester Morris and Walter Huston were also considered, and DeMille looked at a screen test Fox had made of Burgess Meredith. Morris was too expensive, Huston unavailable, and Meredith apparently incompatible with the image DeMille had in mind. Agent Phil Berg suggested English actor Lionel Atwill, stating that he was confident Atwill could play the role because he had played "low type Americans" on stage.[5] Berg, it would seem, was working hard for a commission. Eventually, DeMille would settle for his *Dynamite* discovery Charles Bickford, who was a fine actor and an adequate choice, but lacked the underlying sense of menace that another performer might have brought to the role.

DeMille interviewed Gloria Stuart for the part of the high school girl, Gay Merrick, and said she was "extremely enthusiastic," and he also considered Paramount contract player Grace Bradley, but ultimately he selected a former model who called herself Mari Colman. In April 1933 Colman won a Paramount screen test in a New York beauty competition, and DeMille was apparently delighted by the innocent image she projected.

In a comic sequence in David O. Selznick's 1937 production of *A Star Is Born,* the studio's latest discovery, Esther Blodgett, is given a new name more in keeping with her status as a movie starlet. As *This Day and Age* was getting ready to roll, Mari Colman was subjected to the same treatment as DeMille and Paramount tested long lists of potential screen names. Among the suggestions were Betty Barnes, Doris Bruce, Alice Harper, Grace Gardner, Chloris Deane, and Marie Blaire. Colman herself suggested Pamela Drake or Erin Drake. On May 15, Jack Cooper wrote DeMille that he had tried several names on seventeen people. Eleven voted for the name Doris Manning; the other six held out for Doris Drake. Somehow, the name ultimately bestowed upon her was Judith Allen. DeMille and Paramount had high hopes for Allen, and she was even seen around town in the company of Gary Cooper, one of the studio's biggest stars.

Then, on July 13, a day before the first preview screening of *This Day and Age*, a headline in the *Los Angeles Times* proclaimed: "ACTRESS CONFESSES HOAX." It was revealed that the picture's leading lady, Judith Allen, was in fact Marie Elliot Sonnenberg, a "former Boston society girl" and current wife of onetime wrestling champion Gus Sonnenberg. It seems that while recovering from a drubbing in the wrestling ring at St. Vincent's hospital in Los Angeles, Sonnenberg saw a gossip column item about Judith Allen and Gary Cooper. Supposedly breaking a vow to keep quiet, Gus blabbed to the press. At first the newly named actress denied even knowing Sonnenberg, then a reporter confronted her with a honeymoon picture. "The reporter placed a finger on the actress's neck mole and pointed another to the unmistakable skin blemish at the exact spot on the girl in the photograph."[6] While the story hardly lived up to the newspaper's claim that this was "one of the most sensational Hollywood hoaxes in film history," it didn't help matters when Bill Cunningham, a sports reporter friend of Sonnenberg, offered the observation, "I don't know where they get this 'Boston society darling' business, except that in Hollywood a dinner coat, a bottle of Listerine and a $10 bill change a bindle bum into a gentleman." Cunningham went on to suggest that Allen and her family had soaked Sonnenberg for his dough and took him for a buggy ride.[7]

DeMille was understandably furious over being deceived by his new discovery, and after a promising debut in a Cecil B. DeMille production, Judith Allen's career soon evaporated with a slow descent into Westerns and Poverty Row quickies as the director exerted his influence to keep her from being cast in major studio films.[8]

After the changes that came out of the July 14 preview, Anne Bauchens reported that the final cut of *This Day and Age* was 7,641 feet. Paramount's editorial department head George Arthur suggested that DeMille "cut out the silly actions of the [newspaper] editor," and DeMille agreed to eliminate another minute and a half of film.[9]

As if coming up with a name for the leading lady wasn't challenge enough, no one seemed to be able to agree on a title for the picture. The usual call went out to studio personnel, but the short list did not mark the work of geniuses. Suggestions included *High School Men*, *Battle Cry*, *High and Mighty*, *Pay Day*, *Live and Learn*, *May Day*, *We Want Action!*, *The Young March On!*, *The Snare*, *These Young Sinners*, *No Kidding*, *Over Here*, *We Accuse*, *Innocent Blood,* and *Against the Rules*. But ultimately effects cinematographer Gordon Jennings, who prepared the titles for Paramount Pictures, had the main title card set with Bartlett Cormack's original choice: *This Day and Age*.

The film performed adequately at the box office, and after distribution costs and other expenses were deducted and the sale of *When Worlds Collide* was eventually added to the balance sheet, *This Day and Age* showed a thin profit of $21,733.48. It would mark DeMille's final venture in contemporary social drama.

# Four Frightened People

A Paramount Picture. A Cecil B. DeMille Production. Director: Cecil B. DeMille. Screenplay by Lenore Coffee and Bartlett Cormack, from a book by E. Arnot Robertson. Assistant directors: Cullen B. "Hezie" Tate, James Dugan, and David MacDonald. Art director: Roland Anderson. Photography: Karl Struss. Film editor: Anne Bauchens. Music: Karl Hajos. Additional music by Milan Roder, Heinz Rhoemheld, and John Leipold

Picture started: September 16, 1933. Picture completed: November 3, 1933. Length: 7,028 feet (eight reels). Negative cost: $509,006.96. Released: January 26, 1934. Gross film rentals: $494,425.97 (to 1937). Net Loss: $260,765.35 (to 1950)

Cast: Claudette Colbert (Judy Cavendish), Herbert Marshall (Arnold Ainger), Mary Boland (Mrs. Mardick), William Gargan (Stewart Corder), Leo Carrillo (Montague), Nella Walker (Mrs. Ainger), Tetsu Komai (native chief), Chris Pin Martin (native boatman), Joe De La Cruz (native), Minoru Nisbeda (first Sakai), Teru Shimada (second Sakai), E.R. Jinadas (third Sakai), Delmar Costello (fourth Sakai), and Ethel Griffies (Mrs. Ainger's mother)

*F*our Frightened People harks back to DeMille's comedies of the late 1910s, and because it is a departure from most of his sound films, many have taken it to be a tolerably stupid adventure yarn rather than the highly amusing social satire that it is. Who but DeMille would give audiences a Pekincse-toting feminist lecturing South Sea natives on the liberating rewards of birth control? Or a character like the native Montague, the "most white man on the island" (brilliantly played by Leo Carrillo), who believes that his borrowed necktie grants him immunity from savage violence? Or Judy Cavendish, the prim school teacher with hornrimmed glasses who blossoms into a liberated woman clad in jungle leaves and leopard skins?

Cecil B. DeMille began negotiating for the rights to *Four Frightened People,* the second film to be produced under his new three-picture deal with Paramount, even before the revised contract was signed. The Elizabeth Marbury Agency first brought the property to his attention, and on February 14, 1933, DeMille's office sent out an order to secure an option on E. Arnot Robertson's novel. The owners held out for an outright sale of the screen rights, and Russell Holman and A.M. Botsford in the Paramount story department suggested a $5,000 payment for those rights.[1] The deal was closed on February 17, 1933, and script-writing chores were handed over to Lenore Coffee and Bartlett Cormack, who delivered the first script on August 11.

Under consideration for the role of Judy from the beginning, Claudette Colbert was scheduled to finish her current picture, *Torch Singer*, on July 29, 1933, and production plans on *Four Frightened People* were tailored to her availability. Paramount contract actor Herbert Marshall was also set from the inception of the project, but DeMille had made no decisions for the other male roles. As was his custom, he began casting by looking at various actors in earlier screen roles. On Friday, July 21, 1933, he screened *The Story of Temple Drake* (Paramount, 1932) to look at William Gargan, and he liked what he saw; but he also watched *Crime of the Century* (Paramount, 1933) for Gordon Westcott, *Disgraced* (Paramount, 1933) for Bruce Cabot, and *Ladies They Talk About* (Warner Bros., 1933) for Preston Foster.

However, on July 24, after taking a second look at Westcott in *Private Detective 62* (Warner Bros., 1932) and Preston Foster in *The Man Who Dared* (Fox, 1933), DeMille lost interest in using either of them, but during this same marathon screening session he became intrigued with Leo Carrillo for the role of Montague after seeing *Broken Wing* (Paramount, 1932).

Leo Carrillo's previous salary was noted as $2,500 per week with a four-week guarantee, but the deepening Depression brought a general lowering of salaries throughout the industry, and on August 1, the casting department informed DeMille that Carrillo would be willing to work three weeks for $5,000 flat. DeMille okayed the figure and allowed the studio to sign a contract with the actor. William Gargan would be paid $6,500 for a six-week guarantee, prorated at $1,250 per week thereafter. Charles Morton was hired to double for William Gargan, a major comedown for an actor who had starred at Fox in F.W. Murnau's *4 Devils* only four years earlier.

According to the original schedule, DeMille was to leave for Honolulu on August 19 and arrive on August 24 to scout locations, with the rest of the cast and crew leaving Los Angeles on August 25 and arriving on August 31. But in fact he was already registered at the Royal Hawaiian Hotel by August 22, and in a letter to fellow Paramount director

Eddie Sutherland, DeMille noted, "[O]ur departure was something like an amateur first night." Word of DeMille's arrival spread quickly, and he received notes from Hollywood refugees Babe London and Lois Weber, who were then living in Honolulu. London, a heavyweight comic actress of the silent era, hoped that DeMille might have a part for her—but the limited roles in the script offered few parts for bit players. Director Lois Weber, although experiencing hard times in her own career, wrote to introduce a former studio worker in hopes that DeMille would hire him, but there is no evidence that he acted on Weber's suggestion.

DeMille's assistant director, Cullen B. "Hezie" Tate, boarded a ship for Hawaii on September 8, and the revised final script was completed by Bartlett Cormack in Kialua, Hawaii, on September 11.

While DeMille has often been pictured as a tyrant on the set, an image he did little to dispel because it gave him an edge in dealing with the egos and personalities of cast and crew, he could also be concerned and thoughtful of even the tiniest details. As he prepared to roll camera, Cecil had production secretary Emily Barrye issue the following order to the costume department: "MR. deMILLE WANTS US TO HAVE WRAPS AT LOCATION TOMORROW IN CASE MISS COLBERT AND MISS BOLAND'S DOUBLES GET WET IN GETTING OUT OF BOAT AND WE HAVE TO DRY THEIR CLOTHES OFF."[2]

As one might expect on distant location, the production had its ups and downs. When the first "day for night" scenes were processed and printed, the Hollywood studio expressed concern over the quality of the photography. These scenes were intentionally underexposed to enhance the night effect, but DeMille had cinematographer Karl Struss review his footage and defend it with a written opinion. "I feel that the negative for night effect that we have shot to date in the night sequence, in the boats and on the beach, is perfectly satisfactory as to negative quality, which scenes were shot in sunshine, sun behind clouds and in rain," wrote Struss.[3]

But, while DeMille supported his cinematographer, he was not so happy with the still pictures he was getting. On September 26 Emily Barrye conveyed to production manager Roy Burns, "Mr. deMille is not pleased with the contrasty stills we have gotten the last couple of days."[4] Always keeping an eye on publicity and promotion, DeMille felt that the still pictures taken during production were nearly as important as the motion pictures. He arranged for the developing of the still negatives to be entrusted to another photographer and to reshoot the stills that did not meet his standards.

The story of *Four Frightened People* concerns a quartet of travelers to the Far East who jump ship to avoid an outbreak of plague and end up trekking through deep jungles with the help of a native guide to reach civilization. The Hawaiian locations lend a reality to the plight of the characters, but because movies are at least 80 percent illusion, shooting the jungle scenes necessitated a certain amount of eye trickery. At one point in the film, the four frightened people are surrounded by tiny Sakai natives who hover overhead in trees armed with deadly blowguns. One of the natives is shot and topples to the ground from his perch. On-screen the scene appears to be photographed in the remotest part of the forest, but in fact part of it was shot within reach of the most modern creature comforts. On October 1, Emily Barrye noted to assistant directors "Hezie" Tate and Jimmie Dugan that DeMille "looked at the big tree in front of the hotel with the thought of using it for the shooting of the Sakai. . . . They are planning to miss the top of the building across the street but will want some of the small bamboo that we used in the Mardick village to silhouette in the F.G. [foreground]. He wants two or three small boys that climb trees well. Puff of smoke comes into scene before he falls."[5]

Still, the tropical location was no picnic, and a number of the cast and crew were taken ill during the shoot. In reviewing cost overruns after *Four Frightened People* had wrapped, Emily Barrye outlined delays encountered when Claudette Colbert became sick:

On 9/25/33 we did not shoot in the daytime on account of Miss Colbert's illness but, rehearsed the doubles at the Banyan tree and hau[6] and that night shot at the Banyan tree with Miss Colbert's double and cast from six until 11:45 PM, taking two pages of dialogue.

On 9/26/33, had a 12:30 call with the doubles and shot our long shots in the hau.

On 9/27/33 we again shot in the hau without Miss Colbert. On these two days we shot three-quarters of a page of dialogue each day.

On 9/30/33 we moved equipment back to this location and shot another five hours and forty-five minutes with Miss Colbert, necessitating re-lighting of set for long shot, taking three and one-half pages at dialogue.

On 9/29/33 we moved equipment back to the hau location after a half day's work at the Mardick village, and re-lighted set to get

close-ups of Miss Colbert and give her an entrance,
approximately two and a half hour's shooting and two and one-
quarter pages of dialogue.

On 10/8/33 we moved equipment back to Kamani Grove on
Warm Springs Rd. at Kapoho, and shot with Miss Colbert until
four PM, getting three and one-quarter pages of dialogue. Had
we moved into this location when we finished Mardick village
it would have saved double moving of equipment and half a
day, I believe, as the two locations were within a few yards of
each other.[7]

Problems with equipment compounded the usual comedy of errors
that can infect even the best-planned human endeavors. A September 29
report by Emily Barrye outlines the previous day's disasters:

9/28/33 Shooting Mardick Village. 8:30 Call. Miss Boland half
hour late leaving the hotel, at 9:27 only four boys made up and
dressed. At 9:35 grass tiger built by prop shop not ready. Miss
Boland saw a rehearsal with the double and then went to
location dressing room to have her eye lashes put on and
wardrobe. Had refused to allow anyone but Monty Westmore,
who was getting the natives made up, to put them on. At
10:58 Miss Boland did not have her sandals. Milo Anderson
brought one sandal. Mr. DeMille was informed that Vicky
[Williams] was bringing the second. The second sandal
arrived at 11:07. 1st crank turned at 11:12 but camera noise
too great to shoot. It was the same camera that was repaired
yesterday at the hau location. This delay caused us to have to
go back to the Mardick Village again today and shoot for
another half day.[8]

On October 3, the eighteenth day of shooting, getting the mechanical
cobra to work caused a twenty-five-minute delay, and a typical tropical
downpour required an additional twenty-minute wait.

The picture finished shooting in Hollywood on November 3, and on
November 14 George M. Arthur, head of the Paramount cutting department, sent DeMille a postproduction schedule that anticipated a January
5, 1934, release date. The work print was to be shown to the music and
sound departments on November 25. The following day the first nega-

tive cutting would take place, and dubbing prints would be made for sound editing and music.[9]

Sound mixing and music scoring would occur between November 27 and December 4, and the scored scenes cut into the sound negative on December 5, when the picture negative would be re-cut, if necessary, and a first trial composite picture and sound print made ready for a scheduled December 11 preview.

DeMille looked at the first two assembled reels on November 13 and screened the full picture with his staff on December 1 and again on December 3, offering specific notes for changes he wanted to make in the editing. Before he was able to finish supervising the cutting, he was called to Washington, D.C., to testify before the Board of Tax Appeals in an action brought by the federal government against Cecil B. DeMille Productions seeking back taxes in the sum of $1.6 million. Not knowing how long he would be tied up in the East, the director appointed a hand-picked committee to steer the picture through completion in his absence, including editor Anne Bauchens, long-time associate Mitchell Leisen, Adolph Zukor's brother-in-law Albert Kaufman, secretary Emily Barrye, assistant director Cullen Tate, and writer Bartlett Cormack.

Only a few days behind schedule, *Four Frightened People* was previewed, at a length of ninety-six minutes, in Huntington Park, California, on Friday, December 15. For DeMille the occasion was "like giving birth to baby with mother away."[10] The screening was not helped by the fact that it was raining, the house was only two-thirds full, and the audience was made up mostly of kids waiting to see the Richard Dix war aviation picture *Ace of Aces*, when Paramount had been told by Fox West Coast Theaters that the second picture on the bill would be *The Masquerader*, a sophisticated drama starring Ronald Colman.

Reaction at the preview was mixed. The audience didn't seem to appreciate the fact that the picture was shot in actual locations, and they had a general sense that the characters were not properly set up. These concerns would be addressed by adding title cards announcing that *Four Frightened People* was shot in the South Seas and giving brief background biographies of the four principal characters. Beyond this, the film seemed at least ten minutes too long, laughter erupted in some places where a more serious tone was intended, and the music sounded weak overall. After a meeting of the committee, Anne Bauchens prepared a six-page list of suggested cuts.

A print of the picture was airmailed to New York, and DeMille took this print to Stamford, Connecticut, for his own preview on Monday, December 18. In a telegram to Paramount production head Emanuel Cohen he noted, "Reactions of audience in main same as Huntington Park. Agree must eliminate thousand feet."[11] He instructed George M. Arthur to follow through with the cuts suggested by Bauchens, and suggested additional cuts of his own. In all nearly sixteen hundred feet of film were eliminated, and the picture finally went out with a seventy-eight-minute running time.

After screening the picture for himself, Emanuel Cohen weighed in with suggestions of his own, much to the disgust of writer Bartlett Cormack. "Unkindest cut of all," Cormack wired DeMille, "was elimination of Little Miss Muffet line occasioned by Mr. Cohen's bewilderment because Judy [Claudette Colbert] had said her name was Jones and here was somebody calling her Muffett. That finished me. They say there is a good living to be made in raising alfalfa."[12]

The final hurdle for *Four Frightened People* was the New York censor review. They were aghast at scenes of a seemingly nude Claudette Colbert bathing under a jungle waterfall. In an impassioned plea to James Wingate of the Motion Picture Producers and Distributors of America, DeMille wrote:

> Because of the objections raised by the New York censors to
> two scenes in my picture, FOUR FRIGHTENED PEOPLE, I
> telegraphed our New York office as follows: "Advise Board
> of Censors there are no nude shots in the bathing scenes. . . .
> Girl under waterfall wears Annette Kellerman bathing suit,
> and all parts of body are covered." I am surprised that the
> Board requests these eliminations as surely the scenes are
> staged in good taste, and all who have seen picture class these
> scenes as ones of artistry. I have never made a personal
> request to any censor board, but in this case I beseech you to
> reconsider, particularly as it cost us a great sum of money to
> take the company to Hawaii in an effort to obtain accuracy,
> artistry, and authenticity.[13]

The scenes remained in the film, but DeMille was not entirely honest with the censors. It is true that Colbert's double wears a form-fitting body suit in the long shots, but in a closeup of Colbert, she is clearly topless—if only partially revealed for just a frame or two.[14] One hesitates to call Frank Capra a liar, but in his book *The Name above the Title*, he writes of Claudette Colbert's unwillingness to raise her skirt for the hitch-hiking scene in her next picture, *It Happened One Night* (Columbia, 1934). Surely Capra was remembering a press agent's fable—or perhaps DeMille had greater powers of directorial persuasion.

Part of a minor cycle of "back to nature" films, *Four Frightened People* was not a box-office success, and DeMille never again ventured into full-length comedy.

# 59

# Cleopatra

A Paramount Picture. A Cecil B. DeMille Production. Produced and directed by Cecil B. DeMille. Screenplay by Waldemar Young and Vincent Lawrence, from an adaptation of historical material by Bartlett Cormack (additional, uncredited writing by Manuel Komioff, Jeanie Macpherson, and Finley Peter Dunne Jr.). Costumes: Travis Banton. Art directors: Hans Dreier and Roland Anderson. Assistant directors: Cullen B. "Hezie" Tate and David MacDonald. Montage sequences: William Cameron Menzies. Photography: Victor Milner, A.S.C. Film editor: Anne Bauchens

Picture started: March 12, 1934. Picture finished: May 2, 1934. Montage and special effects shots: May 11 through June 12 and June 20, 1934. Preview length: 9,191 feet. Final length: 9,046 feet (eleven reels). Cost: $842,908.17. Released: August 16, 1934 (New York premiere). Gross: $1,929,161.10

Cast: Claudette Colbert (Cleopatra), Warren William (Julius Caesar), Henry Wilcoxon (Marc Antony), Gertrude Michael (Calpurnia), Joseph Schildkraut (Herod), Ian Keith (Octavian), C. Aubrey Smith (Enobarbus), Ian MacLaren (Cassius), Arthur Hohl (Brutus), Leonard Mudie (Pothinos), Irving Pichel (Apollodorus), Claudia Dell (Octavia), Eleanor Phelps (Charmian), John Rutherford (Drussus), Grace Durkin (Iras), Robert Warwick (Achillas), Edwin Maxwell (Casca), Charles Morris (Cicero), and Harry Beresford (the soothsayer)

On February 10, 1938, after seeing a revival of *Cleopatra*, movie fan Hildegarde Merta of Chicago wrote Cecil B. DeMille questioning the historical accuracy of the women's costumes. It seemed to her that they looked remarkably modern. Answering for DeMille, Frank Calvin replied on February 16:

> For your information, over six months were spent in the research work on this picture, including a very careful study of the costumes and head dresses of the period, and you can rest assured that they were correct.
>     Quite often modern clothes designers copy ancient costumes, and it is for that reason that you noticed a similarity.

DeMille always made a great point of stressing the effort he and his staff put into historical research for his films, but Hildegarde Merta's suspicion that *Cleopatra*'s gowns owed more to Hollywood than ancient Alexandria were well founded. While Travis Banton was certainly "inspired" by Egyptian and Roman art, he did his best to make sure his designs were *à la mode* and would reveal as much of Claudette Colbert's 5'3", 34" x 26½" x 37" figure as industry censors permitted in the last days before a toughened Production Code took effect on July 1, 1934.[1]

In a letter to his niece, dancer-choreographer Agnes deMille, Cecil outlined his approach to Cleopatra's story, noting that he was consciously attempting to avoid characters that were painted only in tones of black and white. "The treatment may be a little startling to you at first," he wrote, "because it is neither the Shavian [George Bernard Shaw] treatment, nor the Shakespearian treatment. It is an endeavor to humanize characters, and . . . I am confident that I am giving the characters their first really human chance. They have always been ponderous and pompous, villains and heroes."[2]

Indicative of his take on the characters were some of the actors he considered for the picture. In a quick note to Al Kaufman, DeMille asked, "Don't faint! Do you think Menjou could play Julius Caesar?" Adolphe Menjou had risen to stardom in the silent era playing a lovable cad—a relentless, womanizing lounge lizard who still managed to command audience sympathy. His image changed somewhat with the coming of sound, and he was often cast as a seemingly respectable character with a slightly seedy edge. The idea of the distinctly modern Menjou brought a derisive comic reply from Kaufman. "I did faint. That's why it's taken me until now to say I don't think so."[3] But DeMille did not alter his basic concept of Caesar's character. He looked at film on former silent screen lover John Gilbert, an actor who occasionally enjoyed going against his romantic image to play manipulative scoundrels in films like *Man, Woman and Sin* (M-G-M, 1927) and *Downstairs* (M-G-M, 1932). Ultimately, after screening *The Mouthpiece* (Warner Bros., 1933), DeMille settled on Warren William to play Caesar. William carved a unique place in precode Hollywood, playing a series of hustlers, con men, unscrupulous politicos, and ambulance chasers who had no redeeming social value but who nevertheless delighted audiences with the sheer audacity of their guile.

DeMille discussed the role of Marc Antony with Richard Dix and Charles Bickford and offered William Gargan a test. One day DeMille was scheduled to look at some footage in a Paramount screening room. Arriving early he caught a screen test of English actor Henry Wilcoxon, who had been brought to the States by producer Benjamin Glazer. On December 8, 1933, DeMille wrote Al Kaufman, "So far Harry Wilcoxon is the nearest thing to Marc Antony I have seen and if it can be arranged with Mr. Glazer, whose discovery I understand he is, I should like to have him for Antony."[4]

After *The Sign of the Cross* and her Oscar-winning performance in Frank Capra's *It Happened One Night* (Columbia, 1934), Claudette Colbert was considered ideal for the role of Cleopatra, and no one else was seriously considered. But the glorified ingenue of two years before was now a bona fide superstar, and Colbert's new status would create problems on the set during production.

As part of his research and preparation, DeMille asked to see the 1917 William Fox production of *Cleopatra,* starring silent screen icon Theda Bara. On January 5, 1934, DeMille was told that there was no print in Los Angeles, but that there was one in Fox's East Coast storage facility at Little Ferry, New Jersey. On February 13, 1934, George M. Arthur reported: "A print of the original version of CLEOPATRA, made by Fox, is in from New York. Will you please look at it as soon as possible, as they have requested that it be returned immediately?"[5] DeMille's screening of the picture on February 15 may have been the last time anyone saw Theda Bara's *Cleopatra.* On July 9, 1937, a nitrate fire at Little Ferry destroyed virtually all of Fox's pre-1935 negatives and protection masters.[6]

It became DeMille's custom to have his secretaries take note of his statements for future reference and to call them up as needed. As he prepared to start shooting, Emily Barrye kept a steady stream of reminders coming. Among them, on March 1, 1934: "CB you want to talk to Wilcoxon about 'abandon'—so he will lose some of that British reserve." And on March 8: "CB: Don't forget Gertrude Michael's funny southernish accent when you are seeing her as Calpurnia."[7]

As *Cleopatra* was about to go before the camera, problems arose behind the scenes. On March 9, 1934, costumer Victoria Williams resigned from the picture, unhappy with what she perceived to be a lack of organization in the costume department. Three days later, on the first day of shooting, the daily production report noted that "costumes not ready"; the following day witnessed a "Costume delay owing to shoes not being ready."[8] March 17 began with a rehearsal "with principals in morning. After lunch Mr. DeMille ordered Miss Colbert's head dress changed which occasioned a delay of 2 hrs. 15 minutes." Even with this delay DeMille and company managed to shoot six script pages that day. But wardrobe problems continued throughout the production. On March 23 there was a "delay owing to wardrobe not being ready in particular C. Aubrey Smith's."

April 4 was scheduled for a night shoot with a call at 7:00 P.M., but "Miss Colbert was late on the set. She was sent for at 7:10 & asked to be ready to come immediately when called which was at 7:40 She arrived at 8:10 not in costume." Shooting finally wrapped at 5:20 A.M. the following day. On April 5, "There was a 2 1/2 hour delay while the crown worn by Miss Colbert was changed." And on the 6th, "There was a 3 hour delay whilst Miss Colbert's costume was got ready." The assistant director suggested that there might have been an element of star temperament in some of the delays, noting that "The 3 hours delay in the 4/6/34 was due to the fact that Miss Colbert did not fit the night before, thus at 8:30 am of the 4/6/34 she found her costume unsatisfactory to her."

On the following day, April 7, "The company dismissed at 12:30 p.m. Miss Colbert came back to the set at 1:40 reporting that she had sent back her costume as being unsatisfactory to her. The previous evening Mr. deMille released her from the final long shot in order that she might have a fitting. She gave 20 minutes of her time at the end of which she ok'd costume. At 1:30 she sent it back as not being satisfactory, thus occasioning a 2 hour delay."

As of April 7 *Cleopatra* was half a day behind schedule. DeMille managed to pick up the lost time by April 10, but Claudette Colbert went home at 4:15 P.M. that afternoon complaining of illness. She remained at home on the eleventh, "necessitating the shooting of odd pick up shots in which she did not figure thus causing the loss of a day." Colbert remained absent on the twelfth, thirteenth, and fourteenth, leaving the picture three days behind schedule.

She returned to the set on April 16, which proceeded as scheduled, but on April 18 the company lost another half day because the rear-projection apparatus would not synchronize with the camera. By April 20 DeMille had picked up a day; and by the twenty-fourth, two of the three and a half days had been made up, but "84 mins [were] lost owing to Miss Colbert not answering her calls on time."

On April 25, one and a half hours were lost because Ralph Jester was not on hand to supervise the makeup of the "bull man" in the barge sequence. Another half hour was lost when Claudette Colbert was late returning from lunch, and yet another one and a half hours evaporated due to the food in a scene not being as DeMille wished. Further frustrations arose on the twenty-sixth, and DeMille shot off a quick memo to the casting office: "I am unable to shoot on time this morning because the dancers are not ready. Leroy Prinz [the dance director] stating that girls were here at 7 o'clock this morning but the gate man would not let them in and there was nobody in the casting office to okay them."[9]

The "bull man" and dancers were part of the visual centerpiece of the film, Cleopatra's seduction of Marc Antony on her barge. "Cleopatra is here putting on a show deliberately, with the intention of so astonishing the tough, hard soldier Antony that he will have to remain long enough for her to get in her deadly work," Cecil advised Agnes deMille, as he offered her the job of staging dances for the sequence. "This entire barge sequence should be the most seductive, erotic, beautiful, rhythmic, sensuous series of scenes ever shown. I do not mean by numbers of characters, and I do not mean an Albertina Rasch Ballet."[10] He added, "LeRoy Prinz [is] in charge of dancing but am not sure of his capability of handling so difficult a subject."[11]

Cecil proposed that Agnes do a solo dance number, supervise "certain other numbers," and act as "a general assistant to me through Cleopatra's barge episode," but just as she was scheduled to come to California she received an offer from Oscar Hammerstein to do the choreography on a show he was opening on April 6 in Drury Lane, London. Cecil advised, "If Hammerstein offer more beneficial, suggest she take it as do not want to jeopardize her future there." Still he managed to delay shooting the barge sequence so that Agnes's schedule could be accommodated.[12]

DeMille's interest in having Agnes work on *Cleopatra* was genuine. "You are the most interesting dancer I know," he wrote. "Your dances are different and have drama in them and something to make one stop, look, and listen." Still, he had a clear vision in his mind's eye of what he wanted to see before Agnes ever set foot on the sound stage in Hollywood. "The incident of the clams will show you what I mean, and the type of novelty that I am looking for," he advised in sending her the script.

> Antony had seen all the regular dancers in the world, so they could not interest him. Cleopatra would not have made the mistake of just staging a dance, therefore, when the first

course, which was clams, is to be served, she has a net dragged over the side of the ship dripping with water and seaweed and dragged by slaves before the table and couch of Cleopatra and Antony, and then the net is opened and with the kelp wrapped around them, beautiful girls come to life, their hair still dripping with the sea water, and lay before Antony the clams. . . . This should be a beautiful, intriguing, and different "number."

Another possibility is a fire dance, using in some way the astonishing man, whom you may have seen, who blows lighted gasoline from his mouth. . . . Then, perhaps, a nymph and fawn dance . . . the "Bubble Dance," which is probably not Egyptian at all, but which is picturesque, you may be able to make Egyptian. I saw it done here with a single girl and a balloon, which in our case, of course, would be a blown bladder.

Again, later, when Antony tries to free himself from the spell being cast over him, I see a bull led before him, on the back of which lies a beautiful dancer, whose costume suggests, perhaps, the mate of the bull. Perhaps her headgear is horns, and her shoes are hoofs, like Edmund Dulac's EUROPA AND THE BULL. . . ."[13]

Although the director presented these ideas as suggestions, the mention of specific wardrobe makes it clear that Cecil already knew what he wanted to see, as the costumes would already be in the works to meet production deadlines. In later years, Agnes dismissed her uncle's artistic sensibilities and snorted that he wanted her to ride in naked on the back of a bull, but in her March 28, 1934, memo to music director Rudolph Kopp, she seemed to embrace the idea. Her early notation for "The Dance of the Bull and the Lotus" included

1. Entrance on the back of the bull. Tympani accompaniment only—slow, low, and in rhythm with the animal's feet.
2. The descent from the bull. A quickening rhythm.
3. The appearance of the girls. A cymbal crash.
4. The Dance. . . .[14]

The first suggestion of a problem between uncle and niece came in an April 4, 1934, memo:

Mr. deMille does not want any of the stills made of Agnes deMille today used or sent out, as the costume worn and the makeup used were incorrect.

Mr. deMille did not like the makeup on Agnes deMille's mouth and the costume was not right. Mr. deMille states that if you wish to make some stills of Miss deMille to drape her in silver cloth, but do not use any of the stills made this afternoon, as the costume worn would give the wrong impression.[15]

Paramount's publicity department shot new stills of Agnes to meet a deadline for *American Magazine*, but these stills would prove to be the extent of Agnes deMille's participation in *Cleopatra*. Cecil and his niece agreed to disagree, and she returned to New York where she would make her mark as a choreographer on Broadway.

DeMille finished principal photography on *Cleopatra* on May 2, shooting retakes and additional closeups, but the film still required footage for the big battle scenes, which he began shooting on May 11. Incorporating footage shot by DeMille, the battle montages for *Cleopatra* were "scripted" by optical effects expert Gordon Jennings and production designer and sometime-director William Cameron Menzies, who proposed additional scenes based on notes from the director. Menzies began work on May 22 and finished on June 17, and although DeMille was involved in discussions and made written notes about the montages, he apparently was not directly involved with the footage Menzies shot. Henry Wilcoxon was injured on May 29, 1934, while shooting the montages when he slipped and an extra's sword struck his thigh. Closeups of Ian Keith, intended to be superimposed over the montage action, were shot in New York by Paramount test director Oscar Serlin.[16]

As with *The Sign of the Cross*, DeMille had trouble getting what he wanted from the music department. On June 4, 1934, writing for DeMille, Emily Barrye tried to lay down the law to music director Rudolph Kopp with a dose of her rather arch sense of humor:

HARPS HARPS HARPS

Mr. deMille wants harps used in the love themes, let them predominate and bring wood winds in and out as you need them. . . .

## HARPS HARPS HARPS

MUSIC FOR PARTY IN ATRIUM should be much lighter and gayer. As it is CB would have to dissolve the music out when the dialogue starts—he wants harps—guitars—lyres—native instruments with harps predominating.

Get set on harps and see what other instruments you can bring in without hurting the harps—don't worry about the harps hurting the other instruments. He wants exactly the instruments that were used in Poppea's bedroom in SIGN OF THE CROSS.[17]

On June 8 DeMille was angered when Roy Fjasted and Dick Johnston in the music department notified him of a four thousand dollar increase in music costs. In a memo to Roy Burns, DeMille raged that if they had followed his instructions there would be no cost overruns, and the next day, still unsatisfied, DeMille wrote Kopp directly: "Can't use music of atrium at all. It is mournful, sounds like a dirge, and all I want is three harps and a flute and no other instruments at all, or else I will use no music at all."[18]

After the June 20, 1934, preview, DeMille and editor Anne Bauchens trimmed about a minute and a half of footage. DeMille's meticulous planning and production paid off; sneak previews for paying audiences rarely resulted in major revisions to his films.

For all the problems during production, *Cleopatra* was worth the effort. After the less-than-enthusiastic reception accorded *Four Frightened People*, DeMille looked for *Cleopatra* to repeat the success of *The Sign of the Cross*—and it did. The afternoon after the New York premiere, he telegraphed his staff:

At nine o'clock this morning there was a line from the box office to the Paramount Theatre around the Times building. It is now two o'clock in the afternoon and I am standing in the theatre. Every seat in the entire building is sold. There is a crowd of at least two hundred and fifty people standing. Another two or three hundred are outside in the lobby waiting to get in and still another crowd in the street waiting to get in. The Manager says he hasn't seen a sight like this in the Paramount Theatre for a long time.[19]

# 60

# The Crusades

A Paramount Picture. A Cecil B. DeMille Production. Produced and directed by Cecil B. DeMille. Screenplay by Harold Lamb, Waldemar Young, and Dudley Nichols (additional, uncredited writing by Howard Higgin, Jeanie Macpherson, and Charles Brackett). Photography: Victor Milner, A.S.C. Music: Rudolph Kopp. Technical effects: Gordon Jennings. Costumes: Travis Banton. Art directors: Hans Dreier and Roland Anderson. Assistant directors: George Hippard (first assistant), David MacDonald (second assistant), and Cullen B. "Hezie" Tate. Production manager: Roy Burns. Script clerk: Emily Barrye. Film editor: Anne Bauchens

Picture started: January 30, 1935. Picture closed: April 16, 1935. Picture reopened: April 30 to May 13, 1935, and again May 20, 1935. Picture finished: June 4, 1935. Preview length: 11,262 feet. Final length: 11,265 feet (thirteen reels). Negative cost: $1,376,260.87. Released: August 21, 1935 (New York premiere), October 25, 1935 (general release). Gross film rental (through March 31, 1951): $1,491,471.83

Cast: Loretta Young (Berengaria), Henry Wilcoxon (King Richard), Ian Keith (Saladin), C. Aubrey Smith (hermit), Katherine DeMille (Alice), Joseph Schildkraut (Conrad), Alan Hale (Blondel), C. Henry Gordon (Philip II), George Barbier (Sancho, king of Navarre), Montagu Love (blacksmith), William Farnum (Hugo of Burgundy), Hobart Bosworth (Frederick), and Lumsden Hare (Robert, earl of Leicester)

With the success of *The Sign of the Cross* and *Cleopatra*, Paramount was willing to loosen the budgetary purse strings for another historical epic, and DeMille obliged with his biggest production to date. *The Crusades* telescoped the seven historic Holy Land campaigns, which occurred between 1096 and 1291 A.D., into a single narrative, although Harold Lamb, a screenwriter for the film and the author of the book that inspired the project, noted:

It is the third Crusade with which story is concerned 1187 A.D. the year Saladin captured Jerusalem.
    The failure of this crusade was caused by the personal quarrel of the leaders. This, in turn, was due to the bitter

wrangle between Richard and Phillip of France, after Richard refused to marry Alice of France, and his strange marriage with Berengaria of Navarre en route to the Holy Land.

Aggravated, of course, by Richard's arrogance and his assumption of leadership over the other princes, this quarrel became an open breach at the capture of Acre. The embittered princes returned home leaving Richard to march on Jerusalem with Hugo of Burgundy and a remnant of the once formidable crusade.[1]

Shortly after completing the script, DeMille and writers Harold Lamb and Waldemar Young attended a production meeting in Mannie Cohen's office on January 7, 1935, to get reactions from Paramount producers and executives Benjamin "Barney" Glazer, E. Lloyd Sheldon, Jeff Lazarus, Mel Schauer, Bogart Rogers, and William Wright. The discussion was transcribed, and offers a sense of DeMille's approach to bringing history and spirituality to the screen, as well as a sense of his ideas about dramatic construction:[2]

> EMANUEL COHEN: This is a very important picture and will cost a lot of money. Have you anything you want to say Mr. DeMille?
>
> CECIL B. DeMILLE: The prosecution usually presents its case first.
>
> EMANUEL COHEN: Barney?
>
> BARNEY GLAZER: I like it too much to prosecute. I think it is a very, very fine job indeed. My criticisms all relate to minor points, but there is one major question. Will we get in trouble with England and the English colonies for your suggestion that Berengaria, queen—or near queen, was desired of and spent some time in the tent of Saladin? It is a daring invention.
>
> CECIL B. DeMILLE: I would think not. Even in England they thought Berengaria was a steamship until we started the picture. I did not know it until I read Harold Lamb's book.
>
> WALDEMAR YOUNG: English people as a people are not afraid . . . of their bloody history. Was Berengaria ever crowned Queen of England?
>
> HAROLD LAMB: As a matter of fact, we know nothing about her except where she came from, where she was crowned and where she was married to Richard, and she appeared to the

Pope in Rome—but everything else in her history is a blank. . . . On her return after his [Richard's] death, she just disappeared.

CECIL B. DeMILLE: . . . I want a cut to get 13 or 14 pages out of the script. . . . Did it impress you as being long?

BARNEY GLAZER: No. I didn't think it was as long as Wally [Waldemar Young] said it was at lunch.

E. LLOYD SHELDON: I have Barney Glazer's enthusiasm for the script and I think it is a swell picture and a swell job. My concern [is] . . . I am rather anxious to see a stronger spiritual impulse—a stronger underscoring of theme . . . beginning [with the] desecration of [the] relics of Christ. There is a great dearth of common people. . . .

CECIL B. DeMILLE: . . . We had it in the scene of the populace rising to a high pitch of fervor for the Crusade. But the moment you take rulers and show . . . the King of France and the King of Germany, Richard of England . . . and Hugo, a double-crossing bastard, . . . The little bickerings they [the audience] may know about are shown through [the] personal story . . . the only way that people would believe today that people would give up their lives for a piece of wood is to put in a personal story to hold them. To carry a character like Richard, who is the audience, to carry him through and show his acquirement of God and spiritual understanding and let the audience take it from that.[3]

E. LLOYD SHELDON: . . . I got a certain inconsistency of character with Saladin. First he comes on a proud and vengeful Turk, trampling people under horses hoofs. Is that gap bridged—Saladin here and Saladin later? I would rather have Saladin left out of the first scene. To see some other [Moslem] representative have that [anti-Christian] attitude. . . . You have a world wide hero in Saladin because he allowed Christians to go into Jerusalem. . . . You alienate your audience at the start by having him the representative of desecrations. . . .

CECIL B. DeMILLE: . . . when Saladin comes along [at the beginning] with his attitude [it is] to make the audience feel the Crusade—to make them want to get up and fight. If we talk about relics or freeing Jerusalem, they [the audience] won't care. Kids could understand Saladin's attitude with the monk is there to show to the audience that it is going to be a great fight.

JEFF LAZARUS: It's terrific stuff. The question of whether it is going to gross one million or five million is going to be decided by how spiritual the thing is going to be. . . . Without a picture that says here is the greatest fight that decent people have ever waged—how bitterly they wanted to wage it—you won't gross five millions. . . . We're not spending much time with the soldiers of the Lord, but with the Kings. You have already given them the tarbrush. Richard had no purpose—he went into it to get out of the way of one wife and to get meat for his men. . . . One group should tell the Crusade story . . . some group must have a great invincible, clean purpose. . . .

WALDEMAR YOUNG: If anybody in this room doubts the spirituality of this story, let him read it without choking up. . . .

JEFF LAZARUS: Could I be permitted to disagree for a minute . . .

WALDEMAR YOUNG: . . . at Acre—crawling to the Cross . . . at Windsor Castle—in the public square—people, not soldiers. It's all through the story.

CECIL B. DeMILLE: If we don't give out that spiritual thing we can start with a Cross and a rope around and it crashes to the street and go to a cut of a great bonfire and sacred books burning and then go to the slave market.

JEFF LAZARUS: I think it is superb.

WALDEMAR YOUNG: It is there [already in the script].

BARNEY GLAZER: If it doesn't come out on the screen it will be C.B.'s fault. It's in the story. . . .

CECIL B. DeMILLE: All that sounds like I'm going to have to put back the . . . ride of the Crusaders across France. [It] was eliminated because of the cost. The little squire saying good-bye to his old mother—the young boy bidding his sweetheart good-bye—that shot is maybe what you are all missing. . . .

E. LLOYD SHELDON: It is awfully important. . . . The danger may be that you have lost the Crusades feeling. . . . You think of these wretched souls that went over there and went through privations, when actually the Kings were only thinking of another province.

CECIL B. DeMILLE: That would be fatal.

JEFF LAZARUS: Fatal.

CECIL B. DeMILLE: The first part of the picture is developed to show the rise of the Crusades. . . . We have the hermit in the street with Saladin at the square—[later] with Phillip [of France]—and [in England at] the courtyard [of the Castle]. Then, if we gave them more [of the hermit] they [the audience] are going to say: "What the Hell?" Then . . . we carry them with the dramatic love story [between Richard and Berengaria] through the middle and they have had their relief through the middle part. And then we are at our climax of love and religion into Jerusalem and into the Holy Sepulcher and you end your story. . . . If the Hermit or anyone else goes on talking about God and religion through eleven reels, you are going to be in trouble at the box office.

JEFF LAZARUS: Just get it long enough so they can't double feature it.

Although some minor revisions were made, the script remained essentially unchanged as DeMille brought *The Crusades* from page to screen. Fervor for the Crusade among commoners was depicted in large crowd scenes but was never really personalized through individual characters, although DeMille did add a brief cutaway of Richard's young squire, played by future director Oscar Rudolph, saying good-bye to his mother and made sure that there were several other farewells spotted throughout the departure of the Crusaders from England. In the finished picture one can't help but agree with the comments of Jeff Lazarus and Lloyd Sheldon. The venal motivations of the kings through much of the film's running time make them all rather unsympathetic and tend to undercut Richard's last-reel conversion.

Henry Wilcoxon had a lock on the role of Richard the Lion Heart from the beginning, and DeMille notified production manager Roy Burns that "I want Harry Wilcoxon to start carrying the falcon around. Pick out the best of the birds we have, and have him start carrying him around until the bird knows him. Perhaps he should also feed him."

Finding a leading lady for the role of Berengaria proved more of a chore. When Claudette Colbert's name was floated, it was noted that she would be used only "if we are absolutely stuck for someone to play the part." Madeleine Carroll was a strong contender in DeMille's mind, but her home studio, Gaumont British, did not want her to do a costume picture. As late as December 6, 1934, he expressed a desire to interview Merle Oberon. However on December 10, he had Emily Barrye notify the casting department that "Mr. deMille does not think it will be neces-

288 / Cecil B. DeMille's Hollywood

sary to bring Merle Oberon in after looking at *Broken Melody*." Constance Cummings was rehearsing a play in New York, Ann Harding was ill, and Helen Twelvetrees was considered to be "good in one picture—then poor in the next."[4]

Olivia de Havilland was considered early on. She attracted attention for her role as Hermina in Max Reinhardt's stage production of *A Midsummer Night's Dream*, but Florence Cole's September 25, 1934, report was not encouraging:

> Mr. Datig [Paramount casting director] says she is a San Francisco society girl—has never done any picture work, and has not made any screen tests.
> Mr. Datig says she was in his office today—they are not interested in her, and he doesn't think you would be.[5]

On October 27, 1934, Fred Datig wrote DeMille that "There is a possibility that we can borrow Miss [Loretta] Young from 20th Century [Pictures], but Mr. Zanuck would like to read the script first. M-G-M want her too but no definite promise has been made. She will not be needed for 20th Century picture after January 15th."[6]

As the starting production date pushed back from late fall into the end of January 1935, Young became the clear choice for Berengaria. The price to borrow her from Joseph Schenck and Darryl F. Zanuck's 20th Century Pictures was $2,500 per week with an eight-week guarantee and $1,923 per week thereafter. She brought one advantage that another performer might not. Although she was busy, having made a half-dozen pictures in the previous year, she was technically still a featured player and had not yet achieved star status. Young could be billed under the title, and not take thunder away from Henry Wilcoxon, who also had not yet earned star billing.

For the role of Blondel the Troubadour, DeMille wanted a singer who could act—or an actor who could sing. Character comedian Lynne Overman was rejected when he claimed to be only a "sporting house tenor." Paramount had an option on the services of Everett Marshall, who had starred in RKO's 1930 production *Dixiana*, but his price per picture was $15,000, and his name added little or no box-office value. DeMille asked casting to check with M-G-M about Nelson Eddy, who had yet to make a mark in films, and was advised by Fred Datig that "Nelson Eddy is a baritone, under contract to M.G.M. Studio and is scheduled to play opposite Jeanette MacDonald starting approximately October 15th for about eight weeks. Although Eddy has an excellent singing voice, he is pretty bad as an actor and M.G.M is anticipating plenty of trouble before their picture is finished. I hesitate taking a chance on him for Blondel."[7]

While DeMille relied on Paramount's casting department during the making of *The Crusades*, he continued his long-held practice of accepting personal solicitations from actors. In responding to a request from actor Hobart Bosworth for a role in *The Crusades,* the director wrote: "I am looking forward with unusual joy and some trepidation to the making of the CRUSADES. It is probably the biggest yet undertaken, and I have put your name down at once to see where I can fit you in. It will be a pleasure to have you with me once again."[8]

Bosworth had been the first true movie star, receiving "above the title" billing on *The Roman* (Selig Polyscope, 1909) at a time when virtually all film actors were anonymous. He had worked several times with DeMille in the 1910s, but by 1934 the sixty-seven-year-old actor had fallen on hard times, working only three days in his chosen profession during the year. He would eventually be cast as King Frederick of Germany in *The Crusades* and earn $1,000 for ten-days' work out of three weeks. When every casting director in Hollywood had forgotten, Cecil B. DeMille remembered and offered work to actors who longed once again for the smell of greasepaint. Among those on DeMille's "preferred list" for *The Crusades* were actors like Billy Elmer and H.B. Carpenter, who had worked in some of his earliest films and who were now reduced to playing occasional bits in low-budget Westerns. Former silent stars like William Farnum, Charles Ray, Betty Blythe, Grace Cunard, Bessie Eyton, Maude Fealy, Pauline Garon, Ella Hall, Florence Lawrence, Alice Lake, Florence Turner, and Clara Kimball Young were also on the list—insuring that, if available and willing to play a bit part or an extra role, they would land at least a few days work in the latest Cecil B. DeMille Production.

In the Depression-bound 1930s things were especially grim for Hollywood's bit players, as studios sought to scale back budgets for their program pictures. Most extra people subsisted on six dollars per week. Dress extras, who supplied their own wardrobe, earned an average of $17.20 per week, and only forty-two of the thousands of registered extras earned over $35 weekly.[9] With a budget for bits and extras of $72,208.32, *The Crusades* provided well over three thousand man-weeks of employment for Hollywood's legion of extras.

The joy and trepidation DeMille expressed to Hobart Bosworth were both justified. Clearly the director was in his element, recreating history on a massive scale, but the sheer size of *The Crusades* made the production an ordeal. On September 26, 1934, DeMille expressed his concern to Roy Burns about progress on the costumes:

> It appears to me now that we are heading for exactly the same difficulty that we had in Cleopatra. For that there was some excuse, because you had a designer leave you just prior to starting.
>
> For The Crusades there will be no excuse if we are not ready, and my guess from present progress is that we will not be ready unless reorganization is made in that department.[10]

Costume designer Travis Banton was on thin ice over his slow work, but DeMille was reluctant to replace the well-respected designer. On January 5, 1935, Emily Barrye wrote Roy Burns: "Wait until we see what happens on Monday on the Loretta Young costumes, before anything is done about Banton." Banton's talent ultimately overcame his lack of management skills, and he completed the costumes for the picture.

On January 29, 1935, the day before the cameras were to roll, DeMille received word that Paramount had authorized a $40,000 increase in expenditures, bringing the budget to $1,040,000; but on the first day of shooting the budget went out the window as the picture fell a full day behind schedule. Three days later, the company was two days behind. And so it went. For the most part the assistant director's daily reports noted no extraordinary delays, but the picture kept veering further and further from schedule, as DeMille took his time lining up and rehearsing shots and other things conspired to slow things down. On February 11, 1935, DeMille noted:

> We had a man in foreground with a cheap part in his wig. He was right in the foreground and had a dead white part in his wig which was faky.
>
> We save 8¢ on a wig like this that may cost us the retake of this scene.

This incident would serve as the inspiration for the production short *Hollywood Extra Girl* in which DeMille is shown in a staged scene berating assistant director David MacDonald for allowing an extra with a "1935 head dress" into a scene set in the twelfth century. But at least some of the production delays may have been calculated, with DeMille playing for time to solve one problem by creating a diversion in another area. On February 13, the thirteenth camera day, there was a fifty-five minute delay "due to the fact Mr. DeMille was not satisfied with head dresses & wigs of the Christian slave women." The following day, Emily Barrye noted the real reasons for such delays: "Mr. deMille had some trouble with Philo McCullough reading a line today and said to send you a note about hiring stock actors who couldn't speak lines." And:

WE WILL HAVE TO RETAKE THE SLAVE MARKET

Mr. deMille wants you to get a very good actor for the man who buys the girl and take[s] her down the stairs—not a $12 a day man.
Anne Sheridan [sic] was very good.
The girls around the Nun are okay if they are roughed up a bit.
Will need 5 to 6 new girls to carry the right hand line and front line.
Get the best actor you can for the auctioneer—not another Jewish comedian.[11]

During outdoor shooting on the re-dressed Roman street built for *Cleopatra* on February 20, four takes were spoiled by whistles from the set of Lewis Milestone's production of *Paris in Spring*. And so it went. By March 5, the thirtieth camera day, *The Crusades* was nine days behind schedule. On March 14, and now twelve days behind, George Hippard recorded: "9 am call Mr. DeMille arrived at 9:25 & 25 minutes late after lunch call. 9:25 to 12:16 rehearsing and lining up & rewriting script on account of illness of Wilcoxon since Wednesday & Miss Young being unavailable had to shoot scenes in which they were not in, out of continuity. 1 1/2 pps shot."[12] On April 4 DeMille complained to Roy Burns, "Again and again we have had scenes spoiled by trucks passing through outside of stage although red lights were on. Would suggest that attention be called to this."[13]
Preparations to shoot some of the big nighttime battle scenes on April 11, with catapults lobbing firebombs at the city of Acre, prompted

Emily Barrye to advise the production staff to "Have plenty of men to put out fire balls on the ground. The . . . surcoats and capes should be fireproofed."[14]

Principal photography finally closed on April 16, 1935, eighteen days behind schedule, shooting scenes in the ship's galley and on the hill above Jerusalem. The picture was reopened twice to complete the battle montages. The final cost came in $336,000 over budget, with much of the overage covered by Cecil B. DeMille Productions.

As film editor Anne Bauchens cut the picture DeMille advised, "Assemble long shots. Don't use so many closeups on first cut."[15] The edited picture clocked in at about 125 minutes' running time. In all, some 387,788 feet of picture negative were used in making *The Crusades* (including special effects and transparencies), and 374,805 of sound track negative—making for an astonishing shooting ratio of thirty-four feet of film exposed for every foot that ended up on the screen. Five hundred and forty-seven still pictures were taken during production.

*The Crusades* was screened for two different groups of critics in the Paramount studio theater on Wednesday, July 31, and Wednesday, August 7, 1935. On August 5, 1935, DeMille was informed by Rodney Bush of Paramount's exploitation department that, despite its length, the picture would be released without an intermission. It opened August 21, 1935, at the Astor Theatre in New York on a road-show basis. General release followed in October.

*The Crusades* performed well at the box office, but ultimately failed to achieve commercial success, showing a loss of $443,986.65 as of a 1951 producer's settlement statement. Still, DeMille was proud of *The Crusades*, and when he wasn't promoting one of his current releases he would sometimes refer to it as his favorite film. He believed in the message of religious tolerance he felt he had injected into the story, and in his autobiography he stated that "Thanks to our treatment of the subject and the wonderfully sensitive performance of Ian Keith as Saladin, *The Crusades* has been one of my most popular pictures in the Middle East."[16] But in fact, when the film was offered by Paramount's foreign department in 1936, censors in Egypt, Syria, and Palestine rejected it outright.[17] Eventually, it did play Egypt and Palestine and some other Middle Eastern markets, but the income tallies from these territories could hardly be considered impressive: Egypt—$19,234.53; Palestine—$6,291.20; Iraq—$232.68; Iran $1,254.67; and $134.75 in the rest of the Arab world.[18]

# 61

# The Plainsman

A Paramount Picture. A Cecil B. DeMille Production. Produced and directed by Cecil B. DeMille. Screenplay by Waldemar Young, Harold Lamb, and Lynn Riggs. Material compiled by Jeanie Macpherson, based on stories by Courtney Ryley Cooper and Frank J. Wilstach (additional, uncredited writing by Wallace Smith, Stuart Anthony, and Virginia Van Upp). Art direction: Hans Dreier and Roland Anderson. Musical direction: Boris Morros. Original music: George Antheil. Photography: Victor Milner, A.S.C. Film editor: Anne Bauchens

Picture started: July 21, 1936. Picture closed: September 8, 1936. Picture reopened: September 13, 1936. Picture closed : September 23, 1936. Length: 10,154 feet (twelve reels). Cost: $974,084.85. Released: January 1, 1937. Gross: $2,278,533.33

Cast: Gary Cooper (Wild Bill Hickok), Jean Arthur (Calamity Jane), James Ellison (Buffalo Bill Cody), Charles Bickford (John Lattimer), Helen Burgess (Louisa Cody), Porter Hall (Jack McCall), Paul Harvey (Yellow Hand), Victor Varconi (Painted Horse), John Miljan (Gen. George Custer), and Frank McGlynn Sr. (Abraham Lincoln)

I n early 1936 Paramount commissioned a review of its business activities. The report was not particularly flattering regarding DeMille's track record in the past three years:

|  | Paid DeMille | Estimated Net |
|---|---|---|
| *The Sign of the Cross* | $310,000 | $517,000 profit |
| *This Day and Age* | 40,000 | 12,000 profit |
| *Four Frightened People* | 50,000 | 305,000 loss |
| *Cleopatra* | 50,000 | 215,000 profit |
| *The Crusades* | 75,000 | 795,000 loss |
| Totals: | $525,000 | $358,000 loss[1] |

Nor was the report particularly favorable toward Paramount's dealings with DeMille. *The Crusades* had been made under a two-picture contract, with the second scheduled picture to be *Samson and Delilah*. DeMille had been advanced $60,000 of the $75,000 due under the contract for

*Samson and Delilah* and had spent $142,000 in preliminary costs, exclusive of studio overhead charges, preparing the script and getting ready for production before it was decided to abandon the project.

On February 10, 1936, Paramount president John Edward Otterson and vice president Watterson R. Rothacker began negotiations with DeMille for a nine-picture contract. The negotiations did not result in a new agreement, but Otterson ordered that DeMille be paid $3,000 per week by Paramount until further notice. Adolph Zukor intervened and finally worked out an arrangement whereby DeMille would keep the advances he had received and produce a Western to be titled *Buffalo Bill* at a cost not to exceed $600,000, exclusive of star Gary Cooper's salary. DeMille was to receive an additional advance of $36,000 against 50 percent of the profits, grouping *Buffalo Bill* with *The Crusades* in a revision of the original two-picture deal, and was to be responsible for any costs exceeding the $600,000 budget. "The result," concluded the report, "is that DeMille and his unit actually cost the company $269,300, excluding overhead, from the date CRUSADES was completed to May 16, 1936 while Paramount was trying to make up its mind."

Although *The Crusades* performed rather respectably at the box office, it would never recoup its costs. The studio wanted DeMille's big pictures, but they also wanted to curb expenses and avoid a repeat of the overruns on *The Crusades*. In canceling *Samson and Delilah* Paramount avoided what it perceived would be another expensive historical drama. And by insisting that DeMille work with Gary Cooper, the company hoped to add star power and box-office insurance.

Although B-Westerns and stars like Gene Autry, Buck Jones, and George O'Brien were popular with movie audiences, big-budget studio Westerns had been more or less in limbo since the box-office failures of *The Big Trail* (Fox, 1930), *Billy the Kid* (M-G-M, 1930), and *Cimarron* (RKO-Radio, 1931).[2]

*Buffalo Bill,* a film to be based on the life of William F. Cody, no doubt appealed to DeMille because he claimed to have met Sitting Bull and Buffalo Bill as a small boy when Buffalo Bill's Wild West Show came to New York. But RKO's *Annie Oakley* (1935) dealt with Cody's later years as a showman, and so DeMille turned to his earlier years as a frontier scout for the basis of his story. Inspired by the film version of *The Last Frontier* (Metropolitan-P.D.C., 1926), which was based on a 1921 novel by Courtney Ryley Cooper, DeMille decided to weave history and fiction into a rousing, idealized Western adventure pitting gun runners and Indians against Wild Bill Hickok and Buffalo Bill Cody, with a romance between Wild Bill and Calamity Jane added for spice.

*The Last Frontier* had originally been planned as a Thomas H. Ince production, and Ince had sent director B. Reeves "Breezy" Eason to Canada to shoot footage of buffalo herds. Ince's death halted the project, but it was revived when Producers Distributing Corporation took over the Ince studio interests. Cowboy star Jack Hoxie played Buffalo Bill in the silent film, which had been successful enough that E.B. Derr had initiated the making of several sound sequences for a revival of the film when he took over the production reins at Pathé after DeMille's departure for M-G-M. The part-talking version was never released, and although the newly shot footage survived in the RKO-Pathé Culver City vaults at the time of DeMille's inquiry in April 1936, all known prints of the original silent production had been junked.[3] But, even though he was unable to re-screen *The Last Frontier*, DeMille apparently remembered the picture well enough that he told his casting director that the actor selected to play Buffalo Bill in his new film "should be played by a Jack Hoxie type."[4]

Although DeMille and his writers were dealing with incidents that had occurred only sixty years earlier, they discovered they had a great deal of creative latitude because there were few surviving primary accounts of Wild Bill Hickok's career. Historians, surviving old-timers, and even contemporary official records often could not agree on how many, or even the correct names, of men Hickok was said to have killed in his line of duty as town marshal of Hays City, Kansas. Hickok's romance with Calamity Jane was based on the flimsiest evidence. "It is known that he bought her a dress once," DeMille recalled many years later. "That is definitely known. How and why he bought her the dress is not known."[5]

One fact that was known was that Wild Bill Hickok had been shot from behind by Jack McCall. Paramount was appalled at the idea that Gary Cooper, as Hickok, would be killed at the end of the film, but DeMille was adamant in serving history on this point, although he seemed willing to compromise if there was any compelling evidence that Hickok's death would hurt the picture's box-office potential. DeMille asked fellow director Frank Lloyd to read the script for *The Plainsman* while the film was in production, and on August 3, 1936, Lloyd suggested:

> The last scene which shows Hickok in Calamity's arms
> should show Hickok coming to sufficiently to say, "I reckon

it's going to be lonely for me from now on, Calamity." And Calamity saying, "No, Bill, you've always kept good company and you always will." Bill's eyes close, which we know is in death. The sound of the Plainsman's song should start on the sound track—and you Lap Dissolve to a plainsman advancing to the camera, happy and carefree, with the music in crescendo, and you see the spectral form of Hickok riding with them in a glorified exit. In other words, he has joined the throng of the pioneer plainsmen of the west who have passed on.[6]

DeMille ignored Lloyd's sappy dialogue suggestions, but he did incorporate the idea of a "phantom curtain call" for Gary Cooper and a rousing, printed on-screen afterword about Wild Bill Hickok's contribution to the winning of the West.

*The Plainsman* would mark a distinct shift in DeMille's approach to filmmaking. Former Paramount publicist William Pine became DeMille's associate producer, taking on many of the day-to-day production chores that DeMille or production secretary Emily Barrye had assumed in the past. DeMille's extensive use of carefully planned second-unit footage also began with this film.

For a tale of the Old West and wide-open spaces, it is surprising that so much of *The Plainsman* was shot on Paramount studio sound stages. Twenty-nine of the forty-six originally scheduled shooting days were set in the great indoors. Thirteen days were to be spent on the studio back lot. Only four days of principal photography were to be shot on locations near the studio. Most of the outdoor action was shot in Montana and Wyoming by second-unit director Arthur Rosson. DeMille would increasingly rely on Rosson to shoot location scenes for his next several pictures, and they developed a close working relationship, but the second-unit director's initial efforts did not meet with DeMille's favor. A June 20, 1936, telegram to Rosson in Birney, Montana, is typical of the direct and specific instructions the filmmaker would offer to those who worked with him:

CONFIRMING TELEPHONE CONVERSATION THE CAVALRY CHARGE HAS NO THRILL WHATEVER stop APPEARS TO BE CRANKED NORMAL stop FOR MOST OF THE CHARGE IT IS IMPOSSIBLE TO TELL

WHETHER THEY ARE INDIANS OR CAVALRY stop IT
IS IMPOSSIBLE TO GET A THRILL FROM A CHARGE
COMING DIRECTLY AT CAMERA stop APPROACH
SHOULD BE DIAGONAL SO THAT WE CAN SEE MEN
ARE GALLOPING. . . . THE EFFECT OF THIS SCENE
MUST BE FAST SPEED AND THUNDERING HORSES
NOT LITTLE TOY PUPPETS TWO OR THREE MILES
AWAY stop YOU HAD BETTER NOT HAVE THEM
DRAW THEIR SABRES BUT USE REVOLVERS AND
RIFLES stop LOCATION OF CHARGE IS NOT GOOD stop
SHOT WITH TREE IS BEST. USE SOMETHING TO
BREAK THE FOREGROUND. DON'T HAVE ANY
TROTTING stop THIS MUST BE THE CLIMAX OF AN
EXCITING SEQUENCE PHOTOGRAPHED AS SUCH stop
BE SURE AND UNDERCRANK INDIAN CHARGE. . . . I
WOULD PUT A CAMERA CAR IN FRONT OF CUSTER
AND THE FLAGS AND LET ME SEE SOMETHING THAT
WILL MAKE AN AUDIENCE GET UP AND CHEER
INSTEAD OF THE SLEEPY HOLLOW SCENE THAT
YOU SENT DOWN. REGARDS[7]

Much of Rosson's footage was designed to be incorporated in rear-screen process scenes. Rear projection was common in the 1930s, but DeMille stretched the use of process photography to the limit in *The Plainsman*, even staging battle scenes on sound stages with major elements derived from second-unit footage projected behind his principal players. The results were certainly economical, though not always convincing to the eye.

One of the things that kept DeMille from going on extended location jaunts was his new role as on-air host of the *Lux Radio Theatre*. The program aired live from Hollywood on Monday evenings from 9:00 to 10:00 P.M. over the CBS radio network. DeMille was credited as "producer" of the show, but more accurately he would be described as "master of ceremonies," introducing the stars and the stories and conducting scripted interviews with various celebrities between acts. In truth the program required little of his time, a dress rehearsal and two broadcasts (for the East and West Coasts), but, for the most part, it did necessitate his being in Hollywood during the broadcast season. Although he was already well-known for his film work through the years, DeMille's tenure on the *Lux Radio Theatre* made him a familiar household friend to millions of listeners as he promised the glamour of movieland with his weekly "Greetings from Hollywood."

The reaction by audiences in various cities who previewed *The Plainsman* was as much as DeMille and Paramount could hope for. The November 23, 1936, screening in New Orleans "did not start until eleven forty last night and finished at one thirty and not one person of the audience left the theatre," DeMille wired his wife the following day.[8] Audience member Fred Wendt wrote: "I think this picture is perfect—congratulations! The only disappointing incident is when Gary Cooper is killed. However, when thinking it over I conclude that if 'Wild Bill' were not killed, 'The Plainsman' would be just another cowboy picture and the public would forget the whole thing almost immediately."[9]

On December 9, 1936, Everett R. Cunnings, district manager of the Tri States Theatre Corporation, wired Paramount in New York: "Our Omaha theatre previewed The Plainsman last night with Cecil B. DeMille in person stop Large audience applauded and cheered picture and DeMille was showered with congratulations stop Newspapers so impressed they ran reviews of picture in news sections stop My entire staff joins me in congratulating DeMille and Paramount for producing not only the finest picture of the season but what will prove the biggest grosser stop It is replete with running comedy stop Add together The Virginian, Texas Rangers, Covered Wagon and Trail of the Lonesome Pine and you have The Plainsman[.]"[10]

When *The Plainsman* hit theaters in early 1937, the charges of reckless financial abandon and inept bungling leveled at Paramount executives only months before now seemed short-sighted and off the mark. The picture was a tremendous hit, wiping out the deficits piled up by DeMille's previous Paramount pictures, and inspiring a new cycle of epic Westerns including *Wells Fargo* (Paramount, 1937), *Stagecoach* (Wanger-United Artists, 1939), *Destry Rides Again* (Universal, 1939), *Dodge City* (Warner Bros., 1939), *The Westerner* (Goldwyn-United Artists, 1940), and DeMille's own *Union Pacific* (1939). After years of uneven success, DeMille hit his stride with *The Plainsman* and once again became a consistently potent box-office force. Not surprisingly, he returned to American historical themes for five of his next six films.

# The Buccaneer

A Paramount Picture. A Cecil B. DeMille Production. Produced and directed by Cecil B. DeMille. Screenplay by Edwin Justus Mayer, Harold Lamb, and C. Gardner Sullivan, based on Jeanie Macpherson's adaptation of *Lafitte the Pirate* by Lyle Saxon (additional, uncredited writing by Preston Sturges, Emily Barrye, Grover Jones, and Jesse Lasky Jr.). Associate producer: William H. Pine. Second-unit director: Arthur Rosson. Photography: Victor Milner, A.S.C. Art direction: Hans Dreier and Roland Anderson. Musical score: George Antheil. Editor: Anne Bauchens

Picture started: August 9, 1937. Picture finished: October 19, 1937. Second-unit work: July 19–30, 1937. Length: 11,297 feet (thirteen reels). Cost: $1,395,752.08. Released: February 4, 1938

Cast: Fredric March (Jean Lafitte), Franciska Gaal (Gretchen), Akim Tamiroff (Dominique You), Margot Grahame (Annette de Remy), Walter Brennan (Ezra Peavey), Ian Keith (Crawford), Spring Byington (Dolly Madison), Douglas Dumbrille (Governor Claiborne), Hugh Sothern (Andrew Jackson), Fred Kohler (Gramby), and Anthony Quinn (Beluche)

*T*he Buccaneer had a long journey to the screen that DeMille documented to stave off a plagiarism lawsuit by Zelma B. Tiden, who claimed that the film borrowed elements from her play *Captain What-the-Devil*.

As early as 1918 DeMille was interested in making a pirate story based on the life of Henry Morgan. Famous Players-Lasky rejected the notion based on exhibitor aversion to costume pictures, but DeMille returned to the idea several times through the years. In 1924 writer Hugh Wiley proposed a story called *The Republic of Texas* that among other things promised: "Pirates: Galveston Gang, Jean Lafitte, terror of the Gulf, pardoned by President Madison for his help in winning the battle of New Orleans."[1] DeMille rejected Wiley's broader story, but, intrigued with the idea of doing a film about Lafitte, hired the writer to prepare a story treatment for the newly formed DeMille Pictures, Inc. He wrote:

I have your letter of May sixth and am delighted that you will go ahead with the Lafitte idea.

For the straight romance of the tale, I would suggest
having the girl aboard Lafitte's ship when the British are
taking New Orleans, and even though there is a price that has
been placed on Lafitte's head by the American government,
she persuades him to fight for America, which he does, and is
victorious, saving New Orleans for America. Then, because of
his romance with the girl, he gives himself up, believing that
he may be hanged, but instead, at the girl's instigation or help
from General Jackson, he is pardoned and restored to citizen-
ship instead of being hanged.

If my idea does not appeal to you, don't let it worry you at
all—but go ahead and throw your own Lafitte.[2]

Wiley completed his story, but plans for production hit a snag when
Famous Players-Lasky purchased the screen rights to *Captain Sazarac*,
Charles Tenney Jackson's 1922 novel dealing with the life of Lafitte, and
produced a film based on it called *The Eagle of the Sea* in 1926.

DeMille's interest in Lafitte was rekindled in 1933 when he read
Lyle Saxon's 1930 biography *Lafitte the Pirate*. But Lafitte's story was
in the air in Hollywood. Between 1930 and 1937 M-G-M, Fox, Warner
Bros., First National, and RKO all registered stories about the pirate with
the Motion Picture Producers and Distributors of America, the trade
association led by Will H. Hays that sought to bring some sense of regu-
larity to the motion picture industry.

In 1934 DeMille again turned his attention to the life of Henry Morgan after completing *Cleopatra*. On May 8, 1934, Paramount purchased
Laurence Stallings and Maxwell Anderson's 1925 play *The Buccaneer*
as a basis for this proposed production. DeMille had little interest in the
play itself, but he liked the title and it became his practice, based on
advice from the studio, to buy the rights to a published underlying property to forestall nuisance suits for plagiarism. Bartlett Cormack was assigned to develop the Morgan story, but DeMille's note on Cormack's
draft of June 16, 1934, showed his displeasure: "What story are you
going to tell (not continuity or dialogue). Present treatment entirely un-
real and to me uninteresting. Spain cannot be the villain. The people and
dialogue must be real."[3]

While on a promotional tour for *Cleopatra*, DeMille and publicist
William Pine visited New Orleans. As DeMille recalled the experience:

Mr. E.V. Richards, one of the Paramount partners, took me tarpon fishing about the first of September at Grand Terre and Grand Isle.

To reach these two islands, we went by boat through the Louisiana Bayou. . . . I noticed an old ruined fort and asked Mr. Richards about it. He explained it was Fort Livingston and that the United States Government had built the fort to prevent Lafitte from returning to his island kingdom. When we tied up to Grand Terre in the evening, the shrimp fishing fleet was in. Many of these fishermen are descendants from the Lafitte pirates and in talking to them I became fascinated with the exploits of the pirate patriot whom they almost revere, and I decided then to make the Lafitte picture instead of Captain Morgan . . . but to utilize the title "The Buccaneer" for the Lafitte picture.[4]

The one roadblock was Warner Bros.' June 22, 1934, registration of the novel *Black Ivory* by Polan Banks, a story about Jean and Pierre Lafitte. Under M.P.P.D.A. rules, a registration of previously copyrighted material precluded other member producers from touching a similar subject for a period of two years.[5]

Finally, on October 12, 1936, DeMille assigned Jeanie Macpherson to develop the Lafitte story, and on November 16, 1936, he registered a story called *Jean Lafitte* with the M.P.P.D.A. A presumably revised story of the same title was re-registered on January 1, 1937. Story conferences on the project began on January 6, and on January 18 DeMille hired screenwriter Edwin Justus Mayer to write the screenplay.

"It is my custom in constructing a story," DeMille noted, "to put a large blank piece of cardboard on the office wall, and start construction on that so that I can observe the picture as a whole during the time of writing. The date of last notation on the blackboard [for *The Buccaneer*] is February 7, 1937 . . . and shows the outline of the story proceeding along the lines in which it was eventually concluded."

On February 15, 1937, DeMille, Edwin Justus Mayer and an entourage from DeMille's office went to New Orleans and conducted extensive research among primary historical documents in various libraries, museums, and private collections in the area. While in Louisiana, DeMille also met with Lyle Saxon and arranged to buy the screen rights to *Lafitte the Pirate*.

In April 1937 DeMille hired screenwriter Preston Sturges to work on *The Buccaneer*. "He preferred to draft his own story without working upon the scenario that I already had and consequently I used none of the Sturges material," DeMille recalled. However, even if his script was tossed out, Sturges did have some impact on the film. He recommended Akim Tamiroff for the role of Dominique You, the Napoleonic gunner who sails with Lafitte.[6] Tamiroff's performance in *The Buccaneer* became one of the picture's delights.

On May 11, 1937, Edwin Justus Mayer was taken off the project and DeMille assigned Harold Lamb and C. Gardner Sullivan to revise and rewrite the script. On June 14, 1937, screenwriter Grover Jones was hired to work in parallel with Lamb and Sullivan because, according to DeMille, "I was dissatisfied with the progress being made with some of the characterization and situations being evolved by Lamb and Sullivan."

Grover Jones wrote his own version based on the Mayer-Lamb-Sullivan screenplay. His work was completed on July 15 and, as DeMille recalled, "I then took both the Jones version and the Mayer-Lamb-Sullivan version and combined them to my own satisfaction which was the final script as shot." Jesse Lasky Jr. sought work as a screenwriter and provided a few revisions. DeMille had no need for another writer but promised Lasky an assignment on his next production.

DeMille was unequivocal in dismissing Zelma Tiden's claim that *The Buccaneer* infringed on her play. "Going back in our records ten years," he wrote, "we don't find any record of correspondence with Miss Zelma B. Tiden, either of manuscripts submitted or subjects suggested by Miss Tiden. The policy of DeMille Productions is not to receive any original or unpublished material. I have not read Miss Tiden's manuscript, 'Captain What The Devil,' nor have I heard of it until the announcement of Miss Tiden's suit in the trade papers. . . . I know nothing of the production of Miss Tiden's play in New Orleans and did not see any of the advertising mentioned . . . nor did I . . . hear any radio announcements advertising such play."

Paramount's attorneys finally settled with Zelma B. Tiden for $450 on November 2, 1939. The sum probably covered her legal expenses and saved the studio the cost of going to trial.

Compared to the struggle to develop the script, production on *The Buccaneer* was relatively uneventful. Robert Donat was DeMille's first choice to play Lafitte, but he was unavailable. Laurence Olivier was suggested as a substitute by Paramount's casting department, but as yet Olivier had no box-office standing in the United States. Fredric March had the star power, and he was in transition from the swaggering leading man of his early films to the restrained and deeply effective character actor he would become. This tension in his evolving temperament added depth to his performance, but the balance was sometimes uneasy. March's French accent, for example, seems more an affectation that one gets used to rather than a fully internalized vocal characteristic.

Franciska Gaal, who played the Dutch girl Gretchen, was a Hungarian actress who had made a picture with producer Joe Pasternak and director Henry Koster in Budapest. When Koster and Pasternak were signed by Universal Pictures, they tried to sell Gaal to the studio, and failing in that they pressed other studios to look at her. During Ernst Lubitch's brief tenure as head of production at Paramount, Adolph Zukor, who was originally from Hungary, asked Lubitsch to look at Koster and Pasternak's film with an eye to hiring the pair for a Paramount project. Lubitsch came away from the screening declaring that Gaal was a sensation.[7]

According to Paramount's publicity releases, playwright Ferenc Molnar wrote *The Good Fairy* and *Violet* especially for Gaal, and her eight European films, starting with *Paprika* (1933), were all "international successes." She spent a year being groomed by Paramount, a process depicted somewhat comically in the production short *Gretchen Comes Across* (Paramount, 1937), and DeMille is said to have declared, "I felt instantly that she 'had something'; that the qualities possessed by Helen Hayes, Mary Pickford, Elisabeth Bergner and mischievous, vivacious Clara Bow at the height of her international renown, were also Miss Gaal's."[8] DeMille gets points for showmanship, but the public didn't share his grandiloquent discernment, and Gaal quickly disappeared from the American screen.

Lafitte's pirate ship was the *Pandora*, rented from M-G-M at $4,000 for the first week and $500 per day thereafter. It plied the waters off Catalina Island, which made do for the coast of Louisiana with the aid of some well-placed flora from studio greensmen. The other local location was the Baldwin Ranch in Arcadia, California, now the Los Angeles County Arboretum.

Art Rosson's second unit shot most of the pirate stuff in the Louisiana swamps under the supervision of associate producer William Pine. Early in Rosson's shooting schedule on location in New Iberia, Louisiana, he nearly faced disaster. The unit reported: "CAUGHT IN THUN-DER AND RAIN STORM EQUIPMENT NEARLY LOST IN SWAMP FROM WATER GETTING IN BARGES NO ACCIDENTS OVER 200 MEN WORKING IN SMALL BOATS AND CANOES AT TIME"[9]

In general DeMille was pleased with the unit's work. He wired Pine on July 28:

> JUST RAN THIRD DAY'S STUFF STOP WITH THE
> EXCEPTION OF FOLLOW SHOTS WHERE FOUR
> HUMAN WINDMILLS ARE REVOLVING
> SIMULTANEOUSLY IN A ROW FOR EVERY FOOT OF
> EVERY TAKE THE ACTION IS GOOD AND THE
> LOCATIONS MAGNIFICENT. . . . THERE ARE ENOUGH
> CUTS THROUGH THIS STUFF WITHOUT THE WAVING
> OF ARMS TO GIVE ME WHAT I REQUIRE STOP
> THEREFORE RETAKES NOT WORTH THE
> ADDITIONAL COST. . . . SOME OF THE SHOTS ARE AS
> BEAUTIFUL AS ANYTHING I HAVE EVER SEEN ON
> THE SCREEN[.][10]

The surprising thing about the DeMille spectacles is just how little spectacle there is. The battle scenes, for example, are usually set pieces of editorial montage—effectively, even brilliantly done, but not the kind of thing the word "spectacle" usually conjures up. He staged the Battle of New Orleans in *The Buccaneer* rather effectively but with great economy. Taking advantage of the British army tactic of marching soldiers to battle in strict formation, DeMille was able to shoot comparatively little footage and reuse the shots of the advancing soldiers several times since the basic action remained the same. He even managed to swell the ranks of his British troops by several hundred phantom soldiers with the benefit of mirrored reflections—an illusion familiar to anyone who has sat in a barbershop and watched multiple images recede into infinity.

For DeMille, spectacle was a means, not an end in itself, and *The Buccaneer* spends the majority of its screen time exploring the nature of honor and respectability. One of DeMille's most disturbing sequences occurs when Gretchen is forced to walk the plank. The scene is basically a narrative device, allowing her to be rescued by the returning Lafitte and establishing her love for him. DeMille's emphasis is on Gretchen's agony as she begs for her life. It is one of those haunting moments that abound

[*Above*] DeMille discusses design sketches for *The Ten Commandments* (1923) with art directors Paul Iribe (left) and Francis McComas. (Unless otherwise noted, all photographs are from the author's collection.) [*Below*] An indication of the cold weather encountered on location for *The Ten Commandments* are DeMille's gloves and the overcoat worn by Estelle Taylor during rehearsal.

[*Above*] DeMille directs Leatrice Joy and Rod LaRocque as Julia Faye looks on in background. Scenes for *Triumph* were shot in an actual canning factory, adding a touch of realism to an extravagant story. (Marc Wanamaker/Bison Archives) [*Below*] Cast and crew for *Feet of Clay*. (Seated) Cinematographer J. Peverell Marley (second from left), Cecil B. DeMille, Julia Faye, Anne Bauchens, and Vera Reynolds (to the right of Marley). Latin lover Ricardo Cortez (nee Jacob Krantz) is seated fourth from right, and assistant director Frank Urson is to the right of Cortez. Among those standing in the rear are second cameraman Fred Westerberg (in white shirt and bow tie), Mitchell Leisen (fifth from left), and Rod LaRocque (with towel over his shoulders).

Legendary stage and screen actress Alla Nazimova (left) visits the DeMille studio during production of *The Road to Yesterday* as DeMille looks on with admiration and actress Jetta Goudal plays to the camera. Nazimova was leaving Hollywood to return to the stage after nearly ten years in pictures.

Theodore Kosloff (right), a longtime associate of DeMille (center), urged the director to make a film with a Russian theme and served as a consultant on *The Volga Boatman*. The bit actor on the left is unidentified.

[*Above*] D.W. Griffith (center) visits Cecil B. DeMille and Jeanie Macpherson on the set of *The King of Kings.* Movie and still photographers captured the moment, and judging from the backlighting, the meeting was carefully staged for the cameras. (Courtesy Danny Schwartz)  [*Below*] One of the more peculiar elements in *Dynamite* is this competition in which uniformed participants race these giant double-hoops, powered only by shifting body weight. Here DeMille shows Kay Johnson (foreground) and Julia Faye how the camera will follow the action as they move along the outdoor track.

An elaborate multistoried set built for *The Godless Girl*. DeMille, cinematographer J. Peverell Marley, and art director Mitchell Leisen ride the elevator at right. *The Godless Girl* utilized moving camera to a much greater extent than most DeMille films.

[*Above*] DeMille introduces his 1931 Diana to the 1914 model. Eleanor Boardman (left) played the role in the sound version of *The Squaw Man*—Winifred Kingston (right) took the part in the 1914 original and played a bit part in the second remake.   [*Below*] *The Sign of the Cross* gave work to many of Hollywood's struggling extras and bit players in the depths of the nation's economic depression. Here Cecil B. DeMille (behind camera on boom) lines up a crowd reaction shot during the spectacular Roman games. (Marc Wanamaker/Bison Archives)

[Left] DeMille (in apron) rehearses the scene for *This Day and Age* in which Herman's tailor shop will be bombed by gangsters. Cinematographer J. Peverell Marley stands behind DeMille; actors Oscar Rudolph (left) and Harry Green are in the foreground.

[Below] DeMille chats with Herbert Marshall and Claudette Colbert between takes in Hawaii during production of *Four Frightened People*.

[*Above*] Preparing to shoot a close-up of Julius Caesar (Warren William). Emily Barrye is working as production secretary, and cinematographer Victor Milner is beside camera at right. (Courtesy Mark Viera) [*Below*] DeMille never clocked out and even worked from his sick bed, although this scene is clearly staged for the publicity camera. Costumer Ralph Jester visits the director in the hospital to present some medieval pieces for his approval.

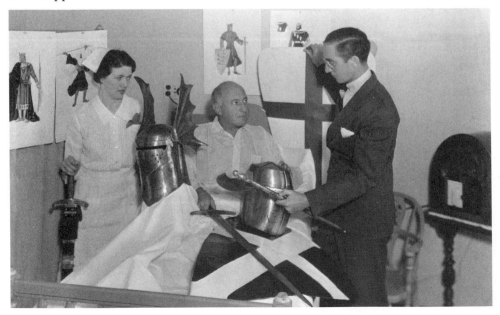

On the set of *The Crusades*, DeMille gives Loretta Young and Anna Demetrio their sight lines for a two-shot in which they will ultimately interact with Henry Wilcoxon, who will be shot from a reverse angle. Wilcoxon (in turtleneck) looks on. (Marc Wanamaker/Bison Archives)

The ruler of all he surveys, Cecil B. DeMille rides a camera boom during production of *The Plainsman*. Cinematographer Victor Milner, A. S. C. (wearing visor), is behind the camera. Screenwriter Grover Jones (wearing hat and glasses) sits beside DeMille. In the mid-1930s, Jones edited a lively "Movie Magazine By Movie Makers" first called *Jones' Wheeze* and later shortened to *Jones'*.

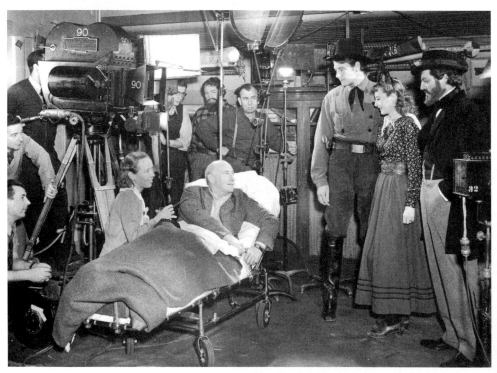

Production on *Union Pacific* was shut down for three weeks while DeMille underwent surgery and recovery. When the picture reopened for five days of shooting, DeMille arrived at the studio in an ambulance and directed from a stretcher. Here he offers pre-scene guidance to Joel McCrea, Barbara Stanwyck, and Francis J. McDonald.

DeMille and film editor Anne Bauchens, who cut every DeMille film from 1918 to the end of his career, and who was the first woman to win an Oscar for film editing. Here DeMille demonstrates the mysteries of an overlapping sound cut for the benefit of the publicity camera. In reality he rarely set foot in the cutting room, preferring to screen the work prints of his films in the studio theater and offering Bauchens specific written notes.

May 13, 1940, the scheduled final day of principal photography. Preston Foster and Gary Cooper are on horseback at left. Madeleine Carroll in black hat in middle and Cecil B. DeMille is in white shirt and hat beside the blimped Technicolor camera. *North West Mounted Police* tells the story of Dusty Rivers (Cooper), a Texas Ranger who travels to Canada to apprehend a killer. While in the north, Rivers becomes the rival of Mountie Jim Brett—both for the killer and for the woman, April Logan (Carroll).

[*Above*] Jeanie Macpherson and Jesse L. Lasky Jr. confer with DeMille over a draft script as Gladys Rosson stands by to take notes. The director's office on the Paramount lot came to be known as the DeMille Bungalow, and was much less ostentatious than his quarters at Famous Players-Lasky or M-G-M. (Marc Wanamaker/Bison Archives)
[*Below*] The port of Tjilatjap, Java, recreated for *The Story of Dr. Wassell* at the Paramount studio in Hollywood, miles from the nearest body of water. DeMille sits atop the precariously perched camera crane. Art directors Hans Dreier and Roland Anderson managed to come up with impressive settings despite wartime restrictions that limited producers to only $5,000 worth of new construction materials per film.

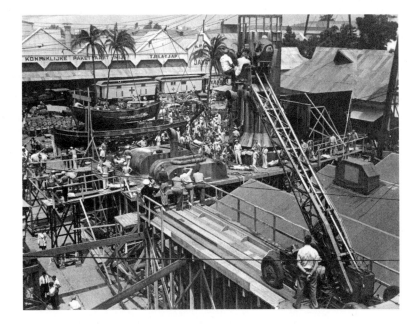

[*Above*] DeMille speaks to his cast during production of *Unconquered* as his current "chair boy" holds the public address microphone for him. Gary Gooper is on the right with his hand to his chin. Cooper's double, dressed identically, stands with his arms crossed. Henry Wilcoxon's face is visible behind Cooper's double. [*Below*] (Left to right) dialogue coach Frances Dawson, prop man Sam Miller, wardrobe woman Julie Cockerill, prop man Dwight Thompson, hairdresser Lenore Weaver, and dance director Theodore Kosloff (head and shoulders only) listen attentively as DeMille explains what he is looking for in the next setup with Hedy Lamarr for *Samson and Delilah*.

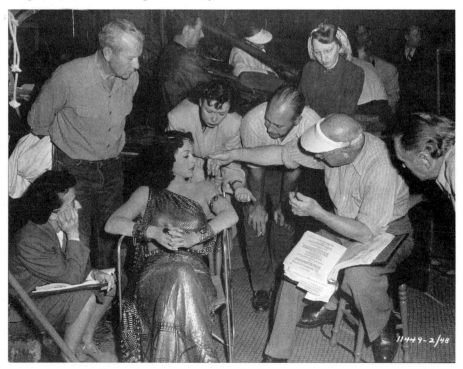

[*Above*] DeMille chats with writer-director Billy Wilder on the set of *Samson and Delilah* as cinematographer George Barnes listens. Wilder would cast DeMille to play himself in *Sunset Boulevard*. [*Below*] DeMille watches with amusement as Betty Hutton gives William "Hopalong Cassidy" Boyd a big kiss as he visits the set of *The Greatest Show on Earth*. Boyd was one of the director's closest friends. Hutton adored DeMille and has said she would have married the director in a minute if he had asked. (Courtesy Karl Thiede)

[*Above*] Cecil B. DeMille with Pauline Kessinger, manager of the Paramount studio commissary. DeMille customarily dined with a large entourage of co-workers and guests when he ate at the studio. He praised the bean soup once, and Kessinger made sure it was always on the menu. She was nearly apoplectic one day when she ran out of the soup before DeMille arrived, and she rushed over to apologize. "Thank god," he replied, "I hate bean soup." [*Below*] DeMille and Charlton Heston on location in Egypt near Mt. Sinai. The effects of DeMille's heart condition are evident in his thin and tired appearance.

[*Above*] H.B. Warner reminisces with DeMille on the set of *The Ten Commandments*. Warner played Jesus in DeMille's *The King of Kings* in 1927, and put on his grease paint one final time in a small role for the director before retiring. [*Below*] On the back lot at Paramount setting up a scene for *The Ten Commandments* with a VistaVision camera, DeMille grabs a sandwich. Cinematographer Loyal Griggs stands beside the director. In the background is the barn in which DeMille had his first Hollywood office in 1913.

in his films—like the final shot of *Cleopatra*, or the gangster poised over a well full of rats in *This Day and Age*, or Pharaoh carrying his dead child through the temple in *The Ten Commandments*, or Kay Johnson fingering her wedding ring in *Dynamite*—the images unobtrusively support the narrative and do not necessarily call attention to themselves, but they remain with the viewer long after the final fade-out.

*The Buccaneer* opened at the Saenger Theatre in New Orleans on January 7, 1938. According to *Variety,* more than 15,000 people crowded Canal Street hoping to catch a glimpse of DeMille and the other Hollywood celebrities on hand for the premiere. After the film, the audience applauded for five minutes before DeMille got up on stage with Margot Grahame, Akim Tamiroff, Hugh Sothern, and Evelyn Keyes. Tamiroff was clearly the hit of the evening; his comic portrayal of Dominique You delighted the audience, and he was mobbed as he left the theater. DeMille seldom resorted to comic relief characters in his films, but the Russian actor was so well received as a Frenchman in *The Buccaneer* that the director would bring him back, with only slight variations, as a Mexican in *Union Pacific* and a French Canadian in *North West Mounted Police.*

For many years *The Buccaneer* was the rarest of DeMille's sound films. When the picture was remade in 1958, Paramount was preparing to sell the television rights to its pre-1948 sound film library. The studio withheld the original version of *The Buccaneer* from the sale, and it has only recently become available again for television.

# 63

# Union Pacific

A Paramount Picture. A Cecil B. DeMille Production. Produced and directed by Cecil B. DeMille. Screenplay by Walter DeLeon, C. Gardner Sullivan, and Jesse Lasky Jr., based on Jack Cunningham's adaptation of the novel "Trouble Shooter" by Ernest Haycox (additional, uncredited writing by Frederick Hazlitt Brennan, Stanley Raub, Jeanie Macpherson, Stuart Anthony and Harold Lamb). Associate producer: William H. Pine. Second-unit director: Arthur Rosson. Art direction: Hans Dreier and Roland Anderson. Music: Sigmund Krumgold and John Leipold. Photography: Victor Milner, A.S.C. Film editor: Anne Bauchens

Picture started: November 15, 1938. Temporarily closed: January 31, 1939. Picture reopened: February 20, 1939. Picture closed: February 24, 1939. Second unit opened: October 19, 1938. Second unit closed : February 18, 1939. Length: 12,159 feet (fourteen reels). Cost: $1,451,268.47. Released: April 28, 1939 (Omaha, Nebraska, premiere)

Cast: Barbara Stanwyck (Mollie Monahan), Joel McCrea (Jeff Butler), Robert Preston (Dick Allen), Lynne Overman (Leach Overmile), Akim Tamiroff (Fiesta), Brian Donlevy (Sid Campeau), Henry Kolker (Asa M. Barrows), Anthony Quinn (Jack Cordray), and Lon Chaney Jr. (Dollarhide)

Following *The Buccaneer* DeMille planned to make a film dealing with the history of Canada's Hudson Bay Company and, true to his earlier word to Jesse Lasky Jr., he assigned the young screenwriter to conduct research and outline a story for the film. The idea was abandoned when DeMille discovered that 20th Century-Fox had a similar project in preparation.[1]

Industry trade magazine publisher Martin Quigley suggested a film based on the building of the transcontinental railroad, and DeMille was not dissuaded when he learned that Warner Bros. had already registered the title *Union Pacific* with the Motion Picture Producers and Distributors of America on February 7, 1938. Somehow managing to skirt M.P.P.D.A. regulations regarding noninterference with another producer's registered property, Cecil B. DeMille Productions signed a letter of agreement with W.M. Jeffers, president of the Union Pacific

Railroad, on March 2, 1938. Jeffers agreed to open up the Union Pacific business archives and to supply consultants and the U.P.'s top track-laying crew.

Joel McCrea received his first break in the picture business with DeMille as a bit player on *Dynamite* in 1929, and his stock had risen considerably since then. McCrea once proclaimed that he was never anyone's first choice for a part, but apparently he was DeMille's first choice to play the role of Jeff Butler in *Union Pacific*. The actor first learned he was under consideration for the role by reading a newspaper, and on July 1, 1938, he wired DeMille to express his surprise and delight. "I don't know whether to believe what I read in the papers or not," he wrote, " but I can't think of a type of story or a man I would rather work with. So I hope it's true. Could I talk with you some time?"[2]

Claudette Colbert, DeMille's first choice to play the part of Mollie Monahan, was not nearly so eager to work with him again, apparently believing that the temperaments of star and director had grown too similar to permit a comfortable working relationship. While the star was apparently willing to burn bridges, Cecil B. DeMille was not, and on August 14, 1938, he poured some oil on the water:

Dear Claudette:

While naturally I was terribly disappointed to read your decision not to play Molly in UNION PACIFIC, I understand perfectly your viewpoint and must admit the justness of your position.

The blow was somewhat assuaged by the charming way in which you put it and by your acknowledgment of the fact that we have something in common as director and star.

I assure you there is no one in this industry whose artistry I hold in greater esteem than yours, and I shall live in hope that in the not too distant future, I may direct you in a part that will add another jewel to your already well-filled crown of achievements.[3]

Although Barbara Stanwyck may have been his second choice, DeMille would give her his highest praise. "I am sometimes asked who is my favorite actress, among those I have directed," he later wrote. "I always dodge the question by explaining that I have to continue living in

Hollywood. But if the tortures of the Inquisition were applied and an answer extracted from me, I would have to say that I have never worked with an actress who was more co-operative, less temperamental, and a better workman, to use my term of highest compliment, than Barbara Stanwyck." Perhaps anticipating that Colbert, and others, might read his book, DeMille added, "[W]hen I count over those of whom my memories are unmarred by any unpleasant recollection of friction on the set or unwillingness to do whatever the role required or squalls of temperament or temper, Barbara's name is the first that comes to mind, as one on whom a director can always count to do her work with all her heart."[4]

As usual, when word went out that Cecil B. DeMille was starting a picture, Hollywood's hopefuls let the director know they were ready for the call. "I want to help you build your railroad or perhaps join the element that tries to stop it,"[5] wrote Lane Chandler, a former Paramount contract player who spent much of his career playing supporting roles in B-Westerns. Chandler, one of DeMille's favorites, played small parts in many of the director's films, and was cast as a train conductor in *Union Pacific*.

Among the former silent stars who landed bits in DeMille's railroad epic was former Hal Roach Studio comic Max Davidson as the "6th Card Player." The screen's first Tarzan, Elmo Lincoln, was the "11th Card Player." Monte Blue had become a star after featured roles in several DeMille films; but his career faltered with the coming of sound. His Native American blood helped land him a role as an Indian. Buddy Roosevelt, a Poverty Row cowboy star in the 1920s, shoveled coal as a railroad fireman. Maude Fealy, who gained some screen fame in the 1910s as a leading lady for the Thanhouser Film Company, played a laborer's wife. DeMille remembered Fealy from his days as an actor at Elitch's Gardens in Denver, Colorado, and she and her mother would land small roles in nearly all of DeMille's later films. Black actor Noble Johnson, who had played an Indian in the 1914 *Squaw Man*, put on war paint again for *Union Pacific*; and when *The Squaw Man*'s villainous Cash Hawkins, Billy Elmer, suggested that a role with DeMille would "put me back on the picture map," DeMille made the notation "must use" as he sent Elmer's name to casting director Joe Egli.

Few of DeMille's early associates in the picture business found any lasting success as the years rolled by. His *Girl of the Golden West* sent a note on October 13, 1938:

My dear Mr. DeMille

As usual when in trouble I turn to you. I have been ill for over a year, so I can't work. I don't even belong to the [Screen Actors] Guild, so am asking a big favor. Could you and will you put Jim to work. He is strong and willing, but things have gone against us so hard we need help so turn to you as I understand you are using a lot of men. If you could see your way clear to put him in stock extra work I would be most grateful and so would he. He can get nothing from Central [Casting], as they have their favorite ones whom they keep working all the time and CB we need the money so badly. I am writing as I feel I can explain better than he. You know him, Jim Gordon, and know his work. If you will do this and want to see him would love to come over and say hello too. Thanking you for anything you can do for us.

I remain sincerely,
Mabel Van Buren Gordon[6]

Two days later Gladys Rosson told Joe Egli, "If Jim Gordon is in good condition (and doesn't drink) he [DeMille] would like him to be used in the picture if possible. He is the husband of Mabel Van Buren (who used to be under contract to the old Lasky studio)."[7]

As the script for *Union Pacific* was nearing completion, DeMille looked for a unique solution to facilitate the rescue of the train crew after a spectacular wreck and an impending Indian attack. Mollie Monahan is a telegraph operator, but the Indians have cut the wires. Gladys Rosson gave researcher Frank Calvin his marching orders:

Mr. deMille wants you to talk to some telegraph operator and find out if a makeshift telegraph key has ever been rigged up and if so, out of what?

Mr. deMille would like to find some interesting thing of a hammer and nail—or stove lifter and monkey wrench that could be rigged together in Mollie's car by which she could send the message during the Plum Creek Massacre. . . .[8]

Eventually DeMille settled on using a rifle. One end of the broken wire is attached to the barrel and, holding the insulated wooden gunstock, Mollie is able to tap out a crude message to alert the rescuers.

In addition to the several days that second-unit director Art Rosson spent shooting in Cache, Oklahoma, nineteen days of location work were done in Utah; but most of *Union Pacific* was shot on Paramount sound stages in Hollywood. The building of Cheyenne, Wyoming, and Omaha, Nebraska, and the scenes at "End of Track" were shot in Canoga Park, California, near the Southern Pacific right-of-way and on the adjoining RKO ranch.

One of the marvels of the Hollywood studio system was its efficiency. *Union Pacific* went before the cameras in November 1938, and was on theater screens by April 1939—a schedule that few, if any, current feature schedules could hope to meet. Continuity of staff and crew had much to do with this, of course, but DeMille spent a great deal of effort in preproduction planning.

What makes the schedule on *Union Pacific* even more remarkable is that the production was shut down for three weeks when DeMille collapsed and was hospitalized for an operation. He directed the last five days of shooting while reclining on a stretcher, much to the horror of his doctors and the delight of the studio publicity department.

In early December 1938 it was anticipated that *Union Pacific* might be ready for an Easter release. Paramount editorial head Charles West told associate producer Bill Pine that in order to have fifty release prints completed by April 7, 1939, DeMille would have to have to allow a minimum of fifty-seven days for postproduction. West reminded Pine that *The Plainsman* had required sixty-three days from close of shooting to final negative match and that *The Buccaneer* required seventy-three days for the same work.

The delay caused by DeMille's hospitalization put the schedule well past West's proposed February 18 deadline for a first negative cut, but DeMille and West managed to compress the postproduction schedule, and though they didn't quite meet the April 7 date, two weeks later Anne Bauchens was able to report to DeMille that the prints to be used for the April 28 premiere had been checked and were "excellent in every regard."[9]

The premiere was the culmination of a well-coordinated publicity campaign that saw DeMille and a company of Hollywood celebrities make a whistle-stop train tour from Los Angeles to Omaha. However, all the extra effort put into getting the picture ready was nearly undone by poor presentation. After the screening DeMille wired Charles West:

OMAHA PRINT BADLY SCARRED BY
PERPENDICULAR STREAKS GOING FROM SIDE TO
SIDE AT BEGINNING OF REEL TWO AND
CONTINUING UNTIL AFTER EXIT OF ROSE FROM
CAFE. . . . TELL [Paramount sound department head]
LOREN RYDER THAT AS ENGINE SLID FROM TRACK
IN SNOW I PRESUME A VALVE WAS BLOWN IN MR.
BLANK'S SUPPOSEDLY NEW EQUIPMENT AT OMAHA
THEATRE AND THE FILM CONTINUED TO PLAY
SILENTLY UNTIL AFTER SCENE IN MOLLIE'S CAR. IN
SPITE OF THAT PICTURE TREMENDOUS SUCCESS.
PROJECTION WAS SO POOR IT WAS HARD TO JUDGE
WHETHER FAULT WAS BAD PRINT OR BAD
PROJECTION. CONSIDERABLE GRAIN WAS EVIDENT
IN SEVERAL PLACES. SUGGEST WRITTEN
INSTRUCTIONS TO PROJECTIONISTS BE SENT WITH
ALL PRINTS AND ADVISE MANAGERS OF PRINTS
ALREADY SHIPPED THAT CUSTOMARY COLOR
SLIDE OVER MAIN TITLE SHOULD NOT BE USED AS
IT RUINS EFFECT OF MAIN TITLE WHICH IN UNION
PACIFIC IS PART OF PICTURE ITSELF.[10]

Despite the technical failures at the premiere screening, *Union Pacific* was yet another spectacular DeMille success. The May 8, 1939, issue of *National Box Office Digest* estimated the film would do 170 percent of normal business for theater owners and declared: "The Picture has everything—size and sweep, laughs and tears, great acting performances, and corking writing. . . . And to top it all, Cecil B. DeMille has played with his materials with consummate skill—with hooey and hokum where hooey and hokum serve, with deftness where that was the requirement. His twenty-five years of picture making have been crammed into one grand prize package."[11]

Two weeks later the same magazine noted that *Union Pacific* was playing at 172 percent, "which places it as third biggest moneymaker so far this year."[12]

# 64

# North West Mounted Police

A Paramount Picture. A Cecil B. DeMille Production. Produced and directed by Cecil B. DeMille. Original screenplay by Alan LeMay, Jesse Lasky Jr., and C. Gardner Sullivan, derived in part from *The Royal Mounted* (1908), a play by Cecil B. DeMille and William C. deMille (additional, uncredited writing by Jeanie Macpherson, Frank Wead, Clements Ripley, and Bartlett Cormack). Associate producer: William H. Pine. Second-unit director: Arthur Rosson. Assistant directors: Eric Stacey and Eddie Salven. Rehearsal director: Cullen B. "Hezie" Tate. Art direction: Hans Dreier and Roland Anderson. Music: Victor Young. Photography: Victor Milner and W. Howard Greene. Film editor: Anne Bauchens

Picture started: March 7, 1940. Picture closed: May 13, 1940. Picture re-opened and closed: May 24, 1940. Second-unit schedule: March 25–26, April 5–19, April 24–28, and April 30–May 9, 1940. Length: 11,301 feet (thirteen reels). Released: October 21, 1940 (Regina, Canada, premiere)

Cast: Gary Cooper (Dusty Rivers), Madeleine Carroll (April Logan), Paulette Goddard (Louvette Corbeau), Preston Foster (Sgt. Jim Brett), Robert Preston (Ronnie Logan), George Bancroft (Jacques Corbeau), Lynne Overman (Tod McDuff), Akim Tamiroff (Dan Duroc), Walter Hampden (Big Bear), Lon Chaney Jr. (Shorty), Montagu Love (Inspector Cabot), Robert Ryan, Regis Toomey, Wallace Reid Jr., Rod Cameron, and Richard Denning

Although DeMille had long been interested in color effects and had included two-color Technicolor sequences in *The Ten Commandments* (1923) and *The King of Kings* (1927), *North West Mounted Police* was DeMille's first picture to be shot entirely in color. It set the photographic style for all of his future productions. Brightly lit, with rich, saturated hues, the film has a story-book quality that is vivid and pleasing to the eye, but also rather stylized and theatrical.

The decision to shoot in color was no casual option in 1940. The only viable full-spectrum color process was Technicolor's three-strip system, first demonstrated in 1932, which exposed three rolls of black-and-white film simultaneously through color filters to create red, green, and blue color records. From these records, printing matrices were generated and soaked in complementary dyes, which for various technical reasons were actually magenta, yellow, and cyan. These dyes were transferred to a blank print-film in a procedure that owed more to lithography than photography. In addition to requiring three times the footage in principal photography, the release prints were much more expensive. Going into production the estimated cost of release prints for *North West Mounted Police* was $200,000, compared with only $56,000 if the picture was shot in black and white.[1]

Producers were locked into using Technicolor's proprietary three-strip camera and the Technicolor laboratory. Technicolor also required that producers hire a color consultant, and preferably use one of its own cinematographers either as first cameraman or as a "lighting expert."

Seeking advice from Arthur Rosson, who had experience with Technicolor as a second unit director on *Gone with the Wind* (Selznick International/M-G-M, 1939), DeMille received a quick lesson in the process. Rosson recommended shooting in three-quarter light to get modeling in the actors faces, and also advised that lights should be on hand at all times—even outdoors. "Particular attention must be taken of the sky," Rosson informed DeMille.

> Where sky is shown . . . all scenes for that incident showing
> sky should be taken against the same sky. . . . To illustrate, if
> you photograph two people straight on, (south we say) and
> show sky—the chances are if you made individuals of each
> [actor in close-up] you would normally show the eastern sky
> behind one and the western sky behind the other—chances are
> all three skys would be a different tone of blue. The difference
> on the screen is intensified and should be avoided. Move the
> people [in relation to the camera so that the same southern sky
> will be seen in the closeups as in the two shot].

But if the sky presented problems, the Technicolor process did offer certain advantages. In shooting night scenes in daylight ("day for night" as it is known in the industry), Rosson stated, "It is not essential to eliminate the sky. The sky can be made almost a jet black [in printing] if desired."

With regard to Technicolor's cameramen, Rosson told DeMille that Ray Rennahan, who had shot the two-color Technicolor sequences for *The Ten Commandments* in 1923, was the most experienced Technicolor cameraman and that Howard "Duke" Greene was the "best man for exteriors." He also advised DeMille to avoid using Technicolor cinematographer William V. Skall, and suggested that a Technicolor lighting expert was not essential to achieve quality photography. "On G.W.T.W. [*Gone with the Wind*] contract called for a Technicolor expert for lighting to go with the picture and work with the cameraman. After two weeks company could not dismiss with his services because of contract so he was relegated to whatever unit was working off the stage or was sent to check up locations. . . . Cameraman [Ernest] Haller did all the lighting of the sets alone. When Hal Rosson took retakes, the color expert was off the picture so he did the lighting alone and had to match what Haller had done. The picture speaks for itself."[2]

Under terms of its contract with Paramount, Cecil B. DeMille Productions, Inc., received a cash advance of $100,000 for *North West Mounted Police* against 50 percent of net profits. In return, DeMille Productions was responsible for putting up 15 percent of the overall production budget, although they were able to recoup their investment in first position with Paramount from dollar one of gross film rentals. The arrangement gave DeMille Productions working capital in preparing the film, but also acted as a constraint against cost overruns as DeMille was on the hook for 15 percent of whatever the picture cost.

DeMille had worked in the motion picture financing department of the Bank of America in years past, so he was a familiar figure; but even so his arrangement with the bank for borrowing hundreds of thousands of dollars at a time was incredibly informal. DeMille didn't even meet with the bank's motion picture finance manager himself. He sent secretary Gladys Rosson to firm up the transactions, and she reported back with a written summary of her meeting:

Mr. [J.H.] Rosenberg [of Bank of America] was cordial as always. He thought your subject and cast and color splendid. He asked the cost. I quoted $1,576,000 as the budget and that you and [Paramount executive] Mr. [William] Lebaron expected to get it down to $1,400,000 or $1,450,000, he said, "Whew—that's a lot of money—but you can have whatever you want—you know that." He asked how much we were allowing for color. I said $300,000. He said, "He ought to be okay with that." He said, "Are you paying Cooper $150,000" and I assented.

He said that neither the Bank of America nor the Guaranty

Trust were furnishing picture money for less than 5%. . . . He said you were their oldest picture account, and that "with all due regard for our other accounts," they felt pretty close to you and valued your business, the way you did business and the cooperation you never hesitated to give the bank; he wanted you to feel happy and satisfied and to have no mental reservations with regard to the interest charged you.

He gave me a package of blank notes and said to fill them out and send them in whenever you wanted to start drawing.

We set $217,500—15% of $1,450,000. as the probable amount we would borrow. I told him that I would notify him of any more or less required as the picture progressed. . . .

He asked if your deal with Paramount had changed any. I told him that we had given Paramount an extension of our present contract to cover 2 more pictures. . . . Also, that our advance was now $100,000 per picture and 50/50 on the net profits. He said "You have about the sweetest deal in pictures—you can't lose the way you are set up."

He asked what the radio [Lux Radio Theatre] was bringing you in, and I said $80,250. last year. He shook his head as if to say, "Marvelous."[3]

Eventually DeMille Productions' 15 percent share in the cost of *North West Mounted Police* amounted to $221,964.77; but on December 16, 1940, less than two months after its release, the director's company received $81.06 from Paramount to finish paying off the investment. The picture was one of the studio's biggest talking picture hits to date.[4]

# Reap the Wild Wind

A Paramount Picture. A Cecil B. DeMille Production. Produced and directed by Cecil B. DeMille. Screenplay by Alan LeMay, Charles Bennett, and Jesse Lasky Jr., from a story by Thelma Strabel (additional, uncredited writing by Jeanie Macpherson). Associate producer: William Pine. Second-unit director: Arthur Rosson. Art direction: Hans Dreier and Roland Anderson. Music: Victor Young. Photography: Victor Milner, A.S.C., and William V. Skall, A.S.C. Underwater photography: Dewey Wrigley, A.S.C. Film editor: Anne Bauchens

Picture started: June 2, 1941. Picture closed: August 19, 1941. Picture reopened: September 9–12, 1941. Second unit opened: April 28, 1941. Second unit closed: August 31, 1941. Length: 11,094 feet (thirteen reels). Cost: $2,038,210.91. Released: March 18, 1942 (Hollywood premiere). Gross: over $4,000,000

Cast: Ray Milland (Stephen Tolliver), John Wayne (Capt. Jack Stewart), Paulette Goddard (Loxi Claiborne), Raymond Massey (King Cutler), Robert Preston (Dan Cutler), Lynne Overman (Capt. Phillip Philpott), Susan Hayward (Drusilla Alston), Charles Bickford (mate of the *Tyfib*), Walter Hampden (Commodore Devereaux), Louise Beavers (Maum Maria), Martha O'Driscoll (Ivy Devereaux), Hedda Hopper (Aunt Henrietta), Victor Varconi (Lubbock), Raymond Hatton (master shipwright), Milburn Stone, Barbara Britton, Julia Faye, George Melford, Mildred Harris, Claire McDowell, Dorothy Sebastian, Monte Blue, Max Davidson, and Billy Elmer

In his autobiography Cecil B. DeMille felt compelled to comment on "a subject which has added to Hollywood's merriment for many years: the DeMille chair boy." It was his custom to have a designated person follow him around the set during production with his director's chair. The legend was that DeMille never looked to see if his chair was at hand, he merely sat—and the chair had better be there! DeMille's chair boy bccame a symbol of Hollywood's vainglorious obsessions, and virtually every parody on filmmaking sported a young character holding a chair in lockstep behind a tyrannical director charging around the set with great energy barking orders to actors and technicians. Invariably a pretty young extra or makeup girl passes by and catches the chair boy's eye just as the director sits, providing the desired result of seeing pride landing on its keister.

For DeMille the chair boy was more a matter of practicality than pretense. "When a director is working on a motion picture set from morning till night, day after day," he wrote, "his work demands every ounce of his energy and constant attention. If he has a chance to sit down for a few moments, he should take it; and he should not have to search around for his chair. . . ."[1]

The designated chair boy on *Reap the Wild Wind*, Olaf Bolm, was called to military service, and he left a job description for his replacement. It seems there was more to the job than just carrying a chair:

The following is a list of the duties which should be done by whoever takes over my job.

File and keep track of all pictures, research photos and notes in Mr. deMille's office. Also maps and any other loose material.

Keep an accurate check and list of all [production artist Dan Sayre] Groesbeck and other original sketches, including [Natalie] Visart fashion and costume sketches. Have all the sketches photographed and put a copy of each in a loose leaf binder, and keep them numbered consecutively and correspondingly, such as A-1, etc.

On the set always carry the finder, color glass, magnifying glass, colored pencils, and pad, red and blue crayons, chalk, and tape measure. (The last three to be obtained from Prop Dept.)

Always have copies of the research pictures, and photographic copies of all the sketches in Mr. deMille's dressing room on the set.

Have a good idea of the shooting schedule, and know the lines and scenes for the days shooting, and also be familiar with the next two or three days work.

Always have one of Mr. deMille's chairs or stool close by, for him when he wants to sit down in a hurry.

Handle the PA mike [public address microphone] when necessary.

Always carry two sticks of gum to lunch to be given to him after he finishes eating, also white pad and pencil.

Take and type up all of your own notes.

Help Marion and Bernie [Berenice Mosk] in any research or other work that has to be done.

Sort and paste into books all the production stills and publicity stills at the end of the picture.

Have Mr. deMille's dressing room well supplied with pencils,
pads, paper, cough drops, and visor (clean white ones to be
gotten from Arthur Umiker)
Check with Arthur Umiker whenever more gum is required.
Beech-nut peppermint flavored gum.[2]

On September 13, 1940, some ten months before the cameras started
to turn on *Reap the Wild Wind*, DeMille had a meeting with the Paramount special effects wizards to outline what he would need from them
for his upcoming picture. Without a script available, the effects men had
read the *Saturday Evening Post* story on which the film was to be based.
"That gives you the background," DeMille told them, "but does not in
any way give you the story; and even the character relationship is entirely
different. I expect to start the picture somewhat along the same lines as
North West Mounted Police. . . ."[3]

Although DeMille's decision to tell essentially the same story in
*Reap the Wild Wind* as he had *Union Pacific* and *North West Mounted
Police* may seem odd, it should be remembered that before major studio
feature films made their way to television in the late 1950s there was little
chance that one would be able to see a screen favorite after its initial
theatrical run. Films were occasionally reissued, but such instances were
relatively rare. Denied reruns and videotape, audiences would flock to
see new films that contained familiar elements they had enjoyed before
in other films.

Speculating what a film might have been like with other actors in the
leading roles is always interesting. For the role of Loxi, DeMille's "ideal
casting" list for *Reap the Wild Wind* included Vivien Leigh, Katharine
Hepburn, Joan Fontaine, and Lana Turner. In a sort of ironic door prize,
he would eventually give the role to Paulette Goddard, who had campaigned heavily for the role of Scarlett O'Hara in *Gone with the Wind*
only to lose out to Vivien Leigh.

DeMille wanted Hattie McDaniel to play Maum Maria and Paramount even arranged to borrow the first African American Oscar-winner
from Warner Bros. But ultimately McDaniel proved too expensive. She
was to receive $8,000 for seven weeks' work, although it was stipulated
she would work the eighth week for free, and thereafter her salary would
be $1,000 per week. She also required featured billing on the main title and
on all advertising under Paramount's control.[4] Louise Beavers eventually
landed the role. Her salary was $450 for a week with a six-week guarantee.

The most intriguing possibility was Errol Flynn for the role that eventually went to John Wayne. DeMille had wanted Flynn for what became the Preston Foster role in *North West Mounted Police*, but Warner Bros. would not loan him out. By coincidence William Pine found himself flying on the same plane with Flynn. On December 6, 1940, Pine called the DeMille office to report on his conversation with Flynn. Pine's comments were summarized by one of DeMille's secretaries:

Bill Pine called Mr. deMille from Chicago today and said Errol Flynn was on the plane with him flying east last night.

Mr. Flynn is anxious to play for us.

Charles Feldman is his new agent

Mr. Flynn told Bill Pine that Warner Bros. told him no one wanted him. They never told him that Mr. deMille wanted him for NORTH WEST MOUNTED POLICE. Mr. Flynn says he will be a good boy if they will let him do one outside picture.

Bill Pine discussed the part of Jack with Mr. Flynn.

Have Mr. Freeman call Warner Bros. and ask for Mr. Flynn and be turned down—then Mr. Flynn will raise hell.

Mr. Flynn says he may be able to arrange his lay-off from Warner Bros. to come in time for our picture.[5]

DeMille called Pine back the same day after speaking with the Paramount casting department:

Mr. deMille's telephone call to Bill Pine in Chicago

[They] Tried to sell me [on the idea of using] Ray Milland. Told them about Flynn. [They were] Inclined to believe that it is an act of talking to be sociable. They thought it was impossible. It was an act of talking.

Did not know what [Flynn's agent Charles] Feldman would do, but if Warner Bros. did not want to do it that would be that.

[I'm] Going after Vivien Leigh as number one choice for the girl.

Next to that were trying to sell Joel McCrea. Do not think he is right for the part of Jack. Could play Steve. He is not perfect, would give a good performance.

Melvyn Douglas was discussed. Franchot Tone. He would give a great performance.

George Brent, there is a possibility of borrowing, but they say he is not nearly as good as Milland at the box office. [Paramount studio head Y. Frank] Freeman insists, but I was inclined to doubt it.[6]

One of DeMille's well-documented habits was to not allow actors under consideration for a role to read the script. Instead he would discuss the part with the prospective performer in terms of what their character would mean to the film. When John Wayne was finally cast in the role of Jack Stewart (called Jack Martin in early drafts of the script), he wrote to his agent Leo Morrison:

Reading the script for the first time I was disappointed in the lack of color and character in "Jack Martin." However, I recalled the picture of Martin that Mr. DeMille painted for us in his office, so I disregarded the play of the character as painted by the writers. They presented a character in the first few pages that would be both by situations and dialogue, attractive to Loxi. But at the entrance of Steve into the story Jack becomes negative in all scenes that include the three principals. I think there is a possibility of developing him into a great character without detracting from Steve or Loxi and will add color to the script as a whole and will make Loxi's part more believable. This can be done simply by making him an individualist played boldly and impulsively instead of being played as a plodding dullard.[7]

Many filmmakers have said that casting is the most important aspect of a director's job—DeMille certainly agreed. He expected his players to bring their skill and insight to the set. When asked by actors how to play a scene, DeMille would say that he wasn't running an acting school, that they were hired because he felt they could do the job, and he expected them to do the job. DeMille's faith in John Wayne was justified in the actor's thoughtful analysis of how to make the role come alive without taking away from the story or the other actors.

DeMille and his second unit and special photographic effects crew used 882,566 feet of film in shooting *Reap the Wild Wind*; even dividing by three for the three-strip Technicolor camera, the shooting ratio was a hefty twenty-seven to one. The film was completed and ready for preview just after the December 7, 1941, Japanese attack on Pearl Harbor that catapulted the United States into World War II. Meeting with J.H. Rosenberg to discuss various financial matters related to the picture, Gladys Rosson asked the movie banker his opinion about when the film should be released. Reporting to DeMille, she wrote: "Mr. Rosenberg is delighted with news of the [well-received] preview, and he would most certainly favor Washington's birthday [as a release date] over Easter week. He thinks that by the end of February, if the jittery nerves of the people haven't quieted, then all the more the public will need a smash hit. He says he is telling everyone that the glowing example set by the British and particularly the Londoners should be followed. He says his reports of business, in London particularly, are splendid."[8]

Critical reaction to *Reap the Wild Wind* was enthusiastic. The April 11, 1942, issue of *Liberty* magazine gave the film:

**** 4 stars Excellent (for DeMille Showmanship)

Cecil B. DeMille's new super-spectacle is exactly that. It's a fabulous historical show, combining romance, maritime melodrama, brawls and undersea shots in a whopping entertainment. It makes no pretense of being a co-ordinated artistic achievement. That isn't DeMille's field. He has preferred here, as so often in the past, to pack a picture full of spectacle, excitement, color and comedy. The result is a production which should prove extremely popular.

But there were naysayers as well. One anonymous moviegoer was willing to share his thoughts with the director, even if he wasn't willing to share his name.

Dear Mr. DeMille,

The parade passed you up years ago. Your pictures always were and still are "TRIPE." Why don't you give up. Your "Reap the Wild Wind" STUNK. You're smart to drag in everything but the kitchen sink, and yet it died. It's a damn good thing the Civil War didn't occur during "Reap the Gale"

or we would have been sitting in that theatre yet. I'd like to
see you try your hand directing a picture with 2 characters in a
single room and see where you end up. "DeMille Tripe"
should be emblazoned on your coat of arms.

A Movie Fan[9]

Most movie fans disagreed with this assessment, however, and they made
their opinions known at the box office. On February 18, 1944, nearly two
years after the picture's first release, Neil Agnew of Paramount distribution reported:

The week ending January 22nd, the United States gross film
rental of REAP THE WILD WIND passed the $3,800,000
figure previously estimated.
    As the Canadian rentals are now in excess of $160,000 the
ultimate domestic income will reach $4,000,000.[10]

# 66

# The Story of Dr. Wassell

A Paramount Picture. A Cecil B. DeMille Production. Produced and directed by Cecil B. DeMille. Screenplay by Alan LeMay and Charles Bennett, based on the story of Commander Corydon M. Wassell, U.S.N., (MC [Medical Corps]), as related by him and fifteen of the wounded sailors involved, and also upon the story by James Hilton (additional, uncredited writing by Jeanie Macpherson). Associate producer: Sidney Biddell. Assistant director: Eddie Salven. Second assistant director: Oscar Rudolph. Unit manager: Frank Caffey. Assistant unit manager: Ted Leonard. Dialogue supervisor: Edwin Maxwell. Dialogue director: Arthur Pierson. Second-unit director: Arthur Rosson. Art direction: Hans Dreier and Roland Anderson. Music: Victor Young. Photography (in Technicolor): Victor Milner, A.S.C. and William Snyder, A.S.C. Film editor: Anne Bauchens

Picture started: July 6, 1943. Picture closed: October 7, 1943. Second unit opened: April 5, 1943. Second unit closed: August 12, 1943. Length: 12,239 feet (fifteen reels). Cost: $2,744,991.71. Released: April 26, 1944 (Little Rock, Arkansas, premiere). Gross rentals: $6,222,192.33 (gross receipts: $4,209,968.54). Net profit: $205,639.04 (to March 31, 1951)

Cast: Gary Cooper (Corydon M. Wassell), Laraine Day (Madeline), Signe Hasso (Bettina), Dennis O'Keefe (Hopkins), Carol Thurston (Tremartini), Carl Esmond (Lt. Dirk van Daal), Paul Kelly (Murdock), Elliott Reid (Anderson), Stanley Ridges (Commander Bill Goggins), Renny McEvoy (Johnny), Oliver Thorndike (Alabam), Philip Ahn (Ping), and Barbara Britton (Ruth)

Paramount trade ads announcing the studio's product for the 1941–1942 season promised "3 big DeMille Productions in 2 years—In addition to *Reap the Wild Wind* Mr. DeMille has promised to deliver for Paramount two other equally important pictures between now and the close of the '41–'42 Season." One of the two promised pictures was *Rurales* (sometimes called *The Flame*), a film with a Mexican theme that was to be shot in black and white. Although Arthur Rosson actually shot some second-unit location footage, the picture was shelved in favor of a Technicolor production of Ernest Hemingway's *For Whom the Bell Tolls*. But John Hay Whitney and the federal government persuaded DeMille to turn the project over to Paramount, where it was eventually directed by

Sam Wood, and to return to *Rurales* as a "good neighbor" picture—part of the campaign to keep the Latin American neighbors of the United States from siding with the Axis.

But DeMille again changed his plans when he heard one of Franklin D. Roosevelt's radio chats on April 28, 1942. The president told listeners about the heroic exploits of navy surgeon Dr. Corydon Wassell who, in defiance of orders to leave them behind, led a group of wounded men to safety before the island of Java was completely overrun by the Japanese.

Excited about the picture possibilities of the Wassell story, DeMille rousted Paramount studio head Y. Frank Freeman from home and dinner and together they drafted a telegram to President Roosevelt's secretary, Stephen Early, requesting permission to make what they hoped would be "a magnificent inspirational motion picture."

"If you could suggest method of obtaining proper approval," Freeman and DeMille assured Early that they "would pay liberally for rights to this story. Disposition of such payments could be worked out in reference to distribution to Armed Forces Relief Agencies and Dr. Wassell."[1]

Preliminary details were worked out, and a somewhat bewildered Corydon Wassell found himself whisked from Australia with no knowledge of why he was being ordered Stateside until he met Cecil B. DeMille in Hollywood.

Born in Arkansas on July 4, 1884, Corydon Wassell completed one year of high school before becoming a plumber. In 1904 he decided to quit working with his hands and start working with his brain. Bitten by his sister's rabies-infected dog, Wassell was sent to Baltimore to receive the Pasteur treatment, and after his experience there he decided to become a doctor. Wassell studied with his aunt to pass his needed high school equivalency test, and after graduating from medical school he entered private practice in Arkansas. He later went to China with his first wife to work with the Episcopal Missions. She died in 1926 as the result of a freak accident, slipping on wet pavement, hitting her head, and falling into a pool of water. Wassell was forced to leave China in 1927 during an uprising by Chiang Kai-shek and the Cantonese. He later returned to the Far East and was stationed in Java with the U.S. Navy at the time of the events depicted in the film.[2]

Although basing the film on fact, DeMille decided to improve on history in adapting Dr. Wassell's story. In real life, Madeline was already Wassell's second wife during their adventure. It was felt that a budding on-screen romance would add to the box-office appeal, so in the script the characters were unwed for the duration!

Landing the role of Dr. Wassell's love interest was a bit of sweet revenge for Laraine Day, who was borrowed from M-G-M for the picture. "I had been under contract to Paramount in 1937 in the talent school when Mr. DeMille was making *The Buccaneer*," she recalled.

> There was a tiny speaking part in the picture, and my agent asked DeMille if he would use me in the role. DeMille said that he wouldn't consider it, that I had no talent and shouldn't even be on the lot.
> Now it's 1942 and I'm under contract to M-G-M and DeMille can't find anybody in all of Hollywood to play a nurse. I'd been playing nothing but nurses in the Dr. Kildare pictures, and so I got the part. Of course, he didn't remember the earlier incident.[3]

In an example of the sort of tie-in that would become common later in Hollywood, novelist James Hilton was commissioned to write a story about Wassell's exploits. This was a classier form of novelization designed to add luster to the project before the film's release and also provide a copyrighted "source" to forestall potential plagiarism suits.

Cecil B. DeMille later claimed that only one actor was "ideally qualified" to play Dr. Wassell—Gary Cooper, but in fact Albert Dekker was announced for the role. Dekker withdrew because he felt, for public consumption at least, that the role was unsuitable for him. The truth is that Dekker was only an ace in the hole in the event that Cooper was not available when *The Story of Dr. Wassell* went into production.

Gary Cooper was working at Warner Bros. on *Saratoga Trunk*, and it was believed that he would be finished by May 3, 1943. But as early as February 26, DeMille's assistant director, Eddie Salven, noted that *Saratoga Trunk* director "Sam Wood averages about 2 pages [of script] a day in shooting, which he has not yet done on this picture, having shot about 4 pages in 3 1/2 days."[4]

In early March, Salven went to the Warner studio in Burbank to obtain firsthand information on when Cooper might be available. He reported:

> The company is carrying this production on a 60–day sched-

ule which was made from an unfinished script. Estimated finish date, May 3, 1943.

The 60–day schedule is not a true schedule inasmuch as Warner Brothers do not schedule pictures day by day. Rather, a picture in a certain bracket goes into so many days, to wit:

A picture comparable to our "B" or program product would go into a 12 to 28 day schedule; and our "A" productions would go from 40 to 50 days; on rare occasions, such as "SARATOGA TRUNK," they have a 60–day schedule.

In the case of "Sergeant York," [Warner Bros., 1941] when the script was read by the producer and production office, it was automatically put into a 48–day schedule and came in in 72 days.

As of Wednesday, March 3, Sam Wood had shot 12 pages [of script] in 7 days. Yesterday, Thursday, March 4, they took credit for [shooting] 2 1/4 pages of script, which they were still shooting this afternoon at 2:00 PM.

From careful figuring with script and average shooting of Mr. Wood, we assumed the picture would come in 27 days over the 60–day figure, thereby making a new finish date of Friday, June 4, 1943, as compared with May 3, previously.

If Mr. Wood should beat this 27–day overage, the time between whatever he picked up and June 4th would be consumed by Mr. Cooper's rest between productions. Therefore we would still not be able to start the STORY OF DR. WASSELL before Tuesday, June 8th.[5]

Eddie Salven made at least four trips to Warner Bros. over several weeks to try to ascertain a finish date for *Saratoga Trunk*. On April 21 he reported that a June 5 completion date still seemed possible, "excluding weather conditions, which are slowing up the company on location."

During the last two weeks, while I was on my vacation, there was some talk of doing all the shots concerning Mr. Cooper and Miss [Ingrid] Bergman and then cleaning up Cooper after Miss Bergman was off salary. This . . . was not given much consideration in that Mr. Cooper's deal with Warners is on a flat basis, whereas Miss Bergman is on a weekly salary of $15,600.00 per week (*please do not quote*).

Mr. Sam Wood assured Mr. [Y. Frank] Freeman that he would finish with Mr. Cooper by the 5th of May, and thereafter work with Miss Bergman. During my visit today, [*Saratoga Trunk* producer] Mr. Hal Wallis, knowing of our set-up here [at Paramount] and our anxiety in knowing just when Mr. Cooper would be free to start THE STORY OF DR. WASSELL, told Mr. Wood that because of Miss Bergman's high salary as against Mr. Cooper's flat deal, the company would definitely concentrate on Miss Bergman and not Mr. Cooper. . . .

The June 5th figure of Mr. Cooper's finishing date does not take in any rest period between the finishing of "SARATOGA TRUNK" and the starting of "THE STORY OF DR. WASSELL," which could not be started without Mr. Cooper even for a few days and then at great cost.[6]

DeMille and Paramount opted to wait for Cooper, pushing back their start date. On June 9, 1943, Eddie Salven was finally able to offer a realistic finish date for Cooper. "Mr. Cooper should finish his regular production shots about Tuesday, June 15th, with two additional days of Transparency [rear projection process] shots, which the company assumes will be ready to photograph about the 17th or 18th."[7] Allowing for a rest period, Cooper was finally able to start on *The Story of Dr. Wassell* in early July.

Laraine Day remembers the making of *The Story of Dr. Wassell* as having been an enjoyable experience. "DeMille was pleasant to work with because we never really worked with him. An assistant did all the rehearsing, then he'd come in, run through it once and shoot it. The only time he really directed was during the crowd scenes. Then he was in complete control—of course he had a number of assistants working with him."[8]

DeMille was no longer just a filmmaker. Through hosting the *Lux Radio Theatre* and the lavish cross-country publicity caravans he conducted when promoting his pictures, he became a semiofficial spokesman for Hollywood. George Mitchell, who later became an industrial filmmaker and wrote a number of historical articles for *Films in Review* and *American Cinematographer*, was a young soldier visiting Hollywood on leave during the production of *The Story of Dr. Wassell*, and he remembered that there were bleachers erected on the set so visitors could see how movies were made.[9]

Cecil B. DeMille's 15 percent share of production costs on *The Story of Dr. Wassell* finally amounted to $408,080.48, and as usual he borrowed the money from the Bank of America, this time at a bargain-basement rate of 4 percent interest.

> Mr. [J.H.] Rosenberg said that we were the only motion picture company borrowing for production that did not have a contract with the Bank, and that we were the only motion picture company borrowing at 4% for production cost. He said that included [Samuel] Goldwyn and the rest of them. He looked me straight in the eye and said, "And I've never told you or Mr. deMille anything you could not depend upon."
> For the first time, he said he would like us to not spread around our arrangement with the Bank because he said the Bank wouldn't think of giving [producer Walter] Wanger, Goldwyn or any of the others a like deal. He said, "We only do business under contract with them."[10]

Several weeks after relaying notes of this meeting to DeMille, Gladys Rosson added: "He asked if the high cost of your cast was the big expense or was it 'because the unions own the picture business—and don't fool yourselves about it.'"[11]

# 67

# Unconquered

A Paramount Picture. A Cecil B. DeMille Production. Produced and directed by Cecil B. DeMille. Screenplay by Charles Bennett, Fredric M. Frank, and Jesse Lasky Jr., based on the novel by Neil H. Swanson (additional, uncredited writing by Jeanie Macpherson and Norman Reilly Raine). Photography: Ray Rennahan, A.S.C. Art direction: Hans Dreier and Walter Tyler. Second-unit director: Arthur Rosson. Music: Victor Young. Film editor: Anne Bauchens

Picture started: July 29, 1946. Picture finished: November 8, 1946. Picture reopened for pickup shots: November 25–26, 1946. Additional pickup shots: December 10 and December 30, 1946. Added scene shot: May 5, 1947. Second-unit location work: June 5–23, 1946, at Cook Forest, Pennsylvania; and July 15 to August 4, 1946, at Ashton and McCall, Idaho. Length: 13,194 feet. Cost: $4,371,593.62. Released: October 3, 1947. Gross rentals: $6,665,992.36 (gross receipts: $4,633,486.25). Unrecouped balance (loss): $1,717,978.82 (to March 31, 1951)

Cast: Gary Cooper (Christopher Holden), Paulette Goddard (Abby), Howard Da Silva (Garth), Boris Karloff (Guyasuta, chief of the Senecas), Cecil Kellaway (Jeremy Love), Ward Bond (John Fraser), Virginia Campbell (Mrs. Fraser), Katherine DeMille (Hannah), Henry Wilcoxon (Capt. Steele), Sir C. Aubrey Smith (Lord Chief Justice), Victor Varconi (Capt. Simeon Ecuyer), and Raymond Hatton (Venango scout)

On August 16, 1944, Cecil B. DeMille received a letter from the American Federation of Radio Artists (A.F.R.A.) informing him that the board of directors of the union had voted to assess its members one dollar each to fight California ballot Proposition 12—a so-called "right to work" initiative that would have abolished the closed shop in California. The assessment was due and payable by September 1, 1944; members not paying the assessment were subject to suspension from the union.

DeMille favored Proposition 12, and he believed A.F.R.A. "was demanding, in a word, that I cancel my vote with my dollar. Even if I were opposed to Proposition 12, I asked myself, did my union, did any organization, have the right to impose a compulsory political assessment upon any citizen, under the pain of the loss of his right to work?"

DeMille refused to pay the dollar, but in an effort to reach a compromise he offered to make a gift to the union of one dollar for every member in the Los Angeles local if the union would agree to return the dollar assessments to the members. "The union refused," DeMille wrote. "I saw then that the fundamental issue was not Proposition 12. It was an issue of union power: the power to control the individual member's political freedom through control of his right to work."

DeMille was suspended by A.F.R.A. and banned from appearing on radio. He made his last *Lux Radio Theatre* broadcast on January 22, 1945, giving up a salary of $100,000 a year. He sued the union for reinstatement but lost in the Los Angeles County Superior Court, the State District Court of Appeals, and the California Supreme Court. He soon formed the DeMille Foundation for Political Freedom to campaign for right-to-work legislation throughout the country.[1]

It was against this backdrop that DeMille began work on *Unconquered*, a tale of slavery and indentured servitude set in the American colonies during the surveying of the Mason-Dixon line and the siege of Fort Pitt. DeMille was inspired by the novel *The Judas Tree,* by Neil H. Swanson. What intrigued him was the fact that in Britain at the time condemned white prisoners were given a choice of hanging or slavery in the colonies for a term of fifteen years. Paramount bought the screen rights to *The Judas Tree* for DeMille; but as with *The Story of Dr. Wassell*, a new work was commissioned to establish literary credentials for the film. According to a confidential memo by DeMille's associate producer, Sidney Biddell, Neil H. Swanson was hired to write a new novel of not less than eighty thousand words to be based on the screenplay then being written by Norman Reilly Raine. Doubleday Doran was set to publish, and Swanson would receive an advance of $5,000 from the publisher. The money for the advance would actually come from Cecil B. DeMille Productions and Paramount, but was to be paid by the publisher. DeMille-Paramount were to be repaid the advance from the first $5,000 of royalties; but they agreed to put up an additional $15,000 to advertise and promote the book, and Doubleday Doran agreed to put up $5,000 of its own in promotional expenses. A 50 percent share of any subsidiary rights in the novel was earmarked for DeMille-Paramount, and the $20,000 advanced by DeMille-Paramount was to be accounted for as an advertising charge against the film. Biddell virtually crowed over the scheme:

As soon as the contracts are signed, Doubleday Doran will announce, having been informed of our title for the picture by

that time, that they will publish on their 1946 list a *new* novel
by Neil Swanson titled _____. Shortly thereafter, through
our own publicity department, we will announce that we have
purchased the picture rights to this book by Neil Swanson. . . .
Once the book is published, we will have behind the picture
all the advantages of a best-selling novel with its attendant
publicity and advertising value for what may finally be either
a nominal sum, nothing, or at a profit to us.[2]

The title *Unconquered* was set by July 23, 1945, but it took Swanson
nearly a year to finish the manuscript, and Doubleday Doran decided to
hold publication until 1947, forcing Paramount to create another white
lie saying they had purchased the rights a year before when the novel was
only in outline form.

During scripting, DeMille was obsessed with bringing something to
the screen that had never been seen before. At a production meeting on
April 26, 1945, DeMille outlined the story and discussed some of its
inherent problems:

The siege of Fort Pitt plays an important part in the story.
There is nothing more boring than a siege in a picture. An
audience doesn't give a damn about it. And it's been well
done in "Drums Along the Mohawk"—fairly well done in
"Howards of Virginia" and "Last of the Mohicans." Each has
something to its credit and all bored the audience. An audience is not interested in a fight over a stockade. So when we
take that on, we take on something that has to be done differently than it's been done before, because it's been a flop
before.

Later in the story, the hero and heroine are captured by Indians. "And
then comes the escape of the two," DeMille said, "which I would be very
happy to have some ideas on. It has to be something never done before."[3]
The writers got as far as having hero and heroine jumping into a
canoe and paddling downriver, racing ever closer to a waterfall. According to Jesse Lasky Jr., DeMille became obsessed with finding a unique
"take out" as the Indians gained on the fleeing captives. "He wanted, he
warned, 'the scene to grab me by the hair of my head (difficult to imagine) and yank me out of my seat!'" Wilfred Buckland, DeMille's friend

and former art director, visited the office one day while the dilemma was being pondered:

> "And so, Wilfred," DeMille concluded, "as usual my writers have failed to find me anything—anything at all—that will enable [Paulette Goddard] and Gary Cooper to survive the redskins, and ME to survive the audience's boredom. Perhaps you could give them some ideas."
> The sparkle in the old man's eye was definitely amusement. "Send 'em over the waterfall, C.B.!" Buckland suggested. . . .
> "The canoe goes over. Like this . . . Then, just as it plunges down, Cooper grabs a tree limb which happens to be stretched across the falls. . . . With one hand he seizes it—and with the other arm he holds the girl. Their weight makes the limb swing—right through the downpour of water—and . . . whips them safely into . . . a cavern! . . . behind the falls."
> "Could an audience believe it?" [Jesse Lasky Jr.] snorted.
> DeMille mused, "An audience will believe what it sees."[4]

Delighted with the suggestion, DeMille gave Buckland a check for his assistance. It would be Buckland's last contribution to a DeMille film.

Wilfred Buckland's son, William, had suffered a nervous breakdown and had been institutionalized at Camarillo State Hospital. He was released, but never fully recovered, and he took to the bottle. In despair that he would die leaving William unable to face the world, on July 18, 1946, Wilfred Buckland shot his son and then turned the gun on himself.

Not quite six weeks later DeMille lost another long-time collaborator when Jeanie Macpherson succumbed to cancer on August 26 at the age of fifty-nine.

Wilfred Buckland's canoe escape was just one of several hoary devices that DeMille incorporated in *Unconquered*. *New York Times* reviewer Bosley Crowther criticized DeMille for lifting the "dead soldiers" rescue from P.C. Wren's *Beau Geste* (written in 1924 and filmed in 1926 and 1939), in which the bodies of the fort's defenders are propped up at their posts to deceive the enemy into believing that their attack has failed. DeMille claimed he wasn't inspired by *Beau Geste*, but instead borrowed the idea from an old stage melodrama "about the Sepoy rebellion, called, I think it was, *Jessie Brown*."[5] Dion Boucicault's play opened at

Wallack's Lyceum Theatre in New York on February 22, 1858, and DeMille claimed that his father had read the play to him as a boy. In admitting his debt to *Jessie Brown or, The Relief of Lucknow,* DeMille said much about his own work, for he never abandoned the conventions of the nineteenth-century theater in constructing his screenplays.

One must wonder if DeMille and perhaps Wilfred Buckland were as familiar with Buster Keaton's 1923 film *Our Hospitality*? It seems more than a coincidence that the daring canoe rescue bears a striking similarity in concept and execution to the waterfall rescue in that picture.

The Pittsburgh premiere audience for *Unconquered* certainly took the scene to be comic in nature, and they laughed it off the screen. Attempts to revise the action by reshooting and re-editing had little impact on later audience reaction. DeMille may have been more prophetic than he knew when he told his associates, "An audience is not interested in a fight over a stockade." *Unconquered* broke DeMille's string of hits based on American history.[6]

# 68

# Samson and Delilah

A Paramount Picture. A Cecil B. DeMille Production. Produced and directed by Cecil B. DeMille. Screenplay by Jesse L. Lasky Jr. and Fredric M. Frank, based on a treatment by Harold Lamb derived from the Book of Judges, chapters 13–16, and on the novel *Judge and Fool* by Vladimir Jabotinsky (additional, uncredited writing by Jeanie Macpherson). Photography: George Barnes, A.S.C. Photographic effects: Gordon Jennings, A.S.C. Unit directors: Arthur Rosson and Ralph Jester. Art direction: Hans Dreier and Walter Tyler. Holy Land photography: Dewey Wrigley, A.S.C. Process photography: Farciot Edouart, A.S.C., and Wallace Kelley, A.S.C. Music: Victor Young. Choreographer: Theodore Kosloff. Film editor: Anne Bauchens

Picture started: October 4, 1948. Picture finished: December 22, 1948. Picture reopened: January 4, 1949, for scenes in plowed field and January 18–21, 1949, for added scenes and close-ups. Cost: $3,097,563.05. Road-show release: December 21, 1949. General release: March 28, 1951. Net profit: $5,564,825.17 (as of December 20, 1969)

Cast: Victor Mature (Samson), Hedy Lamarr (Delilah), George Sanders (the Saran of Gaza), Angela Lansbury (Semadar), Henry Wilcoxon (Ahtur), Olive Deering (Miriam), Russ Tamblyn (Saul), Julia Faye, William Farnum, Lane Chandler, Francis McDonald, Victor Varconi, Frank Reicher, and George Reeves

*S*amson and Delilah was a long-cherished project for DeMille. He first turned his attention to the story in 1932, but studio reluctance and his string of successes with pictures based on American historical themes conspired to keep *Samson and Delilah* from being produced.

Studio executives in 1947 were no more eager to make *Samson and Delilah* than their long-departed predecessors had been in 1935, but DeMille dazzled them with conceptual art by Dan Sayre Groesbeck showing a muscular Samson and a scantily clad Delilah and opening their eyes to the box-office possibilities. DeMille had all the instincts of a carnival pitchman in drumming up interest for his projects, and he would prepare a text suitable for public appearances, magazine articles, or special production trailers to promote his films. Such pieces were largely drafted by his office staff, but the consistency in approach through the years attests

334

to DeMille's involvement in their preparation. Like a Barnum who inspired curiosity with a sign reading This Way to the Egress, DeMille was a spellbinder who made you believe you needed to see his latest offering. And, there was something for everyone. For those anxious that *Samson and Delilah* might play fast and loose with the Bible, he proclaimed: "In 1932 Harold Lamb wrote the treatment which formed the basis of our screenplay. All during those months of preparation one vital fact was kept in mind: the Bible story must not be changed in any particular. It wasn't."[1]

Well, yes and no. The basic Bible story wasn't altered, but it was slicked up a bit. There simply wasn't enough plot in the Bible story to propel a feature-length film. The idea that Samson was first married to Delilah's sister was a dramatic device taken from Vladimir Jabotinsky's 1930 novel *Judge and Fool.*

For those concerned that *Samson and Delilah* might lack artistic aspiration and historical grounding, DeMille assured his audience:

> For inspiration we went to the great painters to see how they
> visualized certain episodes from the Samson story. Dore
> [Gustave Doré], Rubens, Solomon, Michelangelo—each had
> his concept of Samson and Delilah. . . . We took little pieces
> from some of these masterpieces; others were brought to life
> in full on the screen.
>
> Two years were spent in research, and more than 2,000
> volumes were consulted.

For those who suspected that Edith Head and the other members of the costume department were not sufficiently familiar with the particulars of ancient Philistine and Danite clothing, DeMille shared his own astonishment: "There were a number of surprises. We discovered that the Philistines derived their culture largely from the Minoans. . . . We were amazed to see how closely Minoan dress resembled current styles. Their sandals, for example, are exactly like those being worn by the women of today." For those who doubted that Samson could kill an army of a thousand with the jawbone of an ass:

> My chief concern with episodes of this type is to convince
> myself that they are possible. . . . Well, there was a sergeant
> named York in World War I who, single-handed, brought in a

few hundred Germans, some armed with machine guns. There was Dentatus, the Roman Consul, alone in a gorge backed by rocks, doing battle against an army of Pyrrhus soldiers. That fight suggested the setting for the jawbone scene in our picture. We placed Victor Mature, who plays Samson, in a narrow defile between two huge ledges. Under those circumstances, the triumph of one man over many was most convincing.

DeMille made a point of drawing a word picture of "Delilah, the dark-eyed temptress . . . her beauty, her love and her greed on display . . ."[2] What he neglected to mention was that at various times he seriously considered casting a blue-eyed blonde or a redhead in the role.

While in Washington, D.C., on April 5, 1948, DeMille became excited about an item he read in the papers. "Is there any truth to the item in Louella Parsons Column of April 3, that M.G.M. is borrowing Bing Crosby from Paramount—and that Paramount could have in exchange any player they wanted—why couldn't we trade Bing Crosby for Lana Turner—to play Delilah?"[3] He was assured that there was nothing to the story; then on April 20, casting director William Meiklejohn gave C.B. more bad news, "I phoned B.B. Kahane [a vice president of Columbia Pictures] regarding Rita Hayworth. He informed me that she definitely will not be available this year as her pictures are all scheduled and she has no open time."[4]

And, strange as it may seem, girl-next-door-type Nancy Olson was given serious consideration. She auditioned on May 6, and DeMille commented, "She is terrific. . . . She has authority, timing."[5] Then, after screening a Paramount screen test of Olson in a scene from *A Farewell to Arms*, he was equally enthusiastic. "She is," he said, "extremely interesting, awfully good, has amazing timing."[6] He only selected Hedy Lamarr to play his "dark-eyed temptress" after screening two reels of her 1938 film *Algiers* in the Paramount studio theater on August 3, 1948.

For Samson, DeMille made some effort to groom the screen's future Hercules, Steve Reeves, Mr. Universe of 1947, for the role. Reeves shot a screen test in New York on January 30, 1948, that DeMille screened two weeks later. "He has a very good voice—wonderful body. Seems that he might be easy to teach,"[7] was DeMille's initial comment; but after two auditions on March 2 and March 9, he finally concluded that Reeves was "impossible for Samson."[8]

Douglas Fairbanks Jr. was considered, and DeMille even spoke to Cary Grant about playing Samson! Victor Mature finally captured DeMille's attention when he saw *Kiss of Death* (20th Century-Fox, 1947), and a secretary recorded his comment that Mature "gave excellent performance."[9]

Production on *Samson and Delilah* proceeded on schedule, but it did not always go smoothly. DeMille avowed: "Many persons have given so much to bring it to life on the screen. Months of planning, worry, disappointment. But always perseverance. And always a willingness to keep at it."

But DeMille was disappointed at Victor Mature's unwillingness to do some of the strenuous action stuff; and when a group of actors was hired for a fight scene, he wanted to be certain, that unlike Victor Mature, "Mike Mazurki, Robert Barratt, Harry Woods, Ed Hinton—I assume they . . . will do their own fighting in the fight on the stairs where they throw things. If William Farnum can take it at his age—they should be able to do so."[10]

Long-time associate Ralph Jester showed little perseverance or willingness to keep at it. Jester had worked in costuming on DeMille's pictures back to the 1930s. On *Samson and Delilah* he was put in charge of the second unit sent to shoot footage in North Africa. Returning to Hollywood, Jester resumed his chores in the costume department, but problems with the costumes led DeMille to take his frustration out on Jester, who got fed up with DeMille's bullying and quit the production. A somewhat contrite Jester stopped by DeMille's office before he left the lot, but the director wasn't in, so he left a brief note:

C.B.—
Dropped in to say hello and good-bye. No hard feelings here—none with you, I hope. Best of luck on the picture.
Ralph

DeMille replied:

Dear Ralph,
Of course there are no hard feelings—only regret that you couldn't endure me! You are a fine artist and fully capable of executing your ideas. .

Things might not have got so chaotic here if you had not

gone to Africa—but then we might have missed some of the good stuff you brought back from there.

Surely you have known me long enough and well enough to know that, when I am in production, only one thing counts: the picture. But differences about a picture make no difference to friendship ever, as far as I am concerned.
Sincerely,
Cecil B. deMille[11]

Jester would return to work in the costume department for DeMille on *The Ten Commandments* (1956), but his departure from *Samson and Delilah* cost him any chance he might have had for a more responsible role on DeMille's staff and paved the way for Henry Wilcoxon to move into the associate producer's position. But if DeMille's browbeating sent Jester packing, others saw DeMille's on-set rages from a different perspective. Kathleen Key, who had been a minor leading lady in the silent era, had a bit role in *Samson and Delilah*, and as the film was nearing completion, she wired her thanks for her work on the picture:

THOROUGH PLEASURE WORKING WITH YOU AFTER ALL THESE YEARS EVEN IF IT WAS ONLY EXTRA. . . . ALWAYS WISH YOU HAD MADE BEN HUR BECAUSE YOU GIVE ACTORS BREAKS AS THE SISTER OF BEN HUR TIRZAH [I] WAS SO BROKEN HEARTED AT THAT YOUNG AGE WITH AMBITIONS AND ABILITY TO BE CUT TO MERE BIT SO HOPE SOMETIME IN THE FUTURE I CAN DO SOMETHING WORTHWHILE FOR YOU. . . . ASIDE FROM BEING VERY THOROUGH YOU ARE A PANIC TO LISTEN TO FIRING EVERYONE ONE MINUTE AND FORGETTING ABOUT IT THE NEXT THAT IS WHY EVERYBODY LOVES YOU AND GIVES YOU THEIR BEST. . . .[12]

Not all the bit players were happy, however. Whereas in the past DeMille sent favored names to the casting department, now he advised eager actors to contact assistant director Eddie Salven. There were complaints of favoritism among the assistant directors and in the Paramount casting office. Several extras were cut off after working only one day on the picture, and some who were promised work never got called. After the picture closed DeMille learned of the disappointment of another veteran from the silent era:

> Charles Morton called to tell Mr. deMille that he was not used even one day on the picture. That Mr. deMille had said he would use him after seeing the test he made for Mitch Leisen in "A Mask for Lucretia" and that he had told Joe Egli he would take anything—even extra work—as he was badly in need of financial assistance—but that the Casting Office didn't even call him for one day and he would like Mr. deMille to know this. Mr. deMille would remember him as "Hawaii"—the name he used to call him—after he worked for Mr. deMille on the Hawaiian location.[13]

Although DeMille usually welcomed visitors when he was shooting, he drew the line when it came to the climactic scene of *Samson and Delilah*. On November 20, 1948, secretary Berenice Mosk sent out word that

> The miniature Temple set is to be a closed set and a tarp or drape put up to keep anyone from going on the stage, (not directly connected with the set).
>
> No one from the press, no visitors, nor studio employees are to be allowed on this set unless a written okay is first procured from Mr. deMille, Roy Burns or Phil Koury.[14]

Samson's destruction of the Temple of Dagon was a special effects *tour de force* combining full-sized sets of the lower levels of the temple filled with people and a detailed miniature of the entire temple populated with tiny dolls. The illusion on-screen is perfect, but DeMille clearly didn't want the audience to know that the spectacular scene was the result of movie trickery.

The temple scene aside, however, *Samson and Delilah* is a curiously sloppy film overall. No DeMille film since *Manslaughter* had been so crudely put together. The footage of Samson's fight with the lion is so poorly integrated and edited that the sequence looks more like a scene from a Poverty Row quickie than a major studio super production. Even action with the principal players, such as the fight in which the character Semadar is accidentally killed, is staged with an awkwardness that is as mystifying as it is annoying.

Critical reaction to *Samson and Delilah* was not overwhelmingly favorable. Bosley Crowther observed that the picture "is the ultimate distillation of the cinema tradition of Cecil B. DeMille. . . . Unquestionably it has paid off well over a number of years. Whether it has a future remains now to be seen."[15]

DeMille was concerned enough about negative reaction that he ordered cuts in Samson's fight with the lion and shot five days of new material in January 1950, weeks after *Samson and Delilah*'s December 21, 1949, road-show release.

Reporting on a preview screening of the revised version at the Denham Theatre in Denver, Colorado, DeMille wired Florence Cole:

WORD HAD GOTTEN OUT WHAT PICTURE WAS
PREVIEWING SO THE THEATRE WAS PACKED TO
THE LAST SEAT AND THEY HAD TO CLOSE THE BOX
OFFICE AND LOCK THE DOORS TO KEEP BACK THE
CROWD. . . . I HAVE BEEN PREVIEWING PICTURES
FOR THIRTY-SIX YEARS AND BELIEVE IT IS THE
BEST AUDIENCE REACTION I CAN RECALL AT A
FIRST RUNNING. ALL AUDIENCE PREVIEW CARDS
ARE SUPERLATIVE. . . . NOT A SINGLE PERSON LEFT
THE THEATRE OR STIRRED FROM HIS SEAT UNTIL
THE END TITLE CAME ON THE SCREEN. THERE ARE
SEVENTY-FIVE GOOD LAUGHS AND THERE WERE
HANDKERCHIEFS APLENTY AT THE END[16]

Theater manager Dave Cockrill called DeMille to tell the director he had received more than thirty phone calls from patrons after the screening, and added:

For a man in your position, who has given us the greatest
work we have ever seen, to have been so moved by the
appreciation shown you and the picture, shows you are just a
nice person. This was the comment of every single call.

I have never heard expressions of friendship so deep and
warm from a large group of people for one person—that is
true friendship—and the only thing I can say is that they just
love you.

There will be great rejoicing in theatredom over this
picture.[17]

# The Greatest Show on Earth

A Paramount Picture. A Cecil B. DeMille Production. Produced and directed by Cecil B. DeMille. Screenplay by Fredric M. Frank, Barre Lyndon, and Theodore St. John, based upon story by Fredric M. Frank, Theodore St. John, and Frank Cavett (additional, uncredited writing by Stephen Longstreet, Luther Davis, and Sidney Biddell). Associate producer: Henry Wilcoxon. Assistant director: Eddie Salven. Unit director: Arthur Rosson. Art direction: Hal Pereira and Walter Tyler. Music: Victor Young. Photography: George Barnes, A.S.C. Additional photography: J. Peverell Marley, A.S.C., and Wallace Kelley, A.S.C. Film editor: Anne Bauchens, A.C.E.

Picture started in Sarasota, Florida: January 31 to March 9, 1951. Picture resumed at Paramount studio: March 19 to May 11, 1951. Picture resumed in Washington, D.C.: May 16 to May 19, 1951. Picture resumed in Philadelphia: May 21 to May 26, 1951. Process (yellow screen) shots: June 5–6, 1951. Bing Crosby/Bob Hope audience scene shot: June 21, 1951. Additional audience reaction scenes shot: July 25–26, August 1, and August 13, 1951. Length: 13,709 feet (sixteen reels). Cost: $3,873,946.50. Released: January 10, 1952 (New York premiere, Radio City Music Hall). Gross receipts: $15,797,396.36 (to December 29, 1962). Net profit: $6,615,903.31. Producer's share: $3,307,951.66

Cast: Betty Hutton (Holly), Cornel Wilde (Sebastian), Charlton Heston (Brad), Dorothy Lamour (Phyllis), Gloria Grahame (Angel), James Stewart (Buttons), Henry Wilcoxon (detective), Emmett Kelly (himself), Lyle Bettger (Klaus), Lawrence Tierney (Henderson), Julia Faye (Birdie), and John Ringling North (himself)

On July 16, 1946, just days before DeMille went into production on *Unconquered*, Gladys Rosson informed him that J.H. Rosenberg was retiring after twenty years with the Bank of America and thirty-six years in the banking business. She wrote:

> He is familiar with the labor situation and can't see how you derive satisfaction from working as you do against budgets that you cannot control, and with labor demands mounting, and the responsibility of spending 3 to 4 million dollars that have to earn 5½ to 6 millions before there is a profit.

He says the labor situation may put Disney and companies like that out of business; labor is ruining the finest industry on the west coast.[1]

Today, of course, it is easy to laugh at such nonsense. In 2002 the movie business had a banner year with some nine billion dollars in box-office revenue, and the Walt Disney Company has managed to weather the past fifty-six years without closing its doors.

But if Rosenberg's crystal ball was cloudy and he could not see into the distant future, his words certainly reflected the attitudes of the moment. Hollywood was experiencing labor unrest—there was even a pitched battle between picketers and studio police armed with water hoses in front of Warner Bros. in Burbank.[2] Theaters were closing—some 4,500 theaters shut down between 1946 and 1952. Box-office revenues were declining—$1.5 billion in the record-year 1946, $1.2 billion in 1949, heading for $1.075 billion in 1952.[3] Television took the lion's share of the blame—why pay good money to sit in a theater when you could enjoy Milton Berle at home for free?

Hollywood faced other problems as well. Some in Congress were convinced that the movie colony was a haven for Communists who were spewing the party line to unsuspecting popcorn munchers sitting in the dark.

DeMille, with his conservative Republican credentials, should have been above suspicion; but only if one didn't look too deeply. After all, he had worked with "Hollywood Ten" writer John Howard Lawson during his tenure at M-G-M, and had traveled to the Soviet Union in 1931.[4] He had planned to make *For Whom the Bell Tolls*, a tale of left-leaning rebels in the Spanish Civil War; and going further back, *The Volga Boatman* offered a rather open-minded view of the Russian revolution, and socially conscious films like *Kindling* and *The Golden Chance* showed sympathy for the downtrodden. Despite his religious epics, DeMille had made some disturbing films hinting that he didn't exactly embrace the old-time religion: *The Godless Girl* showed some sympathy for the atheist heroine, and *Adam's Rib* had an evolutionary flashback to caveman days. Did DeMille have cause to be concerned that his past might catch up with him? Maybe not, but he made an effort to ensure the House Un-American Activities Committee would not be inclined to look too closely.

"DeMille didn't give a damn about anybody's politics," said Al Rogell, who was first vice president of the Screen Directors Guild

(S.D.G.) in 1950. "What he wanted was to keep Congress away from the Guild."[5]

The 1947 Taft-Hartley Labor Act (also known as the Labor-Management Relations Act) was passed over the veto of President Harry Truman, who called it a "slave labor bill." Taft-Hartley outlawed the closed shop and made it more difficult for unions to organize.[6] The legislation also mandated that union officers sign a loyalty oath declaring that they were not affiliated with the Communist Party. The loyalty oath provision was challenged in a lawsuit, but was upheld by the United States Supreme Court on May 8, 1950. Screen Directors Guild president Joseph Mankiewicz signed the loyalty oath, as did the rest of the S.D.G. board; but when Mankiewicz left on vacation members of the board loyal to Cecil B. DeMille voted to extend the oath requirement to the entire membership.[7] Signing the oath was made a condition of good standing in the Guild. The board's action was overwhelmingly ratified by the membership on a vote of 547 to 14, with 57 abstentions, but this "courtesy" ballot required the voters to sign their names in casting their votes, and some leveled charges of intimidation at the board. On his return, Mankiewicz wanted to call an open meeting of the Guild membership to discuss the issue. The DeMille faction attempted to prevent such a meeting and sought the removal of Mankiewicz as president of the Guild.

Twenty-five names were required on a petition to call the full membership meeting, and in a strange act of irony those who opposed the oath were required to sign in order to establish their good standing in the union and make their signatures valid on the petition. The general membership meeting took place in the Beverly Hills Hotel on Sunday, October 22, 1950.

DeMille found himself in the awkward position of condemning Mankiewicz for opposing the legal actions of the board and the vote of its membership—something DeMille himself had been quite content to do when he drew a political line in the sand with A.F.R.A. over the $1 assessment. Taking the floor DeMille proceeded to question the motives of the twenty-five who had signed the petition. He pointed out that several of the signatories were also known members or supporters of organizations the government claimed to be Communist fronts.

In a filmed interview Joseph Mankiewicz later stated that DeMille pronounced the names of some of his fellow directors emphasizing their European and Jewish heritage—Villiam Vyler, Billy Vilder, etc. Such tactics would be untypical of DeMille, who otherwise abhorred ethnic or racial bigotry, and who was invariably decorous in his public demeanor. His mother was Jewish and he had recently worked closely with Billy Wilder on *Sunset Boulevard*; such insensitivity from DeMille is difficult to imagine. Interestingly, Robert Parrish, who offers a firsthand memoir of the meeting in his book *Growing Up in Hollywood* and who was also interviewed on film in later years, makes no mention of DeMille's pronunciation of the names.

Beyond the political aspects, a personal element also played a role in the dispute. Joseph Mankiewicz was no wild-eyed radical, but a Republican who considered Cecil B. DeMille to be a mentor. It had been Cecil B. DeMille who nominated Mankiewicz for the presidency of the Guild. Both men felt a sense of betrayal in the other's actions, and their personal animosity added fuel to the dispute.

From the hostility in the room it was clear that DeMille lost the support of the membership with his actions, and he submitted an odd compromise offering a motion "that the balloting to recall Mankiewicz be closed and that all the ballots be destroyed without being counted."[8] But director Don Hartman asked if DeMille were willing to take back his charges against the twenty-five, and when he refused, Hartman asked for DeMille's resignation from the Guild.

It was John Ford who offered a solution to the standoff. He observed that forcing DeMille from the Screen Directors Guild would finish the Guild as a viable organization, but he also noted that the board, of which he himself was a member, had lost the support of the membership. He suggested that the board resign and a new one be elected in its place. Mankiewicz and the twenty-five signers were given a vote of confidence, and DeMille's influence in the Guild was broken. Ford later sent DeMille a friendly note, and DeMille responded with gratitude, apparently aware that, as humiliating as his defeat was, Ford had saved him from even greater personal and professional embarrassment. "Attack I am used to," he wrote Ford, and added, "kindness moves me deeply."[9]

While this battle was raging, DeMille was preparing to make *The Greatest Show on Earth*, a film that he hoped would preserve a record of circus life under the big top. The film also turned out to be the salvation of the Ringling Bros. Circus.

DeMille spent three weeks traveling with the circus in August 1949, and in November asked writer Theodore St. John to come in and pitch a circus story.

On December 1, Paramount signed separate agreements with John

Ringling North and the circus, tying up North's services as a consultant and committing the Ringling Bros.–Barnum & Bailey Combined Shows, with its affiliated trade names, to a ten-year exclusive agreement with the studio.[10] North was to receive $25,000 in ten equal annual installments. The circus would receive $75,000 against royalties, which were to be 10 percent of the gross film rentals over and above 1.9 times negative cost (Paramount's recoupment figure) if the picture was filmed in black and white or 2 times negative cost if the picture was shot in color. The royalty would jump to 12 percent on gross rental amounts above $12 million after recoupment. Studio overhead charges were pegged 26 percent—6 percent below Paramount's calculated overhead charge for the year. If the overhead generally applied to other Paramount pictures fell below 32 percent the overhead charges on the circus picture would be adjusted downward accordingly. Cecil B. DeMille's producer's fee was not to exceed $100,000, and DeMille's profit participation was not to be deemed part of the negative cost. No write-offs of material for other pictures were allowed, and Paramount agreed to produce a class "A" dramatic film, not merely a reproduction of circus acts. The studio agreed not to reproduce scenes of the "tragic fire at Hartford, Connecticut or any other circus fire in which patrons were injured." It was further agreed that Paramount would have use of the circus costumes for the 1951 season but would have to supply the costumes for the film's principals. Paramount also retained rights to exploit the film after the exclusive ten-year deal ended.[11]

Another ten months passed before Paramount formally amended its April 27, 1937, contract with Cecil B. DeMille Productions to take in the circus picture. The parties agreed that *Samson and Delilah* and *The Greatest Show on Earth* would be the seventh and eighth pictures under the contract and that Cecil B. DeMille Productions would receive a $100,000 advance on each picture against royalties, but not less than a total of $450,000 advance on both pictures. DeMille Productions requested and Paramount agreed to pay $250,000 on account, and if at the end of three years after release of the eighth picture but not later than five years from the date of the agreement, the share of profits due DeMille Productions was less than $450,000, DeMille Productions agreed to pay the difference but in any event not more than the $250,000 already advanced.

The general decline in box-office revenues caused the studios to not renew contracts with long-established players, and the axe fell heavily on women stars of a certain age. Paulette Goddard's contract with Paramount came to an end in 1949, and it was perhaps a mark of some desperation that she campaigned heavily for a role in *The Greatest Show on Earth*; but, while DeMille remained personally friendly with Goddard, she had walked off the set for a brief time while making *Unconquered*. Fearing a repeat performance, he had no intention of casting her in *Greatest Show*. Dorothy Lamour had not made a film for Paramount since *Manhandled* in 1948 when DeMille signed her for a role in the picture; and after Betty Hutton completed *Annie Get Your Gun* at M-G-M on December 17, 1949, she didn't make another film until she signed with DeMille in June 1951.

DeMille became interested in newcomer Charlton Heston when he met the actor in the studio commissary on April 24, 1950. The following day he asked to be reminded to talk to director William Dieterle about Heston's work in *Dark City,* which was currently filming. DeMille screened a scene from the movie and two Paramount tests of Heston at his home on June 5, 1950. One test showed Heston playing a scene from *The Strange Love of Martha Ivers* opposite Laura Elliot; the other was a scene originally written for *Quantrill's Raiders* with Wendell Corey. DeMille commented, "I think he's awfully good."[12] But on July 19, after screening *Dark City*, DeMille felt "He is not quite right for our picture . . . [he has] a sinister quality. He's sincere—you believe him—he has some power—he's not attractive." He asked his staff to "Find out if he has any humor. Everything I've seen him in he's dour."[13]

According to Heston, one evening he waved and smiled at DeMille when he passed the director as he drove off the lot. Apparently the smile did the trick, and when DeMille watched the actor in *Of Human Bondage*, a Westinghouse Studio One TV production, on October 6, 1950, he noted, "Heston has a funny way of speaking—it's an artificial way . . . like James Mason. [I] Am inclined to give him the part."[14]

DeMille finally signed a nonexclusive three-picture deal with Heston on November 28, 1950. The term was to begin February 5, 1951, at a rate of $20,000 for ten weeks to be paid at $2,000 per week, and pro rata thereafter. The second film was to commence within one year of July 1, 1952, at a rate of $2,500 per week, unless Wallis-Hazen Productions called Heston under his pre-existing contract before DeMille called him; then Heston would receive only $2,000 per week. The third picture was to commence within one year of July 1, 1952, at $3,000 per week, or $2,500 if he was called to work by Wallis-Hazen first. All of the films were to have ten-week guarantees.[15]

For the first time in many years Hollywood extras were disappointed to find they would not be working in DeMille's latest picture. Many letters requesting work were met with a form letter: "We are in an unusual situation relative to offering work on THE GREATEST SHOW ON EARTH, since our extensive location schedule and use of regular circus personnel has practically eliminated our normal use of extra players."[16]

But the circus players presented a special challenge. If the movie company had to pay the circus performers for all the days worked as the film crew traveled with the show, the cost would be prohibitive. On July 11, 1949, the Screen Actors Guild agreed to waive membership requirements and working-condition clauses for the circus acts. They agreed that Paramount and DeMille Productions didn't have to pay acts seen only in long shots or in footage not used in the picture, provided the footage wasn't used in another film; also, the picture company would be required to pay featured acts in closer shots only one day's pay at Guild minimum, and the studio would be credited if the circus paid the acts additional money for their work in the film. It was further understood that if the acts were requested to do special material that was not part of their regular act they would be paid Guild minimum for such work.

Paramount's agreement not to make any reference to the July 6, 1944, tent fire in Hartford, Connecticut, precluded the possibility of DeMille inserting a "trial by fire" in his screenplay, but he was able to incorporate another favorite device—a train wreck. The wreck in *The Greatest Show on Earth* was not merely a bit of spectacle, DeMille was quick to point out, having its basis in a train wreck involving the Hagenbeck-Wallace Circus in 1929.[17]

The Hartford fire had a devastating impact on the Ringling show that nearly scuttled *The Greatest Show on Earth*. Although Paramount's contract with the circus specified that the studio would have the use of the 1951 season's costumes, the Ringling show couldn't afford to lay out the needed cash for its portion of wardrobe expenses. Costumer Stanley Goldsmith phoned associate producer Henry Wilcoxon on January 4, 1951, to say he had spoken with a Mr. Stroock, who was on the hook for items already ordered by the show:

He wouldn't want anyone to know it, but they have just paid out $750,000. in part payment of the Hartford fire and the [circus's recent] engagement in Cuba was not successful. They have not sent 5¢ to LaRay—and he cannot order the 200

pair of shoes until he gets at least a down payment of $2,000.
. . . Brooks Costume Co. wouldn't want any more business
from the Circus because they have to wait too long for the
money. . . . Brooks will go ahead with what the Circus will
need for their opening on March 4th, but for the time being
they are up to their necks in credit with the Circus and they
would rather that we purchase the web sitters' costumes and
then have us deduct them from our bill with the Circus . . . the
Circus has not ordered them and they have no authorization
from the Circus to go ahead with the making of them.[18]

The cash crunch for the circus was eased considerably with the royalty payments it received from Paramount for *The Greatest Show on
Earth*.

DeMille had often campaigned to give his films limited road-show
engagements in advance of general release, but in an October 23, 1951,
meeting to discuss distribution of the film it was decided to go for the
widest possible saturation release:

BARNEY BALABAN: For the last four years, April, May and
June have been consistently bad months for business. Starts to
pick up after July 4. August is big, and from September on it's
all good.
MR. SCHWALBERG: If we start in the middle of July with 500
[prints], or as many as we need, to intelligently handle the
saturation, we'll be a lot better off than we were with
SAMSON AND DELILAH where we started out with 1, then
4, then 9, then 26 and so on.
BARNEY BALABAN: With SAMSON AND DELILAH, you
had to be convinced of what you had. With THE GREATEST
SHOW ON EARTH, you don't have to be convinced. I think
that we are thinking right with saturating the country—and
getting a complete fast liquidation. If you want a pre-release
engagement somewhere, that might be alright—but *NO* test
engagements. . . . Should our terms be 50/50 from the first
dollar—and sell to any exhibitor who is willing to pay from the
first dollar [?]
CECIL B. DE MILLE: I think it would be wonderful not to have
to raise admission prices.

JERRY PICKMAN: AMERICAN IN PARIS is coming out at advanced prices and a percentage basis; STREETCAR [*A Streetcar Named Desire*] is asking $1.30 [for admission]; QUO VADIS? is anybody's guess—I don't know—but THE GREATEST SHOW ON EARTH would look awfully attractive put out at 50/50 and no advance admission prices, and no guaranteed [number of weeks] playing time.

CECIL B. DE MILLE: *PROVIDED* the exhibitor does not think the picture is not good; he'd have to believe that we were offering him a very attractive deal.

I think the way to handle it is for me to make the announcement in an interview—that this picture was made for every child and woman and man in the world—that it is a picture they will take to their hearts—and I might even say it is a good piece of merchandise.

JERRY PICKMAN: If a newspaper has a big story on page one, it doesn't raise the price [from 5¢] to 7¢—so why ask the public to pay more to see a great piece of merchandise in the form of a picture.

We'd give it to [Louella] Parsons or some important outlet perhaps 2 weeks before our opening sales date—make it part of the campaign.[19]

With its liberal distribution policy, *The Greatest Show on Earth* was a phenomenal hit. Of course, even with a good deal, exhibitors wanted an edge in attracting patrons to their theaters, and Arthur M. Concello, general manager of the Ringling show, was outraged when he saw a newspaper ad for *The Greatest Show on Earth* at the Gateway Theatre in Kenosha, Wisconsin, reading "Bigger and Better Than the Circus Itself and a Lots Less Money!" Paramount took immediate steps to suppress the language in future ads.

Once, when asked how many Oscars he had won, DeMille is said to have replied, "Eleven! But they only gave me three." He received a special award in 1949 honoring "Cecil B. DeMille Distinguished Motion Picture Pioneer for 38 Years of Brilliant Showmanship," and he took home two awards at the 1953 Oscar ceremony—the Irving G. Thalberg Memorial Award honoring his contributions as a producer, and a Best Picture Oscar for *The Greatest Show on Earth*. Some have suggested that the awards were given to applaud DeMille's conservative political beliefs in keeping with the mood of the era, but more likely the film industry was aware that at age seventy-three, DeMille would have few opportunities for future honors, and Hollywood genuinely sought to recognize the contributions of its most successful citizen.[20]

# The Ten Commandments

A Paramount Picture. A Cecil B. DeMille Production. Produced and directed by Cecil B. DeMille. Screenplay by Aeneas MacKenzie, Jesse L. Lasky Jr., Jack Gariss, and Fredric M. Frank, from *Prince of Egypt* by Dorothy Clark Wilson, *Pillar of Fire* by the Rev. J.H. Ingraham, and *On Eagle's Wings* by the Rev. A.E. Southon, in accordance with the ancient texts of Philo, Josephus, Eusebius, the Midrash, and the Holy Scriptures (additional, uncredited writing by Edmund Penney). Associate producer: Henry Wilcoxon. Art direction: Hal Pereira, Walter Tyler, and Albert Nozaki. Unit director: Arthur Rosson. Assistant directors: Francisco Day, Michael Moore, Edward Salven, Daniel McCaulay, and Fouad Aref. Music: Elmer Bernstein. Photography: Loyal Griggs, A.S.C. Additional photography: J. Peverell Marley, John Warren, and Wallace Kelley. Film editor: Anne Bauchens, A.C.E.

Picture started (Egyptian unit): October 14, 1954. Picture finished: December 3, 1954. Hollywood unit started: March 28, 1955. Hollywood unit finished: August 13, 1955. Length: 19,994 feet (twenty-four reels). Cost: $13,272,381.87. Released: November 8, 1956 (New York premiere). Gross receipts: $90,066,230.00 (to June 23, 1979). Producers share: $11,412,640.00

Cast: Charlton Heston (Moses), Yul Brynner (Rameses), Anne Baxter (Nefretiri), Edward G. Robinson (Dathan), Yvonne De Carlo (Sephora), Debra Paget (Lilia), John Derek (Joshua), Sir Cedric Hardwicke (Sethi), Nina Foch (Bithiah), Martha Scott (Yochabel), Judith Anderson (Memnet), Vincent Price (Baka), John Carradine (Aaron), Olive Deering (Miriam), Ian Keith, H.B. Warner, Julia Faye, Woodrow Strode, and George Melford

THOSE WHO SEE THIS MOTION PICTURE
## PRODUCED AND DIRECTED
## BY
## CECIL B. DE MILLE
WILL MAKE A PILGRIMAGE OVER THE VERY GROUND
THAT MOSES TROD MORE THAN 3,000 YEARS AGO

So reads Cecil B. DeMille's on-screen credit in *The Ten Commandments*. In his filmed introduction he says, "Our intention was not to create a story, but to be worthy of the Divinely inspired story created three thousand years ago—the five Books of Moses." Titles proclaim the film is based on the Holy Scriptures, the Midrash, and works by Philo, Josephus, and Eusebius, historians who, DeMille tells the audience, "had access to documents long since destroyed—or perhaps lost—like the Dead Sea Scrolls."[1] But more recent works were consulted as well: *Prince of Egypt* (1949) by Dorothy Clark Wilson, *Pillar of Fire* (1872) by the Rev. J.H. Ingraham, and *On Eagle's Wings* (1937) by the Rev. A.E. Southon. These various works helped fill in "thirty missing years" of the life of Moses, and as with *Samson and Delilah*, Cecil B. DeMille and his writers did not attempt to change the Bible, but they did augment it considerably.

"I have sometimes likened the producer to the restorer of a broken mosaic," wrote DeMille in his introduction to *Moses and Egypt*, a book by Henry Noerdlinger compiling his research for *The Ten Commandments*. "Some parts of the mosaic can be supplied by historians. The missing parts . . . the producer must supply; but the integrity of the whole work demands that what the producer supplies must fit in with what history knows."[2]

In the case of Moses, what history knows is—not much. *Moses and Egypt* outlines what is known historically about Egypt and offers a manifesto explaining how and why decisions were made in adapting the story of Moses for the screen; but, although he dressed it up with some elusive prose, the conscientious Noerdlinger felt compelled to note that no archaeological evidence had been found to suggest when, where—or even if—the events described in the Five Books of Moses took place:

> To relate the biblical events of Moses' birth and the signifi-
> cant Exodus with Egyptian history has proved to be a most
> difficult puzzle. No conscientious scholar has been able to set
> an exact date with absolute certainty for these events. . . .
>
> The problem with which we deal here has received
> considerable attention. We can state that neither the period nor
> the pharaohs chosen for the picture *The Ten Commandments*
> have been picked by whim. Among scholars there are those
> who favor the thirteenth century B.C. as the general era of the
> Exodus. Of course, this or any other proposed solution will
> remain controversial until conclusive evidence can be estab-
> lished.[3]

In relating the "back story" of Moses, *The Ten Commandments* turns to the most basic of DeMille's themes—two brothers vying for the same woman. Moses, adopted into Pharaoh Sethi's house, and Rameses, the Pharaoh's son by birth, compete to wed the Princess Nefretiri. The one who wins her hand will ascend to the throne of Egypt after Sethi's death. Moses gains the admiration of his adopted father, and Rameses resents the loss of his father's respect. When Moses finally learns of his Hebrew heritage and discovers he is the Chosen One who will lead the people of Israel from bondage, the conflict becomes deeper—will man be ruled by the laws of God, or the whims of a dictator? But until the Egyptian forces are destroyed when the Red Sea closes in on them, the conflict is framed as a sibling rivalry as compelling as it is simple and elemental. DeMille portrays Moses and Rameses as people that the audience can understand.

"No critical appraisal [of The Ten Commandments] can be pure rave," observed one reviewer. "While DeMille has broken new ground in terms of size, he has remained conventional with the motion picture as an art form. Emphasis on physical dimension has rendered neither awesome nor profound the story of Moses. The eyes of the onlooker are filled with spectacle. Emotional tug is sometimes lacking."[4]

Shot in VistaVision, *The Ten Commandments* was DeMille's first wide-screen film, and he may have been influenced by prevailing attitudes of the time that the bigger screen lent itself to long, continuous takes that eliminated the need for editing and breaking the action into shorter shots. Still, from DeMille's "curtain speech" prologue, it is evident that he intended the theatrical effect and gave the film's words and ideas equal importance with its visual style.

Literal in conception, highly stylized in execution, staged more like a Victorian pageant than a film, and sporting long passages of expository dialogue, *The Ten Commandments* is a curious production. On virtually every level one can understand why critics were lukewarm, and yet seeing the film in a theater with an audience, one becomes aware that for many it is a very moving, even spiritual experience.

With his three-picture contract and the strong box-office performance of *The Greatest Show on Earth*, there was never any question that Charlton Heston was the actor born to play Moses, although his ten-week guarantee was upped to twenty-five weeks for *The Ten Commandments*—this amounted to a flat $50,000 deal because Heston committed to working for free after twenty-five weeks if his services were required to complete the film.

DeMille was less certain about who should play Rameses. On July 24, 1952, he was convinced that Michael Rennie was right for the part. On December 8 he believed James Mason would make a wonderful Rameses—an interesting choice considering DeMille's early impression that Mason and Heston shared certain characteristics of vocal inflection. The Paramount casting department recommended Yul Brynner, who was currently starring on Broadway in *The King and I.*

"He saw some film footage of Yul Brynner with receding hair and was not terribly impressed," recalls DeMille's granddaughter, Cecilia Presley. "But someone told him to go see *The King and I* and we went to New York." Cecilia sat with her grandfather in the St. James Theatre on February 26, 1953. "In the second act he grabbed my arm. We went back stage and DeMille said to Yul Brynner, 'How would you like to play the most powerful man in the world?'"[5]

DeMille was so convinced that Brynner was his ideal Rameses that he committed to postponing his start date for almost two years when he signed the actor (*The King and I* was a hit that looked to run indefinitely). Brynner and his theatrical producers agreed that DeMille could have the actor anytime in 1955 on ninety-days' preliminary notice and forty-five days' formal notice. Brynner's deal was much more generous than Heston's—$75,000 for ten-weeks' work to be paid at the rate of $7,500 per week. The eleventh and twelfth week were to be free, the thirteenth and fourteenth week would be paid at the rate of $2,000 per week, and anything over fourteen weeks would be prorated on the $2,000 rate.[6]

Production on *The Ten Commandments* began in Egypt in October 1954 with DeMille and a crew of some eighty technicians and craftsmen from Hollywood shooting scenes of Moses in the wilderness and at locations around Mt. Sinai, as well as the exteriors of the Pharaoh's great city, the beginning of the Exodus, and the pursuit by Pharaoh's charioteers.

Charlton Heston apparently made enough money in 1954 that he sought to avoid moving into a higher tax bracket. He agreed to make the Egyptian trip without compensation. Brynner was able to arrange to be on location with the Egyptian unit for up to ten days, for which he would be paid $7,500. Other principal actors were doubled on the location. The Screen Actors Guild agreed to a waiver relaxing the rules for doubling actors on what was called a preproduction unit. Normally, actors who are doubled are paid on days when their doubles perform. S.A.G. agreed that actors making more than $25,000 for the picture would not have to be paid for days when only their doubles worked. Actors making less than

$1,250 a week would be paid for the days their doubles worked, plus two days of travel; actors making over $1,250 a week would be paid for the days their doubles worked, plus one day of travel.

Conditions were severe on the Egyptian locations. On Thursday, October 21, 1954, publicist Rufus Blair reported to Art Arthur in DeMille's Hollywood office from a camp maintained by the Egyptian National Petroleum Company:

> Am spanking this out under most trying conditions in a
> loosely thrown-up Arabian tent, with the heat already crawl-
> ing past ninety, and it's only 7 a.m. . . .
>
> We are now camped at Abu Rudeis . . . about 310 kilome-
> ters southeast of Cairo and about 150 kilometers inside the
> Sinai Peninsula where you cross the Red Sea at Suez. This is
> where the yellow-jacks and flies dive-bomb at you with
> voracious intent, for the Americans must be fresh meat. . . .
>
> The American manager of the outfit was kind enough to let
> our professional caterer put up his tents on the company's ground
> near the Red Sea, and we are able, at times, to use the toilet
> facilities, whenever his own huge crew isn't using them. . . .

Blair had nothing but admiration for Charlton Heston's endurance and professionalism:

> He had to do each scene several times, and every time he
> stumbled and fell, he had to land on these sharp, three-cornered
> stones. His legs, thighs, arms and chest are a welter of bruises. . . .
>
> Not only that, but do you know what the guy did all the
> time yesterday? When he had to do a scene over—and the old
> tracks had to be covered up—he decided, inasmuch as he
> already was way down below the crew and far away, to save
> the property man the arduous task of crawling up and down all
> the time. So as he retraced his steps back to the starting point,
> he rubbed out the tracks himself in all that heat by brushing
> his robe back and forth across each footstep until the surface
> was virgin again. . . .
>
> Bedouins, the nomadic tribesmen of the desert, had to be
> detoured yesterday as they sought to pass our location sight.
> The regular course lay directly between the VistaVision

cameras and Heston's performance. They were routed behind
the cameras along a hastily built jog of road. Most of them
stopped to watch, of course. . . .

[Head grip Dominic Seminerio] along with ten of his crew
including several local laborers, packed the dolly truck
equipment all the way up Sinai last Saturday [October 16]
from the point where the camels found the steep trail non-
negotiable. Something like 1000 feet, and almost straight up.
Then they twice laid a 40–foot track for the moving camera
shot of Moses receiving the Commandments. . . .

Trouble with dolly stuff here is that there's hardly a
stretch level enough to lay the track. Altogether, there have
only been three dolly shots [so far]—two on Sinai and one
along a strip of desert today. . . .

After finishing with the big tough job of laying that 80–
foot track out there last evening, Dominic's jeep driver got
stuck in the sand on the way in. The guys didn't get supper
until almost midnight.

After their midnight meal, the crew was up in time to make the forty-
five minute drive from camp to location and was ready to start work at
6:30 in the morning. Blair explained:

The sun's no good for shooting here this time of year after
4:30 [P.M.]. . . . That's the reason for the early morning calls
every day. We all roll out at 4:30 a.m., shoot till 4:30 p.m.,
and then come in. . . . DeMille goes over the next day's
production plans with the head technicians and never turns in
before 11 o'clock, sometimes later, and he's the first guy up
in the morning. Today the crew was in the mess tent sweeping
sleep from our eyes, when he walked in chuckling, after his
swim [in the Red Sea], all dressed up and ready to roll. The
jeeps left at 5:45.[7]

DeMille's report to Paramount studio head Y. Frank Freeman nine
days later gave an equally bleak description of the conditions under which
The Ten Commandments company worked in Egypt:

The Mt. Sinai location was hard and rugged. The country is

little visited and no roads from Abu Rudeis to the Monastery
of St. Catherine. For 65 miles we painted rocks white and set
them up in the desert in order that our cars and trucks could
follow by day and night the way to the Monastery . . . which is
the oldest continuous Monastery in the world. . . . We lived in
the Monastery. It has changed little in a thousand years. The
Arch Bishop graciously gave me his suite of office, bedroom,
dining room and bath. The bath had a tub in it, but no running
water either in or out. It had a nice toilet, but no running water
into it; we flushed it with a bucket.

DeMille recounted that, despite the primitive conditions, things were
going well in Egypt. By October 30, Yul Brynner had shot his scenes and
returned to the States on schedule. He assured Freeman, "Heston is doing
fine work and is an impressive Moses." He also reported that his old
friend William Boyd "showed up on the set—as he did at the circus—but
I could not get him in the chariot charge." However, with all the positive
news, DeMille noted that the location work was taking its toll on him and
the crew:

When I got back to Cairo I had lost 21 pounds and weigh at
present 151 pounds, which was my weight when I was
married 52 years ago.
    Most of us have suffered from dysentery, which we did
not seem to be able to cure, so I sent for Dr. Max Jacobson to
come on from New York. He flew out here with Yul Brynner.
I did not mention to the New York office or anyone why I was
sending for him. He has been here now for four days and we
are all in much better shape. As you know, he is one of the
best doctors in America, and I felt the situation was sufficiently important to bring him on at my personal expense,
which I did. He will return on the 3rd of November, and I
believe will have all of us in pretty good shape by then.[8]

Why send to New York for a doctor to treat a condition that was
certainly familiar to doctors in Egypt? There was more to the story than
DeMille was willing to put in a letter. While shooting at the Gates of
Tanis set near Giza, DeMille started to climb a ladder to the top of the
structure to check a camera placement. Partway up he was seized with a

wrenching pain in his chest, and it was all he could do to climb back down. He had suffered a heart attack. One of Egypt's best heart specialists, Dr. Hussein Ibrahim, suggested weeks of recuperation time; but someone recommended DeMille consult an American physician, and Dr. Max Jacobson was called.

DeMille's introduction to Max Jacobson came through actor Albert Dekker, who recommended DeMille talk to him when Gladys Rosson was taken ill with cancer. Rosson passed away on June 14, 1953, before Jacobson could be consulted. But DeMille called for Jacobson after his heart attack.[9] "Dr. Jacobson came into my room alone," DeMille recalled. "He told me, with no polite varnish on his words, the risk I would be taking. . . . 'It is a calculated risk,' he said, 'but with medication, and if you will agree not to walk upstairs in this apartment more than once a day and to ride in a car or jeep instead of walking on the set, in my judgment you can get up tomorrow. . . .'" DeMille went on to say, "I do not recommend anyone else to follow my example, for not everyone else has a Max Jacobson by his side."[10]

"Max Jacobson was sort of creepy," recalls Cecilia Presley, "and the Egyptian doctors thought he was a quack."[11] It was an astute observation. Dr. Max Jacobson, described as "Max with his filthy fingernails" by singer Eddie Fisher, was "one of the best doctors in America" only in the sense that he had an elite clientele of celebrities and politicians.[12] He was in fact a notorious "Dr. Feel-Good," who made an unscrupulous living pumping his clients full of amphetamines and other dubious nostrums. He would later have his license to practice medicine revoked.[13]

DeMille made a pact with God, feeling certain that "if my motives in making the film were what I thought they were, I would be given the strength to finish it." But, hedging his bets, he also made a pact with the Devil, in the guise of Max Jacobson, to complete his labor in Egypt.

With much of the location work being the sort of action and background stuff that he might normally have the second unit shoot, the production continued without significant interruption. DeMille's daughter Cecilia, cinematographer Loyal Griggs, and makeup man Frank Westmore stepped in to take on some of the director's burden, and many in the company remained unaware of DeMille's health crisis.

Max Jacobson accompanied DeMille on his return to Hollywood in December, but with the director at home under the care of his personal physician, Jacobson left for New York and the family saw no need to call him in again. With production on *The Ten Commandments* set to resume on the Paramount sound stages several months later in March 1955, DeMille was able to recover sufficiently to continue the picture. But *The Ten Commandments* suffered another blow on January 22, 1955, when DeMille's long-time assistant director, Eddie Salven, died of pneumonia. Francisco "Chico" Day assumed Salven's duties as first assistant director.

As the Hollywood start date neared, DeMille turned his attention to more conventional filmmaking problems. On February 9, 1955, mindful that he would need children in his Exodus pickup shots, and that labor laws precluded working children for more than four hours a day, DeMille had a brainstorm:

> Today when Mr. deMille saw the dozen or so midgets on THE COURT JESTER set he had the idea that they might be useful for us to use as children provided we did not get too close to them.
>
> Mr. deMille added that we would of course only choose those who have perfect little bodies.[14]

Two days later Bud Brill, of the Paramount casting office, was forced to report that certain requested performers were not to be had.

> Last week we had a special interview to find out if Central Casting was able to supply us with women capable of carrying baskets and props on their heads—naturally, without effort. The results were very disappointing. Out of approximately 150 women we only found three or four who could be classed as fair.
>
> I thought you would like this information in case Mr. deMille asks you what we have been doing in this matter. We will probably have to take a group and rehearse them for about a week to see if we can develop this "talent."[15]

It was DeMille's practice to run his casting ideas by his family and office staff, and when he was looking for an actor to play Dathan, he sought his granddaughter's reaction.

"I'm thinking of casting George Sanders in the role of Dathan."

"Lucky Debra!" was Cecilia's response, Debra being actress Debra Paget, who would play the role of Lilia.

A startled DeMille asked, "Why do you say that?"

Cecilia explained, "Why would Lilia want a boy like John Derek if she could have a man of the world like George Sanders?"[16]

DeMille immediately gave up the idea of using Sanders and signed Edward G. Robinson for the role—a move that took some courage in the days of the Red Scare in Hollywood, for Robinson was—if not black-listed—certainly grey-listed for what were perceived to be left-leaning politics. "An Interested Viewer" made his thoughts known to DeMille in no uncertain terms:

Dear Mr. DeMille,

Hasn't Edward G. Robinson been linked with the Red?

We were so disappointed you had chosen him for The Ten Commandments. Is he the one to do it? We haven't been to a Edward G. Robinson picture in years & have never wanted to see him because of his connections—

We hope this isn't authentic about his having a part unless he could be converted in doing it.[17]

Edward G. Robinson recalled:

It was obvious that while I was forgiven for my premature antifascism, I was doomed both by age and former political leanings to a slow graveyard. The top directors and producers wouldn't have me . . . what I needed was recognition again by a top figure in the industry. . . .

No more conservative or patriarchal figure existed in Hollywood [than Cecil B. DeMille], no one more opposed to communism. . . . And no fairer one, no man with a greater sense of decency and justice. I'm told that when the part [of Dathan] was discussed . . . somebody suggested that I would be ideal, but that under the circumstances I was, of course, unacceptable. Mr. DeMille wanted to know why, coldly reviewed the matter, felt I had been done an injustice, and told his people to offer me the part.

Cecil B. DeMille returned me to films. Cecil B. DeMille restored my self respect.[18]

After casting Edward G. Robinson as Dathan, DeMille was not happy with his performance. At home he told his granddaughter that Robinson wasn't giving him what he wanted.

"Why don't you tell him what you want?" Cecilia asked.

And DeMille, the man who parted the Red Sea twice (once more than God), the tyrant who ate actors and crew people for breakfast, the filmmaker who demanded total dedication to the project at hand, asked: "How could I dare say anything to so talented and respected an actor?"

Later, when he ran Robinson's first scenes on the screen in dailies, DeMille was surprised to see that the actor brought more to the part than had been evident on the set, and he was delighted with the sardonic humor Robinson managed to inject into an otherwise serious role.[19]

DeMille's working methods on the set were as meticulous as his preproduction planning. Charlton Heston observed, "You usually begin with a master shot of the entire scene, sometimes a tracking shot, setting the geography for the closer angles. As he worked through this coverage, he'd weigh each setup as they lit it against the [storyboard] frame sketches or paintings he had of most scenes. He'd rehearse enough to set the moves for the camera and the actors, then shoot it, usually printing in less than six takes. Oddly, he'd often do an entire scene without close-ups, almost unheard of now." Heston also noted that "When DeMille wrapped the company at the end of the day's shoot, he kept the cameraman, the [camera] operator, the sound mixer, the script supervisor, and the first assistant director on the set until he'd picked the first shot for the next morning."[20]

After shooting was completed, several months were spent recording "walla"—added lines, vocal reactions, voice replacements for the Egyptian extras who spoke no English, and even voice replacements for a few actors who spoke English but not nearly well enough. Ed Penney wrote much of this added dialogue, and the sessions were largely directed by associate producer Henry Wilcoxon. The sessions gave DeMille a chance to keep some of his old favorites working. Julia Faye and Maude Fealy were among the actors regularly called for these sessions. They also afforded an opportunity to help out a few younger actors. Richard Gilden was one of those who worked in the walla group.

"I managed to get one day's work acting as a bit player on *The Ten Commandments*," Gilden remembered.

> I was way in the back, you couldn't even see me. During rehearsal I made some grand gesture looking off into the

distance and it caught DeMille's eye. He pointed me out to the other bit players and extras saying that I was the only one in the crowd who was giving him what he wanted. At the end of the day the assistant director came up to me and said, "You'll be back, the old man likes you." And I came back. A one day job turned into months of employment, and then I continued in the walla sessions. We had a ball. It was hardly like work, we had fun all the time during those sessions.[21]

Composer Elmer Bernstein was another relative newcomer whose term of employment extended well beyond his initial assignment. Victor Young had composed the scores for every DeMille film since *North West Mounted Police*, but he was too ill to take on *The Ten Commandments*.[22] Roy Fjastad, of the Paramount music department, recommended Bernstein to write some Egyptian dance music that was needed for playback while shooting a scene. Bernstein's melody—and its orchestration with "plinky things, bells, wooden flutes and other devices that would at least make sound like ancient instruments"[23]—earned DeMille's approval, and the composer remained on *The Ten Commandments* week-to-week for several months before he finally received the assignment to score the entire film.

When time came for the Academy Award nominations, *The Ten Commandments* received Oscar nominations for Best Picture, Best Color Cinematography, Best Color Art Direction, Best Color Costume Design, Best Sound Recording, Best Film Editing, and Best Special Effects, but it was not recognized for Best Musical Score or Best Director.[24]

"Apparently, the members of the Academy saw the picture as an act of God and were not willing to acknowledge any of the human achievements responsible for creating something they thought worthy of a nomination as the best motion picture," Elmer Bernstein later wrote. Visiting DeMille in his office, Bernstein expected to find the director "in a towering rage"; but,

His first concern was that I might be disappointed for failing to be nominated for my work on the score. . . .
I expressed dismay for his sake that the picture did not achieve the honor that he might have hoped for and in that moment I saw sadness in him for the first time. Instead of his characteristically incisive reaction to expressions of sympa-

thy, he hesitated for a long moment and finally said, "I guess we will just have to be satisfied with the grand award of the peoples of the world at the box office."[25]

In a ceremony on December 27, 1956, shortly after *The Ten Commandments* was released in its first road-show engagements, the barn where Cecil B. DeMille first set up offices and dressing rooms for the Jesse L. Lasky Feature Play Company in 1913 was designated as California State Historic Landmark No. 554.[26] Once again the old partners, Lasky and DeMille, Adolph Zukor and Samuel Goldwyn, came together—but this time to look back. Most of their battles had been fought.

DeMille would be involved with one more film, a remake of *The Buccaneer*. He supervised the casting—Jerry Hartleben, who played the cabin boy in the film, remembers meeting the director—but he was too ill to direct. He gave that assignment to his son-in-law, Anthony Quinn.[27]

Mark Haggard, a young film enthusiast in 1958, visited DeMille in his office during the production. After their chat, DeMille suggested he look in on the shooting. Haggard recalls seeing Anthony Quinn on his knees begging Yul Brynner, who was playing Lafitte, to do what he was asking. No more the disciplined control that had once marked a DeMille set.

DeMille dreamed of making one more film—a story of space exploration tentatively titled *Project X*. It would have been the tenth film under DeMille's 1937 contract with Paramount. He also hoped to develop a film about the formation of the Boy Scouts called *On My Honor*, which Henry Wilcoxon would produce and direct.

Cecil B. DeMille died in his Hollywood home on January 21, 1959. He had some hope that the organization he had built would continue without him, but when the script for *On My Honor* was completed in 1961, Paramount showed no interest in making the project, and the offices in the DeMille bungalow were shut down. Business continued, not quite as usual, for many years at 2010 DeMille Drive in Laughlin Park before the two joined houses were finally sold by the family in the 1980s.

When he received the Milestone Award of the Screen Producers' Guild on January 22, 1956, DeMille offered his thoughts on his career:

Motion pictures have been my life's work. And every foot of it in film, and every minute of it in time, has been an adventure which I would not exchange for anything else in the world.

We in the Industry hold great power. Who else—except the missionaries of God—has had our opportunity to make the brotherhood of man not a phrase, but a reality—a brotherhood that has shared the same tears, dreamt the same dreams, been encouraged by the same hopes, inspired by the same faith in man and in God, which we painted for them, night after night, on the screens of the world? Our influence must be used for good—for truth, for beauty, and for freedom.[28]

"In the end he was what he had always been," said his granddaughter. "His father was a playwright and a lay minister, and he was his father's son—a story teller who felt called to make the world a better place."

# Appendix A

# DeMille Pictures, Inc., Costs and Grosses

These figures were compiled by Cecil B. DeMille's secretary Gladys Rosson on January 30, 1936.

**First-Year Program (1925–26)**

| Title | Cost | Gross as of 7/9/27 |
|---|---|---|
| *Hell's Highroad* | $246,819.19 | $213,208.40 |
| *The Coming of Amos* | $255,040.01 | $227,984.65 |
| *The Wedding Song* | $184,407.45 | $198,487.41 |
| *Three Faces East* | $179,077.80 | $313,768.79 |
| *Braveheart* | $290,195.39 | $249,407.70 |
| *Made for Love* | $226,141.96 | $162,576.79 |
| *Red Dice* | $216,295.38 | $176,311.72 |
| *Silence* | $290,921.58 | $268,630.74 |
| *Eve's Leaves* | $245,782.13 | $176,347.63 |
| *Bachelor Brides* | $177,504.04 | $164,754.19 |

**First-Year Specials**

| | | |
|---|---|---|
| *The Road to Yesterday* | $477,479.29 | $522,663.77 |
| | | (as of 10/25/30) |
| *The Volga Boatman* | $479,356.99 | $1,275,374.78 |

**Second-Year Program (1926–27)**

| | | |
|---|---|---|
| *Sunny-Side Up* | $132,942.56 | $144,845.31 |
| *Her Man o' War* | $148,144.40 | $168,690.77 |
| *The Clinging Vine* | $168,067.42 | $153,545.76 |
| *Gigolo* | $225,857.79 | $218,948.54 |
| *Risky Business* | $122,298.03 | $121,360.68 |
| *Young April* | $198,960.60 | $185,816.46 |
| *For Alimony Only* | $161,497.46 | $134,084.91 |

| Title | Cost | Gross as of 7/9/27 |
|---|---|---|
| *Corporal Kate* | $231,143.85 | $147,790.71 |
| *Cruise of the Jasper B* | $245,782.13 | $119,078.73 |
| *Fighting Love* | $183,865.88 | $ 99,419.25 |
| *Rubber Tires* | $203,589.31 | $110,179.64 |
| *Nobody's Widow* | $201,259.51 | $127,082.62 |
| *White Gold* | $191,658.36 | [not listed] |
| *The Little Adventuress* | $153,092.30 | [not listed] |
| *Vanity* | $204,203.67 | [not listed] |
| *Turkish Delight* | $253,640.57 | [not listed] |

**Second-Year Specials**

| | | |
|---|---|---|
| *The Yankee Clipper* | $436,748.53 | $288,882.42 |
| *The King of Kings* | $1,265,283.95 | $2,602,272.52 |
| | (approximate) | (as of 8/31/35) |

**Third-Year Program (1927–28)**

| | | |
|---|---|---|
| *The Country Doctor* | $239,352.98 | $297,808.87 |
| *His Dog* | $103,604.11 | $158,253.11 |
| *The Fighting Eagle* | $297,384.14 | $336,151.63 |
| *Almost Human* | $180,143.11 | $133,141.76 |
| *The Angel of Broadway* | $172,364.00 | $157,093.82 |
| *Dress Parade* | $220,512.16 | $267,814.15 |
| *The Wise Wife* | $155,098.13 | $152,132.36 |
| *Forbidden Woman* | $219,154.95 | $284,976.11 |
| *The Main Event* | $226,260.43 | $194,210.71 |
| *The Wreck of the Hesperus* | $217,558.73 | $266,602.30 |
| *Let 'er Go, Gallagher* | $100,602.57 | $154,368.94 |
| *The Blue Danube* | $275,383.69 | $270,310.63 |
| *The Leopard Lady* | $209,109.76 | $197,499.10 |
| *A Friend from India* | $ 90,648.69 | $123,720.70 |
| *Stand and Deliver* | $201,477.76 | $213,640.42 |
| *Skyscraper* | $203,163.13 | $280,827.64 |
| *A Ship Comes In* | $194,558.14 | $179,120.70 |
| *Chicago* | $303,306.18 | $483,165.79 |
| *Midnight Madness* | $119,788.43 | $137,577.19 |
| *A Blonde for a Night* | $156,408.25 | $133,054.27 |
| *Hold 'em Yale* | $240,454.96 | $299,485.21 |
| *Walking Back* | $156,796.02 | $169,793.26 |

| Title | Cost | Gross as of 7/9/27 |
|---|---|---|
| *The Cop* | [not listed] | $302,101.76 |
| *Tenth Avenue* | [not listed] | $232,965.71 |
| *Man Made Woman* | [not listed] | $152,599.72 |

**Third-Year Special**

| | | |
|---|---|---|
| *The Godless Girl* | $722,315.17 | $489,095.49 |

# Appendix B

# Other Cecil B. DeMille Film Credits

| | | |
|---|---|---|
| *Brewster's Millions* | (Lasky, 1914) | Co-director with Oscar Apfel |
| *The Master Mind* | (Lasky, 1914) | Co-director with Oscar Apfel |
| *The Only Son* | (Lasky, 1914) | Co-director with Oscar Apfel |
| *The Man on the Box* | (Lasky, 1914) | Co-director with Oscar Apfel and Wilfred Buckland |
| *Ready Money* | (Lasky, 1914) | Scenario only |
| *The Circus Man* | (Lasky, 1914) | Scenario only |
| *The Ghost Breaker* | (Lasky, 1914) | Scenario, and co-director with Oscar Apfel |
| *Cameo Kirby* | (Lasky, 1914) | Scenario only |
| *Snobs* | (Lasky, 1915) | Scenario only |
| *After Five* | (Lasky, 1915) | Co-author of source play only |
| *The Governor's Lady* | (Lasky, 1915) | Scenario only |
| *The Goose Girl* | (Lasky, 1915) | Scenario only |
| *A Gentleman of Leisure* | (Lasky, 1915) | Scenario only |
| *The Country Boy* | (Lasky, 1915) | Scenario only |
| *The Love Mask* | (Lasky, 1915) | Scenario only |
| *Nan of Music Mountain* | (Famous Players-Lasky, 1917) | Directed blizzard sequence only |
| *Broadway Jones* | (Artcraft, 1918) | Supervised preproduction only |

| | | |
|---|---|---|
| *Don't Tell Everything* | (Famous Players-Lasky, 1921) | Film uses sequence deleted from DeMille's *The Affairs of Anatol* |
| *Changing Husbands* | (Famous Players-Lasky, 1923) | Supervisor |
| *The Night Club* | (Famous Players-Lasky, 1925) | Co-author of source play only |
| *Chicago* | (DeMille Pictures-P.D.C., 1927) | Directed in whole or in part, but film credited to Frank Urson |
| *Forgotten Commandments* | (Paramount, 1932) | Film uses sequences from *The Ten Commandments* (1923) |
| *Land of Liberty* | (1939) | Supervised production (but credited as "Edited by Cecil B. DeMille") |
| *California's Golden Beginning* | (1948) | Directed sequences with California governor Earl Warren |
| *The Buccaneer* | (Paramount, 1958) | Executive producer only |

# Appendix C

# Unrealized Projects

*The Deluge.* This was announced as DeMille's special production for 1927, but it was shelved in favor of *The King of Kings*.

*The End of the World.* After *This Day and Age* DeMille wanted to make an original film based at least in part on the novel *When Worlds Collide* by Phillip Wylie and Edwin Balmer. Some preparatory work was done, but the film was never scheduled for production. *When Worlds Collide* was eventually produced by George Pal in 1951.

*Esther* (a.k.a. *The Story of Esther*). MacKinlay Cantor worked on this script from July 9 to August 4, 1934.

*Hudson's Bay Company.* Jeanie Macpherson worked on this script from April 26 to October 20, 1937, and again from November 4, 1937, to July 5, 1938. Jesse Lasky Jr. also worked on the script from November 19, 1937, to April 30, 1938.

*The Flame* (a.k.a. *Rurales*). This film with a Mexican background was a project DeMille worked on for nearly five years. At various times, beginning in July 1939, and continuing through December 1944, the following writers worked on the script: J. Robert Bren, Gladys Atwater, Jeanie Macpherson, Jesse Lasky Jr., Theodore St. John, Albert Maltz, Edgcumb Pinchon, John Howard Lawson, Charles Bennett, Alan LeMay, and Bordon Chase. It was shelved in favor of *For Whom the Bell Tolls* and later revived at the behest of the U.S. government as a "good neighbor" project before it was finally abandoned.

*Queen of Queens.* The story of Mary, mother of Jesus. Jeanie Macpherson worked on the script from November 20, 1939, to July 27, 1940. William C. deMille also worked on the script from March 4, 1940, to June 7, 1941, and William Cowan wrote on the project from September 3 to October 9, 1940. *Queen of Queens* met some resistance from the Catholic Church, and the film was never scheduled for production.

*For Whom the Bell Tolls.* DeMille planned to produce a film of Ernest

Hemingway's novel of the Spanish Civil War after *Reap the Wild Wind*, and Jeanie Macpherson worked on the script from October 28, 1940, to May 13, 1941. At the instigation of John Hay Whitney, DeMille turned the project over to Paramount to devote his attention to a "good neighbor" project with a Latin American setting as a part of the United States' ongoing effort to keep South America from siding with the Axis during World War II. *For Whom the Bell Tolls* was eventually directed by Sam Wood in 1943. DeMille's South American project was never filmed.

*Thou Art the Man.* From September 17, 1945, to November 3, 1945, Jeanie Macpherson worked on the script that was based on the biblical story of David.

*Helen of Troy.* Jack Gariss worked on this script beginning on August 9, 1951, but the project was shelved at some later time.

*The Big Brass Band.* Jesse Lasky returned to Paramount in 1957 with the hope of producing this film. DeMille, as a favor to his old friend, was scheduled to direct, and the development of the picture was carried by DeMille's production company. Lasky was on the project from February 4 to August 10, 1957. Three writers worked on the script: Edward James (March 3–23, 1957), Edward Hope (March 27–April 11, 1957), and Barney Slater (June 24–July 22, 1957). The decline of DeMille's health and the death of Lasky in 1958 brought an end to the project.

*On My Honor.* DeMille was planning this biography of Lord Baden Powell, the founder of the Boy Scouts, although work had not begun on the script at the time of his death in January 1959. DeMille's production company, Motion Picture Associates, sought to continue the project under DeMille's associate producer, Henry Wilcoxon, who worked on it from March 1, 1959, to January 31, 1962. Jesse Lasky Jr. worked on the script from May 5, 1959, to April 30, 1960, and Sydney Box also worked on the script from January 15 to June 16, 1961.

*Project X.* At the time of his death, DeMille was planning an epic of space exploration that he dubbed *Project X*. According to his granddaughter, Cecilia DeMille Presley, *On My Honor* would have been directed by Henry Wilcoxon and DeMille's attention would have been devoted to *Project X*.

# Appendix D

# Film Appearances by Cecil B. DeMille

From the beginning of his career Cecil B. DeMille showed a flair for self-promotion, and having been an actor, he delighted in playing himself on-screen. What is remarkable about many of these appearances is that the director makes no effort to smooth the edges of his personality for the public. In *Hollywood Extra Girl*, for example, he is seen not only as charming, dedicated, and fatherly, but also demanding, arrogant, somewhat insensitive, and forgetful of the young extra's name. To say that DeMille bares his soul in these films would be an overstatement, but, as in his autobiography, these brief portraits demonstrate that he was willing to acknowledge his own shortcomings.

The following listing is certainly incomplete, but it gives an idea of the range of his on-screen appearances.

*Squaw Man* (1914). DeMille's only cameo appearance in one of his own films. He plays a card dealer in the saloon scenes.

*The Call of the North* (1914). DeMille appears in the main titles with his producer's credit.

*A Trip to Paramount Town* (1921). A studio promotional short. DeMille is seen on the set directing.

*Hollywood* (1923). DeMille and Jeanie Macpherson make cameo appearances.

*Arch-Conspirators on Cecil B. DeMille's Next Production* (1925). A special trailer for *The Road to Yesterday*. Jeanie Macpherson and Beulah Marie Dix present the script for *The Road to Yesterday* to DeMille. He argues with them over its length, but the writers prevail. DeMille then conjures up miniature images of the characters coming out of the pages of the script, and when one of them makes a complaint, the director (in subtitle) reminds the character: "Remember, our only aim is to entertain and amuse Mr. and Mrs. Public."

*Free and Easy* (1930). Buster Keaton's first M-G-M talkie has a movie-making theme. DeMille appears as himself in one scene.

*Hollywood on Parade No. 9* (1933).

*This Day and Age—Special Trailer* (1933). In a staged scene for this special trailer, DeMille is shown on a camera crane with his crew as if shooting a scene for the film.

*Paramount News* (various dates). Over the years DeMille appeared in a number of stories for Paramount's news reel, including:

> *DeMille in Boston for the Opening of Cleopatra* (1934). DeMille is greeted by Boston exhibitors on the occasion of the opening of Cleopatra in that city.

> *Bank Opening* (1948). Commemorating the thirty-fifth anniversary of *The Squaw Man* with a reception at a new branch of the Bank of America. Members of *The Squaw Man* cast and crew appear, as does Theda Bara.

> *Barn Dedication* (1956). The dedication of the original Lasky Studio building as a California state historical landmark. Adolph Zukor, Jesse L. Lasky, Samuel Goldwyn, Y. Frank Freeman, and Leo Carillo also appear.

*The Hollywood You Never See* (1934). A special trailer on the making of Cleopatra.

*DeMille—Penn Sunday Trailer* (1935). DeMille is seen dictating a letter, which is actually an appeal to the voters of Pennsylvania to do away with statewide "blue laws" that kept movie theaters closed on Sundays.

*Hollywood Extra Girl* (1935). A special trailer made during the production of *The Crusades*.

*DeMille Homecoming* (1937). A special film prepared by Paramount News covering DeMille's visit to the North Carolina home of his grandparents. Not generally released.

*Gretchen Comes Across* (1938). A special trailer on the discovery of Franciska Gaal, who plays the part of Gretchen in *The Buccaneer*.

*March of Time: The Movies Move On* (1939).

*Glamour Boy* (1941). DeMille makes a cameo appearance in this film.

*Star Spangled Rhythm* (1942). DeMille makes a cameo appearance in this film.

*The Story of a Great Motion Picture* (1942). Trailer for *Reap the Wild Wind.*

*DeMille War Appeal* (ca. 1943). A trailer to promote the sale of War Bonds in theaters.

*The Story of Dr. Wassell—Trailer* (1944). DeMille introduces and narrates this trailer.

*Background of a Great Adventure* (1947). Trailer for *Unconquered.*

*Variety Girl* (1947). DeMille makes a cameo appearance in this feature.

*My Favorite Brunette* (1947). DeMille makes a cameo appearance in this feature.

*Jens Månsson i Amerika* (1947). DeMille is said to make a cameo appearance in this Swedish film.

*Right to Work* (1948). A filmed record of DeMille's appearance before Congress speaking in behalf of right-to-work legislation.

*Screen Snapshots—50th Anniversary of Movies* (1949). DeMille is seen in a brief moment at the end of the film along with fellow directors Edward H. Griffith, William Seiter, A. Edward Sutherland, Sam Wood, Robert Z. Leonard, and George Marshall.

*History Brought to Life* (1950). DeMille appears in and narrates this entry in the Academy of Motion Picture Arts and Sciences film awareness series.

*Sunset Boulevard* (1950). DeMille plays himself and is seen directing scenes from *Samson and Delilah* when former star Norma Desmond (played by Gloria Swanson) pays a visit to the set.

*Screen Snapshots: The Great Director* (1951).

*The House on Any Street* (1951). DeMille appeared in this Technicolor fund-raising appeal for multiple sclerosis research. Joan Taylor, Mary Murphy, and Michael Morehouse also appeared in the film.

*Son of Paleface* (1952). A portrait photographer under a black hood takes his time lining up his camera. Star Bob Hope says, "Who does he think he is, Cecil B. DeMille?" The hood is lifted, and it turns out the photographer is indeed Cecil B. DeMille

*Screen Snapshots: Hollywood Night Life* (1952).

*The Greatest Show on Earth—Trailer* (1952).

*The Great Director* (1956). DeMille is seen directing the remake of *The Ten Commandments*.

*The Ten Commandments—Special Trailer* (1956). DeMille speaks of bringing *The Ten Commandments* to the screen.

*The Ten Commandments—Curtain Speech* (1956). DeMille appears on-screen as a prologue to the film.

*The Buster Keaton Story* (1957). DeMille makes a cameo appearance in this feature.

*The Buccaneer—Special Trailer* (1958). DeMille appears in this trailer for the remake of *The Buccaneer*.

# Notes

## Chapter 1: The Squaw Man

1. Cecil B. DeMille to George Pelton, November 10, 1913, Huntington Library, HM 50986.

2. Throughout his life Cecil used the family spelling of "deMille" in his personal life and the spelling of "DeMille" in his professional career.

3. "Ten, twent', thirt' shows" was a once-common show business term for popularly priced shows with ticket prices ranging from ten to thirty cents each.

4. DeMille to Pelton.

5. Jesse L. Lasky, with Don Weldon, *I Blow My Own Horn,* 90.

6. Ibid., 89.

7. Unsigned agreement between Jesse L. Lasky Feature Play Company and Dustin Farnum outlining terms of employment for *The Virginian,* May 4, 1914, photocopy in author's collection. Agreement states that *The Virginian* and two additional pictures "shall be produced under the same terms and conditions as those now existing between us in our production of 'The Squaw Man.' . . ."

8. While appearing on stage in Los Angeles in 1912, Farnum had visited the Universal studio and appeared in a scene for a short film.

9. Lease agreement between Cecil B. deMille for the Lasky Feature Play Company and L.L. Burns, December 22, 1913, photocopy in author's collection.

10. Bison was a brand name for films produced by the New York Motion Picture Corporation. Other N.Y.M.P.Co. brand names included Keystone, KayBee, and Domino.

11. "Lillian St. Cyr Reaches Back 22 Years in Her Memory When She Was Redwing in the First Feature Film," *New York World Telegram,* 1935 [exact date not known], copy of clipping in author's collection.

12. In early prints of *The Squaw Man* the actors received screen credit in an elaborate cut-out display. The style of the original subtitles for *The Squaw Man* can be seen in a clip used in the 1931 Paramount promotional film *The House That Shadows Built.*

13. DeMille's telegrams to Sam Goldfish during the editing of the picture include the following: "HAVE NOT BEEN TO BED FOR SIXTY HOURS AND STILL UP," and "JUST COMPLETING OUR EIGHTY-SEVENTH CONSECUTIVE HOUR OF ASSEMBLING AND CUTTING." Photocopies of this and other *Squaw Man*–related telegram drafts in author's collection.

14. Lasky, *I Blow My Own Horn,* 98.

15. The cost comes from the files of Cecil B. DeMille. Surviving correspondence

indicates the Lasky Company spent more than this, however. It must be assumed that the $15,450.25 is an accurate accounting of direct costs and that additional costs (which involved setting up the studio and other overhead charges) were shifted to later productions on a prorated basis.

16. Apparently Lasky's first visit to his Hollywood studio did not occur until after *The Squaw Man* was released. *Moving Picture World* reported that he left New York on February 24, 1914.

17. Cecil B. DeMille, interview by Art Arthur, no date, photocopy in author's collection.

18. Frank Paret to Alex E. Beyfuss, July 3, 1914, in author's collection.

19. At least one tally of DeMille's costs and grosses, dating from 1931, states that *The Squaw Man* took in only $35,000.

### Chapter 2: The Virginian

1. *The Catalogue of Copyright Entries MOTION PICTURES 1912–1939* lists *The Only Son* as "picturized by Cecil B. DeMille," though this may have merely meant that he wrote the scenario based on the Winchell Smith play.

2. Bosworth, Inc., took its name from actor-director Hobart Bosworth, who joined with Frank Garbutt and Jack London to produce films based on London's novels and stories. Although Bosworth was to receive 25 percent of the profits of Bosworth, Inc., he was never involved in the financing or business affairs of the company. Hobart Bosworth left Bosworth, Inc., in 1915 to join the Universal Film Manufacturing Company. After Bosworth's departure, Bosworth, Inc., remained a corporate entity until its merger with Famous Players-Lasky in 1916, although the later Bosworth productions were released under the brand name Pallas Pictures.

3. Famous Players controlled the distribution rights to the Bosworth pictures for the territories that included New Jersey, Pennsylvania, Delaware, Maryland, Washington D.C., Virginia, West Virginia, Ohio, Indiana, Illinois, Wisconsin, Kentucky, and Michigan.

4. Agreement between Lasky Feature Play Company and Dustin Farnum, April 2, 1914, photocopy in author's collection.

5. Interview with Art Arthur in preparation for DeMille's autobiography, ca. 1958, photocopy in author's collection.

6. Cecil B. DeMille to Sam Goldfish, July 23, 1914, photocopy in author's collection.

### Chapter 3: The Call of the North

1. Jesse L. Lasky to Cecil B. DeMille, May 26, 1914, photocopy in author's collection.

2. William C. deMille, *Hollywood Saga*, 73.

3. Cecil B. DeMille to Sam Goldfish, July 23, 1914, photocopy in author's collection.

### Chapter 4: What's-His-Name

1. George Barr McCutcheon, *What's-His-Name* (New York, 1911), as abridged and reprinted in *Photoplay Magazine*, December 1914, 82.

2. Cecil B. DeMille to Samuel Goldfish, July 23, 1914, photocopy in author's collection.

## Chapter 6: The Rose of the Rancho

1. Cecil B. DeMille, *The Autobiography of Cecil B. DeMille*, 60. Hereafter abbreviated as DeMille, *Autobiography*.

2. DeMille is exaggerating, of course. The average one-reel film of the time cost between five hundred and eight hundred dollars. Ford Sterling was a former Keystone Film Co. comic who in 1914 was making comedies under the Sterling brand for release through the Universal Film Mfg. Co.

3. Cost figures on D.W. Griffith's 1914 Reliance-Majestic production *The Avenging Conscience* indicate that Griffith spent $17,543.30 on the film, a figure comparable to what DeMille spent on *The Rose of the Rancho*, and in keeping with average feature production costs of the period.

4. The "$35,000 basis" DeMille refers to is the average $35,000 advance the Lasky Company might expect in marketing its pictures on the states rights market, and it represents the expected income from a feature release prior to percentage splits.

5. Cecil B. DeMille to Sam Goldfish, October 10, 1914, photocopy in author's collection.

6. David Belasco to Cecil B. DeMille, quoted in DeMille, *Autobiography*, 111.

7. Beatrice deMille to Cecil B. DeMille, December 2, 1914, photocopy in author's collection.

## Chapter 7: The Girl of the Golden West

1. Jesse L. Lasky to Sam Goldfish, November 4, 1914, photocopy in author's collection.

2. Fairbanks was a leading Broadway juvenile at the time of this initial contact with the movies, but nothing came of this overture. Fairbanks signed with the Triangle Film Corporation in 1915, but later joined the Famous Players-Lasky subsidiary, Artcraft Pictures, in 1917. Wallace Eddinger took the lead in Lasky's *A Gentleman of Leisure*, directed by George Melford and released March 1, 1915.

3. Blanche Sweet was an actress with D.W. Griffith's Reliance-Majestic stock company at the time. According to Lillian Gish in *The Movies, Mr. Griffith, and Me* (181) and several interviews given by Blanche Sweet herself, the actress was offered $500 a week by Lasky. A year later, Sweet's price had increased considerably. In a November 2, 1915, letter to Sam Goldfish, Jesse Lasky wrote:

> As I wired you, we signed Blanche Sweet for one year at $750. She refused to give us an option even when I offered to take an option on $1,000 a week. It would take volumes to tell you of the negotiations and, I assure you, I never tried harder to close a deal than I did in the Sweet case. But I never expected to pay $750. However, I assure you it is a very wise move. I have studied all the reports of the exhibitors received through the Paramount exchanges, and there can be no doubt that she is a valuable star. I am assured that she was offered a thousand dollars by other firms and it was those offers which made it so difficult for me.

The original of this letter was uncatalogued when I read it in the Cecil B. DeMille Collection at BYU.

### Chapter 8: The Warrens of Virginia

1. William C. deMille to Cecil B. DeMille, September 17, 1914, photocopy in author's collection.

### Chapter 9: The Unafraid

1. Purchase agreement between Cecil B. DeMille and Harry Revier, February 21, 1914, and lease agreement between Stern Realty Company and Cecil B. DeMille, February 28, 1914, copies in author's collection.

### Chapter 10: The Captive

1. If this incident did occur, it probably did so during the time DeMille was using the Universal ranch for some *Squaw Man* exteriors.

2. [Barrett C. Kiesling], manuscript of DeMille Pictures studio biography of Jeanie Macpherson, ca. 1927, original in author's collection.

3. For more detailed accounts of the shooting incident, see DeMille, *Autobiography*, 127–28, and William M. Drew, *Speaking of Silents*, 226–27.

### Chapter 11: The Wild Goose Chase

1. Robert Cushman, photo curator of the Academy of Motion Picture Arts and Sciences Margaret Herrick Library, reviewed this manuscript and noted, "I met Ina Claire once and asked her about *The Wild Goose Chase*. She instantly remembered it and said she took the job 'between theatrical engagements.'"

2. The letter of agreement between Famous Players-Lasky and DeMille, listing the titles and the terms of transfer, were examined by the author in the files of the Cecil B. DeMille estate in the 1980s.

3. Although DeMille refers to sixty feet per minute, or sixteen frames per second, Kevin Brownlow has noted that during this period Alvin Wyckoff was cranking his camera at something more like twenty or twenty-one frames per second, or seventy-five feet per minute.

4. *Journal of the Screen Producers Guild* 4, no. 1 (February 1956): 6. However, according to the late James Card of the George Eastman House in Rochester, New York, DeMille rejected the idea of donating his film prints and making them available for study when he was first approached by Card in the late 1950s. The family deposited most of his personal prints of his silent films at Eastman House after DeMille's death.

### Chapter 15: Maria Rosa

1. "Geraldine Farrar—Her Interesting Experience," *Paramount Progress*, July 1915.

2. Morris Gest, "Winning Farrar," *Photoplay* 8, no. 2 (July 1915): 115–17.

3. Emma Calvé was *Carmen* in the minds of most opera fans until Geraldine Farrar's triumph in the role at the Metropolitan Opera during the 1914–15 season.

4. In his article for *Photoplay* Gest quotes Jesse Lasky on the terms of the con-

tract: "You can tell her that for every minute of daylight she is in Southern California, whether she is at the studio or not, I will pay her two dollars—and a royalty, and a share of all profits." William C. deMille recalled that Farrar was to be paid twenty thousand dollars for eight weeks' work and be provided with a house and servants for the duration of her stay. Whatever the terms of the final contract, the titles of the first three films note that Geraldine Farrar appears "By arrangement with Morris Gest."

5. Robert Jameison, "Maria Rosa—The Photoplay That Made Geraldine Farrar a Bride," *Picture Progress*, April 1916, 2–3.

## Chapter 16: Carmen

1. William C. deMille, *Hollywood Saga*, 154–55.

2. Ibid. Lydia E. Pinkham's Vegetable Compound, a patent medicine designed to cure "Prolapsus Uteri or falling of the womb and other female weaknesses," contained "18 per cent of alcohol . . . added solely as a solvent and preservative."

3. Geraldine Farrar, *Such Sweet Compulsion*, 170.

4. DeMille, *Autobiography*, 142; and Farrar, *Such Sweet Compulsion*, 169.

5. Sam Goldfish to Cecil B. DeMille, September 29, 1915, photocopy in author's collection. Although the libretto for the Bizet opera was under copyright, the use of the music was not precluded according to William deMille.

6. Jesse L. Lasky to Samuel Goldfish, November 2, 1915, Cecil B. DeMille Collection. Uncatalogued at time of review by author.

7. Fox's *Carmen* cost $32,269 and had a worldwide gross of $106,086.

## Chapter 17: Temptation

1. Cecil B. DeMille to Sam Goldfish, October 28, 1915, photocopy in author's collection.

2. Cecil B. DeMille to Jesse L. Lasky, ca. 1917, quoted in DeMille, *Autobiography*, 212.

## Chapter 18: Chimmie Fadden Out West

1. Jesse L. Lasky to Cecil B. DeMille, November 30, 1915, photocopy in author's collection. Tally's Broadway Theater was a deluxe first-run house in downtown Los Angeles.

## Chapter 19: The Cheat

1. Maurice Bardeche and Robert Brasillach, *The History of Motion Pictures*, 106.

2. Jeanie Macpherson received no credit on *Temptation*; the only record of her involvement comes from DeMille's own personal filmography that his secretary kept for reference. Macpherson does receive screen credit on *The Cheat*.

3. The spoiled Flora Lee Peake in *The Golden Bed* (1925) bears some relation to Edith Hardy in *The Cheat*, and *Unconquered* (1947) contains an element of white slavery.

4. DeMille outtake reel, Cecil B. DeMille estate. Currently on deposit at UCLA Film and Television Archive.

## Chapter 20: The Golden Chance

1. Jesse L. Lasky, with Don Weldon, *I Blow My Own Horn*, 113–14.
2. Jesse L. Lasky to Samuel Goldfish, November 2, 1915, Cecil B. DeMille Collection. Uncatalogued at time of review by author.

## Chapter 21: The Trail of the Lonesome Pine

1. Frank Paret to Alex E. Beyfuss, May 15, 1914, in author's collection.
2. Frank Paret to Alex E. Beyfuss, June 22, 1914, in author's collection.
3. For a fuller account of DeMille's relationship with Macpherson, see Charles Higham, *Cecil B. DeMille*.

## Chapter 22: The Heart of Nora Flynn

1. "American foreground" refers to the prevailing American style of the early 1910s in which the frame "cut" the actors at the knee or above, as opposed to "French foreground," which kept the actors in frame from head to toe.

## Chapter 23: The Dream Girl

1. Frank A. Garbutt to Jack London, November 3, 1914, in the Jack London Collection at the Huntington Library, file number JL 6531.
2. Telegram from Jesse L. Lasky to Cecil B. DeMille, June 24, 1916, photocopy in author's collection.
3. Telegram from Cecil B. DeMille to Jesse L. Lasky, June 24, 1916, photocopy in author's collection.
4. Telegram from Jesse L. Lasky to Cecil B. DeMille, June 29, 1916, photocopy in author's collection.
5. Will Irwin, *The House That Shadows Built*, 220.
6. Telegram from Jesse L. Lasky to Cecil B. DeMille, August 21, 1916, photocopy in author's collection.
7. Goldfish resigned from Famous Players-Lasky on September 3, 1916.
8. Garbutt bought a printing press for his son, Frank E. Garbutt, but the boy showed no interest in following in his footsteps. His daughter, Melodile, took over the press and built a part-time basement business into a major job-printing company. Her involvement in Garbutt's motion picture interests was real, although she confined her participation almost entirely to business affairs. She remained with Famous Players-Lasky until 1921 as head of studio accounting.
9. "Synopsis of Mr. Garbutt's Transactions in the Film Business for Mr. Baker," in the collection of Frank G. Hathaway.
10. A. Scott Berg, *Goldwyn*, 62–64.

## Chapter 24: Joan the Woman

1. Road shows were exclusive long-term engagements in selected theaters in big cities, usually not more than one theater per city, with two screenings per day at advanced ticket prices. Road-show attractions usually approached three hours in running time and were screened with an intermission. Such engagements preceded, and were separate from, the general release of a film.

2. Clemens's work was published under the dual pseudonym "The Sieur Louis De Conte . . . freely translated . . . by Jean François Alden."

3. Cecil B. DeMille to Jesse Lasky, July 1916, as quoted in DeMille, *Autobiography*, 172–73.

4. Night letter from DeMille to Jesse L. Lasky, October 17, 1916, photocopy in author's collection.

5. Telegram from Jesse L. Lasky to Cecil B. DeMille, October 18, 1916, photocopy in author's collection. At this time, Mary Pickford's films were being made on the East Coast.

6. Telegram from Jesse L. Lasky to Cecil B. DeMille, September 6, 1916, photocopy in author's collection. Griffith's *Intolerance* told four stories each set in a different place and time—Ancient Babylon, Judea in the time of Christ, France during the St. Bartholomew's Day Massacre, and contemporary America. The stories are related thematically and are told simultaneously, rather than consecutively, by cutting from one to another at critical moments in an ever-increasing tempo.

7. Night letter from Jesse L. Lasky to Cecil B. DeMille, October 17, 1916, photocopy in author's collection.

8. Night letter from Cecil B. DeMille to Jesse L. Lasky, October 17, 1916, photocopy in author's collection. James Young was the former husband of film star Clara Kimball Young. Although he continued to direct for another dozen years after his dismissal from the Lasky Company, many of his pictures were low-budget, independent efforts. His biggest projects in the 1920s were *Omar the Tentmaker* (1922) and *Trilby* (1923). He also directed Theda Bara's comeback, *The Unchastened Woman* (1925), and *The Bells* (1926), starring Lionel Barrymore and Boris Karloff at a time when Barrymore was considered a has-been and Karloff was yet to be discovered by the American public.

9. Telegram from Jesse L. Lasky to Cecil B. DeMille, November 2, 1916, photocopy in author's collection.

10. Night letter from Cecil B. DeMille to Jesse L. Lasky, November 3, 1916, photocopy in author's collection.

11. Telegram from Jesse L. Lasky to Cecil B. DeMille, November 2, 1916, photocopy in author's collection.

12. Night letter from Cecil B. DeMille to Jesse L. Lasky, November 3, 1916, photocopy in author's collection.

13. Telegram from Jesse L. Lasky to Cecil B. DeMille, March 13, 1917, photocopy in author's collection.

14. Telegram from Cecil B. DeMille to Jesse L. Lasky, January 5, 1917, photocopy in author's collection.

15. Merritt, an expert on the work of D.W. Griffith, compiled the record of these engagements from contemporary newspaper ads and generously shared them. The final production cost of *Intolerance* was nearly four hundred thousand dollars and that figure inflated to over half a million when the distribution costs were added. The expenditure was astronomical for the time, but a far cry from the two million dollars widely reported spent on the picture. No final gross figures are available for *Intolerance*, but contemporary reports on its first release suggest that the picture did as well or better than *The Birth of a Nation* for the first six months of its run before business

slacked off precipitously. It is highly doubtful that *Intolerance* was the monumental failure that many historians have assumed.

16. Jesse L. Lasky to Cecil B. DeMille, March 13, 1917, photocopy in author's collection.

17. "Negative cost" is the direct cost of producing a film's finished negative exclusive of the costs for prints and advertising.

### Chapter 25: A Romance of the Redwoods

1. Triangle offered a program consisting of a five-reel Ince-KayBee feature, a five-reel Griffith-supervised Fine Arts feature, and a two-reel Mack Sennett Keystone comedy, refusing to let exhibitors break up the packages. The company also insisted that theaters booking the Triangle program charge a $2.00 top admission fee.

2. The picture Pickford completed before her two pictures with DeMille, *The Poor Little Rich Girl*, was released on March 5, 1917, just days before *A Romance of the Redwoods* was completed, and was a huge box-office hit.

3. Pickford eventually made *Rebecca of Sunnybrook Farm* later in 1917 with director Marshall Neilan.

### Chapter 26: The Little American

1. Cecil B. DeMille, "Photodrama a New Art," *Moving Picture World*, July 21, 1917, 374.

2. Wilfred Buckland, "The Scenic Side of the Photodrama," *Moving Picture World*, July 21, 1917, 374.

3. After U.S. entry into the war, anti-German hysteria was such that film star Margarita Fischer felt compelled to change her name to Fisher, and character actor Gustav von Seyffertitz took the Anglicized moniker of G. Butler Clonbough for the duration. Sauerkraut became known as "Liberty Cabbage" and on the East Coast the Kaiser roll was dubbed the "Hard Roll." To this day Kaisers are called hard rolls in New York—strange because the German monarchy is long gone and the rolls are relatively soft and bread-like in texture.

### Chapter 27: The Woman God Forgot

1. Telegram from Jesse L. Lasky to Cecil B. DeMille, March 10, 1917, photocopy in author's collection.

2. Night letter from Cecil B. DeMille to Jesse L. Lasky, March 12, 1917, photocopy in author's collection.

3. Telegram from Jesse L. Lasky to Cecil B. DeMille, March 13, 1917.

4. DeMille took his company to Yosemite for this scene.

### Chapter 28: The Devil Stone

1. Tully Marshall played similar roles in Stroheim's *The Merry Widow* (M-G-M, 1925) and *Queen Kelly* (Swanson-United Artists, not released in the United States). Stroheim's first film as a director, *Blind Husbands*, was made in 1918, after the release of *The Devil Stone*.

2. Geraldine Farrar, *Such Sweet Compulsion*, 179.

### Chapter 29: The Whispering Chorus

1. DeMille, *Autobiography*, 192.
2. Unidentified magazine clipping.
3. Draft of telegram, Cecil B. DeMille to Jesse L. Lasky, April 18, 1918, photocopy in author's collection. Maurice Tourneur's production of *The Blue Bird* was released by Artcraft on March 25, 1918.

### Chapter 30: Old Wives for New

1. Memo from Carl H. Pierce, quoted in DeMille, *Autobiography*, 212.
2. Letters from Jesse Lasky to Cecil B. DeMille, quoted in DeMille, *Autobiography*, 212.
3. *Motion Picture News* 17, no. 24 (June 15, 1918): 3579.

### Chapter 31: We Can't Have Everything

1. *Moving Picture World*, June 29, 1918, 1867.

### Chapter 32: Till I Come Back to You

1. The 1933 Warner Bros. film *Ever in My Heart* is a fascinating study of the indignities many German Americans experienced in the Great War and offers a sense of the era. Written by Beulah Marie Dix and Bertram Millhauser, *Ever in My Heart* ultimately veers off into improbable melodrama, but the anti-German harassment suffered by Otto Kruger has the ring of truth about it.
2. Herbert Hoover was director-general of the American Relief Administration—hence the word "Hooverize."
3. For the record, Arthur Allardt's career as an actor evaporated in the 1920s. His last credited appearance was in *A Man's Man* (F.B.O., 1923)—although this was a reissue of a 1917 film. Seyffertitz resumed his name after the war and worked in pictures nearly until his death in 1940.
4. Kevin Brownlow, *The Parade's Gone By*, 227.
5. Night lettergram from Cecil B. DeMille to Jesse L. Lasky, July 11, 1918, photocopy in author's collection.

### Chapter 33: The Squaw Man (first remake)

1. Telegram from Jesse L. Lasky to Cecil B. DeMille, June 24, 1918, photocopy in author's collection.
2. Telegram from Jesse L. Lasky to Cecil B. DeMille, July 10, 1918, photocopy in author's collection. William Faversham was fifty-one years old in 1918.
3. Night lettergram from Cecil B. DeMille to Jesse L. Lasky, July 11, 1918, photocopy in author's collection.
4. Telegram from Cecil B. DeMille to Jesse L. Lasky, July 27, 1918, photocopy in author's collection. Although William Faversham was not used in *The Squaw Man*, he did make *The Silver King* (released January 12, 1919) for Famous Players-Lasky.

### Chapter 34: Don't Change Your Husband

1. Gloria Swanson, *Swanson on Swanson*. An educated guess would suggest that

DeMille wanted Swanson in the *Old Wives for New* role eventually played by Florence Vidor.

2. Presumably DeMille also wanted Swanson for *Till I Come Back to You*.

3. According to Swanson she replaced another actress on *Don't Change Your Husband*, although the film was in preproduction, not mid-production as she remembered in her autobiography.

4. Swanson, *Swanson on Swanson*.

5. Ibid., 100–101.

6. The practice of preproduction script readings may have begun with *Male and Female*. Swanson does not mention such a session being held before *For Better, For Worse*, but she does make a point of describing the group script session for *Male and Female*, her third DeMille picture.

7. S. Harrison, *Motion Picture News*, February 8, 1919, 921; and *Variety*, February 7, 1919, 61.

## Chapter 35: For Better, For Worse

1. Gloria Swanson, *Swanson on Swanson*, 107.

2. The term "slacker" once meant someone who wore slacks. Today "slacks" are synonymous with "pants" or "trousers," but strictly speaking slacks are worn without puttees—which were part of American military uniforms in 1918. Hence a slacker was one who did not wear puttees, or was not in uniform.

3. The scene has an interesting parallel to DeMille's own life. In the early 1920s he and Constance adopted Katherine Lester, whose father was killed in the war and whose mother died of tuberculosis. As Katherine DeMille she pursued a career as an actress in the 1930s and was married to Anthony Quinn.

4. Telegram from Jesse L. Lasky to Cecil B. DeMille, January 22, 1919, photocopy in author's collection.

5. Telegram from Cecil B. DeMille to Jesse L. Lasky, January 23, 1919, photocopy in author's collection.

6. Cecil B. DeMille in interview with Art Arthur in preparation for his autobiography, ca. 1958, photocopy in author's collection.

7. Telegram from Cecil B. DeMille to Jesse L. Lasky, February 4, 1919, photocopy in author's collection.

## Chapter 36: Male and Female

1. Night lettergram from Jesse L. Lasky to Cecil B. DeMille, December 19, 1917, photocopy in author's collection.

2. Although Adolph Zukor lost Pickford, Fairbanks, and Griffith to United Artists, he maintained some business relationships with them—especially with D.W. Griffith. Zukor contracted with Griffith for a series of Dorothy Gish features to be released through Paramount well after the formation of United Artists. One of the terms of the contract was that Griffith's name would not appear in any way in connection with the films.

3. Telegram from Jesse L. Lasky to Cecil B. DeMille, April 29, 1919, photocopy in author's collection.

4. Telegram from Cecil B. DeMille to Jesse L. Lasky, April 30, 1919, photocopy

in author's collection. Glass-covered stages were common in the East from at least 1910. As improved lighting instruments and panchromatic film became available in the later 1920s most glass stages were painted over to block out the sun. With the coming of sound, glass stages became obsolete. Production began at the Astoria studio in September 1920.

5. William Ernest Henley was a remarkable man. As a child he contracted tuberculosis of the bone and had a foot amputated. While in the hospital he wrote poetry that came to the attention of Robert Louis Stevenson. In later years, Henley became editor of such publications as *London*, the *Magazine of Art,* and the *National Observer*. He also co-authored *Slang and Its Analogues* (1890–1904), one of the earliest dictionaries of British and American slang. He is best remembered for his poem "Invictus":

> It matters not how strait the gate,
> How charged with punishments the scroll,
> I am the master of my fate:
> I am the captain of my soul.

6. See Kevin Brownlow, *Hollywood: The Pioneers*, 171.

7. Jesse Lasky's January 22, 1919, telegram to DeMille read: "Have closed for Admiral Crichton" (photocopy in author's collection).

8. Telegram from Cecil B. DeMille to Jesse L. Lasky, May 14, 1919, photocopy in author's collection.

## Chapter 37: Why Change Your Wife?

1. Telegram from Jesse L. Lasky to Cecil B. DeMille, April 29, 1919, photocopy in author's collection. *Susan Lenox* was finally brought to the screen by Metro-Goldwyn-Mayer in 1931 as a vehicle for Greta Garbo.

2. Telegram from Jesse L. Lasky to Cecil B. DeMille, May 9, 1919, photocopy in author's collection.

3. Telegram from Cecil B. DeMille to Jesse L. Lasky, May 12, 1919, photocopy in author's collection.

4. Telegram from Jesse L. Lasky to Cecil B. DeMille, April 29, 1919, photocopy in author's collection.

5. Telegram from Cecil B. DeMille to Jesse L. Lasky, April 30, 1919, photocopy in author's collection. DeMille's declaration that: "I could take the high spots from half the great Biblical stories of the world such as great chariot race and other smashing incidents of the kind," in which he refers to one of the highpoints of *Ben-Hur*, might seem like blatant plagiarism today, but DeMille and his screenwriters followed the nineteenth-century theater tradition of constructing plays from elements already familiar to the audience. For a discussion of the manner in which Henry C. deMille and David Belasco constructed their plays see: Robert Hamilton Ball, ed., *The Plays of Henry C. DeMille Written in Collaboration with David Belasco,* ix–xxv.

6. Telegram from Cecil B. DeMille to Jesse L. Lasky, May 12, 1919, photocopy in author's collection.

7. Telegram from Jesse L. Lasky to Cecil B. DeMille, May 14, 1919, photocopy

in author's collection. George Melford eventually directed *Everywoman*; Theodore Kosloff did not appear in the film; and Irving Cummings played the role of Passion.

8. Telegram from Cecil B. DeMille to Jesse L. Lasky, May 14, 1919, photocopy in author's collection.

9. Telegram from Jesse L. Lasky to Cecil B. DeMille, May 23, 1919, photocopy in author's collection. Milton Sills was a solid leading man in the manner of Elliott Dexter. He was eventually signed by Famous Players-Lasky for *The Faith Healer* (1921), but he was largely a freelance actor throughout the early 1920s. His only work with DeMille was in *Adam's Rib* (1923). Moving to First National in the mid-1920s, Sills became a top star. He created a strong impression in his first sound films, especially in *The Sea Wolf* (Fox, 1930), but died of a heart attack in 1930 at the age of forty-eight.

10. Telegram from Cecil B. DeMille to Jesse L. Lasky, August 30, 1919, photocopy in author's collection.

## Chapter 38: Something to Think About

1. Telegram from Jesse L. Lasky to Cecil B. DeMille, October 1, 1919, photocopy in author's collection.

2. In 1920 Irvin Willat Productions produced *Dabney Todd* as *Down Home*, which bears striking similarities to the DeMille picture. Both *Down Home* and *Something to Think About* were in production about the same time; so it is unlikely that either director saw the other's work before their films were released. Interestingly, *Down Home* features Leatrice Joy, who later became a DeMille star.

3. *The Wanderer* was eventually produced by Famous Players-Lasky in 1925. It was directed by Raoul Walsh and released through Paramount in February 1926.

4. DeMille, *Autobiography*, 230.

## Chapter 39: Forbidden Fruit

1. The Volstead Act, passed over the veto of Woodrow Wilson in October 1919, provided the legal framework for enforcing the Prohibition amendment.

2. *Motion Picture News*, January 22, 1921, 902.

## Chapter 40: The Affairs of Anatol

1. Charles Higham, *Cecil B. DeMille*, 84.

2. Buckland had directed several plays in New York before coming to Hollywood, and directed at least part of the 1914 Lasky Feature Play production *The Man on the Box*.

3. For a moving account of Wilfred Buckland's final years, see Jesse L. Lasky Jr., *Whatever Happened To Hollywood?*

4. David Chierichetti, *Hollywood Director—The Career of Mitchell Leisen*, 28.

5. The DVD release of *The Affairs of Anatol* distributed by Image Entertainment preserves the Handscheigl stencil color effects.

## Chapter 41: Fool's Paradise

1. In *Vertigo*, a man remakes a woman in the image of a lost love, only to find later that she is in fact the woman he presumed dead.

2. For a loving account of life in early Hollywood, see Evelyn F. Scott, *Hollywood—When Silents Were Golden*. Scott was the daughter of Beulah Marie Dix.

3. David Chierichetti, *Hollywood Director—The Career of Mitchell Leisen*, 28.

4. Telegram from Jesse L. Lasky to Cecil B. DeMille, May 27, 1921, photocopy in author's collection. While production at the Long Island studio of Famous Players-Lasky never reached initial expectations, the facility was not shut down until 1932, when another depression took its toll.

5. Cecil B. DeMille to Jesse L. Lasky, ca. 1921, quoted in DeMille, *Autobiography*, 229.

6. DeMille, *Autobiography*, 229, 264.

## Chapter 42: Saturday Night

1. David Chierichetti, *Hollywood Director—The Career of Mitchell Leisen*, 28.

2. Leatrice Gilbert Fountain, *Dark Star*, 76–80. According to Fountain, her parents' marriage was on-again, off-again, and DeMille insisted that Leatrice Joy remain apart from her husband during shooting.

## Chapter 43: Manslaughter

1. Charles Higham, *Cecil B. DeMille*, 91.

2. Evelyn F. Scott, *Hollywood—When Silents Were Golden*, 70.

3. DeMille was among the first filmmakers to give on-screen technical credits in 1914. However, technical credits are nowhere in evidence on surviving prints of *Saturday Night*, *Manslaughter*, or *Adam's Rib*. Credits are derived from Cecil B. DeMille's personal filmography maintained by his staff.

## Chapter 44: Adam's Rib

1. The absentminded professor surrounded by dinosaur bones played by Elliott Dexter in *Adam's Rib* bears a striking resemblance to the character played by Cary Grant in Howard Hawks's *Bringing Up Baby* (RKO-Radio Pictures, 1938). Howard Hawks began his career as a propman with DeMille's unit at Famous Players-Lasky in 1919 and continued to work with DeMille intermittently and in various capacities through the mid-1920s. DeMille also borrowed from Hawks in later years, using Walter Brennan as a folksy sidekick to Andrew Jackson in *The Buccaneer* (Paramount, 1938) after Hawks established Brennan's screen persona in *Barbary Coast* (Goldwyn-United Artists, 1935) and *Come and Get It* (Goldwyn-United Artists, 1936).

## Chapter 45: The Ten Commandments

1. Jesse L. Lasky, with Don Weldon, *I Blow My Own Horn*, 161–64.

2. Ibid.

3. DeMille, *Autobiography*, 1959, 249. Seven others also suggested stories based on the Ten Commandments. None of the eight suggestions offered a usable story, but each received one thousand dollars for their suggestions.

4. Ibid., 250.

5. Jeanie Macpherson, "How the Story Was Evolved," in the souvenir program for the original release of *The Ten Commandments*, 1923.

6. Cecil B. DeMille, *Autobiography,* 250.

7. Jeanie Macpherson, treatment for *The Ten Commandments*. Paramount Story Files, Margaret Herrick Library, Academy of Motion Picture Arts and Sciences, Beverly Hills, California.

8. Ibid.

9. Jeanie Macpherson, *The Ten Commandments*, screenplay. Paramount story files.

10. Hallett Abend, in *Los Angeles Times*, quoted by Charles Higham, *Cecil B. DeMille,* 118.

11. Telegram from Jesse L. Lasky to Adolph Zukor, July 5, 1923, photocopy in author's collection.

12. In addition to his filmmaking activities, DeMille was also a vice president of the Cherokee Avenue branch of Giannini's Bank of Italy in Hollywood at this time.

13. Cecil B. DeMille, *Autobiography*, 258.

14. Irvin Willat, interview by author for Louis B. Mayer Foundation–AFI Oral History project, June 9, 1971.

15. Curtis was known for his work in recording the lives of American Indian tribes. His 1914 feature-length film, *In the Land of the Headhunters* (Seattle Film Co.-World, 1914), documented vanishing tribal life in the Pacific Northwest. For more on Curtis, see Kevin Brownlow, *The War, the West, and the Wilderness*, 338–44.

16. Technicolor perfected its imbibition process in 1928. In "I.B." prints the two-color dyes were transferred to a single strip of film in two successive printing passes, much as in color lithography. Technicolor introduced a full-spectrum three-color process in 1932.

17. Although the version of *The Ten Commandments* released by Paramount Home Video does not preserve the original tints and tones of the rest of film, it does offer an opportunity to view the color footage. An example of the Handschiegl Process can also be seen in the video release in the bright orange wall of fire that halts the Pharaoh's charioteers.

18. Macpherson, "How the Story Was Evolved."

19. Night letter from Jesse L. Lasky to Adolph Zukor, October 5, 1923. Hugo Riesenfeld's New York premiere score for *The Ten Commandments* has recently been revived by musicologist Gillian Anderson. It is a powerful compiled score and does much to enhance the drama. Interestingly, Riesenfeld treats the opening scenes of the modern story in a very lighthearted manner, softening the sting of some of the heavy-handed dialogue titles, and creating a tone for the film that is very much in keeping with Jeanie Macpherson's written ideas about her intentions.

20. James R. Quirk, review in *Photoplay Magazine*, February 1924.

21. The three-week delay in the New York premiere is an indication that Paramount did not give *The Ten Commandments* its full support. Before television and radio promotion, and to some extent even today, an early New York opening was deemed essential for national media exposure.

22. Jeanie Macpherson, treatment for *The Ten Commandments*, 11.

23. From the description, the eliminated scene in *The Ten Commandments* resembles the final shot in DeMille's *King of Kings* (1927).

## Chapter 46: Triumph

1. Telegram from Jesse L. Lasky to Cecil B. DeMille, quoted in DeMille, *Autobiography*, 247.

## Chapter 47: Feet of Clay

1. Telegram from Jesse L. Lasky to Cecil B. DeMille, March 7, 1924, quoted in Charles Higham, *Cecil B. DeMille*, 130.

2. Ibid., 129–36.

3. A clip from *Feet of Clay* does survive in *The World's Greatest Showman*, a television tribute to DeMille produced by Henry Wilcoxon.

4. *Outward Bound* was eventually brought to the screen by Warner Bros. in 1930.

5. According to Evelyn Scott, daughter of Beulah Marie Dix, her mother was annoyed that Sutton Vane filed suit as she had not filed suit over what she perceived to be Vane's lifting of material she had created for *The Road to Yesterday* and *Across the Border*.

6. Adolph Zukor's business relationship with D.W. Griffith is fascinating. In addition to the six Griffith-directed Artcraft films of 1918–19, Zukor also financed a series of Dorothy Gish films produced anonymously by Griffith. Zukor was involved in financing *Broken Blossoms* (1919), eventually released by United Artists, and also put money into Griffith's *Isn't Life Wonderful?* (United Artists, 1924) and *Sally of the Sawdust* (United Artists, 1925), which was produced by Paramount and distributed by United Artists to settle a contract dispute.

## Chapter 48: The Golden Bed

1. DeMille, *Autobiography*, 263.

2. Telegram from Sidney R. Kent to Cecil B. DeMille, December 18, 1924, quoted in DeMille, *Autobiography*, 264.

3. D.W. Griffith made *The Sorrows of Satan* (Famous Players-Lasky, 1925) after DeMille was fired by the studio.

4. DeMille, *Autobiography*, 269.

5. Fred Datig Jr. to author, 2002. These were common references to Zukor around the studio in Hollywood according to Fred Datig Jr., son of Paramount casting director Fred Datig, who served in that capacity from 1925 to 1937 before taking the same position for M-G-M.

6. DeMille, *Autobiography*, 265.

## Chapter 49: The Road to Yesterday

1. Contrary to popular myth, Ince was not shot or stabbed by William Randolph Hearst or Marion Davies or Charlie Chaplin or anybody else. He died at home in his bed. Quoting DeMille's telegram to Adolph Zukor of November 19, 1924: "TOM INCE DIED OF HEART FAILURE AT FIVE THIRTY THIS MORNING" (photocopy in author's collection).

2. Hattie the hairdresser was a black woman. Unfortunately I have not found a record of her last name.

3. Cecil B. DeMille to Jesse L. Lasky, February 1, 1925, box 260, Cecil B. DeMille Collection, BYU.

4. Jesse L. Lasky to Cecil B. DeMille, February 4, 1925, box 260, BYU.

5. Research librarian Elizabeth (Bessie) McGaffey did join the staff of DeMille Pictures sometime later and conducted research for *The Godless Girl* in 1927.

6. Copy of telegram from Jesse L. Lasky to Victor H. Clarke, March 18, 1925, box 260, BYU.

7. Copy of telegram from Jesse L. Lasky to Cecil B. DeMille, March 26, 1925, box 260, BYU.

8. Compiled from telegrams by Cecil B. DeMille to Oscar M. Bate, April 2, 1925, and to Jesse L. Lasky, March 26, 1925, Boxes 261 and 260, BYU.

9. Telegram from Cecil B. DeMille to Jesse L. Lasky, March 26, 1925, box 260, BYU. *Sackcloth and Scarlet* (Kagor Productions, 1925) was the picture DeMille arranged to finance. It was later picked up for distribution through Paramount.

10. Cecil B. DeMille to Nathan Burkan, draft of telegram, April 3, 1925, box 261, BYU.

11. Telegram from Producers Distributing Corporation attorney Nathan Burkan to Cecil B. DeMille, April 4, 1925, box 260, BYU.

12. Telegram from Nathan Burkan to Cecil B. DeMille, April 8, 1925, box 261, BYU. It is difficult to understand how Burkan could have come to this conclusion. Daniels's existing agreement with Famous Players-Lasky was set to expire on June 30, 1925, according to contract summaries DeMille kept in his files. Nevertheless, Burkan's opinion effectively ended DeMille's efforts to sign Bebe Daniels.

13. Memo to Cecil B. DeMille, 1925, box 260, BYU.

14. Telegram from Nathan Burkan to Cecil B. DeMille, April 3, 1925, box 261, BYU.

15. Telegram from Cecil B. DeMille to Nathan Burkan, April 4, 1925, box 261, BYU.

16. Frederick C. Munroe to Cecil B. DeMille, June 22, 1925, box 260, BYU.

17. Copy of letter from Cecil B. DeMille to Jesse L. Lasky, March 12, 1925, box 260, BYU.

18. Metropolitan Studios was established at the former Hollywood Studio at 1040 North Las Palmas Avenue in Hollywood. The overhead resulting from operating a second studio contributed to the precarious finances of P.D.C.

19. Cecil B. DeMille to [?], 1925, box 260, BYU.

20. Cecil B. DeMille to Frederick C. Munroe, June 29, 1925, box 260, BYU.

21. Telegram from Jesse L. Lasky to Cecil B. DeMille, June 16, 1925, box 260, BYU. Roberts would appear in only a handful of features and one or two shorts before his death in 1928 at age sixty-seven.

22. Draft of telegram from Cecil B. DeMille to Nathan Burkan, July 3, 1925, box 261, BYU.

23. DeMille, *Autobiography*, 259–70.

24. It could be argued, however, that the modern day prologue added to *The Sign of the Cross* for its 1944 reissue cast the original film as an historic flashback.

## Chapter 50: The Volga Boatman

1. Telegram from Cecil B. DeMille to Ella K. Adams, November 7, 1925, box 260, BYU.

2. Telegram from F.C. Munroe to Cecil B. DeMille, October 31, 1925, box 260, BYU.

3. Leonard Maltin, *The Art of the Cinematographer*, 66.

4. Cecilia DeMille Presley (DeMille's granddaughter), interview with author, 2002.

5. Telegram from Cecil B. DeMille to F.C. Munroe, December 7, 1925, box 260, BYU.

6. Telegram from F.C. Munroe to Cecil B. DeMille, December 11, 1925, box 260, BYU.

7. Telegram from Cecil B. DeMille to F.C. Munroe, December 12, 1925, box 260, BYU.

8. Telegram from Cecil B. DeMille to F.C. Munroe, December 15, 1925, box 260, BYU.

9. Telegram from Cecil B. DeMille to F.C. Munroe, December 17, 1925, box 260, BYU.

10. Telegram from F.C. Munroe to Cecil B. DeMille, December 18, 1925, box 260, BYU.

## Chapter 51: The King of Kings

1. See appendix A, p. 365, for costs and grosses on the DeMille Pictures, Inc., releases.

2. Denison Clift wrote the scenario for *The Yankee Clipper* (DeMille Pictures-P.D.C., 1927), which was a spectacular box-office flop.

3. Memo from Denison Clift to Cecil B. DeMille, box 261, BYU.

4. Telegram from Cecil B. DeMille to F.C. Munroe, August 5, 1926, box 260, BYU.

5. Undated document listing costs and grosses found at DeMille estate in 1986, photocopy in author's collection.

6. Daniel A. Lord, S.J., *Played by Ear*, 268.

7. Ibid., 268.

8. Bruce Barton was author of a then-popular book about Jesus called *The Man Nobody Knows*.

9. [Cecil B. DeMille] to various, 1926, box 282, BYU. The surviving carbon or draft of this letter does not have a signature.

10. Transcript of script reading and discussion for *The King of Kings*, August 23, 1926, box 282, BYU.

11. Transcript of Cecil B. DeMille's remarks to his cast, August 31, 1926, box 282, BYU.

12. Various memos from Cecil B. DeMille, August 17 and September 7, 1926, and June 23, 1927, box 262, BYU.

13. Lord, *Played by Ear*, 268–69.

14. Ibid., 271–72.

15. Ibid., 272.

16. Barrett Kiesling to Will H. Hays, December 17, 1926, box 282, BYU. According to Daniel A. Lord, Dorothy Cumming obtained a divorce during the early distribution of *The King of Kings* and was effectively blacklisted in Hollywood as a result.

17. W.G. Crothers to Cecil B. DeMille, March 9, 1927, box 282, BYU.

18. Text of DeMille's radio address, box 282, BYU.

## Chapter 52: The Godless Girl

1. The play was also the basis for the 1942 film *Roxie Hart* and the 1975 Broadway musical *Chicago* and its 2002 film adaptation.

2. Among books referred to by Jeanie Macpherson in doing research for *The Godless Girl*, according to records in the DeMille files, were *Reformatory Reform* by Isaac G. Briggs, *The Child, the Clinic and the Court* by a collection of authors, *Young Gaol Birds* by Charles E.B. Russell, *The Young Delinquent* by Cyril Burt, *The Revolt of Modern Youth* by Judge Ben B. Lindsey and Wainright Evans, and *Judge Baker Foundation Case Studies, Cases 1–20*.

3. Charles Beahan to Cecil B. DeMille, September 27, 1927, box 270, BYU.

4. Memo from Gladys Rosson to Cecil B. DeMille Pictures casting director L.M. Goodstadt, October 3, 1927, box 270, BYU.

5. Gladys Rosson to Ella K. Adams, October 25, 1927, box 270, BYU.

6. Telegram from L.M. Goodstadt to Charles Beahan, November 12, 1927, box 270, BYU.

7. Undated letter from E. Jason Temple to Cecil B. DeMille, box 270, BYU.

8. Box 292, BYU.

9. Quack medicine in the 1920s made great claims for the rejuvenating effects of various animal glands. In the changeover to sound, talking sequences were added to already completed silent films in hopes of making them more commercial. Such scenes in the part-talkies of the period were called "goat gland" sequences.

10. Fritz Feld, interview with author, ca. 1985.

## Chapter 53: Dynamite

1. Bickford also describes his lonely arrival in Hollywood just before Christmas and his attendance at a Christmas party in DeMille's bungalow on the M-G-M lot, but since Bickford didn't leave New York for Los Angeles until December 26, 1928, one must conclude that events had blurred his memory between 1928 and his 1965 autobiography.

2. Draft of letter from Cecil B. DeMille to proposed recipient J. Stuart Blackton, September 24, 1929, Cecil B. DeMille Collection, BYU. This letter was prepared in response to Blackton's charge that *Dynamite* plagiarized his film, *The Glorious Adventure*, and may be somewhat self-serving but it offers a glimpse of how DeMille often turned to newspaper articles for inspiration.

3. Sex Appeal in the Background.

4. Handwritten letter from Carole Lombard to Cecil B. DeMille, undated, box 297, folder 13, BYU.

5. Fred C. Beers to Orville Dull, Irving Thalberg, Eddie Mannix, Cecil B. DeMille, and J.J. Cohn, March 4, 1929, box 297, BYU.

6. Cecil B. DeMille to Roy Burns, August 9, 1929, box 299, BYU.

## Chapter 54: Madam Satan

1. Elsie Janis to Cecil B. DeMille, March 24, 1930, box 299, BYU.

2. Telegrams from Joseph Kennedy to Cecil B. DeMille, and DeMille to Kennedy, December 1929, box 299, BYU.

3. Cecil B. DeMille to Frank Joyce, November 12, 1929, box 300, BYU.

4. Draft of telegram from Cecil B. DeMille to Dorothy Dalton, February 13, 1930, box 300, BYU.

5. Telegram from Cecil B. DeMille to Robert G. Ritchie, January 16, 1930, box 299, BYU.

6. Roth's best-selling 1954 autobiography, *I'll Cry Tomorrow*, written in collaboration with Mike Connolly and Gerold Frank, details her career. The book was made into a film starring Susan Hayward.

7. Cecil B. DeMille to J.J. Cohn, May 3, 1930, box 299, BYU.

8. Memos from Barrett Kiesling to Cecil B. DeMille, ca. August 20, 1930, box 299, BYU.

### Chapter 55: The Squaw Man (second remake)

1. Sidney R. Kent became president of Fox Film Corporation after leaving Paramount.

2. Anne Bauchens to Cecil B. DeMille, May 25, 1932, box 60, BYU.

### Chapter 56: The Sign of the Cross

1. "WORLD GROSSES—estimated final," November 1932, from Cecil B. DeMille's files, photocopy in author's collection.

2. Communications between Emanuel Cohen and Cecil B. DeMille, box 505, BYU.

3. Memo to Roy Burns, August 11, 1932, box 506, BYU.

4. Emanuel Cohen to Cecil B. DeMille, August 19, 1932, box 505, BYU.

5. Excerpts of two memos from Cecil B. DeMille to Mr. Egli, Paramount Casting, September 8, 1932, box 505, BYU.

6. Memo to Paramount Casting Department, September 12, 1932, box 505, BYU.

7. Memo from Cecil B. DeMille to Fred Leahy, August 16, 1932, box 505, BYU.

8. In a memo to Cecil B. DeMille, September 28, 1932, Albert Kaufman suggested that all of Joyzelle Joyner's dialogue be re-recorded by another actress (box 505, BYU).

9. Memo from Cecil B. DeMille to Sam Katz, September 19, 1932, box 505, BYU.

10. Sam Katz to Cecil B. DeMille, October 7, 1932, box 505, BYU.

11. Cecil B. DeMille to Sam Katz, October 7, 1932, box 505, BYU.

12. Undated memorandum written by James Wingate in the *Sign of the Cross* file in the M.P.A.A. Production Code Administration Collection, Academy Library, Beverly Hills, California.

13. Christian F. Reisner to A.L. Selig, October 3, 1932, in *The Sign of the Cross* file in the M.P.A.A. Production Code Administration Collection, Academy Library, Beverly Hills, California.

14. Telegram from Adolph Zukor to Cecil B. DeMille, November 14, 1932, box 505, BYU.

15. DeMille shot the World War II prologue for *The Sign of the Cross*, which takes place largely in a bomber flying over Germany, on a Paramount sound stage from March 20 to March 25, 1944, at a reported cost of $125,000.

## Chapter 57: This Day and Age

1. Cecil B. DeMille to John Flinn, November 14, 1932, box 505, BYU.

2. Cecil B. DeMille to John Flinn, November 14, 1932, box 505, BYU; Cecil B. DeMille to Adolph Zukor, November 14, 1932, box 505, BYU.

3. Notes from Horace Hahn to Cecil B. DeMille, May 12, 1933, box 505, BYU.

4. Fred Datig to Cecil B. DeMille, April 4, 1933, box 505, BYU.

5. Phil Berg to Cecil B. DeMille, May 10, 1933, box 505, BYU.

6. *Los Angeles Times*, July 13, 1933, clipping in the Judith Allen biography file at the Margaret Herrick Library, Academy of Motion Picture Arts and Sciences, Beverly Hills, California.

7. Bill Cunningham, "'Sonny' Spent Riches on Wife," *Boston Post*, July 15, 1933.

8. In later years, Judith Allen claimed that Paramount knew of her marriage, that she kept it quiet at the studio's insistence, and that she had just done what she was told. She also claimed that she was cast in a later DeMille film, only to arrive on the set the first day of shooting to learn that she had been fired.

9. DeMille office memos, July 20, 1933, and July 22, 1933, box 505, BYU.

## Chapter 58: Four Frightened People

1. Russell Holman will be familiar to collectors of "Photoplay Edition" novelizations as the adapter of such films as *Speedy, The Freshman, The Fleet's In!, The Love Parade, Cobra, The Cheat* (1923), and *Manhandled*.

2. Memo from Emily Barrye to Milo Anderson, September 15, 1933, box 513, BYU.

3. Memo from Karl Struss to Cecil B. DeMille, September 22, 1933, box 513, BYU.

4. Memo from Emily Barrye per Cecil B. DeMille to Roy Burns, September 26, 1933, box 513, BYU.

5. Memo from Emily Barrye to "Hezie" Tate and Jimmie Dugan, October 1, 1933, box 513, BYU.

6. Hau (*Hibiscus tiliaceus*): Curved soft wood used to make outriggers for Hawaiian canoes. In one sequence the *Four Frightened People* make their way through a tortuous entanglement of these twisted plants.

7. Memo from Emily Barrye to Roy Burns, November 15, 1933, box 513, BYU.

8. Memo from Emily Barrye per Cecil B. DeMille to Roy Burns, September 29, 1933, box 513, BYU.

9. Postproduction schedule, box 513, BYU.

10. Undated copy of telegram from Cecil B. DeMille to Albert Kaufman, box 513, BYU.

11. Draft of telegram from Cecil B. DeMille to Emanuel Cohen, December 18, 1933, box 513, BYU.

12. Telegram from Bartlett Cormack to Cecil B. DeMille, December 21, 1933, box 513, BYU.

13. Draft of telegram from Cecil B. DeMille to James Wingate, December 29, 1933, box 513, BYU.

14. When *Four Frightened People* was sold to televison in the early 1960s, these offending frames were physically spliced out of all the 16mm TV prints.

## Chapter 59: Cleopatra

1. Hildegarde Merta to Cecil B. DeMille, February 10, 1938, and Frank Calvin to Hildegarde Merta, February 16, 1938, box 514, BYU. DeMille associate David MacDonald headed the research team on *Cleopatra*. Colbert's measurements were reported to DeMille's office on January 16, 1934.

2. Cecil B. DeMille to Agnes deMille, March 6, 1934, box 519, BYU.

3. Undated handwritten note from Albert Kaufman to Cecil B. DeMille in response to a November 22, 1933, memo from DeMille, box 515, BYU.

4. Al Kaufman to Cecil B. DeMille, December 8, 1933, box 515, BYU.

5. George M. Arthur to Cecil B. DeMille, February 13, 1934, box 515, BYU.

6. The 1917 *Cleopatra* is considered one of the ten lost films that are most anxiously sought by the American Film Institute. Today only a few seconds of Theda Bara's *Cleopatra* are known to survive.

7. Emily Barrye to Cecil B. DeMille, March 1 and March 8, 1934, box 515, BYU.

8. *Cleopatra* daily production reports, box 516, BYU.

9. Cecil B. DeMille to Fred Leahy, April 26, 1934, box 516, BYU.

10. Albertina Rasch choreographed a number of Broadway shows, including *Rio Rita*, *Three Musketeers,* and *The Band Wagon*. She also created balletic set pieces for such films as *The Merry Widow* (M-G-M, 1934) and *Rosalie* (M-G-M, 1937).

11. Telegram from Cecil B. DeMille to Anna George deMille [mother of Agnes deMille], March 5, 1934, box 516, BYU.

12. Night letter from Cecil B. DeMille to Agnes DeMille [via her agent, Mr. Graham], March 2, 1934, box 516, BYU.

13. Cecil B. DeMille to Agnes DeMille, March 6, 1934 [excerpted and rearranged], box 519, BYU. The work of French illustrator Edmund Dulac (1882–1953), who was best known for a series of pre-World-War-I, deluxe illustrated editions of literary classics like *The Tempest* (1908). *The Rubaiyat of Omar Khayyam* (1909), and *The Sleeping Beauty and Other Tales* (1910), was a strong influence on DeMille's sense of costume, decor, and staging.

14. Memo from Agnes deMille to Rudolph Kopp, March 28, 1934, box 519, BYU.

15. Memo from Florence Cole to Tom Baily, April 4, 1934, box 516, BYU.

16. Keith had left Hollywood after shooting *Cleopatra* to tour in a play.

17. Memo from Emily Barrye to Rudolph Kopp, June 4, 1934, box 516, BYU.

18. Memo from Cecil B. DeMille to Rudolph Kopp, June 9, 1934, box 516, BYU.

19. Telegram from Cecil B. DeMille to [?], August 17, 1934, box 516, BYU.

## Chapter 60: The Crusades

1. Harold Lamb, draft of letter answering questions about script for *The Crusades,* August 24, 1935, box 519, BYU.

2. Transcription of January 7, 1935, *Crusades* production meeting, Box 520, BYU. The rough transcript of this conversation runs thirty-two typewritten legal-sized pages. I have edited and condensed it to an essence of the wide-ranging discus-

sion, and added punctuation to make the text more comprehensible. Emanuel Cohen was Paramount's head of production. E. Lloyd Sheldon and Benjamin Glazer were Paramount producers with backgrounds as writers. Jeff Lazarus was chairman of Paramount's editorial board.

3. The "piece of wood" DeMille refers to is the "True Cross" supposedly residing in the City of Acre during the Third Crusade.

4. Casting notes, December 6, 1934, box 515, BYU; and memo from Emily Barrye to Fred Datig, December 10, 1934, box 519, BYU.

5. Florence Cole to Cecil B. DeMille, September 25, 1934, box 518, BYU.

6. Fred Datig to Cecil B. DeMille, October 27, 1934, box 519, BYU.

7. Fred Datig to Cecil B. DeMille, undated, box 519, BYU.

8. Cecil B. DeMille to Hobart Bosworth, July 19, 1934, box 519, BYU.

9. Early draft script of *Hollywood Extra Girl*, April 22, 1935, box 519, BYU.

10. Cecil B. DeMille to Roy Burns, September 26, 1934, box 519, BYU.

11. Emily Barrye to Roy Burns and Emily Barrye to George Hippard, David MacDonald, Holly Morse, and Joe Egli, February 14, 1935, box 519, BYU. Future star Ann Sheridan played an unbilled bit as a woman who kisses a cross before being sold into slavery. The attention she gained in the slave market scene earned her a featured bit in *Hollywood Extra Girl*, a production short detailing the making of *The Crusades*. The unidentified "Jewish comedian" playing the auctioneer was replaced by J. Carroll Naish.

12. *The Crusades* daily production schedules, box 520, BYU.

13. Cecil B. DeMille to Roy Burns, April 4, 1935, box 519, BYU.

14. Emily Barrye to Roy Burns, et al., April 11, 1935, box 520, BYU.

15. Cecil B. DeMille to Anne Bauchens, April 13, 1935, box 520, BYU.

16. Cecil B. DeMille, *Autobiography*, 344.

17. Overseas report from the Paramount office in France, April 16, 1936, box 521, folder 3, BYU.

18. Cost, loss, and territorial figures from Producer's Settlement Statement prepared by Paramount for Cecil B. DeMille Productions, Inc., as of March 31, 1951, box 751, BYU.

## Chapter 61: The Plainsman

1. Figures were reported as of May 1936. Copy in collection of Karl Thiede.

2. *The Big Trail* and *Billy the Kid* were unequivocal flops. *Cimarron* was popular with audiences and grossed $1,383,000, but the picture cost $1,433,000 and showed a loss on RKO's books of $565,000.

3. Information from memos by Jeanie Macpherson, September 23, 1935, and Emily Barrye, April 30, 1936, box 526, BYU.

4. Undated casting suggestions for *The Plainsman*, box 526, BYU.

5. Transcribed interview between publicist Ann Del Valle and Cecil B. DeMille, October 30, 1958, box 528, BYU.

6. Frank Lloyd to Cecil B. DeMille, August 3, 1936, box 526, BYU.

7. Telegram from Cecil B. DeMille to Arthur Rosson, June 20, 1936, box 527, BYU.

8. Cecil B. DeMille to Constance DeMille, November 24, 1936, box 526, BYU.

9. Preview card returned by Fred Wendt, November 27, 1936, box 527, BYU.

10. Everett R. Cunnings to Robert Gillham, December 9, 1936, box 527, BYU.

## Chapter 62: The Buccaneer

1. Hugh Wiley to Cecil B. DeMille, December 11, 1924, box 535, BYU.

2. Cecil B. DeMille to Hugh Wiley, May 7, 1925, box 535, BYU.

3. Note on Bartlett Cormack's draft of June 16, 1934, box 533, BYU.

4. Cecil B. DeMille, dictated notes intended for attorney Jack Karp, May 6, 1938, box 535, BYU. All of the subsequent narrative by DeMille regarding the development of the screenplay for *The Buccaneer* derive from this document.

5. Such rules were instigated by the Hays office to avoid situations such as DeMille had experienced in 1915 when his version of *Carmen* competed with a separate version made by the Fox Film Corporation.

6. Memo from Dixie Davis to Florence Cole, April 28, 1937, box 533, BYU. Dominique You was an historic character who died November 15, 1830. DeMille borrowed "Mr. Peavey," another comic relief character in *The Buccaneer*, from his brother William C. deMille's play *The Warrens of Virginia*.

7. Director Ernst Lubitsch was appointed to replace Emanuel Cohen as head of production at Paramount in 1935 when Cohen was fired for signing several Paramount players to personal service contracts, ignoring his responsibilities to the company. The choice of Lubitsch seems an odd one. Although his pictures were highly regarded for their artistic merits and the so-called "Lubitsch touch," virtually all of Lubitsch's films, with rare exceptions like *Ninotchka* (M-G-M, 1939) and *To Be Or Not To Be* (United Artists, 1942), were box-office flops. Lubitsch returned to directing in 1936.

8. Cecil B. DeMille quoted in British press book for *The Buccaneer,* in author's collection.

9. Telegram from unnamed still photographer to Cecil B. DeMille's office, July 24, 1937, box 534, folder 1, BYU.

10. Telegram from Cecil B. DeMille to William Pine, July 28, 1937, box 533, BYU.

## Chapter 63: Union Pacific

1. 20th Century-Fox released *Hudson's Bay* in 1940.

2. Joel McCrea to Cecil B. DeMille, July 1, 1938, box 546, BYU.

3. Cecil B. DeMille to Claudette Colbert, August 14, 1938, box 546, BYU.

4. DeMille, *Autobiography*, 364–65.

5. Lane Chandler to Cecil B. DeMille, November 7, 1938, box 546, BYU.

6. Mabel Van Buren Gordon to Cecil B. DeMille, October 13, 1938, box 546, BYU.

7. Gladys Rosson to Joe Egli, October 15, 1938, box 546, BYU.

8. Gladys Rosson to Frank Calvin, September 16, 1939, box 546, BYU.

9. Anne Bauchens to Cecil B. DeMille, April 22, 1939, box 548, BYU.

10. DeMille was referring to the then-common practice of theaters leaving the color-tinted curtain lights up as the curtain opened and the house lights dimmed during a film's opening titles.

11. *National Box Office Digest* 9, no. 13 (May 8, 1939): 7.

12. *National Box Office Digest* 9, no. 14 (May 22, 1939): 5.

## Chapter 64: North West Mounted Police

1. *North West Mounted Police* budget estimate, box 561, folder 4, BYU.

2. Memo from Art Rosson to Cecil B. DeMille, January 25, 1940, box 561, folder 9, BYU.

3. Gladys Rosson to Cecil B. DeMille, January 25, 1940, box 561, folder 2, BYU.

4. Box 561, folder 7, BYU.

## Chapter 65: Reap the Wild Wind

1. DeMille, *Autobiography*, 355–56.

2. Job description dated August 14, 1942, box 586, folder 5, BYU.

3. Transcription of first production meeting for *Reap the Wild Wind,* September 13, 1940, box 571, folder 11, BYU.

4. Memo from William Meiklejohn to Jack Karp, April 10, 1941, box 571, BYU.

5. Rough transcript of phone conversation between Bill Pine and DeMille's office, December 6, 1940, box 571, folder 6, BYU.

6. Rough transcript of phone conversation between Cecil B. DeMille and Bill Pine, December 6, 1940, box 571, folder 6, BYU.

7. John Wayne to Leo Morrison (passed on to DeMille's casting director Joe Egli on April 8, 1941, and later shared with DeMille), box 571, folder 11, BYU. Wayne included two pages of specific, but rather minor suggestions for script revisions.

8. Gladys Rosson to Cecil B. DeMille, December 20, 1941, box 572, BYU.

9. Handwritten postcard from "A Movie Fan" to Mr. DeMille, July 13, 1942, box 573, folder 18, BYU.

10. Neil Agnew to Barney Balaban, Y.F. Freeman, and C.B. DeMille, February 18, 1944, box 571, folder 11, BYU.

## Chapter 66: The Story of Dr. Wassell

1. Copy of telegram from Y. Frank Freeman and Cecil B. DeMille to Stephen Early, April 28, 1942, box 587, folder 1, BYU.

2. Corydon Wassell died on May 12, 1958, at age seventy-four.

3. Laraine Day to author, 2003. DeMille was notoriously averse to dealing with agents, which may have had something to do with his rather harsh judgment at the time.

4. Eddie Salven to Cecil B. DeMille, February 26, 1943, box 587, folder 4, BYU.

5. Eddie Salven to Cecil B. DeMille, March 3, 1943, box 587, folder 4, BYU.

6. Eddie Salven to Cecil B. DeMille, April 21, 1943, box 587, folder 4, BYU.

7. Eddie Salven to Cecil B. DeMille, June 9, 1943, box 587, folder 4, BYU.

8. Dialogue supervisor Edwin Maxwell and dialogue director Arthur Pierson would have conducted these rehearsals.

9. George Mitchell in conversation with author, ca. 1990.

10. Gladys Rosson reporting comments of J.H. Rosenberg, Vice-president Bank of America, Los Angeles Main office, to Cecil B. DeMille, May 19, 1942, box 587, BYU.

11. Gladys Rosson to Cecil B. DeMille, July 9, 1942, box 587, BYU.

## Chapter 67: Unconquered

1. DeMille, *Autobiography*, 384–88. The *Lux Radio Theatre* continued on the air for another ten years, first with director William Keighley (1945–52) and then director Irving Cummings (1952–55) as hosts.

2. Sidney Biddell to George Brown, March 23, 1945, box 600, folder 3, BYU. Norman Reilly Raine did not receive screen credit on *Unconquered* and is listed only as an additional writer in DeMille's log of credits. Swanson's novel was to be based on the first-draft screenplay that Raine was expected to finish in June 1945. Swanson's *The Judas Tree* was also to be drawn upon in writing the new novel, but all character names, except for historical figures, were to be changed.

3. Transcript of production meeting, April 26, 1945, box 602, folder 7, BYU. In attendance were DeMille, Sidney Biddell, Roy Burns, Kenny DeLand, Farciot Edouart, Gordon Jennings, Walter Tyler,and Arthur Rosson.

4. Jesse L. Lasky Jr., *Whatever Happened to Hollywood?*, 197. Lasky misremembers the incidents he describes as having taken place during the writing of *North West Mounted Police*.

5. DeMille, *Autobiography*, 398.

6. DeMille's granddaughter, Cecilia Presley, recalled the reaction of the audience in an interview with the author. She said DeMille was aware the scene needed additional work but that he ultimately lost patience with trying to fix it.

## Chapter 68: Samson and Delilah

1. This and following comments by DeMille ballyhooing *Samson and Delilah* come from an undated article under DeMille's byline titled "Binding Samson with Film" in an unattributed publication, box 628, folder 12, BYU.

2. DeMille, "Binding Samson with Film."

3. Transcript of a phone call from Cecil B. DeMille to Russell Holman, April 4, 1948, box 618, BYU.

4. William Meiklejohn to Cecil B. DeMille, April 20, 1948, box 618, BYU.

5. Transcript of Cecil B. DeMille's comments regarding Nancy Olson's audition, May 6, 1948, box 618, BYU.

6. Transcript of Cecil B. DeMille's comments regarding Nancy Olson after viewing her screen test, undated, BYU box 618, BYU.

7. Transcript of Cecil B. DeMille's comments regarding Steve Reeves, February 12, 1948, box 618, BYU.

8. Transcript of Cecil B. DeMille's comments regarding Steve Reeves, March 9, 1948, box 618, BYU.

9. Transcript of Cecil B. DeMille's comments regarding Victor Mature, undated 1948, box 621, BYU.

10. Cecil B. DeMille to assistant director Eddie Salven, September 24, 1948, box 618, folder 6, BYU. William Farnum, brother of *Squaw Man* star Dustin Farnum, gained screen fame with his brutal fight scene in *The Spoilers* (Selig Polyscope, 1914), and was noted for fight scenes in later pictures. Cowboy stuntman Ted French fought with Farnum on-screen and commented, "That old boy, when he put on a

fight you'd better have your hands up, because he was in there to make pictures and to make it look good and to see that he didn't get hurt."

11. Ralph Jester to Cecil B. DeMille, ca. August 28, 1948, and Cecil B. DeMille to Ralph Jester, August 31, 1948, box 622, folder 4, BYU.

12. Telegram from Kathleen Key to Cecil B. DeMille, December 20, 1948, box 618, BYU.

13. Virginia [last name omitted] to Cecil B. DeMille, December 31, 1948, box 618, folder 5, BYU. Morton had starred in F.W. Murnau's *4 Devils* (Fox, 1928) and was William Gargan's stand-in on DeMille's *Four Frightened People*.

14. Memo from Berenice Mosk to Gordon Jennings, Bob Osborne, Roy Burns, Eddie Salven, and Phil Koury, box 623, folder 9, BYU.

15. *New York Times*, January 8, 1950.

16. Cecil B. DeMille to Florence Cole, box 622, folder 1, BYU.

17. Transcript of Cecil B. DeMille's phone conversation with Dave Cockrill, box 622, folder 1, BYU.

### Chapter 69: The Greatest Show on Earth

1. Gladys Rosson to Cecil B. DeMille, July 16, 1946, box 600, folder 9, BYU.

2. "The Battle of Warner Bros." occurred in October 1945 during a lengthy strike by the Conference of Studio Unions.

3. These figures come from an untitled 1953 film the motion picture industry made to show members of Congress in a campaign to repeal the 20 percent federal excise tax on theater admissions then in place.

4. The "Hollywood Ten," a group of writers and directors sentenced to federal prison terms for contempt of Congress and alleged Communist ties, included Alvah Bessie, Herbert Biberman, Lester Cole, Edward Dmytryk, Ring Lardner Jr., John Howard Lawson, Albert Maltz, Samuel Ornitz, Adrian Scott, and Dalton Trumbo. DeMille also employed Albert Maltz as a writer on the aborted project called *The Flame* (a.k.a. *Rurales*).

5. Al Rogell to author, ca. 1981.

6. The Taft-Hartley Labor Act actually made it illegal for unions to suspend members for failing to pay political assessments, but the law was not retroactive, and the union refused to lift the suspension it had placed on DeMille.

7. The Screen Directors Guild Board at this time included Seymour Berns, Claude Binyon, Frank Borzage, Clarence Brown, David Butler, Merian C. Cooper, Cecil B. DeMille, Harvey Dwight, John Ford, Tay Garnett, Walter Lang, Frank MacDonald, John F. Murphy, Mark Robson, William Seiter, Richard Wallace, and John Waters. Al Rogell served as First Vice President, and Lesley Selander was Second Vice President. See Scott Eyman, *Print the Legend—The Life and Times of John Ford*, 377–86, for a fuller account of the Screen Directors Guild proceedings in this matter.

8. Eyman, *Print the Legend*, 382.

9. Ronald L. Davis, *Duke, the Life and Image of John Wayne* (Norman, Oklahoma: University of Oklahoma Press, 1998), quoted in Eyman, *Print the Legend*, 386.

10. The affiliated trade names included the Al G. Barnes Amusement Company, Sells Floto Circus Company, Sparks Circus Company, Hagenbeck-Wallace Shows

Company, and John Robinson Shows Company, which had been acquired by the Ringling organization through the years.

11. Contract amendment dated September 19, 1950, box 643, BYU.

12. Transcript of DeMille's comments regarding Charlton Heston's screen tests, June 6, 1950, box 646, BYU.

13. Transcript of DeMille's comments regarding Charlton Heston after seeing *Dark City*, July 19, 1950, box 646, BYU.

14. Transcript of DeMille's comments regarding Charlton Heston's performance in *Of Human Bondage*, October 6, 1950, box 646, BYU.

15. Contract summary, box 642, BYU.

16. Undated draft of form letter replying to actors looking for extra work on *The Greatest Show on Earth*, box 642, BYU.

17. For a harrowing account of the Hartford fire and its aftermath see Stewart O'Nan, *The Circus Fire*.

18. Transcript of phone conversation between Stanley Goldsmith and Henry Wilcoxon, January 4, 1951, box 644, folder 17, BYU.

19. Excerpted from a transcription of an October 23, 1951, meeting, box 646, folder 3, BYU. Ultimately, Paramount chose not to hold the picture for a July release.

20. DeMille's films received a number of Academy Award nominations in various categories through the years, but won only the following Oscars: Victor Milner, A.S.C., Best Cinematography for *Cleopatra* (1934); Anne Bauchens, Best Film Editing for *North West Mounted Police* (1940); Farciot Edouart, Gordon Jennings, William L. Pereira, and Louis Mesenkop, Best Special Effects for *Reap the Wild Wind* (1942); Hans Dreier, Walter Tyler, Sam Comer, and Ray Moyer, Best Color Art Direction for *Samson and Delilah* (1950); Edith Head, Dorothy Jeakins, Elois Jenssen, Gile Steele and Gwen Wakeling, Best Color Costume Design for *Samson and Delilah*; and Fredric M. Frank, Theodore St. John, and Frank Cavett, Best Motion Picture Story for *The Greatest Show on Earth* (1952).

## Chapter 70: The Ten Commandments

1. The Holy Scriptures referred to in the titles include the Koran as well as the Bible.

2. Cecil B. DeMille, introduction to Henry S. Noerdlinger, *Moses and Egypt*, 2.

3. Noerdlinger, *Moses and Egypt*, 8–9. For a recent and more thorough examination of biblical archaeology, see Israel Finkelstein and Neil Asher Silberman, *The Bible Unearthed*.

4. *Variety*, October 10, 1956.

5. Cecilia Presley to author, 2002.

6. DeMille was so pleased with Brynner's performance that on June 23, 1955, he agreed to eliminate the two free weeks and to pay Brynner $7,500 per week for the two weeks.

7. Rufus Blair to Art Arthur, October 21, 1954, photocopy in author's collection.

8. Cecil B. DeMille to Y. Frank Freeman, October 30, 1954, photocopy in author's collection.

9. Anne Edwards, *The DeMilles: An American Family*.

10. DeMille, *Autobiography*, 430.

11. Cecilia Presley to author, 2002.

12. Eddie Fisher, with David Fisher, *Been There, Done That*. Eddie Fisher made his first visit to Max Jacobson on April 17, 1953.

13. "On April 25, 1975, after more than two years of hearings and 5,000 pages of testimony, the New York State Board of Regents revoked Max Jacobson's medical license. He was found guilty on 48 counts of unprofessional conduct in 11 specifications, and an additional count of fraud" (*St. Louis Post-Dispatch*, June 18, 1989).

14. Henry Wilcoxon to Chico Day, February 9, 1955, box 675, BYU. *The Court Jester* starred comedian Danny Kaye.

15. Bud Brill to Henry Wilcoxon, February 11, 1955, box 675, folder 8, BYU.

16. Cecilia DeMille Presley to author, 2002.

17. "An Interested Viewer" to Cecil B. DeMille, undated, box 675, BYU.

18. Edward G. Robinson, with Leonard Spigelgass, *All My Yesterdays*, 272. DeMille also hired others who had been threatened with blacklisting, including Elmer Bernstein, Olive Deering, and Nina Foch.

19. Cecilia Presley to author, 2002.

20. Charlton Heston, *In the Arena*, 142–43.

21. Richard Gilden to author, 2002.

22. Victor Young would die on November 10, 1956.

23. Elmer Bernstein, "The DeMille Legend," quoted in Gabe Essoe and Raymond Lee, *DeMille: The Man and His Pictures,* 279–80.

24. It won only Best Special Effects.

25. Bernstein, "The DeMille Legend," 278–79.

26. The barn had been moved from the old Lasky studio location at Selma Avenue and Vine Street to the new Paramount studio on Marathon Street in 1926. In 1985 the barn was moved to its present location at 2100 North Highland Avenue and is maintained and operated as the Hollywood Heritage Museum by Hollywood Heritage, Inc.

27. Jerry Hartleben to author, ca. 1980.

28. *Journal of the Screen Producers Guild* 4, no. 1 (February 1956).

# Bibliography

## Manuscript and film collections

Cecil B. DeMille Collection. L. Tom Perry Special Collections Library, Harold B. Lee Library. Brigham Young University (BYU), Provo, Utah.

M.P.A.A. Production Code Administration Collection, Academy Library, Beverly Hills, California.

## Periodicals

*Journal of the Screen Producers Guild*
*Motion Picture News*
*Motion Picture Story Magazine*
*The Moving Picture World*
*National Box Office Digest*
*Paramount Progress*
*Photoplay Magazine*
*Picture Play Magazine*
*Picture Progress*

## Books

Ball, Robert Hamilton, ed. *The Plays of Henry C. DeMille Written in Collaboration with David Belasco*. Princeton: Princeton University Press, 1941.

Bardeche, Maurice, and Robert Brasillach. *The History of Motion Pictures*. Translated by Iris Barry. New York: Norton, 1938.

Basquette, Lina. *LINA, DeMille's Godless Girl*. Fairfax, Va.: Denlinger's, 1990.

Berg, A. Scott. *Goldwyn*. New York: Knopf, 1989.

Brownlow, Kevin. *Hollywood: The Pioneers*. New York: Knopf, 1979.

———. *The Parade's Gone By*. New York: Knopf, 1968.

———. *The War, the West, and the Wilderness*. New York: Knopf, 1978.

Chierichetti, David. *Hollywood Director—The Career of Mitchell Leisen*. New York: Curtis Books, 1973.

DeMille, Cecil B. *The Autobiography of Cecil B. DeMille*. Englewood Cliffs, N.J.: Prentice-Hall, 1959.

deMille, William C. *Hollywood Saga*. New York: E.P. Dutton & Co., 1939.

Drew, William M. *Speaking of Silents*. Vestal, N.Y.: Vestal Press, 1989.

Edwards, Anne. *The DeMilles: An American Family*. New York: Harry N. Abrams, Inc., 1988.

Essoe, Gabe, and Raymond Lee. *DeMille: The Man and His Pictures*. New York: A.S. Barnes & Co., 1970.

Eyman, Scott. *Print the Legend—The Life and Times of John Ford*. New York: Simon & Schuster, 1999.

Farrar, Geraldine. *Such Sweet Compulsion*. New York: Greystone Press, 1938.

Finkelstein, Israel, and Neil Asher Silberman. *The Bible Unearthed*. New York: Free Press, 2001.

Fisher, Eddie, with David Fisher. *Been There, Done That*. New York: St. Martin's, 2000.

Fountain, Leatrice Gilbert. *Dark Star*. New York: St. Martins, 1985.

Gish, Lillian. *The Movies, Mr. Griffith, and Me*. Englewood Cliffs, N.J.: Prentice-Hall, 1969.

Heston, Charlton. *In the Arena*. New York: Simon & Schuster, 1995.

Higashi, Sumiko. *Cecil B. DeMille and American Culture: The Silent Era*. Berkeley: University of California Press, 1994.

Higham, Charles. *Cecil B. DeMille*. New York: Scribner's, 1973.

Irwin, Will. *The House That Shadows Built*. New York: Doubleday, 1928.

Koury, Phil. *Yes, Mr. DeMille*. New York: G.P. Putnam's Sons, 1959.

Lasky, Jesse L., with Don Weldon. *I Blow My Own Horn*. Garden City, N.Y.: Doubleday, 1957.

Lasky, Jesse L., Jr. *Whatever Happened to Hollywood?* New York: Funk & Wagnalls, 1975.

Lord, Daniel A., S.J. *Played by Ear*. Chicago: Loyola University Press, 1956.

Macpherson, Jeanie. "How the Story Was Evolved." In souvenir program for the original release of *The Ten Commandments*. 1923.

Maltin, Leonard. *The Art of the Cinematographer*. New York: Dover Press, 1978.

Noerdlinger, Henry S. *Moses and Egypt*. Los Angeles: University of Southern California Press, 1956.

O'Nan, Stewart. *The Circus Fire*. New York: Doubleday, 2000.

Parrish, Robert. *Growing Up in Hollywood*. New York: Harcourt Brace Jovanovich, 1976.

Ringgold, Gene, and DeWitt Bodeen. *The Films of Cecil B. DeMille*. New York: Citadel Press, 1969.

Robinson, Edward G., with Leonard Spigelgass. *All My Yesterdays*. New York: Hawthorn Books, 1973.

Roth, Lillian, with Mike Connolly and Gerold Frank. *I'll Cry Tomorrow*. New York: Frederick Fell, 1954.

Scott, Evelyn F. *Hollywood—When Silents Were Golden*. New York: McGraw-Hill, 1972.

Swanson, Gloria. *Swanson on Swanson*. New York: Random House, 1980.

Wilcoxon, Henry, with Katherine Orrison. *Lionheart in Hollywood*. Metuchen: Scarecrow Press, 1991.

# Index